Good
Housekeeping

400 CALORIE MEALS

400 CALORIE MEALS

Easy Mix-and-Match Recipes for a Skinnier You!

HEARST BOOKS

New York

HEARST BOOKS
New York

An Imprint of Sterling Publishing
387 Park Avenue South
New York, NY 10016

GOOD HOUSEKEEPING
Rosemary Ellis
EDITOR IN CHIEF

Courtney Murphy
CREATIVE DIRECTOR

Susan Westmoreland
FOOD DIRECTOR

Samantha B. Cassetty, MS, RD
NUTRITION DIRECTOR

Sharon Franke
KITCHEN APPLIANCES
& FOOD TECHNOLOGY DIRECTOR

Book Design: Memo Productions
Cover Design: Jon Chaiet
Project Editor: Sarah Scheffel
Photography credits on page 476

The Good Housekeeping Cookbook Seal guarantees that the recipes in this cookbook meet the strict standards of the Good Housekeeping Research Institute. The Institute has been a source of reliable information and a consumer advocate since 1900, and established its seal of approval in 1909. Every recipe has been triple-tested for ease, reliability, and great taste.

www.goodhousekeeping.com

For information about custom editions, special sales, and premium and corporate purchases, please contact Sterling Special Sales at 800-805-5489 or specialsales@sterlingpublishing.com.

Distributed in Canada by
Sterling Publishing
c/o Canadian Manda Group, 165 Dufferin Street
Toronto, Ontario, Canada M6K 3H6

Distributed in Australia by
Capricorn Link
(Australia) Pty. Ltd.
P.O. Box 704, Windsor, NSW 2756, Australia

Manufactured in Canada

4 6 8 10 11 9 7 5

ISBN: 978-1-61837-125-6

CONTENTS

CONTENTS

FOREWORD

In *400 Calorie Meals*, we collect our favorite low-cal recipes from the pages of *Good Housekeeping*. You won't believe the delectable dishes you can enjoy for 400 calories (or less!). This book includes sections on Italian, Vegetarian, and Chicken. To make meal planning easy, the first part of each section focuses on main courses, while the second includes appetizers, sides, and desserts. Each recipe includes complete nutritional information; icons indicate recipes that are heart healthy or high fiber, as well as thirty minute or less, slow-cooker, and make-ahead meals.

In Italian, the chapter on pastas, polenta, and risottos includes light versions of favorites like Fettucini Alfredo, Beef Ragu, and lasagna. And, for your next Sunday dinner, try Braciole with Grape Tomatoes or Roman Chicken Sauté with Artichokes. Seafood is an Italian specialty, too. The Roast Salmon with Capers and Parsley is perfect company fare.

Vegetarian opens with recipes for delicious veggie burgers, burritos, pizza, and other fare you can eat without a fork. Then it's on to comforting soups and stews, from Gazpacho with Cilantro Cream to Red Chili with Fire-Roasted Tomatoes. Our stuffed, stacked, and stir-fried dishes lend a sense of play to mealtimes: Choose from Green Tomato Stacks, Stuffed Portobellos, Fast Fried Rice, and then some. We've also included fresh takes on pasta and grain dishes to keep things interesting. And why not enjoy vegetarian breakfast specialties around the clock?

For Chicken, we've picked an irresistible collection of our favorite skinny go-to dishes. Fast and easy recipes like Tangerine Chicken Stir-Fry and Chicken and Veggies on Polenta are sure to become regulars at your house. Chicken and White Bean Chili, and other long-simmering soups and stews, will warm you up on cold days, while great grills like Chicken Bruschetta and Chicken Parm Stacks are perfect for leisurely summer meals. For the kids, we've included fun casseroles and bakes, as well as other creative tosses and sandwiches. Enjoy!

SUSAN WESTMORELAND
Food Director, *Good Housekeeping*

400
CALORIE
ITALIAN

INTRODUCTION

Ask Americans what their favorite ethnic food is, and the majority will answer "Italian." Of course, we owe the Italians a big thanks for sharing two of our most beloved dishes—pizza and spaghetti and meatballs. But it's their reverence for fresh, healthful ingredients, simply prepared, that's truly responsible for the cuisine's ever-increasing popularity. Italian cooks employ wholesome, top-quality ingredients, including fresh produce, cheese, meat, and fish, and treat them with care. Whatever the preparation, cooks strive only to enhance, never transform, what nature has already provided. It's this respect for the ingredients that makes Italian food so special—and so popular.

The simplicity and wide appeal of *la cucina Italiana* also makes it a natural subject for *Good Housekeeping 400 Calorie Meals*. In this section, we share approximately 60 recipes for Italian favorites, from hearty soups and colorful salads to rustic pasta, calzone, and panini and best-loved meat, chicken, and seafood entrées, paired with cooking secrets from the Italian kitchen. You'll find low-cal takes on satisfyingly familiar dishes like fettucine, lasagna, and pizza, along with tasty recipes for traditional Italian recipes like pasta e fagioli and bracciole.

As the title of the book promises, every single main dish is 400 calories or less, and as a bonus, we've included chapters on starters, sides, and desserts that will help you round out your meals in true Italian style. From bruschetta and marinated mixed olive antipasti to sides like Sicilian-style Swiss chard and eggplant caponata to sweet finales like biscotti and granita, an icy Italian treat, the 30-plus add-on recipes are organized by calorie count—from lowest to highest. Simply choose your entrée, then use your surplus calories to select an add-on (or two!) that will make it a meal.

For example, if you're watching your weight and limiting dinners to 450 calories total, begin with a chilled Tuscan-style soup (145 calories), then enjoy our light Cod Livornese (250 calories), and finish with a refreshing coffee granita (55 calories). 145 + 250 +55 = 450 calories. With this section, it's easy to build a satisfying low-calorie Italian meal. See "Skinny Italian Meal Planning," opposite, for examples and tips.

SKINNY ITALIAN MEAL PLANNING

Planning low-calorie brunches, lunches, and dinners is easy with this section. Prepare the add-ons we've suggested under "Make It a Meal" with each main-dish recipe to make 500-calorie dinners, 400-calorie lunches, or 300-calorie breakfasts or brunches. Or get creative and choose from the antipasti, side dish, and dessert recipe lists on pages 113, 125, and 139 to make your own satisfying meal combos. Here are some tasty examples to whet your appetite.

SAMPLE BRUNCH MENU

MAIN: Asparagus-Romano Frittata	235 calories
ADD-ON: 1 medium tomato, sliced, with 1 teaspoon olive oil	65 calories
Total calories per meal	**300 calories**

SAMPLE LUNCH MENU

MAIN: Tuscan Tuna Salad Sandwich	330 calories
ADD-ON: Pignoli Cookie	75 calories
Total calories per meal	**405 calories**

SAMPLE DINNER MENU

MAIN: Veal Shoulder Chops, Osso Buco Style	270 calories
ADD-ON 1: Creamy Polenta	175 calories
ADD-ON 2: Balsamic-Glazed Baby Carrots	65 calories
Total calories per meal	**510 calories**

STAYING SLIM THE ITALIAN WAY

There are lots of things about the Italian way of eating that are naturally healthy—and slimming. In fact, researchers have learned that the Mediterranean diet, with its emphasis on healthy fats and fresh fruits and vegetables, helps to lower the risks of heart disease, type 2 diabetes, obesity, cancer, and Alzheimer's. All that, and it tastes delicious! So while you're eating the low-calorie Italian recipes that follow, try incorporating some of these Mediterranean diet habits into your routine, too.

• **Load up on fruits, vegetables, beans, and whole grains.** They're all good sources of minerals and vitamins (especially heart-healthy antioxidants), low in fat and sodium, and full of fiber. Our barley minestrone (page 38) has 9 grams of fiber per serving and is brimming with fruits and vegetables.

• **Choose seafood over red meat.** Fish, especially oily types like tuna and salmon, supply omega-3 fatty acids, which help lower blood pressure and reduce other risk factors for heart disease. Our Sicilian tuna (page 101), featuring a robust tomato, olive, and caper sauce, is a mouthwatering way to eat fish.

• **Indulge in olive oil.** The monounsaturated fat in olive oil helps lower LDL (bad) cholesterol without reducing the HDL (good) kind—which, by the way, can be diminished by a low-fat diet. Enjoy olive oil in our hearty pasta dishes (page 55) and as a cooking oil for many of the other recipes in this book.

• **Snack on nuts.** These delicious nuggets contain antioxidants and are high in healthy fat. Reach for walnuts, pecans, pistachios, and hazelnuts. Or try pignoli, the fragrant Italian nut we call pine nuts, used in Pignoli Cookies (page 146), Cauliflower with Raisins and Pine Nuts (page 132), and other Italian-style sides.

• **Drink wine—in moderation.** Alcohol raises HDL, and the grape skins used to make red wine contain the antioxidant resveratrol, which may help prevent blood clots. If you're inclined, enjoy a glass of Italian wine with dinner. We sprinkle wine pairing suggestions in the "Make It a Meal" boxes throughout the book.

• **Relax and enjoy your food!** Italians relish leisurely eating and socializing at the table with friends and family. Follow their lead and savor your food and company—it will reduce your stress. If you're like us, you'll find that cooking is another great way to enjoy downtime. We hope that the recipes in this book will inspire you to do just that!

THE HEALTHY ITALIAN PANTRY

The following products are essential to great Italian cooking. We use them generously in the recipes that follow, so stock up!

Olive oil: Used in Mediterranean cooking since antiquity, olive oil is fundamental to Italian cuisine. (See page 12 for details about its health benefits.) You'll see it's the primary cooking oil called for in this section, and it's used in vinaigrettes and brushed on our bruschetta, too. Pressing tree-ripened olives produces the prized liquid. Its flavor, color, and fragrance depend on the region of origin and the quality of the harvest. Once opened, olive oil can be stored in a cool, dark place for up to six months.

Extra-virgin olive oil comes from the first pressing; it is the highest quality, nutritious—and the most expensive. Its luscious fruity flavor and aromatic bouquet make it ideal for salad dressings and for drizzling over finished dishes.

Regular olive oil (sometimes called pure olive oil) is from subsequent pressings. The light golden oil has a milder but still fruity flavor and makes a good everyday budget choice. "Light" olive oil has been specially treated to remove much of the characteristic olive taste; it is not lower in calories or fat than extra virgin or pure.

Balsamic vinegar: The process for making balsamic vinegar, cooking and aging fresh grape must (juice), has been handed down from generation to generation in Italy since the eleventh century. Artisanal balsamic vinegar is famous for its syrupy consistency and sweet tangy flavor, which is achieved by aging it in several varieties of progressively smaller wooden barrels. This precious condiment is best reserved for drizzling over meat or berries; in Italy, it is sometimes served after dinner as a digestive. Commercial balsamic vinegar typically consists of a small amount of artisanal vinegar mixed with wine vinegar and caramel color. It lends a sweetness and depth of flavor to vinaigrettes, sauces, and more.

Pasta: The Chinese may have invented noodles, but Italians have turned pasta into a favorite worldwide. In this book, we use dried Italian-style pasta rather than fresh, since it's readily available and easy to turn into a quick meal. Made from flour and water, dried pasta is not only more economical but lower in fat than fresh pasta; it's a good match for robust, strong-flavored sauces. For creamy or light-bodied sauces, homemade or prepared fresh pasta is also an excellent choice. Made with eggs, fresh pasta has a silky surface and a delicate texture. Store it in the refrigerator up to one week, or freeze up to one month.

For the best taste and texture, buy dried pasta made from durum wheat flour or semolina flour. Or, to up your fiber quotient, consider making whole-wheat or multigrain pasta a habit (see "White versus Whole-Wheat Pasta," below). Store dried pasta in a cool, dry, dark place for up to one year and whole-wheat pasta for up to six months. Don't store pasta in clear containers: Although it looks attractive, exposing pasta to light destroys riboflavin, a key nutrient in pasta. Buy pasta in cardboard boxes, which keeps out light, rather than in clear packaging.

WHITE VERSUS WHOLE-WHEAT PASTA

Although whole-wheat and multigrain pastas are usually slightly more expensive than regular (semolina) pasta, they pack a nutritious punch. Enriched brands of whole-wheat pasta have more thiamin, riboflavin, and folic acid than regular pasta and contain five times the amount of fiber. And the nutty taste of the whole wheat makes it a great choice for fall and winter cooking.

Some brands have a strong grainy taste and a chewy texture, so experiment until you find one that suits your palate. We like Bionaturae Organic Spaghetti: It's 100 percent whole wheat and has a nutty, slightly sweet taste and a firm texture. Note: Unless the label says 100 *percent whole wheat*, the product is actually a blend of whole wheat and white, which still provides a higher fiber content than regular pasta. Whole-wheat and multigrain pastas have a shorter shelf life than semolina pasta; use them within six months of purchase.

HOMEMADE MARINARA SAUCE

This versatile tomato sauce is used in recipes throughout this section, but feel free to substitute a good-quality marinara from a jar for convenience's sake.

In nonreactive 3-quart saucepan, heat **2 tablespoons oil** over medium heat; add **1 small chopped onion** and **1 finely chopped garlic clove** and cook, stirring, until onion is tender, about 5 minutes. Stir in **1 can (28 ounces) plum tomatoes** with their juice, **2 tablespoons tomato paste, 2 tablespoons chopped fresh basil or parsley (optional)**, and **½ teaspoon salt**. Heat to boiling, breaking up tomatoes with side of spoon. Reduce heat; partially cover and simmer, stirring occasionally, until sauce has thickened slightly, about 20 minutes. Makes 3½ cups.

---

65 CALORIES PER ½-CUP SERVING. 1G PROTEIN | 7G CARBOHYDRATE
4G TOTAL FAT (1G SATURATED) | 1G FIBER | 0MG CHOLESTEROL | 388MG SODIUM

Rice: Arborio, Carnaroli, and Vialone Nano are all types of round, short-grained rice grown in northern Italy. All are used to prepare risotto, a rich, creamy dish often amplified with vegetables, seafood, or cheese that's popular on Italian restaurant menus. The traditional method of preparing risotto is not complicated, but it does require a bit of time. The goal is to make the rice absorb hot broth until it swells and turns the rice into creamy yet still slightly firm grains, which requires the slow addition of broth and continual stirring. We offer two convenient twists on this labor-intensive method: Risotto Milanese made in the microwave (page 71) and Butternut Squash Barley Risotto prepared in a slow cooker (page 72).

Polenta: The Italian term for cornmeal, polenta comes in two types: finely and coarsely ground. The choice is a matter of personal preference, although coarsely ground polenta will contribute a more interesting texture. If you've never prepared polenta before, try the Polenta Casserole (page 70) or our Creamy Polenta (page 136) plus the broiled and microwave variations.

Beans: Whenever fresh fava (broad beans), cannellini (white beans), and garbanzo beans (chickpeas) are not available, most Italian cooks will use dried beans. These keep for a year, but since they are not stamped with a "sell-by" date, buy them from bulk bins or a store with a high turnover rate.

To save time, you can use canned beans in the following recipes instead. They're a boon to busy cooks because they don't require soaking or further cooking, and some people find them easier to digest than freshly cooked dried beans. Different brands vary in texture and sodium content, so stock up on your favorite label. Canned beans should be rinsed and drained under cold water before being used. This quick rinse refreshes their flavor and removes some of the sodium added during the canning process.

Cheese: Italian cheese is not just about Parmesan and mozzarella. The recipes in this book also share the joys of creamy ricotta, available as a whole-milk or (skinny!) skimmed-milk product, and ricotta salata, which is a lightly salted, slightly crumbly Sicilian sheep's milk cheese that's no relation to the soft ricotta. We also use Pecorino-Romano, a tangy grating cheese akin to Parmesan, and Provolone, a southern Italian cheese with a mild smoky flavor that's terrific melted in panini. Important: Do as the Italians do and use all cheeses in moderation, as an accent rather than a main ingredient.

Vegetables: Italy would not be Italy without its markets, where a panoply of fresh-picked vegetables lure cooks on a daily basis. We make generous use of the following Italian favorites in both the mains and add-ons in this book: artichokes, arugula, broccoli rabe (blanching before sautéing brings out this green's sweetness), eggplant, escarole, fennel (delicious raw in salads or cooked to bring out its subtle licorice flavor), tomatoes (use fresh when in season, otherwise consider canned), and zucchini. For winning results, choose recipes that feature seasonal vegetables and purchase the freshest examples you can find.

FAVORITE ITALIAN MAINS

To make skinny Italian meal planning a cinch, each main dish is paired with suggestions for add-on recipes that will make it a meal. Or to choose your own add-ons, see the complete recipe lists in the second half of the section, conveniently organized by calorie count, from lowest to highest: Antipasti & Other Starters, page 113; Vegetables & Sides, page 125; and Dolci Desserts, page 139.

355 CALORIES

Tomato, Portobello, and Mozzarella Melts (page 31)

PIZZAS, PANINI & FRITTATAS

Of the many things to thank Italy for, pizza is near the top of our list. Although pepperoni and sausage pizza did not make the skinny Italian list, we offer recipes for two yummy veggie and cheese pizzas and an equally delicious calzone. Our tuna sandwich is dressed up with capers, fresh lemon juice, and basil, and we have included several inspiring Italian takes on grilled cheese, too. For brunch, try our frittatas or spinach strata, an easy breakfast casserole made with bread, eggs, and cheese.

KEY TO ICONS

30 minutes or less   Heart healthy   High fiber   Make ahead   Slow cooker

RICOTTA, YELLOW PEPPER, AND ASPARAGUS PIZZA

Fresh ricotta pairs with yellow and green veggies for a pizza worthy of any Italian pizzeria. Choose part-skim ricotta to keep it skinny.

ACTIVE TIME: 20 MINUTES PLUS TIME TO MAKE DOUGH · **TOTAL TIME:** 40 MINUTES
MAKES: 8 MAIN-DISH SERVINGS

HOMEMADE PIZZA DOUGH
(OPPOSITE; SEE ALSO TIP)

1   POUND THIN ASPARAGUS, TRIMMED
    AND CUT INTO 2-INCH PIECES

1   TEASPOON OLIVE OIL

¼   TEASPOON SALT

1   MEDIUM YELLOW PEPPER,
    CUT INTO THIN STRIPS

1   CUP PART-SKIM RICOTTA CHEESE

2   TABLESPOONS FRESHLY GRATED
    PARMESAN CHEESE

¼   TEASPOON COARSELY
    GROUND BLACK PEPPER

1   Prepare Homemade Pizza Dough. Preheat oven to 450°F; position rack at bottom.
2   In small bowl, toss asparagus with oil and salt. Top pizza dough with pepper strips and asparagus. Dollop with teaspoons of ricotta; sprinkle with Parmesan and black pepper.
3   Bake pizza until crust is golden and crisp, 20 to 25 minutes.

215 CALORIES

PER SERVING. 10G PROTEIN | 35G CARBOHYDRATE | 4G TOTAL FAT (2G SATURATED)
4G FIBER | 11MG CHOLESTEROL | 405MG SODIUM ❤️

MAKE IT A MEAL: For a gourmet pizza dinner that's 500 calories or less, start with two chilled slices of honeydew or cantaloupe topped with thin slices of prosciutto and fresh ground pepper (110 to 160 calories). Finish with a refreshing scoop of your favorite store-bought sorbet (about 120 calories).

HOMEMADE PIZZA DOUGH

Use this basic dough and method to make the pizza opposite and on the next page. Want to add some whole-grain goodness to your pizza crust? Substitute whole-wheat flour for half of the all-purpose. You can also freeze homemade dough, so you may want to make a double recipe. Shape it into a disk, wrap it tightly in plastic, then freeze it in a zip-tight plastic bag. Thaw it in the refrigerator overnight and remove it 30 minutes before you want to roll it.

TOTAL TIME: 20 MINUTES
MAKES: ENOUGH DOUGH FOR 1 (15-INCH) PIZZA

2½ CUPS ALL-PURPOSE FLOUR

1   PACKAGE (¼ OUNCE) QUICK-RISE YEAST

1   TEASPOON SALT

1   CUP VERY WARM WATER (120 TO 130°F)

2   TEASPOONS CORNMEAL

1   In large bowl, combine 2 cups flour, yeast, and salt. Stir in water until dough is blended and comes away from side of bowl.
2   Turn dough onto floured surface and knead until smooth and elastic, about 8 minutes, working in more flour (about ½ cup). Shape dough into ball; cover with plastic wrap and let rest 10 minutes.
3   Grease 15-inch pizza pan; sprinkle with cornmeal. Pat dough onto bottom of pizza pan, shaping ½-inch-high rim at edge of pan. Dough is now ready to top as desired.

TIP   If you're short on time, you can purchase ready-made pizza dough at your neighborhood pizza shop and many supermarkets. The dough is sold raw and raised; just roll it out and top it.

BROCCOLI AND RED PEPPER PIZZA

Pizza topped with mixed veggies is always popular. We've contained the calories without sacrificing the flavor by sautéing the veggies in light corn-oil spread and sprinkling the pizza with part-skim mozzarella.

ACTIVE TIME: 20 MINUTES PLUS TIME TO MAKE DOUGH · **TOTAL TIME:** 40 MINUTES
MAKES: 8 MAIN-DISH SERVINGS

HOMEMADE PIZZA DOUGH (PAGE 23)

2   TEASPOONS OLIVE OIL

1   LARGE RED PEPPER (6 TO 8 OUNCES), CUT INTO THIN STRIPS

1   LARGE GARLIC CLOVE, CRUSHED WITH GARLIC PRESS

1   PACKAGE (16 OUNCES) BROCCOLI FLOWERETS

¼   TEASPOON SALT

½   CUP TOMATO SAUCE

½   CUP PACKED BASIL LEAVES, CHOPPED

4   OUNCES PART-SKIM MOZZARELLA OR MONTEREY JACK CHEESE, SHREDDED (1 CUP)

1 Prepare Homemade Pizza Dough. Preheat oven to 450°F; position rack at bottom.

2 In nonstick 12-inch skillet, heat olive oil over medium-high heat. Add red pepper and garlic; cook until softened. Meanwhile, in 10-inch skillet, heat 1 *inch water* to boiling over high heat. Place steamer basket in skillet; add broccoli. Reduce heat to medium; cover and steam until tender.

3 Remove broccoli from water; transfer to skillet with red pepper, add salt, and toss well to mix.

4 Spread dough with tomato sauce. Spoon broccoli mixture on top. Sprinkle with basil and cheese. Bake until crust is golden and crisp, 20 to 25 minutes.

225 CALORIES

PER SERVING. 10G PROTEIN | 37G CARBOHYDRATE | 4G TOTAL FAT (2G SATURATED) 4G FIBER | 8MG CHOLESTEROL | 554MG SODIUM

MAKE IT A MEAL: A 400-calorie lunch can be as simply delicious as a slice of this mixed veggie pizza plus a baby spinach salad tossed with a tablespoon each of olive oil and lemon juice.

RICOTTA-SPINACH CALZONE

No one can resist the cheesy goodness that is a calzone. This one is a delightfully devious way to make sure you eat your spinach.

ACTIVE TIME: 10 MINUTES · **TOTAL TIME:** 30 MINUTES

MAKES: 4 MAIN-DISH SERVINGS

1 PACKAGE (10 OUNCES) FROZEN CHOPPED SPINACH

1 CUP PART-SKIM RICOTTA CHEESE

4 OUNCES MOZZARELLA CHEESE, SHREDDED (1 CUP)

1 TABLESPOON CORNSTARCH

½ TEASPOON DRIED OREGANO

1 TUBE (10 OUNCES) REFRIGERATED PIZZA-CRUST DOUGH

½ CUP BOTTLED MARINARA OR HOMEMADE MARINARA SAUCE (PAGE 16)

1 Preheat oven to 400°F.

2 In small microwave-safe bowl, heat spinach in microwave on High for 2 to 3 minutes, until spinach is mostly thawed but still cool enough to handle. Squeeze spinach to remove excess water.

3 Meanwhile, in small bowl, combine ricotta, mozzarella, cornstarch, and oregano; set aside.

4 Coat large cookie sheet with nonstick cooking spray. Unroll pizza dough on center of cookie sheet. With fingertips, press dough into 14" by 10" rectangle.

5 Sprinkle cheese mixture lengthwise over half of dough, leaving 1-inch border. Spoon marinara sauce over cheese mixture; top with spinach. Fold other half of dough over filling. Pinch edges together to seal.

6 Bake calzone until well browned on top, 20 to 25 minutes. Cut into 4 equal pieces to serve.

400 CALORIES

PER SERVING. 21G PROTEIN | 43G CARBOHYDRATE | 15G TOTAL FAT (5G SATURATED) 4G FIBER | 19MG CHOLESTEROL | 1,055MG SODIUM

MAKE IT A MEAL: This makes a stellar lunch on the run; reheat in the toaster oven, wrap in a paper towel, and you're good to go. Or, for a hearty weeknight dinner, pair the calzone with a side of Cauliflower with Raisins and Pine Nuts (95 calories; page 132).

MOZZARELLA IN CARROZZA

Mozzarella in carrozza—"mozzarella in a carriage"—is usually deep-fried, but we pan-fry ours to keep the calories in check. According to tradition, it is served with a drizzle of buttery anchovy sauce.

ACTIVE TIME: 20 MINUTES · **TOTAL TIME:** 25 MINUTES
MAKES: 4 SANDWICHES OR 8 SERVINGS

8 OUNCES PART-SKIM MOZZARELLA CHEESE	½ CUP PLAIN DRIED BREAD CRUMBS
8 SLICES FIRM WHITE BREAD, CRUSTS REMOVED	3 TABLESPOONS VEGETABLE OIL
	4 TABLESPOONS BUTTER OR MARGARINE
2 LARGE EGGS, WELL BEATEN	8 ANCHOVY FILLETS, DRAINED
¼ CUP MILK	1 TABLESPOON CHOPPED FRESH PARSLEY
¼ CUP ALL-PURPOSE FLOUR	
½ TEASPOON SALT	1 TEASPOON CAPERS, DRAINED
¼ TEASPOON GROUND BLACK PEPPER	1 TEASPOON FRESH LEMON JUICE

1 Stand mozzarella on short side and cut lengthwise into 4 equal slices. Place each slice cheese between 2 slices bread to form 4 sandwiches.

2 Preheat oven to 200°F. In pie plate, with wire whisk, beat eggs and milk. On waxed paper, combine flour, salt, and pepper; spread bread crumbs on separate sheet of waxed paper. Dip sandwiches, one at a time, in flour mixture, shaking off excess, then in egg mixture, and finally in bread crumbs, shaking off excess.

3 In nonstick 12-inch skillet, heat oil over medium heat until hot. Add sandwiches; cook until golden brown, about 1½ minutes per side. Cut each sandwich on diagonal in half. Arrange on platter in single layer. Keep warm in oven.

4 In same skillet, melt butter; add anchovies and cook, stirring constantly, 1 minute. Add parsley, capers, and lemon juice; cook 30 seconds longer. Transfer sauce to small bowl. Serve sauce with sandwiches.

310 CALORIES

PER SERVING. 13G PROTEIN | 22G CARBOHYDRATE | 19G TOTAL FAT (8G SATURATED) 0G FIBER | 89MG CHOLESTEROL | 713MG SODIUM

MAKE IT A MEAL: For an Italian take on grilled cheese and tomato soup, pair these sandwiches with Chilled Tuscan-Style Tomato Soup (145 calories; page 116). At 455 calories, it's a comfort food meal your waistline can afford.

CARAMELIZED ONION AND GOAT CHEESE PANINI

With their savory, aromatic fillings and a flavor-charred crunch, these melty, satisfying sandwiches are grilled cheese for grown-ups. A heavy skillet does the work of a panini press.

ACTIVE TIME: 35 MINUTES · **TOTAL TIME:** 45 MINUTES
MAKES: 4 SANDWICHES, OR 4 SERVINGS

- 2 TABLESPOONS OLIVE OIL
- 2 JUMBO SWEET ONIONS (1 POUND EACH), THINLY SLICED
- ½ TEASPOON SALT
- ¼ TEASPOON GROUND BLACK PEPPER
- ½ TEASPOON CHOPPED FRESH THYME LEAVES
- 8 CENTER SLICES (½ INCH THICK) COUNTRY-STYLE BREAD
- 4 OUNCES SOFT FRESH GOAT CHEESE

1 In nonstick 12-inch skillet, heat oil over medium heat. Stir in onions and salt and pepper; cover and cook 15 minutes or until very soft, stirring occasionally. Uncover and cook 15 to 25 minutes longer or until onions are golden brown, stirring frequently. Stir in thyme; remove pan from heat.

2 Prepare outdoor grill for direct grilling over medium heat.

3 Meanwhile, assemble panini: Place 4 slices bread on work surface. Spread one-fourth of goat cheese on each slice and top with one-fourth of onion mixture. Top with remaining bread slices.

4 Place 2 panini on hot grill grate. Place heavy skillet (preferably cast iron) on top of panini, press down, and cook 7 to 8 minutes or until bread is toasted and browned on both sides, turning over once. Repeat with remaining panini.

380 CALORIES

PER SERVING. 14G PROTEIN | 48G CARBOHYDRATE | 16G TOTAL FAT (6G SATURATED) 6G FIBER | 14MG CHOLESTEROL | 750MG SODIUM

MAKE IT A MEAL: Giardiniera (35 calories; page 114), a pickled mixed-vegetable antipasto, is just the thing to pair with either of these panini for a quick and satisfying lunch.

RED PEPPER AND PROVOLONE PANINI

ACTIVE TIME: 15 MINUTES · **TOTAL TIME:** 20 MINUTES

Prepare panini as above, but omit step 1. In step 2, while grill is preheating, in small bowl, combine **1 jar (7 ounces) roasted red peppers,** drained and sliced; **¼ cup white wine vinegar; 1 clove garlic,** crushed with press; and **¼ teaspoon ground black pepper**. Set aside 10 minutes; drain. In step 3, divide **4 ounces sliced Provolone, 4 ounces sliced Genoa salami,** and **marinated red peppers** evenly among **4 bread slices;** top with remaining bread. Complete as in step 4.

370
CALORIES

PER SERVING. 18G PROTEIN | 32G CARBOHYDRATE | 18G TOTAL FAT (8G SATURATED) 2G FIBER | 48MG CHOLESTEROL | 1,232MG SODIUM

TUSCAN TUNA SALAD SANDWICHES

Tuna and cannellini beans are a popular combination in Italy. Tossed with a piquant dressing, they make a great sandwich filling.

TOTAL TIME: 15 MINUTES

MAKES: 4 SANDWICHES OR 4 SERVINGS

1 CAN (15 TO 19 OUNCES) WHITE KIDNEY BEANS (CANNELLINI), RINSED AND DRAINED

½ CUP CHOPPED FRESH BASIL

3 TABLESPOONS CAPERS, DRAINED AND CHOPPED

2 TABLESPOONS FRESH LEMON JUICE

2 TABLESPOONS OLIVE OIL

½ TEASPOON SALT

¼ TEASPOON COARSELY GROUND BLACK PEPPER

1 CAN (6 OUNCES) TUNA PACKED IN WATER, DRAINED AND FLAKED

1 BUNCH (4 OUNCES) WATERCRESS, TOUGH STEMS TRIMMED AND SPRIGS CUT IN HALF

4 (6- TO 7-INCH) WHOLE-WHEAT PITA BREADS

2 RIPE MEDIUM TOMATOES (6 TO 8 OUNCES EACH), THINLY SLICED

1 In large bowl, mash 1 cup beans. Stir in basil, capers, lemon juice, oil, salt, and pepper until well blended. Add tuna, watercress, and remaining beans; toss to mix.

2 Cut pita breads in half. Spoon tuna mixture onto pita halves; top with tomato slices.

330 CALORIES

PER SERVING. 20G PROTEIN | 44G CARBOHYDRATE | 10G TOTAL FAT (1G SATURATED) 9G FIBER | 15MG CHOLESTEROL | 724MG SODIUM

MAKE IT A MEAL: Keep lunchtime simple: Munch on 10 baby carrots (40 calories total) in between bites of this tricked-out tuna sandwich. Or top 2 cups watercress with this tuna salad and lose the pita. Either way, you'll have a satisfying lunch for well under 400 calories.

TOMATO, PORTOBELLO, AND MOZZARELLA MELTS

These luscious open-faced focaccia sandwiches are topped with peppery arugula, thickly sliced grilled tomatoes and portobellos, and melted mozzarella cheese. For photo, see page 20.

ACTIVE TIME: 10 MINUTES · **TOTAL TIME:** 20 MINUTES
MAKES: 2 SANDWICHES OR 4 SERVINGS

---

2   CUPS LOOSELY PACKED ARUGULA OR WATERCRESS, TRIMMED

2   TABLESPOONS BALSAMIC VINEGAR

1   LOAF (ABOUT 1 INCH THICK) FOCACCIA OR CIABATTA BREAD

4   LARGE PORTOBELLO MUSHROOMS (ABOUT 1 POUND TOTAL), STEMS REMOVED AND EACH CUT IN HALF

2   RIPE MEDIUM TOMATOES (6 TO 8 OUNCES EACH), EACH CUT INTO ¾-INCH-THICK SLICES

2   TABLESPOONS EXTRA-VIRGIN OLIVE OIL

¼   TEASPOON SALT

¼   TEASPOON COARSELY GROUND BLACK PEPPER

4   OUNCES FRESH MOZZARELLA CHEESE, THINLY SLICED

1   Prepare outdoor grill for direct grilling over medium-high heat.

2   In small bowl, toss arugula and vinegar until evenly coated. From loaf of focaccia, cut two 8" by 2" pieces, using serrated knife. Slice each piece horizontally in half to make four 8" by 2" pieces.

3   Brush mushrooms and tomatoes on both sides with oil; sprinkle with salt and pepper. Place mushrooms, stem sides up, and tomato slices on hot grill rack and cook until tender and charred, 6 to 8 minutes, turning over once. Transfer tomatoes to plate. Arrange mozzarella on mushrooms; cover and cook until cheese melts, 1 to 2 minutes longer.

4   Place bread, cut sides up, on work surface; top with arugula mixture, grilled tomatoes, and cheese-topped mushrooms. Cut each sandwich into 2 portions and serve immediately.

355 CALORIES

PER SERVING. 14G PROTEIN | 43G CARBOHYDRATE | 15G TOTAL FAT (5G SATURATED) 6G FIBER | 22MG CHOLESTEROL | 595MG SODIUM 💙 🌼

MAKE IT A MEAL: You've already fired up the grill. Why not make Grilled Eggplant Caponata Salad (75 calories; page 128)? Finish with 1 cup cubed watermelon (45 calories) for a memorable al fresco dinner for just 475 calories.

EGGS—A NATURAL DIET FOOD

You may be steering clear of eggs because of their cholesterol content, but consider the following: When researchers tracked people on a low-cal diet, they found that those who ate two eggs for breakfast lost 65 percent more weight than those who had a bagel. (The egg eaters' cholesterol levels didn't even go up!) They shed the extra pounds because they felt fuller after breakfast so they ate fewer calories throughout the day.

ASPARAGUS-ROMANO FRITTATA

Consider this frittata a rite of spring. Asparagus plays the starring role, of course, but you could substitute sautéed potatoes, peppers, and onions; spinach and fresh basil; or even rice and a chopped plum tomato or two.

ACTIVE TIME: 15 MINUTES · **TOTAL TIME:** 35 MINUTES
MAKES: 6 MAIN-DISH SERVINGS

12 LARGE EGGS

¾ CUP FRESHLY GRATED PECORINO-ROMANO CHEESE

½ CUP WHOLE MILK

¾ TEASPOON SALT

⅛ TEASPOON GROUND BLACK PEPPER

1 TABLESPOON BUTTER

1 POUND ASPARAGUS, CUT INTO 1-INCH PIECES

1 BUNCH GREEN ONIONS, THINLY SLICED

1 Preheat oven to 375°F. In medium bowl, whisk eggs, Romano, milk, ½ teaspoon salt, and pepper.

2 In nonstick 12-inch skillet with oven-safe handle, melt butter over medium heat. Stir in asparagus and remaining ¼ teaspoon salt; cook 5 minutes. Add onions; cook 3 to 4 minutes, stirring often. Spread vegetable mixture evenly in skillet.

3 Reduce heat to medium-low. Pour egg mixture into skillet; cook 4 to 5 minutes, without stirring, until egg mixture sets around edge. Place skillet in oven; bake 9 to 10 minutes or until set. Invert frittata onto serving plate; cut into wedges.

235 CALORIES

PER SERVING. 18G PROTEIN | 5G CARBOHYDRATE | 16G TOTAL FAT (7G SATURATED) 1G FIBER | 443MG CHOLESTEROL | 580MG SODIUM

MAKE IT A MEAL: For a light brunch with some zip, add a small side salad of mixed greens and grape tomatoes (40 calories) tossed with a tomato-orange vinaigrette: Whisk together ½ cup tomato juice, 1 tablespoon balsamic vinegar, ¼ teaspoon grated orange peel, ¼ teaspoon sugar, and ¼ teaspoon ground black pepper. The dressing is just 5 calories per tablespoon, so the whole meal comes in well under 300 calories.

FLORENTINE FRITTATA

This frittata is a cheesy wonder, combining the smooth creaminess of mozzarella and the salty tang of feta.

ACTIVE TIME: 10 MINUTES · **TOTAL TIME:** 20 MINUTES
MAKES: 4 MAIN-DISH SERVINGS

- 4 LARGE EGGS
- 4 LARGE EGG WHITES
- 1 PACKAGE (10 OUNCES) FROZEN CHOPPED SPINACH, THAWED AND SQUEEZED DRY
- 2 GREEN ONIONS, THINLY SLICED
- ¼ CUP CRUMBLED FETA CHEESE
- 3 OUNCES PART-SKIM MOZZARELLA CHEESE, SHREDDED (¾ CUP)
- ¼ TEASPOON SALT
- 1 TABLESPOON OLIVE OIL
- 1 CUP GRAPE OR CHERRY TOMATOES

1 Preheat broiler.

2 In large bowl, with wire whisk or fork, beat whole eggs, egg whites, spinach, green onions, feta, ½ cup mozzarella, and salt until blended.

3 In broiler-safe nonstick 10-inch skillet, heat oil over medium heat until hot. Pour egg mixture into skillet; arrange tomatoes on top, pushing some down. Cover skillet and cook frittata until egg mixture just sets around edge, 5 to 6 minutes.

4 Place skillet in broiler 5 to 6 inches from source of heat and broil until frittata just sets in center, 4 to 5 minutes. Sprinkle with remaining ¼ cup mozzarella; broil until cheese melts, about 1 minute longer.

5 To serve, gently slide frittata out of skillet and onto serving plate; cut into wedges.

230 CALORIES **PER SERVING.** 18G PROTEIN | 6G CARBOHYDRATE | 14G TOTAL FAT (6G SATURATED) 2G FIBER | 233MG CHOLESTEROL | 570MG SODIUM

MAKE IT A MEAL: Pair this colorful frittata with a mixed greens and tomato salad. Toss 2 cups spinach (15 calories) and ½ cup chopped tomato (15 calories) with 2 tablespoons nonfat balsamic salad dressing (25 calories). The complete brunch is less than 300 calories per serving.

SPINACH STRATA

Fresh basil and mozzarella lend Italian flair to this breakfast casserole. You can assemble this a day ahead, then pop it in the oven—right from the refrigerator—just an hour before serving.

ACTIVE TIME: 15 MINUTES · **TOTAL TIME:** 1 HOUR 15 MINUTES PLUS CHILLING AND STANDING
MAKES: 6 MAIN-DISH SERVINGS

8 SLICES FIRM WHITE BREAD	2 CUPS MILK
4 OUNCES MOZZARELLA CHEESE, SHREDDED (1 CUP)	6 LARGE EGGS
1 PACKAGE (10 OUNCES) FROZEN CHOPPED SPINACH, THAWED AND SQUEEZED DRY	½ CUP LOOSELY PACKED FRESH BASIL LEAVES, CHOPPED
	½ TEASPOON SALT
1 TABLESPOON BUTTER OR MARGARINE, SOFTENED	¼ TEASPOON GROUND BLACK PEPPER

1 Grease 8-inch square glass baking dish. Place 4 slices bread in dish; top with ½ cup cheese, all spinach, then remaining cheese. Spread butter or margarine on 1 side of remaining bread slices; place in dish, buttered side up.

2 In medium bowl, with wire whisk or fork, beat milk, eggs, basil, salt, and pepper until blended. Slowly pour egg mixture over bread slices. Prick bread with fork and press slices down to absorb egg mixture.

3 Cover baking dish with plastic wrap and refrigerate at least 30 minutes or overnight.

4 To bake, preheat oven to 350°F. Uncover baking dish and bake strata 1 hour or until knife inserted in center comes out clean. Remove strata from oven and let stand 5 minutes before serving.

290 CALORIES **PER SERVING.** 17G PROTEIN | 22G CARBOHYDRATE | 15G TOTAL FAT (6G SATURATED) 2G FIBER | 240MG CHOLESTEROL | 575MG SODIUM

MAKE IT A MEAL: A half a grapefruit (30 calories) or ½ cup cubed watermelon (45 calories) are all you need to round out this yummy one-dish meal.

285
CALORIES
Lentil Stew with
Butternut Squash
(page 41)

HEARTY SOUPS & SALADS

Much of the Italian food we have come to love is peasant fare—hearty soups like minestrone and pasta e fagioli in broth—and in this chapter we provide plenty of soul-satisfying options. Enjoy our recipes for chicken soup with escarole and a chunky fish and tomato stew, each well under 400 calories per serving. All you need to complete these meals is a crusty roll to soak up the broth! Or try one of our substantial main-dish salads: Sopressata and Roma Bean Salad with Pecorino and Warm Farro Salad with Roasted Vegetables are loaded with wholesome, flavorful Italian vegetables, grains, and beans.

KEY TO ICONS

🔵 30 minutes or less　❤️ Heart healthy　🌾 High fiber　🟩 Make ahead　🍲 Slow cooker

BARLEY MINESTRONE WITH PESTO

Top this soup with a dollop of our homemade pesto, which you can make in a mini food processor or blender. In a hurry? Store-bought pesto makes an excellent stand-in—although it's not as light as our version.

ACTIVE TIME: 50 MINUTES · **TOTAL TIME:** 1 HOUR 15 MINUTES
MAKES: 6 MAIN-DISH SERVINGS

MINESTRONE

- 1   CUP PEARL BARLEY
- 1   TABLESPOON OLIVE OIL
- 2   CUPS THINLY SLICED GREEN CABBAGE (ABOUT ¼ SMALL HEAD)
- 2   LARGE CARROTS, PEELED, EACH CUT LENGTHWISE IN HALF, THEN CROSSWISE INTO ½-INCH-THICK SLICES
- 2   LARGE STALKS CELERY, CUT INTO ½-INCH DICE
- 1   ONION, CUT INTO ½-INCH DICE
- 1   GARLIC CLOVE, FINELY CHOPPED
- 3   CUPS WATER
- 2   CANS (14½ OUNCES EACH) VEGETABLE BROTH
- 1   CAN (14½ OUNCES) DICED TOMATOES
- ¼   TEASPOON SALT
- 1   MEDIUM ZUCCHINI (8 OUNCES), CUT INTO ½-INCH DICE
- 4   OUNCES GREEN BEANS, TRIMMED AND CUT INTO ½-INCH PIECES (1 CUP)

LIGHT PESTO

- 1   CUP FIRMLY PACKED FRESH BASIL LEAVES
- 2   TABLESPOONS OLIVE OIL
- 2   TABLESPOONS WATER
- ¼   TEASPOON SALT
- ¼   CUP FRESHLY GRATED PECORINO-ROMANO CHEESE
- 1   GARLIC CLOVE, FINELY CHOPPED

1   Heat 5- to 6-quart Dutch oven over medium-high heat until hot. Add barley and cook until toasted and fragrant, 3 to 4 minutes, stirring constantly. Transfer barley to small bowl; set aside.

2   Add oil to same Dutch oven. When hot, add cabbage, carrots, celery, and onion; cook until tender and lightly browned, 8 to 10 minutes, stirring occasionally. Add garlic and cook until fragrant, 30 seconds. Stir in barley, water, broth, tomatoes with their juice, and salt. Cover and heat to boiling over high heat. Turn heat to low and simmer 25 minutes.

3   Stir zucchini and beans into pot; increase heat to medium, cover, and cook until vegetables are barely tender, 10 to 15 minutes longer.

4   Meanwhile, prepare pesto: In blender container with narrow base or in mini food processor, combine basil, oil, water, and salt; cover and blend until mixture is pureed. Transfer pesto to small bowl; stir in Romano and garlic. Makes about ½ cup pesto.

5 Ladle minestrone into large soup bowls. Top each serving with a dollop of Light Pesto.

230 PER SERVING SOUP WITH 1 TEASPOON PESTO. 7G PROTEIN | 42G CARBOHYDRATE
CALORIES 5G TOTAL FAT (0G SATURATED) | 9G FIBER | 1MG CHOLESTEROL | 725MG SODIUM

MAKE IT A MEAL: Pair this soup with a Broiled Rosemary Polenta Wedge (100 calories; page 137) for a warming 330-calorie lunch.

PASTA E FAGIOLI

Here's a fast-lane version of everyone's favorite Italian bean soup.

ACTIVE TIME: 10 MINUTES · **TOTAL TIME:** 35 MINUTES
MAKES: 8 CUPS OR 4 MAIN-DISH SERVINGS

1 TABLESPOON OLIVE OIL

1 SMALL ONION, SLICED

1 LARGE STALK CELERY, SLICED

1 CAN (14½ OUNCES) CHICKEN BROTH

2 CUPS WATER

1 CAN (15 TO 19 OUNCES) WHITE KIDNEY BEANS (CANNELLINI), RINSED AND DRAINED (SEE TIP)

1 CAN (14½ OUNCES) DICED TOMATOES

2 GARLIC CLOVES, CRUSHED WITH GARLIC PRESS

1 TEASPOON SUGAR

¼ TEASPOON SALT

¼ TEASPOON GROUND BLACK PEPPER

¼ CUP TUBETTINI OR DITALINI PASTA

1 PACKAGE (10 OUNCES) FROZEN CHOPPED SPINACH

1 In 5- to 6- quart Dutch oven, heat oil over medium heat until hot. Add onion and celery and cook until vegetables are tender, about 10 minutes.
2 Meanwhile, in 2-quart saucepan, heat broth and water to boiling over high heat.
3 Add beans, tomatoes, garlic, sugar, salt, and pepper to Dutch oven; heat to boiling over high heat. Add broth mixture and pasta; heat to boiling. Reduce heat to medium and cook 5 minutes. Add frozen spinach; cook, stirring frequently, 3 to 4 minutes longer.

TIP Whether you choose pink beans, garbanzos, pintos, or that classic Italian option, cannellini, beans are packed with protein and insoluble and soluble fiber. Insoluble fiber helps promote regularity and may stave off such digestive disorders as diverticulosis. Soluble fiber can reduce LDL cholesterol levels and help control blood-sugar levels in people with diabetes.

220 CALORIES   **PER SERVING.** 10G PROTEIN | 33G CARBOHYDRATE | 5G TOTAL FAT (1G SATURATED) 9G FIBER | 0MG CHOLESTEROL | 1,265MG SODIUM

MAKE IT A MEAL: To add a little crunch to a 375-calorie lunch, add on three store-bought cheese straws (110 calories) and a Chocolate-Hazelnut Macaron (45 calories; page 141).

LENTIL STEW WITH BUTTERNUT SQUASH

Here's a hearty vegetarian slow-cooker meal that's packed with fiber and low in sodium. For photo, see page 36.

ACTIVE TIME: 20 MINUTES · **SLOW-COOK TIME:** 8 HOURS ON LOW

MAKES: 11½ CUPS OR 8 MAIN-DISH SERVINGS

3 LARGE STALKS CELERY, CUT INTO ¼-INCH-THICK SLICES

1 LARGE ONION (12 OUNCES), CHOPPED

1 LARGE BUTTERNUT SQUASH (2½ POUNDS), PEELED, SEEDED, AND CUT INTO 1-INCH CHUNKS

1 BAG (1 POUND) BROWN LENTILS

4 CUPS WATER

1 CAN (14½ OUNCES) VEGETABLE BROTH

½ TEASPOON ROSEMARY

¾ TEASPOON SALT

¼ TEASPOON GROUND BLACK PEPPER

1 OUNCE PARMESAN OR ROMANO CHEESE, SHAVED WITH VEGETABLE PEELER

¼ CUP LOOSELY PACKED FRESH PARSLEY LEAVES, CHOPPED

1 In 4½- to 6-quart slow-cooker bowl, combine celery, onion, squash, lentils, water, broth, rosemary, salt, and pepper. Cover slow cooker with lid, and cook as manufacturer directs on Low for 8 hours.

2 To serve, spoon lentil stew into serving bowls; top with Parmesan shavings, and sprinkle with chopped parsley.

285 CALORIES

PER SERVING. 20G PROTEIN | 51G CARBOHYDRATE | 2G TOTAL FAT (1G SATURATED) 20G FIBER | 3MG CHOLESTEROL | 420MG SODIUM ♥ 🌿 🍱 🍱

MAKE IT A MEAL: Garlicky Escarole with White Beans (80 calories; page 131) will add some greens and beans to an already wholesome meal. Better still, this stick-to-your-ribs meal comes in well under 400 calories.

ZUPPA DE PESCE

This classic Italian fish soup features fresh mussels and chunks of cod in a tomato and white wine broth spiked with fennel seeds and crushed red pepper.

ACTIVE TIME: 25 MINUTES · **TOTAL TIME:** 35 MINUTES
MAKES: 4 MAIN-DISH SERVINGS

1 TABLESPOON OLIVE OIL	1 CUP WATER
1 SMALL ONION, FINELY CHOPPED	½ TEASPOON SALT
1 SMALL RED PEPPER, CHOPPED	12 OUNCES COD OR ALASKAN POLLOCK FILLET, CUT INTO 2-INCH PIECES
1 LARGE GARLIC CLOVE, CRUSHED	1 POUND MUSSELS, SCRUBBED AND BEARDS REMOVED (SEE TIP)
½ TEASPOON FENNEL SEEDS	
⅛ TEASPOON CRUSHED RED PEPPER	8 OUNCES MEDIUM SHRIMP, SHELLED AND DEVEINED
¾ CUP DRY WHITE WINE	
1 CAN (28 OUNCES) WHOLE TOMATOES IN JUICE, COARSELY CHOPPED	½ CUP FRESH BASIL LEAVES, JULIENNED

1 In 5- to 6-quart Dutch oven over medium, heat oil. Add onion and chopped red pepper; cook 6 to 8 minutes or until tender. Add garlic, fennel, and crushed red pepper; cook 1 minute longer, stirring. Add wine; heat to boiling.

2 Stir in tomatoes with their juice, water, and salt; heat to boiling. Add cod, mussels, and shrimp; heat to boiling. Reduce heat to low; cover. Simmer 8 to 9 minutes or until cod and shrimp turn opaque and mussels open. Discard any unopened mussels. To serve, sprinkle with basil leaves.

TIP To clean mussels, scrub them well under cold running water. Cultivated mussels usually do not have beards, but if you need to debeard the mussels, grasp the hairlike beard with your thumb and forefinger and pull it away from the shell, or scrape it off with a knife.

265 CALORIES

PER SERVING. 37G PROTEIN | 15G CARBOHYDRATE | 6G TOTAL FAT (1G SATURATED) 3G FIBER | 147MG CHOLESTEROL | 805MG SODIUM

MAKE IT A MEAL: Pair this vibrant tomato and fish stew with our light and lemony Zucchini Carpaccio salad (205 calories; page 122). Enjoy it all for just 470 calories.

CHICKEN AND ESCAROLE SOUP

Here's a comforting Italian take on chicken noodle soup. It pairs leftover cooked chicken with tiny orzo pasta and escarole, a mild-flavored green in the endive family that's beloved by Italians. The greens require only brief cooking in the broth.

ACTIVE TIME: 15 MINUTES · **TOTAL TIME:** 35 MINUTES
MAKES: 10 CUPS OR 5 MAIN-DISH SERVINGS

1   TABLESPOON OLIVE OIL

2   CUPS SHREDDED OR MATCHSTICK CARROTS (ABOUT TWO-THIRDS 10-OUNCE BAG)

1   SMALL ONION, FINELY CHOPPED

2   GARLIC CLOVES, MINCED

3   CANS (14 TO 14½ OUNCES EACH) CHICKEN BROTH (5¼ CUPS)

2   CUPS WATER

2   HEADS ESCAROLE (1½ POUNDS), CUT INTO 1-INCH PIECES

½   CUP ORZO PASTA (SEE TIP)

2   CUPS CHOPPED LEFTOVER COOKED CHICKEN (10 OUNCES)

⅛   TEASPOON COARSELY GROUND BLACK PEPPER

½   CUP FRESHLY GRATED PARMESAN CHEESE

1   In 6-quart Dutch oven, heat oil over medium-high heat until hot. Add carrots, onion, and garlic; cook 4 minutes or until onion softens, stirring frequently. Stir in broth and water; heat to boiling. Stir in escarole and orzo; heat to boiling.

2   Reduce heat to medium-low; simmer, uncovered, 6 minutes or until escarole and orzo are tender. Stir in chicken and pepper. Reduce heat to low and simmer 3 minutes or until chicken is heated through. Serve with Parmesan.

TIP   In Italian, *orzo* means "barley," but it's actually a tiny, rice-shaped pasta. It's ideal for soups or can be used as a substitute for rice.

285 CALORIES   **PER SERVING.** 28G PROTEIN | 25G CARBOHYDRATE | 9G TOTAL FAT (3G SATURATED) 6G FIBER | 49MG CHOLESTEROL | 890MG SODIUM

MAKE IT A MEAL: Serve with a crusty Tomato and Ricotta Salata Bruschetta (170 calories; page 119) to create an easy 455-calorie meal.

VEAL AND MUSHROOM STEW

In this recipe, the veal is slowly simmered with mushrooms and a touch of sweet Marsala wine until tender. Peas contribute subtle sweetness and color.

ACTIVE TIME: 30 MINUTES · **TOTAL TIME:** 1 HOUR 30 MINUTES
MAKES: 6 MAIN-DISH SERVINGS

1½ POUNDS BONELESS VEAL SHOULDER, CUT INTO 1½-INCH CHUNKS	¼ POUND SHIITAKE MUSHROOMS, STEMS REMOVED
¾ TEASPOON SALT	½ CUP WATER
¼ TEASPOON GROUND BLACK PEPPER	⅓ CUP SWEET MARSALA WINE
3 TABLESPOONS VEGETABLE OIL	1 PACKAGE (10 OUNCES) FROZEN PEAS, THAWED
1 POUND MEDIUM MUSHROOMS, TRIMMED AND CUT IN HALF	

1 Preheat oven to 350°F. Pat veal dry with paper towels and sprinkle with salt and pepper. In nonreactive 5-quart Dutch oven, heat 2 tablespoons oil over medium-high heat until very hot. Add half of veal and cook until browned, using slotted spoon to transfer meat to bowl as it is browned. Add remaining veal to pot and brown in same way.

2 In Dutch oven, heat remaining 1 tablespoon oil over medium-high heat. Add all mushrooms and cook, stirring occasionally, until lightly browned.

3 Return veal to Dutch oven; pour in water and Marsala, stirring until browned bits are loosened from bottom of pan. Heat to boiling.

4 Cover Dutch oven and bake, stirring occasionally, until veal is tender, 1 hour to 1 hour 15 minutes. Stir in peas and heat through.

250 CALORIES

PER SERVING. 26G PROTEIN | 12G CARBOHYDRATE | 11G TOTAL FAT (2G SATURATED) 3G FIBER | 94MG CHOLESTEROL | 448MG SODIUM ♥ 🍱

MAKE IT A MEAL: Roman-Style Artichokes (185 calories; page 120), topped with Romano- and mint-seasoned bread crumbs, are a classic Italian beginning to an equally classic stew. Who would believe you could enjoy so much goodness for 435 calories?

MAKE YOUR OWN SALAD BAR

Create an entire meal with an Italian accent. These Mediterranean ingredients, complete with calorie counts, will help you fill your bowl.

SELECT YOUR SALAD GREENS

Bibb, romaine, baby spinach, arugula, watercress, mixed baby greens, or frisée— the choice is up to you. Use 2 cups as the base for your salad: just 15 calories.

PICK YOUR PROTEIN

Add substance to your salad with any one of these protein-rich items.

Grilled skinless chicken breast: This low-calorie, protein-rich option will keep you satisfied. For authentic Italian flavor, sprinkle each breast with ¼ teaspoon fresh thyme or rosemary and grill in a ridged grill pan sprayed with nonstick olive oil spray for 11 to 13 minutes, turning once, or until instant-read thermometer registers 165°F. Toss ¼ cup cubed chicken into your salad: 60 calories.

Grilled shrimp: Toss 1 pound shrimp with 1 teaspoon olive oil, 1 teaspoon fresh oregano, and ⅛ teaspoon salt to coat. Grill in a grill pan or outdoor grill over medium-high heat for 3 to 5 minutes, until shrimp are opaque throughout, turning once. Cool for 5 minutes before adding 2 ounces shrimp (two extra-large shrimp) to your salad: 65 calories.

Poached salmon: Arrange a 6-ounce fillet in a glass baking dish, season with salt, and top with thinly sliced lemons and ¼ cup water. Cover with plastic wrap and microwave on High for 8 minutes or until fish just turns opaque throughout. Transfer to paper towels to cool for 15 minutes; shred 2 ounces onto your salad: 105 calories.

Beans: Loaded with protein and fiber, beans make you feel fuller longer. Toss in 2 tablespoons of cannellini, garbanzos, or pink beans: 40 calories.

Hard-boiled egg: Full of protein (6 grams per egg), nutrients, and flavor, eggs are a good salad option if you limit them to 2 tablespoons chopped, or one-half egg: 30 calories.

SELECT YOUR ADD-ONS

These mix-ins will elevate your salad from ho-hum to irresistible.

Fresh veggies: Keep starchy, calorie-dense veggies like corn and potatoes to ¼ cup; otherwise, there's no limit: 30 calories.

Fresh fruit: To add tangy flavor along with phytochemicals, vitamins, and more, toss in ½ cup: 20 to 60 calories.

Nuts and seeds: Toast them to bring out their full flavor. Limit to 1 tablespoon to keep calories in check: 45 calories.

Cheese: Add grated Parmesan, crumbled blue cheese, or slivers of Provolone, but use no more than 1 tablespoon: 25 calories.

Olives: A few go a long way, so limit this calorie-dense pick to around 1 tablespoon sliced, or 3 or 4 whole olives: 30 calories.

DRIZZLE WITH DRESSING

Below is a recipe for a classic Italian vinaigrette. Or, do as the Italians do and toss your salad with 1 tablespoon olive oil, the juice of ½ lemon, and some salt (125 calories).

Classic vinaigrette: Whisk together ¼ cup red wine vinegar, 1 tablespoon Dijon mustard, ¼ teaspoon salt, and ¼ teaspoon ground black pepper. Whisk in ½ cup extra-virgin olive oil in a slow, steady stream until well blended. Toss your salad with 2 tablespoons: 165 calories.

Balsamic vinaigrette variation: Prepare as directed but substitute balsamic vinegar for the red wine vinegar.

Herb vinaigrette variation: Prepare as directed but substitute white wine vinegar for the red. Stir in 1 tablespoons chopped fresh chives and 1 teaspoon chopped fresh tarragon.

PROSCIUTTO-WRAPPED GRILLED FIG SALAD

Grilling adds a delicious charred flavor to prosciutto-wrapped fresh figs stuffed with tangy goat cheese. Serving them atop a bed of lightly dressed greens cuts the richness of the dish.

ACTIVE TIME: 15 MINUTES · **TOTAL TIME:** 35 MINUTES
MAKES: 4 FIRST-COURSE SERVINGS

½   TEASPOON FRESH THYME LEAVES

½   TEASPOON FENNEL SEEDS

4   OUNCES GOAT CHEESE

1   PINCH PLUS ¼ TEASPOON SALT

½   TEASPOON GROUND BLACK PEPPER

10   FRESH FIGS, EACH CUT IN HALF LENGTHWISE

4   OUNCES VERY THINLY SLICED PROSCIUTTO, EACH PIECE CUT IN HALF LENGTHWISE

2   TABLESPOONS SHERRY VINEGAR

1   TABLESPOON PURE HONEY

1   TABLESPOON EXTRA-VIRGIN OLIVE OIL

5   OUNCES MIXED BABY GREENS

1   Prepare outdoor grill for direct grilling over medium heat.

2   Chop thyme and fennel together; combine, in bowl, with cheese, pinch salt, and ¼ teaspoon pepper.

3   Scoop 1 level teaspoon goat cheese mixture onto cut side of 1 fig half. Repeat with remaining cheese and figs. Wrap 1 strip prosciutto around each fig, enclosing cheese. If prosciutto doesn't stick to itself, secure with toothpicks.

4   Grill figs 2 to 3 minutes or until prosciutto is lightly charred and cheese is soft, turning over once.

5   Meanwhile, in bowl, whisk vinegar, honey, oil, and remaining ¼ teaspoon each salt and pepper. Add greens; toss to coat.

6   Remove toothpicks, if used. Divide greens and figs among serving plates.

285 CALORIES

PER SERVING. 15G PROTEIN | 31G CARBOHYDRATE | 13G TOTAL FAT (6G SATURATED) 4G FIBER | 35MG CHOLESTEROL | 1,050MG SODIUM

MAKE IT A MEAL: Company's coming? Serve this salad with some Italian bread and olive oil for dipping (80 calories per slice). Finish with our lemony and refreshing Sgroppino Sorbet with Prosecco and Mint (135 calories; page 149).

WARM FARRO SALAD WITH ROASTED VEGETABLES

If you've never tried farro, this hearty main-dish salad provides the perfect introduction to the nutty flavor and chewy texture of this ancient grain.

ACTIVE TIME: 25 MINUTES · **TOTAL TIME:** 1 HOUR 5 MINUTES
MAKES: 4 MAIN-DISH SERVINGS

---

1 TO 2 LEMONS

2 LARGE CARROTS, PEELED AND CUT INTO ½-INCH DICE

2 SMALL FENNEL BULBS, TRIMMED AND CUT INTO 1-INCH PIECES

1 RED ONION, HALVED AND THINLY SLICED THROUGH ROOT END

3 TABLESPOONS OLIVE OIL

1 TEASPOON SALT

1⅛ TEASPOONS GROUND BLACK PEPPER

1 BUNCH RADISHES, TRIMMED AND CUT INTO ½-INCH DICE

1 TABLESPOON RED WINE VINEGAR

2½ CUPS WATER

1 CUP FARRO

1 CUP LIGHTLY PACKED FRESH BASIL LEAVES, CHOPPED

1 Preheat oven to 400°F. From lemons, grate 2 teaspoons peel and squeeze 3 tablespoons juice; set aside.

2 In large bowl, combine carrots, fennel, onion, 1 tablespoon oil, ½ teaspoon salt, and 1 teaspoon pepper; toss. Turn onto 15½" by 10½" jelly-roll pan and spread evenly. Roast 20 minutes, stirring once. Stir in radishes and roast until vegetables are tender, about 10 minutes. Stir in vinegar.

3 Meanwhile, in medium saucepan, bring water, farro, and ¼ teaspoon salt to boiling over high heat. Reduce heat to medium-low; cover and simmer until farro is tender and water is absorbed, 25 to 30 minutes.

4 In large bowl, whisk together reserved lemon juice and peel, along with remaining 2 tablespoons oil, ¼ teaspoon salt, and ⅛ teaspoon pepper. Add farro, roasted vegetables, and basil; toss to combine. Serve warm.

---

320 CALORIES

PER SERVING. 9G PROTEIN | 51G CARBOHYDRATE | 10G TOTAL FAT (2G SATURATED) 9G FIBER | 0MG CHOLESTEROL | 708MG SODIUM ♥

MAKE IT A MEAL: Like to finish your lunch with something sweet? Pair this wholesome salad with a Pignoli Cookie (75 calories; page 146), and you have a guilt-free 395-calorie meal.

SOPRESSATA & ROMA BEAN SALAD WITH PECORINO

Slightly sweeter than green beans, broad beans are the oldest bean in existence. Look for those that are pale green, soft, and tender. These beans are best eaten within a few days of purchase.

ACTIVE TIME: 10 MINUTES · **TOTAL TIME:** 25 MINUTES
MAKES: 4 MAIN-DISH SERVINGS

1¼ POUNDS ROMA BEANS OR GREEN BEANS, TRIMMED

1 LEMON

2 TABLESPOONS EXTRA-VIRGIN OLIVE OIL

¼ TEASPOON SALT

⅛ TEASPOON COARSELY GROUND BLACK PEPPER

4 OUNCES SOPRESSATA OR GENOA SALAMI, SLICED INTO ½-INCH STRIPS

2 SMALL BUNCHES (4 OUNCES EACH) ARUGULA, TOUGH STEMS TRIMMED, OR 2 BAGS (5 OUNCES EACH) ARUGULA

1 (2-OUNCE) WEDGE PECORINO-ROMANO CHEESE

1 If beans are very long, cut crosswise into 2½-inch pieces. In 12-inch skillet, heat 1 *inch water* to boiling over high heat. Add beans; heat to boiling. Reduce heat to low; simmer 6 to 8 minutes or until beans are tender-crisp. Drain beans and rinse with cold running water to stop cooking; drain again.

2 Meanwhile, from lemon, grate ½ teaspoon peel and squeeze 2 tablespoons juice. In large bowl, with wire whisk, mix lemon peel and juice with oil, salt, and pepper.

3 Add beans, sopressata, and arugula to dressing in bowl; toss to coat.

4 To serve, spoon salad onto platter. With vegetable peeler, shave thin strips from wedge of Romano to top salad.

280 CALORIES

PER SERVING. 14G PROTEIN | 14G CARBOHYDRATE | 21G TOTAL FAT (7G SATURATED) 5G FIBER | 41MG CHOLESTEROL | 845MG SODIUM

MAKE IT A MEAL: For an anything-but-ordinary 400-calorie lunch, end the meal with an espresso and two Crunchy Chocolate Biscotti (100 calories; page 143).

HERBED PORK MEDALLIONS WITH ASPARAGUS SALAD

Rubbed with rosemary and parsley and roasted in a 400°F oven, this trim tenderloin is mouthwateringly moist and served atop a fiber-rich salad of crunchy carrots, asparagus, and greens.

ACTIVE TIME: 20 MINUTES · **TOTAL TIME:** 40 MINUTES
MAKES: 4 MAIN-DISH SERVINGS

½ CUP PACKED FRESH FLAT-LEAF PARSLEY LEAVES	¼ TEASPOON GROUND BLACK PEPPER
1 TABLESPOON FRESH ROSEMARY LEAVES, FINELY CHOPPED	4 TEASPOONS EXTRA-VIRGIN OLIVE OIL
1 PORK TENDERLOIN (12 OUNCES)	1 BUNCH RADISHES, TRIMMED AND CUT INTO THIN WEDGES
2 LARGE CARROTS, PEELED AND LEFT WHOLE	1 GREEN ONION, THINLY SLICED
1 POUND ASPARAGUS, ENDS TRIMMED	1 PACKAGE (5 OUNCES) BABY GREENS-AND-HERBS MIX
¼ TEASPOON SALT	¼ CUP BALSAMIC VINEGAR

1 Preheat oven to 400°F. Heat large pot of *water* to boiling over high heat.

2 Finely chop one-third of parsley. Rub chopped parsley and rosemary all over tenderloin and let stand while oven heats.

3 Fill large bowl with ice and water. Add carrots to boiling water. Cook 5 minutes. With tongs, transfer to ice water. When cool, remove with tongs to cutting board. Add asparagus to boiling water. Cook 3 minutes or until bright green and crisp-tender. Transfer to ice water. When cool, drain well.

4 Sprinkle ⅛ teaspoon each salt and pepper all over pork. In 12-inch oven-proof skillet, heat 1 teaspoon oil over medium-high heat. Add pork; cook 6 to 8 minutes or until evenly browned, turning. Transfer to oven. Roast 8 to 10 minutes or until meat thermometer inserted in thickest part of pork registers 145°F; let rest 5 minutes.

5 While pork cooks, cut carrots into 2-inch-long matchsticks. Cut asparagus into 2-inch-long pieces. In large bowl, toss carrots, asparagus, radishes, onion, greens, and remaining parsley with remaining ⅛ teaspoon each salt and pepper and 1 tablespoon oil. Add vinegar; toss to combine. Divide salad among serving plates. Slice pork; arrange on top of salads.

235 CALORIES

PER SERVING. 26G PROTEIN | 14G CARBOHYDRATE | 8G TOTAL FAT (2G SATURATED) 5G FIBER | 62MG CHOLESTEROL | 255MG SODIUM

MAKE IT A MEAL: This substantial salad is dinner worthy without embellishment. But add two pieces of Tuscan White-Bean Bruschetta (140 calories each; page 119) and you'll have a meal to remember for just over 500 calories.

385 CALORIES
Spaghetti and Meatballs
(page 66)

PASTA, POLENTA & RISOTTO

Ask almost anyone what their favorite Italian food is, and they'll answer without hesitation, "Pasta!" Whether you long to twirl your fork in spaghetti and meatballs or crave a square of cheesy lasagna, we offer lots of satisfying pasta options—you won't believe they're 400 calories or less! And, of course, we've included polenta and risotto. Our versions take a few liberties—we make one risotto in the microwave, the other in a slow cooker—but the results are as soul satisfying as the originals.

KEY TO ICONS

⏱ 30 minutes or less ♥ Heart healthy 🌾 High fiber 🟩 Make ahead 🍲 Slow cooker

WHOLE-WHEAT PENNE GENOVESE

An onion-flecked white bean sauté adds heft to this fresh and healthy pesto pasta dish, making it light yet satisfying.

ACTIVE TIME: 20 MINUTES · **TOTAL TIME:** 30 MINUTES
MAKES: 6 MAIN-DISH SERVINGS

12 OUNCES WHOLE-WHEAT PENNE OR ROTINI

1½ CUPS PACKED FRESH BASIL LEAVES

1 GARLIC CLOVE

3 TABLESPOONS WATER

3 TABLESPOONS EXTRA-VIRGIN OLIVE OIL

¼ TEASPOON SALT

¼ TEASPOON GROUND BLACK PEPPER

½ CUP FRESHLY GRATED PARMESAN CHEESE

1 SMALL ONION, CHOPPED

1 CAN (15 TO 19 OUNCES) WHITE KIDNEY BEANS (CANNELLINI), RINSED AND DRAINED

1 PINT GRAPE TOMATOES (RED, YELLOW, AND ORANGE MIX IF AVAILABLE), EACH CUT INTO QUARTERS

1 Cook pasta as label directs.

2 Meanwhile, make pesto: In food processor with knife blade attached, blend basil, garlic, water, 2 tablespoons oil, salt, and pepper until pureed, stopping processor occasionally and scraping bowl with rubber spatula. Add Parmesan; pulse to combine. Set aside.

3 In 12-inch skillet, heat remaining 1 tablespoon oil over medium heat until very hot; add onion and cook 5 to 7 minutes or until beginning to soften. Stir in white beans and cook 5 minutes longer, stirring occasionally.

4 When pasta is done, reserve ¼ cup *pasta cooking water*. Drain pasta and return to saucepot; stir in white bean mixture, pesto, cut-up tomatoes, and reserved cooking water. Toss to coat.

375 CALORIES

PER SERVING. 15G PROTEIN | 59G CARBOHYDRATE | 10G TOTAL FAT (2G SATURATED) 9G FIBER | 5MG CHOLESTEROL | 435MG SODIUM ♥ ♥ ✿

MAKE IT A MEAL: Whole-wheat pasta, beans, veggies, and cheese mean this meal-in-a-bowl needs little to complete it. So, why not indulge in something just because it's luscious? An icy Coffee Granita (55 calories; page 145) is just the thing.

PASTA PRIMAVERA

This dish is traditionally made in spring, when the first tender young vegetables appear—thus the name *primavera*, which means "spring" in Italian. With an abundance of first-of-the-season veggies and fiber-rich whole-grain spaghetti, you'll never miss the cream sauce—or the calories.

TOTAL TIME: 30 MINUTES
MAKES: 6 MAIN-DISH SERVINGS

2 LEEKS (1¼ POUNDS)

1 TABLESPOON EXTRA-VIRGIN OLIVE OIL

½ TEASPOON SALT

½ TEASPOON GROUND BLACK PEPPER

1 POUND THIN ASPARAGUS

1 PACKAGE (12 OUNCES) WHOLE-GRAIN SPAGHETTI

1 CUP FROZEN PEAS

1 PINT GRAPE TOMATOES, EACH CUT IN HALF

¼ CUP PACKED FRESH FLAT-LEAF PARSLEY LEAVES, FINELY CHOPPED

¼ CUP FRESHLY GRATED PARMESAN CHEESE

1 Heat large covered saucepot of *water* to boiling over high heat. Meanwhile, trim and clean leeks, cutting leeks lengthwise in half, then crosswise into ¼-inch-wide slices.

2 In 12-inch skillet, heat oil over medium heat until hot. Add leeks and ⅛ teaspoon each salt and pepper; cook 9 to 10 minutes or until tender and golden, stirring occasionally. While leeks cook, trim asparagus and cut into 1½-inch-long pieces.

3 Cook pasta as label directs. Meanwhile, increase heat under skillet to medium-high. Add asparagus and ⅛ teaspoon each salt and pepper; cook 1 minute or until bright green, stirring. Add peas, tomatoes, and remaining ¼ teaspoon each salt and pepper. Cook 2 minutes or until peas are bright green. From saucepot with pasta, scoop 1 *cup water;* pour into skillet with vegetables. Cook 5 minutes or until liquid has reduced and tomatoes have softened.

4 Drain pasta; transfer to large serving bowl. Add vegetable mixture. With tongs, toss until well combined. To serve, top with parsley and Parmesan.

325 CALORIES

PER SERVING. 15G PROTEIN | 60G CARBOHYDRATE | 5G TOTAL FAT (1G SATURATED) 8G FIBER | 35MG CHOLESTEROL | 320MG SODIUM ❤ ♥ 🌾

MAKE IT A MEAL: What a delightful Italian-style dinner party this pasta makes paired with our Healthy Makeover Tiramisu (175 calories; page 150). No one needs to know that this 500-calorie meal is anything but an indulgence.

RAVIOLI WITH RIPE TOMATOES

Who knew you could prepare pasta in a microwave? What's more, the simple, from-scratch sauce uses the perfectly ripe tomatoes of late summer—and doesn't require any cooking. Whipped up fresh and fast and tossed with ricotta ravioli, it's a flavorful send-off to the season.

ACTIVE TIME: 20 MINUTES · **TOTAL TIME:** 30 MINUTES PLUS STANDING
MAKES: 4 MAIN-DISH SERVINGS

1½ POUNDS RIPE TOMATOES, CHOPPED (4 CUPS)

½ CUP PACKED FRESH BASIL LEAVES, CHOPPED

3 TABLESPOONS OLIVE OIL

¼ TEASPOON FRESHLY GRATED LEMON PEEL

¼ TEASPOON SALT

¼ TEASPOON GROUND BLACK PEPPER

1 BAG (13 TO 16 OUNCES) FROZEN CHEESE RAVIOLI

2½ CUPS WATER

¼ CUP FRESHLY GRATED PARMESAN CHEESE

1 In large bowl, combine tomatoes, basil, oil, lemon peel, salt, and pepper. Let stand at room temperature at least 15 minutes or up to 30 minutes to blend flavors.

2 Meanwhile, place ravioli in large bowl with water; cover with vented plastic wrap and microwave on High for 10 minutes or until cooked through, stirring once.

3 Add hot pasta to tomato mixture and toss to coat. Sprinkle with Parmesan to serve.

375 CALORIES

PER SERVING. 14G PROTEIN | 45G CARBOHYDRATE | 16G TOTAL FAT (4G SATURATED) 4G FIBER | 19MG CHOLESTEROL | 535MG SODIUM

MAKE IT A MEAL: This easy main dish deserves an equally simple-to-prepare side. Build a salad with a bit of crunch—kale, almonds, and lemony dressing—and you'll have a colorful meal for less than 500 calories.

CREAMY MUSHROOM CAVATAPPI

This tasty pasta dish combines mushrooms with cavatappi, or spiral macaroni, for a quick and easy dinner. Instead of cream, we used low-fat milk and cornstarch to lend a velvety texture to the sauce.

ACTIVE TIME: 15 MINUTES · **TOTAL TIME:** 30 MINUTES
MAKES: 6 MAIN-DISH SERVINGS

- 12 OUNCES CAVATAPPI PASTA
- 2 TEASPOONS OLIVE OIL
- 1 SMALL ONION (4 TO 6 OUNCES), CHOPPED
- 1 PACKAGE (8 OUNCES) SLICED CREMINI MUSHROOMS
- 1 TABLESPOON CORNSTARCH
- 1½ CUPS LOW-FAT (1%) MILK
- ½ CUP FRESHLY GRATED PARMESAN CHEESE PLUS ADDITIONAL FOR SERVING
- ¼ TEASPOON SALT
- ¼ TEASPOON GROUND BLACK PEPPER
- 1 PACKAGE (10 OUNCES) FROZEN PEAS
- 8 OUNCES DELI-SLICED HAM, CUT INTO ½-INCH-WIDE STRIPS

1 Cook pasta as label directs.

2 Meanwhile, in 12-inch skillet, heat oil over medium heat until hot. Add onion and cook 3 minutes or until beginning to soften. Increase heat to medium-high and stir in mushrooms; cook 8 to 10 minutes or until mushrooms are golden and most liquid has evaporated, stirring frequently. Transfer mushroom mixture to small bowl.

3 In 2-cup liquid measuring cup, whisk cornstarch into milk; add to same skillet and heat to boiling over medium heat, whisking frequently. Boil 1 minute, stirring constantly to prevent scorching on bottom of skillet. Remove skillet from heat and whisk in ½ cup Parmesan, salt, and pepper.

4 Place peas in colander. Pour pasta over peas; drain and pour pasta mixture into saucepot. Stir in mushroom mixture, cheese sauce, and ham; toss to coat. Serve with freshly grated Parmesan.

400 CALORIES

PER SERVING. 23G PROTEIN | 57G CARBOHYDRATE | 8G TOTAL FAT (3G SATURATED) 5G FIBER | 28MG CHOLESTEROL | 880MG SODIUM

MAKE IT A MEAL: Want to add some greens to your meal? Steam 2 cups spinach per person and give it a squeeze of lemon juice and a sprinkle of salt and pepper. At 15 calories per serving, it'll hardly tip the scale.

LIGHT FETTUCCINE ALFREDO

For a weeknight family supper, try this low-fat version of the classic Alfredo sauce. We shaved off calories—and added sautéed garlic, onion, and broccoli flowerets—while keeping the sauce smooth and cheesy.

ACTIVE TIME: 15 MINUTES · **TOTAL TIME:** 30 MINUTES
MAKES: 6 MAIN-DISH SERVINGS

2	TEASPOONS VEGETABLE OIL	½	TEASPOON SALT
1	SMALL ONION (4 TO 6 OUNCES), FINELY CHOPPED	¼	TEASPOON COARSELY GROUND BLACK PEPPER
1	LARGE GARLIC CLOVE, CRUSHED WITH GARLIC PRESS	½	CUP FRESHLY GRATED PARMESAN CHEESE
2	CUPS FAT-FREE MILK	1	PACKAGE (16 OUNCES) FETTUCCINE
1	CUP CHICKEN BROTH	1	PACKAGE (16 OUNCES) BROCCOLI FLOWERETS
3	TABLESPOONS ALL-PURPOSE FLOUR		

1 In nonstick 12-inch skillet, heat oil over medium heat. Add onion and garlic and cook until onion is golden, about 8 minutes. In bowl, with wire whisk, whisk milk, broth, flour, salt, and pepper until smooth. Add to onion mixture and cook, stirring, until sauce has thickened and boils; boil 1 minute. Stir in Parmesan.

2 Meanwhile, in large saucepot, cook pasta as label directs. After pasta has cooked 7 minutes, add broccoli to pasta water. Cook until pasta and broccoli are done, 3 to 5 minutes longer. Drain pasta and broccoli.

3 In warm serving bowl, toss pasta and broccoli with sauce.

275 CALORIES

PER SERVING. 12G PROTEIN | 46G CARBOHYDRATE | 4G TOTAL FAT (1G SATURATED) 3G FIBER | 5MG CHOLESTEROL | 436MG SODIUM ❤️

MAKE IT A MEAL: We've already dressed up this Alfredo sauce, but consider adding one or even two of the following pasta perk-ups along with the broccoli and onion: 2 tablespoons drained capers; ½ cup pitted and chopped Kalamata or green Sicilian olives; ⅓ cup chopped sun-dried tomatoes; and/or 2 to 4 tablespoons chopped fresh basil, oregano, or parsley. Each of these add-ons is 100 calories or less, so you can finish the meal with an Almond Macaroon Finger (30 calories; page 140) and still come in around 500 calories.

ITALIAN WEDDING PASTA

Rich enough to celebrate a special occasion, our baked pasta lightens up the calories with reduced-fat milk and lean turkey.

ACTIVE TIME: 30 MINUTES · **TOTAL TIME:** 50 MINUTES
MAKES: 8 MAIN-DISH SERVINGS

1 POUND GROUND TURKEY

¼ CUP PLAIN DRIED BREAD CRUMBS

¼ CUP LOOSELY PACKED FRESH PARSLEY LEAVES, CHOPPED

3 GARLIC CLOVES, 1 CLOVE CRUSHED WITH GARLIC PRESS AND 2 THINLY SLICED

1 LARGE EGG

1 CUP FRESHLY GRATED PECORINO-ROMANO CHEESE

1 PACKAGE (16 OUNCES) FARFALLE OR BOW-TIE PASTA

1 TABLESPOON CORNSTARCH

1½ CUPS REDUCED-FAT (2%) MILK

1 CAN (14½ OUNCES) REDUCED-SODIUM CHICKEN BROTH

1 BAG (9 OUNCES) BABY SPINACH

¼ TEASPOON GROUND BLACK PEPPER

1 Preheat oven to 400°F. Line 15½" by 10½" jelly-roll pan with foil.

2 In medium bowl, with fingertips, mix turkey, bread crumbs, parsley, crushed and sliced garlic, egg, and ¼ cup Romano cheese just until blended; do not overmix. Shape turkey mixture into 1-inch meatballs (you will have about 36); place in prepared pan. Bake 20 minutes.

3 Meanwhile, cook pasta as label directs, but drain 2 minutes before indicated cooking time; return to saucepot.

4 In 2-cup liquid measuring cup, whisk cornstarch into milk. Add milk mixture and broth to pasta in saucepot; heat to boiling over medium-high heat, stirring frequently. Boil 1 minute to thicken sauce slightly. Remove saucepot from heat; stir in spinach, ½ cup grated Romano, and pepper. Add meatballs and gently toss to combine. Transfer pasta mixture to 3-quart glass or ceramic baking dish; sprinkle with remaining ¼ cup grated Romano. Bake 20 minutes or until hot in the center and golden brown on top.

390 CALORIES

PER SERVING. 25G PROTEIN | 49G CARBOHYDRATE | 10G TOTAL FAT (4G SATURATED) 4G FIBER | 85MG CHOLESTEROL | 380MG SODIUM ❤

MAKE IT A MEAL: Ground turkey and baby spinach make this pasta dish a stand-alone meal. But if you want something sweet, add an orange (70 calories) to complete your 450-calorie dinner.

BEEF RAGU

We made this classic pasta dish a little healthier by using lean beef and substituting whole-grain penne for regular pasta.

ACTIVE TIME: 15 MINUTES · **TOTAL TIME:** 30 MINUTES
MAKES: 6 MAIN-DISH SERVINGS

- 2½ TEASPOONS SALT
- 1 TEASPOON EXTRA-VIRGIN OLIVE OIL
- 1 POUND LEAN (93%) GROUND BEEF
- ½ TEASPOON GROUND BLACK PEPPER
- 1 LARGE CARROT, PEELED AND FINELY CHOPPED
- 1 LARGE STALK CELERY, FINELY CHOPPED
- 1 SMALL ONION (4 TO 6 OUNCES), FINELY CHOPPED
- ¼ TEASPOON GROUND CUMIN
- ¼ TEASPOON GROUND CORIANDER
- 1 PINCH CRUSHED RED PEPPER
- 1 CAN (28 OUNCES) NO-SALT-ADDED FIRE-ROASTED DICED TOMATOES
- 1 PACKAGE (13¼ OUNCES) WHOLE-GRAIN PENNE
- 1 CUP PACKED FRESH MINT LEAVES, FINELY CHOPPED

1 Cook pasta as label directs, using 2 teaspoons salt, but drain pasta 1 minute before cooking time for al dente is reached.

2 While pasta cooks, in 12-inch skillet, heat oil over high heat. Add beef in even layer. Sprinkle with ¼ teaspoon each salt and black pepper. Cook 2 minutes or until browned; stir, breaking into pieces.

3 Add carrot, celery, and onion. Cook 5 minutes or until tender and golden, stirring occasionally. Add cumin, coriander, and red pepper. Cook 30 seconds, stirring. Stir in tomatoes; heat to boiling. Reduce heat to maintain steady simmer and cook 10 minutes.

4 Return drained pasta to saucepot. Stir in tomato sauce; cook over medium heat 2 minutes or until pasta is al dente and well coated, stirring. Stir in mint and remaining ¼ teaspoon each salt and black pepper.

385 CALORIES

PER SERVING. 27G PROTEIN | 58G CARBOHYDRATE | 6G TOTAL FAT (2G SATURATED) 8G FIBER | 47MG CHOLESTEROL | 385MG SODIUM

MAKE IT A MEAL: Add a whole-grain roll (100 calories) for a filling 485-calorie dinner you will make again and again.

SPAGHETTI AND MEATBALLS

Our leaner take allows you to indulge. For photo, see page 54.

ACTIVE TIME: 1 HOUR · **TOTAL TIME:** 1 HOUR 30 MINUTES
MAKES: 12 MAIN-DISH SERVINGS

MEATBALLS

- 4   SLICES FIRM WHITE BREAD, COARSELY GRATED
- ⅓   CUP WATER
- 2   POUNDS LEAN GROUND BEEF AND TURKEY (1 POUND OF EACH)
- 2   LARGE EGG WHITES
- ¼   CUP FRESHLY GRATED ROMANO OR PARMESAN CHEESE
- 1   GARLIC CLOVE, CRUSHED
- 1   TEASPOON SALT
- ¼   TEASPOON GROUND BLACK PEPPER

TOMATO SAUCE

- 2   TABLESPOONS OLIVE OIL
- 3   CARROTS, FINELY CHOPPED
- 2   ONIONS, CUT INTO ¼-INCH DICE
- 3   GARLIC CLOVES, CRUSHED
- 3   CANS (28 OUNCES EACH) ITALIAN-STYLE PLUM TOMATOES IN PUREE
- ¾   TEASPOON SALT
- ¼   TEASPOON GROUND BLACK PEPPER
- 1½ POUNDS SPAGHETTI

1   Prepare meatballs: Preheat oven to 450°F. In large bowl, with hands, mix grated bread with water until evenly moistened. Add beef and turkey, egg whites, cheese, garlic, salt, and pepper; mix just until combined. With wet hands, shape mixture into twenty-four 2-inch meatballs. Place in 15½" by 10½" jelly-roll pan and bake 18 to 20 minutes, until cooked through and lightly browned.

2   Meanwhile, prepare sauce: In 6-quart Dutch oven or saucepot over medium, heat oil. Add carrots and onions; cook until tender and golden, about 15 minutes. Add garlic and cook 1 minute, stirring. Place tomatoes with puree in large bowl. With kitchen shears, cut up tomatoes until well crushed. Add tomatoes with puree, salt, and pepper to Dutch oven; heat to boiling over high, stirring occasionally. Reduce heat to medium; cover and cook 10 minutes. Uncover, add meatballs, and cook 15 minutes longer, stirring occasionally.

3   Meanwhile, cook spaghetti as label directs, then drain and return to pot. Toss spaghetti with sauce and meatballs. Serve each diner 1 cup cooked spaghetti, ¼ cup sauce, and two meatballs.

385 CALORIES

PER SERVING. 26G PROTEIN | 50G CARBOHYDRATE | 10G TOTAL FAT (2G SATURATED) 3G FIBER | 44MG CHOLESTEROL | 560MG SODIUM

MAKE IT A MEAL: Add the classic side: garlic bread (110 calories; page 115).

SPAGHETTI PIE WITH PROSCIUTTO AND PEAS

Pasta meets pizza: Pour eggs, reduced-fat milk, and part-skim ricotta over pasta, then top with peas and prosciutto. Presto! It's dinner.

ACTIVE TIME: 25 MINUTES · **TOTAL TIME:** 50 MINUTES
MAKES: 6 MAIN-DISH SERVINGS

8	OUNCES THICK SPAGHETTI	¼	TEASPOON SALT
4	LARGE EGGS	¼	TEASPOON GROUND BLACK PEPPER
2	LARGE EGG WHITES	1	TABLESPOON BUTTER OR MARGARINE
1	CONTAINER (15 OUNCES) PART-SKIM RICOTTA CHEESE	1	BUNCH GREEN ONIONS, CUT INTO ¼-INCH PIECES (1 CUP)
¾	CUP REDUCED-FAT (2%) MILK	1	CUP FROZEN PEAS
⅛	TEASPOON GROUND NUTMEG	6	THIN SLICES PROSCIUTTO (3 OUNCES)

1 Preheat oven to 350°F. Prepare spaghetti according to package directions, without using salt and draining 2 minutes before indicated cooking time.

2 Meanwhile, in medium bowl, whisk eggs, egg whites, ricotta, milk, nutmeg, salt, and pepper until blended. Set aside. In oven-safe nonstick 12-inch skillet, melt butter over medium heat. Add green onions and cook about 5 minutes or until softened. Remove skillet from heat.

3 To skillet, add drained spaghetti and frozen peas; toss to combine. Pour egg mixture over pasta and arrange prosciutto slices on top.

4 Place skillet over medium-high heat and cook egg mixture 3 to 5 minutes or until edges just begin to set. Place skillet in oven and bake 15 minutes or until center is set. Slide pie onto large plate to serve.

375 CALORIES

PER SERVING. 25G PROTEIN | 38G CARBOHYDRATE | 13G TOTAL FAT (6G SATURATED) 2G FIBER | 175MG CHOLESTEROL | 700MG SODIUM

MAKE IT A MEAL: Our Arugula and Olive Salad (125 calories; page 116) is just the thing to round out this meal—500 calories will get you a whole lot of satisfaction without a lot of effort in the kitchen.

VEGETARIAN LASAGNA

Everyone loves lasagna, but who likes all the hard work? An easier way? Layer no-boil noodles, sauce, frozen spinach, and shredded cheese in your slow cooker. *Buon appetito!*

ACTIVE TIME: 15 MINUTES · **SLOW-COOK TIME:** 2½ HOURS ON LOW OR 1½ HOURS ON HIGH
MAKES: 8 MAIN-DISH SERVINGS

1 JAR (25 TO 26 OUNCES) MARINARA SAUCE OR HOMEMADE MARINARA (PAGE 16)

1 CAN (14½ OUNCES) DICED TOMATOES IN JUICE

1 PACKAGE (8 TO 9 OUNCES) NO-BOIL LASAGNA NOODLES (12 TO 15 NOODLES)

1 CONTAINER (15 OUNCES) PART-SKIM RICOTTA CHEESE

6 OUNCES SHREDDED ITALIAN CHEESE BLEND OR MOZZARELLA CHEESE (1½ CUPS)

1 PACKAGE (10 OUNCES) FROZEN CHOPPED SPINACH, THAWED AND SQUEEZED DRY

1 CUP FROZEN VEGGIE CRUMBLES (SEE MAKE IT A MEAL, BELOW)

1 In medium bowl, combine marinara sauce and tomatoes with their juice.
2 Spray 4½- to 6-quart slow-cooker bowl with nonstick cooking spray. Spoon 1 cup tomato-sauce mixture into bowl. Arrange one-fourth of noodles over sauce, overlapping noodles and breaking into large pieces to cover as much sauce as possible. Spoon about ¾ cup sauce over noodles, then top with one-third of ricotta (generous ½ cup) and ½ cup shredded cheese. Spread half of spinach over cheese.
3 Repeat layering, beginning with noodles and using frozen crumbles instead of spinach; repeat layering using remaining spinach. Place remaining noodles over spinach, then top with remaining sauce and shredded cheese.
4 Cover slow cooker with lid and cook as manufacturer directs on Low for 2½ to 3 hours or on High for 1½ to 1¾ hours or until noodles are very tender.

380 CALORIES

PER SERVING. 21G PROTEIN | 45G CARBOHYDRATE | 12G TOTAL FAT (6G SATURATED) 5G FIBER | 34MG CHOLESTEROL | 812MG SODIUM 🌱 🟩 🟧

MAKE IT A MEAL: Asparagus Gremolata (65 calories; page 127) pairs prettily with this meatless lasagna—and brings the total up to just 450 calories. Veggie crumbles are a heat-and-serve vegetarian meat alternative found in your grocer's freezer. If you prefer, you can substitute 8 ounces ground turkey for the crumbles; brown the turkey before including it in the layers.

POLENTA CASSEROLE

You can also serve this hearty ragu over pasta.

ACTIVE TIME: 40 MINUTES · **TOTAL TIME:** 1 HOUR 20 MINUTES
MAKES: 2 CASSEROLES OR 8 MAIN-DISH SERVINGS

- 12 OUNCES HOT ITALIAN TURKEY SAUSAGE, CASINGS REMOVED
- 12 OUNCES MEAT LOAF MIX (VEAL, PORK, AND BEEF) OR GROUND BEEF CHUCK
- 1 JUMBO ONION (1 POUND), CHOPPED
- 2 GARLIC CLOVES, FINELY CHOPPED
- 1 CAN (28 OUNCES) TOMATOES IN PUREE
- 1 SMALL EGGPLANT (1 TO 1¼ POUNDS), CUT INTO ½-INCH PIECES

- 4 CUPS WATER
- 1 CAN (14½ OUNCES) CHICKEN BROTH
- 1½ CUPS CORNMEAL
- ½ TEASPOON SALT
- ¾ CUP FRESHLY GRATED PECORINO-ROMANO OR PARMESAN CHEESE

1   In 5- to 6-quart Dutch oven, cook sausage and meat loaf mix over medium-high heat 5 to 6 minutes or until browned, stirring and breaking up meat with spoon. With slotted spoon, transfer meat to medium bowl.

2   To same pan, add onion; cook over medium heat 8 to 10 minutes or until tender. Stir in garlic; cook 30 seconds. Add tomatoes with their puree; heat to boiling over high heat, breaking up tomatoes with spoon. Reduce heat to medium-low; simmer, uncovered, 10 minutes. Add eggplant and meat; cover and cook 5 minutes over medium heat. Uncover and cook 10 minutes longer or until eggplant is tender, stirring occasionally.

3   Meanwhile, preheat oven to 400°F. In microwave-safe 4-quart bowl, with wire whisk, combine water, broth, cornmeal, and salt. Microwave on High 15 to 20 minutes or until cornmeal mixture is very thick. After first 5 minutes of cooking, whisk vigorously until smooth; whisk two more times during remaining cooking time, then whisk in Romano.

4   Spoon 2 cups hot polenta into each of two 1½-quart shallow casseroles. Spread polenta over bottom and up sides of casseroles. Spoon filling over polenta. Spread remaining polenta around casserole edge to form a rim.

5   Bake one casserole 30 minutes until hot. Freeze second casserole.

385 CALORIES   **PER SERVING.** 22G PROTEIN | 34G CARBOHYDRATE | 18G TOTAL FAT (7G SATURATED) 6G FIBER | 65MG CHOLESTEROL | 1,045MG SODIUM

MAKE IT A MEAL: Enjoy with a glass of bold Italian red wine (120 calories).

RISOTTO MILANESE

The traditional preparation of this luscious rice dish always pleases a crowd but rarely pleases the chef. Made the old-fashioned way, risotto requires laboring over a steamy stove without pause for nearly an hour as you stir ladlefuls of hot broth into the rice one by one and wait for the liquid to be absorbed. Our much simpler strategy puts the microwave to work, shaving a whopping 45 minutes off your active time and reducing the constant stirring to just a few strokes.

ACTIVE TIME: 10 MINUTES · **TOTAL TIME:** 35 MINUTES
MAKES: 6 MAIN-DISH SERVINGS

1   CARTON (32 OUNCES) CHICKEN BROTH
1¼ CUPS WATER
½   CUP DRY WHITE WINE
¼   TEASPOON CRUSHED SAFFRON THREADS
1   TABLESPOON BUTTER OR MARGARINE
1   TABLESPOON OLIVE OIL
1   SMALL ONION, MINCED

2   CUPS ARBORIO OR CARNAROLI RICE (ITALIAN SHORT-GRAIN RICE)
⅓   CUP FRESHLY GRATED PARMESAN CHEESE PLUS ADDITIONAL FOR SERVING
½   TEASPOON SALT
½   TEASPOON GROUND BLACK PEPPER

1 In saucepan, heat broth, water, wine, and saffron to boiling.
2 Meanwhile, in microwave-safe 4-quart bowl, combine butter, oil, and onion. Cook, uncovered, in microwave on High for 2 minutes or until onion softens. Add rice and stir to coat; cook, uncovered, on High for 1 minute.
3 Stir hot broth mixture into rice mixture. Cover bowl with vented plastic wrap, and cook in microwave on Medium (50% power) 16 to 18 minutes or until most liquid is absorbed and rice is tender but still firm, stirring halfway through cooking. Do not overcook; mixture will look loose but will thicken to proper creamy consistency after cooking.
4 Stir in ⅓ cup Parmesan, salt, and pepper. Serve with additional Parmesan.

355 CALORIES **PER SERVING.** 9G PROTEIN | 62G CARBOHYDRATE | 6G TOTAL FAT (2G SATURATED) 2G FIBER | 4MG CHOLESTEROL | 620MG SODIUM

MAKE IT A MEAL: Garlic-Crumbed Tomatoes (125 calories; page 133) are a natural mate for this classic Italian rice dish. Enjoy both for just 480 calories.

BUTTERNUT SQUASH BARLEY RISOTTO

This creamy, comforting barley-based risotto is not only delicious and satisfying—it is healthy, too, full of fiber and essential nutrients. A slow cooker makes it blissfully convenient to prepare.

ACTIVE TIME: 15 MINUTES · **SLOW-COOK TIME:** 3 HOURS 45 MINUTES ON HIGH

MAKES: 6 MAIN-DISH SERVINGS

- 2 TABLESPOONS BUTTER OR MARGARINE
- 2 SHALLOTS, THINLY SLICED
- 2 SPRIGS FRESH THYME
- 2 CUPS PEARL BARLEY
- 1 CARTON (32 OUNCES) VEGETABLE BROTH
- 2 CUPS WATER
- 1 LARGE BUTTERNUT SQUASH (2½ POUNDS), PEELED AND SEEDED, CUT INTO ½-INCH CUBES
- 1½ TEASPOONS SALT
- ⅔ CUP FRESHLY GRATED PARMESAN CHEESE
- ¼ TEASPOON GROUND BLACK PEPPER
- 2 TABLESPOONS CHOPPED FLAT-LEAF PARSLEY LEAVES

1 In 12-inch skillet, melt 1 tablespoon butter over medium-high heat. Add shallots and cook 2 minutes or until golden, stirring often. Add thyme; cook 30 seconds. Add barley and cook 2 minutes or until toasted and golden, stirring often.

2 Transfer to 6-quart slow-cooker bowl, along with broth, water, squash, and ½ teaspoon salt. Cover and cook on High for 3½ to 4 hours or until liquid is absorbed and squash is tender.

3 Uncover; discard thyme. Add Parmesan, remaining tablespoon butter, 1 teaspoon salt, and pepper. Gently stir until butter and Parmesan melt. Transfer risotto to serving plates and garnish with parsley. Risotto can be stored, covered, in refrigerator up to 3 days.

355 CALORIES

PER SERVING. 11G PROTEIN | 68G CARBOHYDRATE | 6G TOTAL FAT (2G SATURATED) 15G FIBER | 5MG CHOLESTEROL | 1,005MG SODIUM

MAKE IT A MEAL: A Chianti-Roasted Pear (135 calories; page 148) is a fitting ending to this warm and creamy 490-calorie dinner.

240
CALORIES
*Cornish Hens Milanese
(page 87)*

MEAT & POULTRY

A meal featuring steak, pork chops, and even veal doesn't have to be high in calories if you do as the Italians do and prepare it with plenty of fresh vegetables (don't forget to use heart-healthy olive oil too). Enjoy our version of braciole, a traditional stuffed and rolled beef dish that we've updated with lean flank steak; rosemary-scented lamb chops; and even veal parmigiana—all for 400 calories or less. And if poultry is on your agenda, then savor a feast of herb-roasted chicken or Cornish hens, turkey cutlets wrapped in prosciutto and topped with a melon and basil garnish, or our pretty grilled chicken breast stacks layered with pesto and mozzarella cheese.

KEY TO ICONS

🕐 30 minutes or less   ❤ Heart healthy   🌾 High fiber   🟩 Make ahead   🍲 Slow cooker

FIRE-GRILLED STEAK WITH FENNEL

Grilled steak and vegetables get big flavor from olive oil, tangy vinegar, fresh herbs, and capers.

ACTIVE TIME: 15 MINUTES · **TOTAL TIME:** 35 MINUTES
MAKES: 4 MAIN-DISH SERVINGS

1	BEEF FLANK STEAK (1 POUND)	½	CUP FRESH MINT LEAVES
⅜	TEASPOON SALT	½	CUP FRESH FLAT-LEAF PARSLEY LEAVES
¼	TEASPOON FRESHLY GROUND BLACK PEPPER	3	TABLESPOONS RED WINE VINEGAR
5	TEASPOONS EXTRA-VIRGIN OLIVE OIL	2	TABLESPOONS CAPERS, RINSED AND DRAINED
2	MEDIUM FENNEL BULBS (1½ POUNDS EACH), CORED, AND CUT LENGTHWISE INTO ½-INCH-THICK SLICES	1	SMALL GARLIC CLOVE, CRUSHED
1	LARGE RED ONION (12 OUNCES), CUT INTO ⅓-INCH-THICK ROUNDS	1	TABLESPOON WATER

1 Prepare outdoor grill for covered direct grilling over medium heat. Sprinkle steak on both sides with ¼ teaspoon each salt and pepper. Use 2 teaspoons oil to brush both sides of fennel and onion slices; sprinkle with remaining ⅛ teaspoon salt.

2 Grill steak, covered, 8 to 10 minutes for medium-rare or until desired doneness, turning over once. (Instant-read meat thermometer should register 145°F.) Grill onion alongside steak 7 to 9 minutes or until tender. Transfer steak to cutting board; transfer onion to bowl.

3 Meanwhile, finely chop mint and parsley; place in medium bowl with vinegar, capers, garlic, water, and remaining 1 tablespoon oil. Stir to blend.

4 Place fennel on grill. Cover; cook 3 to 4 minutes or until browned, turning over once. Toss with onion.

5 Thinly slice steak. Serve with fennel, onion and some herb sauce.

290 CALORIES **PER SERVING.** 26G PROTEIN | 16G CARBOHYDRATE | 13G TOTAL FAT (4G SATURATED) 6G FIBER | 67MG CHOLESTEROL | 465MG SODIUM

MAKE IT A MEAL: Pair with Garlic-Crumbed Tomatoes (125 calories; page 133) and finish with ½ cup lemon sorbet sprinkled with ¼ cup fresh blueberries (100 calories) for a 515-calorie dinner.

VEAL PARMIGIANA

Smothered in marinara sauce and topped with mozzarella cheese, this Italian-restaurant favorite is easy to make at home. For a lower-fat take on this classic, substitute 1½ pounds skinless, boneless chicken breast halves for the veal.

ACTIVE TIME: 30 MINUTES · **TOTAL TIME:** 55 MINUTES
MAKES: 6 MAIN-DISH SERVINGS

- 1 CUP PLAIN DRIED BREAD CRUMBS
- ½ TEASPOON SALT
- ⅛ TEASPOON GROUND BLACK PEPPER
- 1 LARGE EGG
- 2 TABLESPOONS WATER
- 6 VEAL CUTLETS (1½ POUNDS)

- 3 TABLESPOONS OLIVE OIL
- 2 CUPS HOMEMADE MARINARA SAUCE (PAGE 16) OR BOTTLED MARINARA SAUCE
- ¼ CUP FRESHLY GRATED PARMESAN CHEESE
- 4 OUNCES PART-SKIM MOZZARELLA CHEESE, SHREDDED (1 CUP)

1 On waxed paper, combine bread crumbs, salt, and pepper. In pie plate, beat egg and water. Dip cutlets in egg mixture, then in bread crumbs; repeat to coat each cutlet twice.

2 In 12-inch skillet, heat oil over medium heat. Add cutlets, a few at a time, and cook until browned, about 5 minutes per side, using tongs to transfer cutlets to platter as they are browned.

3 Return cutlets to skillet. Spoon marinara sauce evenly over cutlets. Sprinkle with Parmesan and top with mozzarella. Reduce heat to low; cover and cook just until cheese has melted, about 5 minutes.

375 CALORIES

PER SERVING. 35G PROTEIN | 19G CARBOHYDRATE | 17G TOTAL FAT (8G SATURATED) 0G FIBER | 154MG CHOLESTEROL | 913MG SODIUM

MAKE IT A MEAL: Whether you make this dish with veal or chicken breasts, either one just begs for some garlic bread. Add on our Garlic and Herb Bread (110 calories; page 115) to create a 485-calorie meal.

VEAL CHOPS, OSSO BUCO STYLE

Tender veal chops are simmered with tomatoes, herbs, and wine.

ACTIVE TIME: 30 MINUTES · **TOTAL TIME:** 2 HOURS 40 MINUTES
MAKES: 8 MAIN-DISH SERVINGS

1 TABLESPOON OLIVE OIL	1 CAN (14½ OUNCES) WHOLE TOMATOES IN JUICE
4 POUNDS BONE-IN VEAL SHOULDER CHOPS	
½ TEASPOON SALT	1 CUP DRY WHITE WINE
¼ TEASPOON GROUND BLACK PEPPER	1 CAN (14½ OUNCES) CHICKEN BROTH
4 CARROTS, PEELED AND CHOPPED	1 BAY LEAF
3 STALKS CELERY, THINLY SLICED	1 PACKAGE (10 OUNCES) FROZEN PEAS, THAWED
2 ONIONS, CHOPPED	½ TEASPOON GRATED FRESH LEMON PEEL PLUS ADDITIONAL FOR GARNISH
4 GARLIC CLOVES, FINELY CHOPPED	

1 Preheat oven to 350°F. In 6-quart Dutch oven, heat oil over medium-high heat until hot. Sprinkle veal chops with salt and pepper on both sides. Add to Dutch oven in three batches, and cook 8 to 9 minutes per batch or until veal is browned on both sides, turning over once. Transfer veal to plate.
2 Add carrots, celery, onions, and garlic to pot and cook over medium heat 12 minutes or until lightly browned and tender, stirring occasionally.
3 Return veal and any juices from plate to Dutch oven. Stir in tomatoes with their juice, wine, broth, and bay leaf. Heat to boiling over high heat, stirring and breaking up tomatoes with side of spoon.
4 Cover Dutch oven; bake 1 hour and 15 minutes or until veal is very tender when pierced. (Instant-read meat thermometer should register 145°F.) Transfer veal to platter. Skim cooking fat from liquid.
5 Cook sauce on range top over medium-high heat about 10 minutes or until slightly thickened, stirring often. Add peas and lemon peel; cook 2 minutes. To serve, discard bay leaf. Transfer veal to dinner plates. Spoon sauce over veal; sprinkle with additional lemon peel for garnish.

270 CALORIES

PER SERVING. 38G PROTEIN | 15G CARBOHYDRATE | 6G TOTAL FAT (1G SATURATED) 4G FIBER | 141MG CHOLESTEROL | 575MG SODIUM

MAKE IT A MEAL: Add a half portion of Risotto Milanese (180 calories; page 71) plus steamed green beans tossed with a little olive oil and lemon juice.

BRACIOLE WITH GRAPE TOMATOES

Braciole is traditionally simmered slowly in tomato sauce. This recipe uses a quicker method: roasting the beef at high heat and pairing it with tiny sweet grape tomatoes.

ACTIVE TIME: 15 MINUTES · **TOTAL TIME:** 40 MINUTES PLUS STANDING
MAKES: 8 MAIN-DISH SERVINGS

½ CUP ITALIAN-STYLE BREAD CRUMBS	4 TEASPOONS OLIVE OIL
1 GARLIC CLOVE, CRUSHED WITH GARLIC PRESS	½ TEASPOON GROUND BLACK PEPPER
	¼ TEASPOON SALT
¼ CUP FINELY GRATED PECORINO-ROMANO CHEESE	1 BEEF FLANK STEAK (1¾ TO 2 POUNDS)
	2 PINTS GRAPE TOMATOES
½ CUP PACKED FRESH FLAT-LEAF PARSLEY LEAVES, FINELY CHOPPED	

1 Preheat oven to 475°F. In small bowl, combine bread crumbs, garlic, Pecorino, parsley, 1 tablespoon oil, and ¼ teaspoon pepper.

2 On large sheet of waxed paper, with flat side of meat mallet or heavy skillet, pound steak to even ½-inch thickness. Spread crumb mixture over steak in even layer; press into meat. Starting at one long side, roll steak into cylinder (about 2½ inches in diameter) to enclose filling completely. (Some bread crumbs may spill out.) With butcher's twine or kitchen string, tie roll tightly at 1-inch intervals. Place roll in center of 18" by 12" jelly-roll pan. Rub salt and remaining 1 teaspoon oil and ¼ teaspoon pepper all over steak. Scatter tomatoes around steak.

3 Roast 25 to 27 minutes or until temperature on instant-read thermometer, inserted into thickest part of roll, registers 145°F. Let steak stand in pan 10 minutes to set juices for easier slicing. Remove and discard twine; cut roll crosswise into ½-inch-thick slices. Transfer meat and tomatoes with their juices to serving platter.

255 CALORIES

PER SERVING. 22G PROTEIN | 10G CARBOHYDRATE | 14G TOTAL FAT (5G SATURATED) 1G FIBER | 54MG CHOLESTEROL | 290MG SODIUM ❤

MAKE IT A MEAL: Add on our Creamy Microwave Polenta (205 calories; page 136), another quick take on a classic. You'll have a 460-calorie meal that's just the thing for last-minute company.

PORK CHOPS MARSALA

A lush but light wine sauce flavors these lean chops, for restaurant-style richness minus the fat and calories.

TOTAL TIME: 25 MINUTES
MAKES: 4 MAIN-DISH SERVINGS

4 BONELESS PORK LOIN CHOPS (4 OUNCES EACH), TRIMMED OF FAT	½ TEASPOON DRIED THYME, OR 1½ TEASPOONS FRESH THYME LEAVES
½ TEASPOON SALT	1 POUND ASPARAGUS, ENDS TRIMMED
¼ TEASPOON GROUND BLACK PEPPER	2 TABLESPOONS WATER
1 TABLESPOON OLIVE OIL	½ CUP REDUCED-SODIUM CHICKEN BROTH
1 PACKAGE (10 OUNCES) SLICED CREMINI OR WHITE MUSHROOMS	⅓ CUP MARSALA WINE, PREFERABLY SEMI-SECCO (SEE TIP)
1 LARGE SHALLOT, CHOPPED	

1 Evenly season pork chops, on both sides, with salt and pepper.

2 In nonstick 12-inch skillet, heat 2 teaspoons oil over medium heat. Add chops and cook 6 minutes or until browned outside and still slightly pink in center, turning over once. (Instant-read meat thermometer should register 145°F.) Transfer chops to platter; keep warm.

3 In same skillet, heat remaining 1 teaspoon oil 1 minute. Add mushrooms, shallot, and thyme; cook 5 minutes or until mushrooms are browned and shallot is softened.

4 Meanwhile, place asparagus in glass pie plate with water; cover and cook in microwave on High for 3 minutes or until fork-tender. Set aside.

5 Add broth and wine to mushroom mixture; cook 2 minutes. Place chops on dinner plates; top with wine sauce. Serve with asparagus alongside.

TIP Marsala, Italy's most famous fortified wine, is available secco (dry), semi-secco (semisweet), and dolce (sweet). Fine is usually aged less than one year, while Vergine e/o Soleras Stravecchio or Riserva is aged at least ten years.

230 CALORIES **PER SERVING.** 29G PROTEIN | 6G CARBOHYDRATE | 9G TOTAL FAT (2G SATURATED) 3G FIBER | 67MG CHOLESTEROL | 460MG SODIUM

MAKE IT A MEAL: You've already opened a bottle of Marsala, so why not drink a glass (120 calories), then finish the meal with our decadent-tasting Healthy Makeover Tiramisu (175 calories; page 150)? Enjoy it all for just 525 calories per serving.

GLAZED ROSEMARY LAMB CHOPS

These rosemary-scented lamb chops are broiled with an apple-jelly and balsamic-vinegar glaze. This glaze is delicious on pork, too.

ACTIVE TIME: 10 MINUTES · **TOTAL TIME:** 20 MINUTES
MAKES: 4 MAIN-DISH SERVINGS

8   LAMB LOIN CHOPS, 1 INCH THICK (4 OUNCES EACH)

1   LARGE GARLIC CLOVE, CUT IN HALF

2   TEASPOONS CHOPPED FRESH ROSEMARY OR ½ TEASPOON DRIED ROSEMARY, CRUMBLED

¼   TEASPOON SALT

¼   TEASPOON COARSELY GROUND BLACK PEPPER

¼   CUP APPLE JELLY

1   TABLESPOON BALSAMIC VINEGAR

1   Preheat broiler as manufacturer directs and position rack close to heating element. Rub both sides of each lamb chop with garlic; discard garlic. Sprinkle lamb with rosemary, salt, and pepper. In cup, combine apple jelly and balsamic vinegar.

2   Place chops on rack in broiling pan. Broil chops, close to source of heat, 4 minutes. Brush chops with half of apple-jelly mixture; broil 1 minute. Turn chops over and broil 4 minutes longer. Brush chops with remaining jelly mixture and broil 1 minute longer for medium-rare or continue cooking to desired doneness. (Instant-read meat thermometer should register 145°F.)

3   Transfer lamb to warm platter. Skim and discard fat from drippings in pan. Serve chops with pan juices drizzled on top.

240 CALORIES

PER SERVING. 26G PROTEIN | 14G CARBOHYDRATE | 8G TOTAL FAT (3G SATURATED) 0G FIBER | 82MG CHOLESTEROL | 223MG SODIUM ✅ ❤️

MAKE IT A MEAL: Serve with Spaghetti Squash with Olives and Pecorino (125 calories; page 134) for a meal so full of contrasting textures and flavors, you'd never guess it's just 365 calories per serving.

CHICKEN SCARPARIELLO

We adapted this traditional Italian dish for the slow cooker. One secret to its extra-rich taste: coffee-colored cremini mushrooms (or baby portobellos), a more flavorful variety of the common cultivated mushroom.

ACTIVE TIME: 20 MINUTES · **SLOW-COOK TIME:** 8 HOURS ON LOW OR 4 HOURS ON HIGH
MAKES: 6 MAIN-DISH SERVINGS

8	OUNCES HOT OR SWEET ITALIAN SAUSAGE LINKS, CUT CROSSWISE INTO 1½-INCH PIECES
1	ONION, CHOPPED
2	GARLIC CLOVES, CRUSHED WITH GARLIC PRESS
2	TABLESPOONS TOMATO PASTE
2	TABLESPOONS BALSAMIC VINEGAR
½	TEASPOON ITALIAN SEASONING OR DRIED THYME

1	PINT GRAPE TOMATOES
1	PACKAGE (8 OUNCES) SLICED CREMINI MUSHROOMS
1	CHICKEN (3½ TO 4 POUNDS), CUT INTO 8 PIECES, SKIN REMOVED FROM ALL BUT WINGS
¼	TEASPOON SALT
¼	TEASPOON GROUND BLACK PEPPER

1 In nonstick 12-inch skillet, cook sausage pieces over medium heat, turning occasionally, until well browned, about 6 minutes. With tongs or slotted spoon, transfer sausages to 5- to 6-quart slow cooker. Add onion to skillet and cook until slightly softened, about 4 minutes. Stir in garlic and cook, stirring, 1 minute. Remove skillet from heat; stir in tomato paste, vinegar, and Italian seasoning until blended, then add tomatoes and mushrooms. Spoon vegetable mixture into slow cooker and stir to combine. Do not wash skillet.

2 Sprinkle chicken pieces with salt and pepper. In same skillet, cook chicken (in two batches, if necessary) over medium heat until well browned, about 10 minutes.

3 Place chicken pieces on top of vegetable mixture in slow cooker. Cover and cook as manufacturer directs, 8 hours on Low or 4 hours on High. Skim fat from juices before serving.

355 CALORIES

PER SERVING. 39G PROTEIN | 9G CARBOHYDRATE | 17G TOTAL FAT (6G SATURATED) 2G FIBER | 120MG CHOLESTEROL | 420MG SODIUM

MAKE IT A MEAL: A chunk of crusty bread (80 calories) is all you need to complete this stew. For dessert, a refreshing Bold Berry Granita (60 calories; page 145) would round out this 495-calorie meal nicely.

ITALIAN HERB-ROASTED CHICKEN

This simple and delicious roasted-chicken recipe combines dried Mediterranean herbs and garlic.

ACTIVE TIME: 10 MINUTES · **TOTAL TIME:** 1 HOUR 10 MINUTES PLUS STANDING
MAKES: 4 MAIN-DISH SERVINGS

---

1 WHOLE CHICKEN (3½ POUNDS)	1 GARLIC CLOVE, CRUSHED WITH GARLIC PRESS
1 TABLESPOON OLIVE OIL OR SOFTENED BUTTER	¾ TEASPOON SALT
½ TEASPOON DRIED BASIL	1¼ TEASPOONS COARSELY GROUND BLACK PEPPER
½ TEASPOON DRIED OREGANO	½ CUP WATER
½ TEASPOON DRIED ROSEMARY	

1   Preheat oven to 450°F. Remove bag with giblets and neck from chicken cavity; discard or reserve for another use.

2   In cup, mix olive oil, herbs, and garlic. With fingertips, gently separate skin from meat on chicken breast. Rub herb mixture on meat under skin. Tie legs together with string. Rub chicken all over with salt and pepper.

3   Place chicken, breast side up, on rack in small roasting pan (13" by 9"). Pour ¼ cup water into pan. Roast chicken 1 hour or until juices run clear when thickest part of thigh is pierced with tip of knife and instant-read thermometer inserted into thickest part of thigh registers 165°F.

4   Lift chicken from pan and tilt slightly to allow juices inside cavity to run into pan. Place chicken on platter; let stand 10 minutes to allow juices to set for easier carving.

5   Remove rack from roasting pan. Skim and discard fat from pan juices. Add remaining ¼ cup water to pan juices; cook 1 minute over medium heat, stirring constantly to scrape up browned bits from bottom of pan. Serve chicken with pan juices.

390 CALORIES

PER SERVING. 41G PROTEIN | 1G CARBOHYDRATE | 23G TOTAL FAT (6G SATURATED) 1G FIBER | 161MG CHOLESTEROL | 700MG SODIUM

MAKE IT A MEAL: About 25 minutes before the chicken is done, stick our Balsamic-Glazed Baby Carrots (65 calories; page 126) in the oven. To complete this cozy meal, add ½ cup steamed broccoli topped with 1 teaspoon olive oil.

CORNISH HENS MILANESE

Gremolata, the name given to the tasty blend of chopped fresh parsley, freshly grated lemon peel, and pungent garlic we use here, is a popular way to finish a meat, poultry, or fish dish in Italy. Try gremolata scattered over steamed green beans or new potatoes. For photo, see page 74.

ACTIVE TIME: 5 MINUTES · **TOTAL TIME:** 55 MINUTES
MAKES: 4-MAIN DISH SERVINGS.

---

2   CORNISH HENS (1½ POUNDS EACH)

3   TABLESPOONS CHOPPED FRESH PARSLEY

1   TEASPOON EXTRA-VIRGIN OLIVE OIL

¼   TEASPOON SALT

⅛   TEASPOON GROUND BLACK PEPPER

1   SMALL GARLIC CLOVE, MINCED

½   TEASPOON FRESHLY GRATED LEMON PEEL

1 Preheat oven to 375°F. Remove giblets and necks from hens; reserve for another use. With poultry shears, cut each hen lengthwise in half. Rinse hen pieces with cold running water; pat dry with paper towels.

2 In small bowl, combine 2 tablespoons parsley with oil, salt, and pepper. With fingertips, carefully separate skin from meat on each hen half; spread parsley mixture under skin. Place hens, skin side up, in large roasting pan (17" by 11½").

3 Roast hens, basting with drippings three times, until instant-read thermometer registers 165°F when inserted into thickest part of thigh, about 50 minutes.

4 Arrange hens on warm platter. In cup, combine remaining 1 tablespoon parsley, garlic, and lemon peel; sprinkle over hens.

---

240 CALORIES

PER SERVING. 32G PROTEIN | 0G CARBOHYDRATE | 27G TOTAL FAT (7G SATURATED) 0G FIBER | 187MG CHOLESTEROL | 236MG SODIUM

MAKE IT A MEAL: Our Cauliflower with Raisins and Pine Nuts (95 calories; page 132) is Sicilian in origin, but it's delightful alongside these Milanese Cornish hens. If you want to incorporate some greens, add ½ cup baby spinach to the cauliflower after cooking and toss to wilt it.

ROMAN CHICKEN SAUTÉ WITH ARTICHOKES

This light and tangy chicken dish, studded with sweet grape tomatoes and garlicky artichoke hearts, is served over a bed of spicy arugula.

ACTIVE TIME: 15 MINUTES · **TOTAL TIME:** 30 MINUTES
MAKES: 6 MAIN-DISH SERVINGS

1¼ POUNDS CHICKEN-BREAST TENDERS, EACH CUT CROSSWISE IN HALF, THEN CUT LENGTHWISE IN HALF

¼ TEASPOON SALT

¼ TEASPOON GROUND BLACK PEPPER

1 TABLESPOON OLIVE OIL

2 GARLIC CLOVES, THINLY SLICED

1 CAN (13¾ TO 14 OUNCES) ARTICHOKE HEARTS, DRAINED, EACH CUT INTO QUARTERS

½ CUP DRY WHITE WINE

½ CUP CHICKEN BROTH

1 PINT GRAPE TOMATOES

1 TEASPOON GRATED FRESH LEMON PEEL PLUS ADDITIONAL FOR GARNISH

1 BAG (5 TO 6 OUNCES) BABY ARUGULA

1 Sprinkle chicken with salt and pepper to season all sides. In 12-inch skillet, heat 2 teaspoons oil over medium-high heat until very hot. Add chicken and cook 8 minutes or until browned on the outside and no longer pink inside, stirring occasionally. With slotted spoon, transfer chicken to bowl.

2 To same skillet, add remaining 1 teaspoon oil. Reduce heat to medium and add garlic; cook 30 seconds or until golden. Stir in artichokes, and cook 3 to 4 minutes or until browned. Stir in wine, and cook 1 minute over medium-high heat.

3 Add chicken broth and tomatoes; cover and cook 2 to 3 minutes or until most tomatoes burst. Remove skillet from heat. Return chicken to skillet; stir in lemon peel until combined. Arrange arugula on platter; top with sautéed chicken mixture. Garnish chicken with additional lemon peel.

165 CALORIES

PER SERVING. 26G PROTEIN | 14G CARBOHYDRATE | 8G TOTAL FAT (3G SATURATED) 1G FIBER | 82MG CHOLESTEROL | 223MG SODIUM

MAKE IT A MEAL: For a light summer dinner, start with our Super-Fast Antipasti (280 calories; page 123). This chicken and artichoke dish is super low-cal, so you can nosh on some olives, mozzarella, and even salami and still not top the 500-calorie mark.

PROSCIUTTO-WRAPPED TURKEY CUTLETS

An Italian-style basil and melon salsa tops these luscious and lean grilled cutlets. When buying cutlets, make sure not to get the ones that are very thinly sliced for scaloppini.

ACTIVE TIME: 20 MINUTES · **TOTAL TIME:** 25 MINUTES
MAKES: 4 SERVINGS

2 LIMES

1½ CUPS CHOPPED, PEELED CANTALOUPE

1½ CUPS CHOPPED, PEELED HONEYDEW MELON

1 SMALL KIRBY CUCUMBER, SHREDDED (½ CUP)

1 JALAPEÑO CHILE, SEEDED AND FINELY CHOPPED

¼ CUP LOOSELY PACKED FRESH BASIL LEAVES, CHOPPED

¼ TEASPOON SALT

4 TURKEY BREAST CUTLETS (1 POUND TOTAL)

¼ TEASPOON COARSELY GROUND BLACK PEPPER

8 THIN SLICES PROSCIUTTO (4 OUNCES)

1 Grease grill rack. Prepare outdoor grill for direct grilling over medium heat.

2 From 1 lime, grate 1 teaspoon peel and squeeze 2 tablespoons juice. Cut remaining lime into 4 wedges and set aside. In medium bowl, combine lime juice, both melons, cucumber, jalapeño, basil, and salt. Makes about 3 cups salsa.

3 Sprinkle turkey cutlets with lime peel and pepper. Wrap each cutlet with 2 pieces prosciutto, pressing prosciutto firmly onto turkey.

4 Place turkey on hot grill rack over medium heat and cook 5 to 7 minutes, until turkey loses its pink color throughout and instant-read thermometer registers 165°F when inserted horizontally into center, turning over once. Transfer turkey to plate; serve with salsa and lime wedges.

195 CALORIES

PER TURKEY CUTLET PLUS ¼ CUP SALSA. 35G PROTEIN | 3G CARBOHYDRATE | 4G TOTAL FAT (1G SATURATED) | 0G FIBER | 86MG CHOLESTEROL | 865MG SODIUM

MAKE IT A MEAL: Grill some lemon-mint potato packets (215 calories per serving): Quarter then toss 4 large red potatoes with 2 tablespoons olive oil, fresh lemon peel and juice, chopped fresh mint, and salt and pepper to taste. Wrap in heavy-duty aluminum foil, cover grill, and cook for 30 minutes, turning over halfway through cooking time.

CHICKEN AND PESTO STACKS

These colorful stacks of chicken breasts, veggies, mozzarella, and a drizzle of pesto are as pretty as they are fun to eat.

ACTIVE TIME: 20 MINUTES · **TOTAL TIME:** 30 MINUTES
MAKES: 4 MAIN-DISH SERVINGS

3   TABLESPOONS PREPARED PESTO

3   TABLESPOONS WATER

1   LARGE SWEET ONION (12 OUNCES), CUT CROSSWISE INTO 4 SLICES

2   MEDIUM YELLOW PEPPERS, EACH CUT INTO QUARTERS

4   MEDIUM SKINLESS, BONELESS CHICKEN BREAST HALVES (1½ POUNDS)

¼   TEASPOON SALT

¼   TEASPOON GROUND BLACK PEPPER

2   TEASPOONS OLIVE OIL

4   SLICES FRESH MOZZARELLA

1   TOMATO, CUT INTO 4 SLICES

1   Preheat broiler and place rack 6 inches from heat source. In small bowl, mix pesto with water. Spray 15½" by 10½" jelly-roll pan with nonstick cooking spray. Arrange onion slices on pan; brush with 2 tablespoons pesto mixture. Broil onion slices 5 minutes. Arrange peppers on pan with onion; broil 12 to 15 minutes longer or until vegetables are tender, turning vegetables over halfway through cooking.

2   Meanwhile, with meat mallet, pound chicken placed between two sheets plastic wrap to even ½-inch thickness; season with salt and pepper.

3   In 12-inch skillet, heat oil over medium heat until hot. Add chicken and cook 6 to 8 minutes or until browned on both sides, turning over once.

4   Top chicken in pan with mozzarella slices; cover and cook 2 to 3 minutes or until cheese melts and chicken is no longer pink throughout; chicken should register 165°F when instant-read thermometer is inserted horizontally into center.

5   To serve, on each dinner plate, stack 1 slice onion, 2 slices pepper, 1 slice tomato, and 1 piece chicken with mozzarella; drizzle with remaining pesto mixture.

400 CALORIES   **PER SERVING.** 48G PROTEIN | 16G CARBOHYDRATE | 16G TOTAL FAT (6G SATURATED) 3G FIBER | 122MG CHOLESTEROL | 345MG SODIUM

MAKE IT A MEAL: For a colorful sweet finale, top a 6-ounce container of plain nonfat yogurt with ⅓ cup raspberries or your favorite type of berry (100 calories).

CHICKEN SALTIMBOCCA

This hearty entrée with prosciutto and Gorgonzola cheese has less than 300 calories. Really!

ACTIVE TIME: 10 MINUTES · **TOTAL TIME:** 30 MINUTES
MAKES: 4 MAIN-DISH SERVINGS

- 4 THIN SLICES PROSCIUTTO (2 OUNCES)
- 1 (2-OUNCE) CHUNK GORGONZOLA CHEESE, CUT INTO THIN SLICES
- 4 MEDIUM SKINLESS, BONELESS CHICKEN BREAST HALVES (1½ POUNDS)
- 2 TEASPOONS OLIVE OIL
- ½ CUP DRY WHITE WINE
- 1 TABLESPOON FRESH LEMON JUICE
- 1 BAG (5 TO 6 OUNCES) MIXED BABY GREENS

1 On large cutting board or cookie sheet, arrange prosciutto slices in single layer. Evenly divide Gorgonzola and place in center of prosciutto slices. Place 1 chicken breast crosswise on each Gorgonzola pile. Wrap each chicken breast with prosciutto, pressing firmly to encase cheese; secure with toothpick if necessary. (Prosciutto will not completely cover chicken.)

2 In 12-inch skillet, heat oil over medium heat until hot. Add wrapped chicken, Gorgonzola side down, and cook 12 to 15 minutes, turning over once, until chicken is browned on both sides, and registers 165°F on instant-read thermometer inserted horizontally into center. Transfer wrapped chicken breasts to platter; cover with foil to keep warm.

3 To same skillet, add wine and lemon juice and heat to boiling over medium-high heat; boil 2 minutes to reduce sauce by half, stirring occasionally and scraping up any browned bits. Remove skillet from heat.

4 Place greens in large bowl and toss with sauce. Arrange greens on dinner plates and top with chicken.

295 CALORIES

PER SERVING. 47G PROTEIN | 3G CARBOHYDRATE | 10G TOTAL FAT (4G SATURATED) 1G FIBER | 119MG CHOLESTEROL | 700MG SODIUM

MAKE IT A MEAL: This delicious dinner already includes a green salad, so all you need to worry about is dessert. How about our Bold Berry Granita (60 calories; page 145)? The chicken dish and the granita come in at just 355 calories per serving!

THE SKINNY ON POULTRY

The breast is the most tender part of the bird—and also the leanest. Consider everyone's favorite, chicken: A 3½-ounce portion of breast meat without skin has about 4 grams of fat. The same amount of skinless dark meat has about 10 grams of fat.

And, whether you're eating chicken, turkey, duck, or Cornish hen, keep in mind that removing poultry skin slashes the amount of fat almost in half. You may prefer, however, to cook poultry with the skin on to keep the moisture in. Then simply remove the skin before eating. The fat reduction is practically the same, but the cooked bird will be juicier and more flavorful.

**375
CALORIES**

*Mediterranean
Seafood Stew
(page 97)*

FISH & SHELLFISH

Italy is surrounded by the sea, so seafood is abundant in its cuisine. Here, we offer a range of healthy and delicious mains, including a seafood salad and a hearty Mediterranean stew, roasted and sautéed fish preparations, and two pasta dishes, one tossed with shrimp and one with clams. If you haven't cooked much seafood at home, give these simple, low-calorie dishes a try. Containing a mere 175 to 380 calories and plenty of heart-healthy omega 3s (see page 105), these flavorful Italian mains are a smart way to add skinny options to your diet.

KEY TO ICONS

🔵 30 minutes or less   ❤️ Heart healthy   🌾 High fiber   🟩 Make ahead   🍲 Slow cooker

ITALIAN SEAFOOD SALAD

Italians often serve this salad on Christmas Eve, but why not enjoy it throughout the year? It's a tasty summer-entertaining dish.

ACTIVE TIME: 50 MINUTES · **COOK:** 55 MINUTES PLUS CHILLING
MAKES: 4 MAIN-DISH SERVINGS

½ POUND SEA SCALLOPS

1 POUND CLEANED SQUID

2 TO 3 LEMONS

1 POUND LARGE SHRIMP, SHELLED AND DEVEINED

¼ CUP OLIVE OIL

1 SMALL GARLIC CLOVE, MINCED

¼ TEASPOON SALT

¼ TEASPOON COARSELY GROUND BLACK PEPPER

2 LARGE STALKS CELERY, CUT INTO ½-INCH PIECES

¼ CUP FRESH PARSLEY LEAVES

¼ CUP GAETA OR NIÇOISE OLIVES (OPTIONAL)

1 Pull tough crescent-shaped muscle from side of each scallop; discard. Rinse squid; slice bodies crosswise into ¾-inch-thick rings. Cut tentacles into several pieces if large. Cut 1 lemon into slices; from remaining lemons, squeeze ⅓ cup juice.

2 In 5-quart saucepot, combine 2½ inches *water* and lemon slices; heat to boiling over high heat. Add shrimp. Reduce heat to medium; cook until shrimp are opaque throughout, 1 to 2 minutes. With slotted spoon, transfer shrimp to colander to drain; transfer to large bowl.

3 To saucepot, add scallops; cook just until opaque, 2 to 3 minutes. With slotted spoon, transfer to colander to drain, then add to bowl. To saucepot, add squid; cook until opaque, 30 seconds to 1 minute. Drain in colander, then add to bowl.

4 In small bowl, whisk lemon juice, oil, garlic, salt, and pepper until blended. Add dressing, celery, parsley, and olives, if using, to seafood in bowl; toss to mix. Cover and refrigerate salad at least 3 hours to blend flavors or up to 8 hours.

380 CALORIES **PER SERVING.** 46G PROTEIN | 9G CARBOHYDRATE | 16G TOTAL FAT (3G SATURATED) 0G FIBER | 423MG CHOLESTEROL | 300MG SODIUM

MAKE IT A MEAL: Serve this chilled salad on some crisp Bibb lettuce, then finish with our Buttermilk Panna Cotta with Blackberry Sauce (115 calories; page 147). This refreshing meal can be enjoyed for a little over 500 calories.

MEDITERRANEAN SEAFOOD STEW

Added in the final half hour, the fresh cod, shrimp, and mussels in this satisfying slow-cooker stew keep their scrumptious flavor and texture. For photo, see page 94.

ACTIVE TIME: 20 MINUTES · **SLOW-COOK TIME:** 3 HOURS 30 MINUTES ON HIGH
MAKES: 6 MAIN-DISH SERVINGS

2 LARGE LEEKS, WHITE AND PALE GREEN PARTS ONLY	8 SPRIGS FRESH FLAT-LEAF PARSLEY, STEMS AND LEAVES SEPARATED
1½ POUNDS FENNEL (1 MEDIUM BULB), TRIMMED AND FINELY CHOPPED	1 POUND MUSSELS, BEARDS REMOVED, SCRUBBED
2¼ POUNDS TOMATOES, CHOPPED	1 POUND SHRIMP (16 TO 20 COUNT), SHELLED AND DEVEINED
2 GARLIC CLOVES, CHOPPED	12 OUNCES SKINLESS COD FILLET, CUT INTO 4-INCH PIECES
1 TEASPOON SALT	
½ TEASPOON FRESHLY GROUND BLACK PEPPER	2 TEASPOONS EXTRA-VIRGIN OLIVE OIL
4 SPRIGS FRESH THYME	4 CRUSTY DINNER ROLLS

1 Cut root ends from leeks. Cut each leek lengthwise in half, then into ¼-inch-thick slices. Place in large bowl of cold water. With hands, swish leeks to remove grit. Repeat process, changing water several times. Drain.
2 Transfer leeks to 6-quart slow-cooker bowl along with fennel, tomatoes, garlic, salt, and pepper. With kitchen twine, tie thyme and parsley stems together, reserving the parsley leaves. Bury in vegetable mixture.
3 Cover with lid and cook on High for 3 hours. Stir in mussels and shrimp, and lay fish on top. Immediately cover and cook 30 to 40 minutes longer, or until mussels open and shrimp and fish turn opaque throughout.
4 Divide mussels among serving dishes. Discard herb bundle. Divide stew among serving dishes. Drizzle oil over stew. Chop reserved parsley leaves and sprinkle over stew. Serve with rolls.

375 CALORIES

PER SERVING. 32G PROTEIN | 46G CARBOHYDRATE | 7G TOTAL FAT (1G SATURATED) 6G FIBER | 112MG CHOLESTEROL | 1,250MG SODIUM

MAKE IT A MEAL: This mouthwatering stew is already paired with a crusty roll to soak up the succulent broth. For a cooling finish, enjoy a scoop of store-bought Italian ice (125 calories) in your favorite flavor.

TRATTORIA-STYLE SHRIMP FETTUCCINE

Classic and quite simple to prepare, this shrimp and pasta dish can be served as a one-dish meal, thanks to the bag of fresh spinach that gets incorporated at the last minute.

ACTIVE TIME: 20 MINUTES · **TOTAL TIME:** 30 MINUTES
MAKES: 6 MAIN-DISH SERVINGS

12 OUNCES FETTUCCINE OR SPAGHETTI

2 TABLESPOONS OLIVE OIL

1 MEDIUM ONION, CHOPPED

2 GARLIC CLOVES, THINLY SLICED

½ CUP DRY WHITE WINE

1 BOTTLE (8 OUNCES) CLAM JUICE

½ TEASPOON SALT

1 POUND SHELLED AND DEVEINED LARGE SHRIMP, TAIL PART OF SHELL LEFT ON IF YOU LIKE

1 BAG (5 TO 6 OUNCES) BABY SPINACH

⅓ CUP LOOSELY PACKED FRESH PARSLEY LEAVES, CHOPPED

1 Cook pasta as label directs.

2 Meanwhile, in 12-inch skillet, heat oil over medium heat until hot. Add onion and garlic, and cook 10 minutes or until golden and tender, stirring often. Add wine; increase heat to medium-high and cook 1 minute. Stir in clam juice and salt; heat to boiling. Stir in shrimp, and cook 2 to 3 minutes or until shrimp turn opaque throughout.

3 Drain pasta and add to skillet with spinach and parsley; toss to coat.

350 CALORIES **PER SERVING.** 24G PROTEIN | 46G CARBOHYDRATE | 7G TOTAL FAT (1G SATURATED) 4G FIBER | 115MG CHOLESTEROL | 515MG SODIUM

MAKE IT A MEAL: This delightful shrimp pasta can stand alone as a quick weeknight meal. But you could also serve it family style, with a pretty platter of our fresh Tomato and Mozzarella Salad (160 calories, page 118). Just be sure to watch your portion size; if you limit yourself to the planned serving size, that's an ample 510-calorie meal.

LINGUINE WITH RED CLAM SAUCE

Here's a beloved Italian classic. If you can't make it to the fish market for fresh clams, you can substitute two 10-ounce cans of whole baby clams plus one-fourth of the clam liquid.

ACTIVE TIME: 20 MINUTES · **TOTAL TIME:** 1 HOUR
MAKES: 6 MAIN-DISH SERVINGS

½ CUP DRY WHITE WINE

2 DOZEN LITTLENECK CLAMS, SCRUBBED (SEE TIP)

12 OUNCES LINGUINE

3½ CUPS HOMEMADE MARINARA SAUCE (PAGE 16) OR BOTTLED MARINARA

1 TABLESPOON BUTTER OR MARGARINE, CUT INTO PIECES (OPTIONAL)

¼ CUP CHOPPED FRESH PARSLEY

1 In nonreactive 12-inch skillet, heat wine to boiling over high heat. Add clams; cover and cook until clams open, 5 to 10 minutes, transferring clams to bowl as they open. Discard any clams that have not opened after 10 minutes. Strain clam broth from skillet through sieve lined with paper towels; reserve ¼ cup. When cool enough to handle, remove clams from shells; discard shells and coarsely chop clams.

2 Meanwhile, in large saucepot, cook the pasta as label directs. Drain.

3 In same clean 12-inch skillet, combine marinara sauce, reserved broth, and clams; cook over low heat until heated through. In warm serving bowl, toss pasta with sauce and butter, if using. Sprinkle with parsley and serve.

TIP With a stiff-bristled brush or other sturdy scrubber, clean clams well under cold running water to remove sand.

395 CALORIES

PER SERVING. 20G PROTEIN | 65G CARBOHYDRATE | 6G TOTAL FAT (1G SATURATED) 6G FIBER | 28MG CHOLESTEROL | 661MG SODIUM ✿

MAKE IT A MEAL: Our Swiss Chard Sicilian Style (80 calories; page 130), studded with yellow raisins and toasted pine nuts, makes a nice accompaniment to this pasta—and a 475-calorie meal.

SICILIAN TUNA WITH PUTTANESCA SAUCE

A robust sauce of tomatoes, Kalamata olives, capers, and chopped fresh basil complements the flavor of the marinated tuna steaks.

ACTIVE TIME: 25 MINUTES · **TOTAL TIME:** 30 MINUTES PLUS MARINATING
MAKES: 8 MAIN-DISH SERVINGS

6 TABLESPOONS OLIVE OIL	1 LARGE STALK CELERY, CHOPPED
5 TABLESPOONS FRESH LEMON JUICE	3 RIPE MEDIUM PLUM TOMATOES, CHOPPED
4 ANCHOVY FILLETS, CHOPPED	
1 GARLIC CLOVE, FINELY CHOPPED	2 GREEN ONIONS, SLICED
¼ TEASPOON DRIED THYME	¼ CUP PITTED KALAMATA OR NIÇOISE OLIVES, COARSELY CHOPPED
⅛ TEASPOON GROUND BLACK PEPPER	
8 TUNA STEAKS, ¾ INCH THICK (5 OUNCES EACH)	2 TABLESPOONS CAPERS, DRAINED
	¼ CUP CHOPPED FRESH BASIL

1 In 13" by 9" baking dish, combine 3 tablespoons oil, 3 tablespoons lemon juice, anchovies, garlic, thyme, and pepper. Add tuna, turning to coat. Cover and marinate at least 45 minutes or up to 2 hours, turning once.

2 In 2-quart saucepan, heat remaining 3 tablespoons oil over medium heat. Add celery and cook 5 minutes. Stir in tomatoes, green onions, olives, and capers; cook until mixture has thickened slightly, about 5 minutes. Stir in basil and remaining 2 tablespoons lemon juice; keep warm.

3 Preheat broiler. Place tuna on rack in broiling pan. Place pan under broiler at closest position to heat source. Broil tuna about 3 minutes per side until pale pink in center (medium) or until desired doneness. (Instant-read thermometer inserted horizontally into center of tuna should register 145°F.) Serve with sauce.

240 CALORIES

PER SERVING. 24G PROTEIN | 3G CARBOHYDRATE | 14G TOTAL FAT (2G SATURATED) 1G FIBER | 39MG CHOLESTEROL | 291MG SODIUM

MAKE IT A MEAL: Round out this meal with our Creamy Polenta (175 calories; page 136). And while you're at it, enjoy a glass of wine (100 calories). A high-acid wine like Chianti Classico or Barbera would pair well with the bold tomato sauce and bring your dinner in at just over 500 calories.

ROASTED HALIBUT WITH FENNEL AND POTATOES

Sambuca is a popular Italian liqueur, but you can use any anise-flavored liqueur, including Pernod. A jigger of these spirits subtly enhances the natural licorice flavor found in the fennel.

ACTIVE TIME: 15 MINUTES · **TOTAL TIME:** 1 HOUR
MAKES: 4 MAIN-DISH SERVINGS

1 LARGE LEEK

1 POUND YUKON GOLD POTATOES, UNPEELED AND THINLY SLICED

1½ POUNDS FENNEL (1 MEDIUM BULB), CORED AND THINLY SLICED, SOME FRONDS FROM BULB RESERVED FOR GARNISH

4 TEASPOONS EXTRA-VIRGIN OLIVE OIL

¾ TEASPOON SALT

⅜ TEASPOON GROUND BLACK PEPPER

4 PIECES SKINLESS HALIBUT FILLET (6 OUNCES EACH)

2 TABLESPOONS ANISE-FLAVOR LIQUEUR (SEE ABOVE) OR WHITE WINE

1 TEASPOON FENNEL SEEDS

1 LEMON, THINLY SLICED

1 Cut off roots and trim dark-green top from leek. Discard any tough outer leaves. Thinly slice leek. Rinse leek thoroughly in bowl of cold water; swish to remove any sand. With hands, transfer leek to colander, leaving sand in bottom of bowl. Drain well.

2 Preheat oven to 425°F. Spray 13" by 9" glass baking dish with nonstick cooking spray. To baking dish, add leek, potatoes, fennel, 1 tablespoon oil, ½ teaspoon salt, and ¼ teaspoon pepper; toss to coat, then spread evenly. Roast vegetables 35 minutes or until tender, stirring once halfway through roasting.

3 Place halibut on vegetables; drizzle with liqueur and remaining oil. Sprinkle with fennel seeds, and remaining ¼ teaspoon salt, and ⅛ teaspoon pepper. Place lemon slices on halibut; return dish to oven and continue roasting 10 to 12 minutes or just until halibut turns opaque in center. To serve, sprinkle with fennel fronds.

365 CALORIES

PER SERVING. 24G PROTEIN | 3G CARBOHYDRATE | 14G TOTAL FAT (2G SATURATED) 1G FIBER | 39MG CHOLESTEROL | 291MG SODIUM

MAKE IT A MEAL: Start off with antipasti—Roasted Prosciutto-Wrapped Asparagus (50 calories; page 115) and the Italian pickled vegetables known as Giardiniera (35 calories; page 114).

COD LIVORNESE

The Tuscan seaport town of Livorno is famous for this simple preparation of white fish featuring Mediterranean favorites: tomatoes, olives, and capers. The dish is classically made with snapper, but we used cod; you can also substitute flounder or tilapia.

ACTIVE TIME: 15 MINUTES · **TOTAL TIME:** 30 MINUTES
MAKES: 4 MAIN-DISH SERVINGS

1 TABLESPOON CHOPPED FRESH OREGANO LEAVES	¼ CUP KALAMATA OLIVES, PITTED AND COARSELY CHOPPED
2 TEASPOONS GRATED FRESH LEMON PEEL	2 TABLESPOONS DRAINED CAPERS
2 TEASPOONS PLUS 2 TABLESPOONS OLIVE OIL	⅛ TEASPOON CRUSHED RED PEPPER FLAKES
¼ TEASPOON SALT	2 GARLIC CLOVES, MINCED
4 PIECES (6 OUNCES EACH) COD FILLET	¼ CUP LOOSELY PACKED FRESH PARSLEY LEAVES, CHOPPED
1 PINT CHERRY TOMATOES	

1 In cup, combine oregano, lemon peel, 2 teaspoons oil, and salt. Rub both sides of cod fillets with oregano mixture.

2 In nonstick 12-inch skillet, heat 1 tablespoon oil over medium heat. Add cod to skillet, and cook 8 to 10 minutes or just until fish turns opaque throughout, turning over once. (Instant-read thermometer inserted horizontally into center of fillet should register 145°F.) Transfer cod fillets to dinner plates.

3 In same skillet, heat remaining 1 tablespoon oil over medium heat. Stir in tomatoes, olives, capers, crushed red pepper, and garlic; cook 6 to 8 minutes or just until tomatoes are heated through and skins split. Stir in parsley; serve with cod.

250 CALORIES

PER SERVING. 31G PROTEIN | 6G CARBOHYDRATE | 11G TOTAL FAT (2G SATURATED) 2G FIBER | 73MG CHOLESTEROL | 450MG SODIUM ♥

MAKE IT A MEAL: This rustic fish dish would be nice with a half-portion of our Sopressata and Roma Bean Salad (140 calories; page 51). Finish with a glass of sparkling Italian white wine, like Prosecco (120 calories) for a 510-calorie meal.

GET YOUR OMEGA-3S

Despite their reputation for clogging arteries and packing on unwanted pounds, not all fats are villainous. Indeed, one type of polyunsaturated fat, omega-3, is thought to combat heart disease. Omega-3s help inhibit the formation of blood clots and reduce the incidence of heartbeat abnormalities. You'll find omega-3s in fish—and the oilier the fish, the more omega-3 it contains. So be sure to include oily fish like salmon, bluefin tuna, mackerel, and sardines in your diet.

ROAST SALMON WITH CAPERS AND PARSLEY

A whole salmon fillet with a crusty crumb-and-herb topping looks festive, tastes fabulous, and is surprisingly quick and easy to prepare.

ACTIVE TIME: 10 MINUTES · **TOTAL TIME:** 40 MINUTES
MAKES: 6 MAIN-DISH SERVINGS

---

3   TABLESPOONS BUTTER OR MARGARINE

⅓   CUP PLAIN DRIED BREAD CRUMBS

¼   CUP LOOSELY PACKED FRESH PARSLEY LEAVES, MINCED

3   TABLESPOONS DRAINED CAPERS, MINCED

1   TEASPOON DRIED TARRAGON, CRUMBLED

2   TEASPOONS GRATED FRESH LEMON PEEL

¼   TEASPOON SALT

¼   TEASPOON COARSELY GROUND BLACK PEPPER

1   WHOLE SALMON FILLET (2 POUNDS)

LEMON WEDGES

1   Preheat oven to 450°F. In 1-quart saucepan, melt butter over low heat. Remove saucepan from heat; stir in bread crumbs, parsley, capers, tarragon, lemon peel, salt, and pepper.

2   Line 15½" by 10½" jelly-roll pan with foil; grease foil. Place salmon, skin side down, in pan and pat crumb mixture on top. Roast until salmon turns opaque throughout and topping is lightly browned, about 30 minutes. (Instant-read thermometer inserted horizontally into center of fillet should register 145°F.)

3   With two large spatulas, carefully transfer salmon to platter, allowing salmon skin to remain attached to foil. Serve with lemon wedges.

325 CALORIES   **PER SERVING.** 28G PROTEIN | 5G CARBOHYDRATE | 21G TOTAL FAT (7G SATURATED) 0G FIBER | 94MG CHOLESTEROL | 407MG SODIUM

MAKE IT A MEAL: For easy 500-calorie entertaining, serve this salmon with Asparagus Gremolata (65 calories; page 127) and some herb-roasted potatoes (125 calories). To make four servings, toss 1½ pounds small red potatoes, cut in half, with 2 tablespoons butter, fresh parsley, lemon peel, and salt and pepper. Wrap in a foil packet and roast them with the fish for 25 minutes, or until tender.

ITALIAN-SPICED SHRIMP CASSEROLE

Both quick and flavorful, this healthful shrimp dish on rice gets its flavor from a variety of Italian herbs and spices.

ACTIVE TIME: 20 MINUTES · **TOTAL TIME:** 40 MINUTES
MAKES: 6 MAIN-DISH SERVINGS

1 CUP LONG-GRAIN WHITE RICE	1 CUP DRY WHITE WINE
1¾ CUPS HOT WATER	1 CAN (14½ OUNCES) NO-SALT-ADDED DICED TOMATOES, DRAINED WELL
1 TABLESPOON OLIVE OIL	
1 SMALL ONION, FINELY CHOPPED	½ TEASPOON SALT
1 TABLESPOON FRESH OREGANO LEAVES, MINCED	½ TEASPOON GROUND BLACK PEPPER
½ TEASPOON CRUSHED RED PEPPER, OR TO TASTE	1 POUND 16- TO 20-COUNT SHRIMP, SHELLED AND DEVEINED, TAIL PART OF SHELL LEFT ON IF YOU LIKE
2 GARLIC CLOVES, CRUSHED WITH GARLIC PRESS	8 LEAVES BASIL, VERY THINLY SLICED, FOR GARNISH

1 Preheat oven to 400°F.

2 In 3-quart shallow baking dish, combine rice and water. Cover tightly with foil and bake 20 minutes.

3 Meanwhile, in 5- to 6-quart saucepot, heat oil over medium heat. Add onion, oregano, and crushed red pepper; cook 3 minutes, stirring occasionally. Add garlic and cook 30 seconds or until golden, stirring. Add wine and heat to boiling; reduce heat to medium-low and simmer 6 minutes or until wine is reduced by half, stirring occasionally. Stir in tomatoes, salt, and black pepper. Remove from heat.

4 Arrange shrimp on top of rice in baking dish, in single layer. Pour tomato mixture evenly over shrimp; cover tightly with foil and bake 15 minutes or until shrimp turn opaque. Garnish with basil.

245 CALORIES

PER SERVING. 16G PROTEIN | 35G CARBOHYDRATE | 4G TOTAL FAT (1G SATURATED) 2G FIBER | 93MG CHOLESTEROL | 300MG SODIUM

MAKE IT A MEAL: A side of Green Beans with Mint (90 calories; page 131) makes for a well-rounded dinner. Afterwards, enjoy a cappuccino (80 calories) and a cookie of your choice (30 to 75 calories; see page 139); your total calorie count will still be well under 500.

BAKED SNAPPER WITH PEPPERS AND MUSHROOMS

This fast fish recipe is both ultra low fat and low cal without missing out on flavor. It's a diet dish that you'll crave.

ACTIVE TIME: 20 MINUTES · **TOTAL TIME:** 35 MINUTES
MAKES: 6 MAIN-DISH SERVINGS

1 TABLESPOON OLIVE OIL

2 MEDIUM ORANGE AND/OR YELLOW PEPPERS, THINLY SLICED

1 MEDIUM ONION, CHOPPED

1 PACKAGE (10 OUNCES) SLICED MUSHROOMS

½ CUP DRY WHITE WINE

1 TEASPOON FRESH THYME LEAVES, CHOPPED, PLUS ADDITIONAL THYME LEAVES FOR GARNISH

6 SKINLESS, BONELESS SNAPPER, SOLE, OR FLOUNDER FILLETS (4 OUNCES EACH)

2 TABLESPOONS FRESH LEMON JUICE

¼ TEASPOON SALT

¼ TEASPOON GROUND BLACK PEPPER

1 Preheat oven to 450°F. In 12-inch skillet, heat oil over medium heat until hot. Add peppers and onion, and cook 10 minutes or until tender, stirring often. Add mushrooms, wine, and thyme; cook over medium-high heat 3 minutes, stirring frequently.

2 Meanwhile, spray 13" by 9" glass or ceramic baking dish with nonstick cooking spray. Arrange fillets in baking dish, folding narrow ends under. Sprinkle with lemon juice, salt, and pepper.

3 Spoon hot vegetable mixture from skillet on top of fish in baking dish. Bake fish 15 to 18 minutes or until opaque throughout. (Instant-read thermometer inserted horizontally into center of fillet should register 145°F.) Garnish with additional thyme leaves.

175 CALORIES

PER SERVING. 26G PROTEIN | 9G CARBOHYDRATE | 4G TOTAL FAT (1G SATURATED) 2G FIBER | 42MG CHOLESTEROL | 175MG SODIUM ❤

MAKE IT A MEAL: For a cozy 455-calorie dinner, pair this baked fish with our Parmesan Brussels Sprouts (145 calories; page 134). Finish with a Chianti-Roasted Pear (135 calories; page 148).

IRRESISTIBLE ADD-ONS

To make your meal planning a breeze, we've organized the add-on recipes in the following chapters by calorie count—from lowest to highest. Choose your main dish from the preceding chapters, then select one or more of these tempting starters, sides, and desserts to round out your meal. So, if you're preparing Pasta Primavera, a 325-calorie main dish, you could add our luscious Healthy Makeover Tiramisu (175 calories) to create a 500-calorie dinner. Or you could enjoy two lower-calorie add-ons instead: an antipasto of Roasted Prosciutto-Wrapped Asparagus (50 calories) and an Arugula and Olive Salad (125 calories) on the side—and your dinner still adds up to 500 calories total. It's that easy!

**170
CALORIES**
Bruschetta, Two Ways
(page 119)

ANTIPASTI & OTHER STARTERS

Antipasto (plural *antipasti*) literally means "before the pasta" and refers to both hot and cold hors d'oeuvres. The contents of traditional antipasto platters varies from region to region and includes everything from cured meats and cheeses, olives and pickled vegetables, to smoked fish. Here, we offer a tempting variety, including asparagus spears wrapped in prosciutto, bruschetta, and a fresh tomato and mozzarella salad. Calories range from a 35-calorie pickle dish to a whole antipasto selection for 280 calories, so you'll find a match to suit whatever main dish you select.

KEY TO ICONS

🕐 30 minutes or less   ❤ Heart healthy   🌾 High fiber   🟩 Make ahead   🍲 Slow cooker

GIARDINIERA

This pickled assortment of vegetables is often served as an antipasto.

ACTIVE TIME: 1 HOUR · **TOTAL TIME:** 1 HOUR 20 MINUTES PLUS CHILLING
MAKES: 10 CUPS OR 20 ANTIPASTO SERVINGS

½ SMALL HEAD CAULIFLOWER, CUT
INTO SMALL FLOWERETS (1½ CUPS)

1 LARGE RED PEPPER,
CUT INTO 1-INCH PIECES

1 CUP THICKLY SLICED CARROT
(2 LARGE)

2 LARGE STALKS CELERY,
THICKLY SLICED

½ (5-OUNCE) JAR GREEN OLIVES,
DRAINED

½ CUP SUGAR

2¼ CUPS DISTILLED WHITE VINEGAR

¾ CUP WATER

1 TABLESPOON KOSHER, CANNING,
OR PICKLING SALT

¼ TEASPOON MUSTARD SEEDS

⅛ TEASPOON CRUSHED RED PEPPER

1 In large bowl, combine cauliflower, red pepper, carrot, celery, and olives. In nonreactive 4-quart saucepan, combine sugar, vinegar, water, and salt; heat to boiling over high heat, stirring occasionally. Reduce heat to low.
2 In container with lid and large enough to hold vegetables, place mustard seeds and crushed red pepper; pack vegetables into container and pour hot brine over, making sure vegetables are completely covered with brine.
3 Allow giardiniera to cool, then chill for 3 hours before serving. Refrigerate pickles in an airtight container for up to 1 week.

35 CALORIES **PER ¼-CUP SERVING.** 0G PROTEIN | 8G CARBOHYDRATE | 0G TOTAL FAT (0G SATURATED) | 1G FIBER | 0MG CHOLESTEROL | 443MG SODIUM

ROASTED PROSCIUTTO-WRAPPED ASPARAGUS

This classic Italian finger food requires only three ingredients. Use medium-sized asparagus spears because they are easier to handle.

ACTIVE TIME: 30 MINUTES · **TOTAL TIME:** 50 MINUTES
MAKES: 12 ANTIPASTO SERVINGS

Place **24 trimmed asparagus spears** and ¼ **cup boiling water** in large roasting pan covered with foil. In a preheated 400°F oven, steam asparagus until tender, 10 to 15 minutes; transfer to paper towels to drain, and wipe pan dry. Assemble **12 thin slices prosciutto (8 ounces),** each cut in half lengthwise, and ½ **cup freshly grated Parmesan cheese**. On waxed paper, place 1 thin strip prosciutto and sprinkle with 1 teaspoon freshly grated Parmesan; roll prosciutto around spear—it will overlap slightly to cover the spear. Repeat with remaining asparagus, prosciutto, and Parmesan. Roast until asparagus is heated through and prosciutto just begins to brown, about 10 minutes.

PER SERVING (2 SPEARS). 7G PROTEIN | 1G CARBOHYDRATE | 2G TOTAL FAT (1G SATURATED) | 1G FIBER | 15MG CHOLESTEROL | 540MG SODIUM

GARLIC AND HERB BREAD

Here's a classic Italian favorite to pair with pasta. We call for dried oregano in this recipe, but you can swap in 1 tablespoon chopped fresh oregano if you prefer.

ACTIVE TIME: 5 MINUTES · **TOTAL TIME:** 20 MINUTES
MAKES: 10 SLICES

Preheat oven to 350°F. Slice **1 loaf Italian bread** in half lengthwise. On cut sides of bread, sprinkle **2 tablespoons olive oil; 2 cloves garlic, finely chopped; 1 teaspoon dried oregano;** and **1 tablespoon freshly grated Parmesan cheese.** Wrap bread in aluminum foil; bake 15 minutes or until top of bread is lightly browned.

PER SLICE. 3G PROTEIN | 16G CARBOHDYDRATE | 4G TOTAL FAT (1G SATURATED) 1G FIBER | 0MG CHOLESTEROL | 188MG SODIUM 💙 ❤️

ARUGULA AND OLIVE SALAD

Peppery arugula, roasted peppers, and salty olives and Parmesan make for a piquant salad.

TOTAL TIME: 10 MINUTES
MAKES: 4 FIRST-COURSE SERVINGS

In large bowl, combine **6 ounces baby arugula, 2 thinly sliced jarred roasted red peppers, ¼ cup halved pitted Kalamata olives,** and **3 tablespoons Balsamic Vinaigrette** (see page 47). Toss to coat. Divide among serving plates. With vegetable peeler, shave **1 ounce Parmesan cheese** into paper-thin slices over salads.

125 CALORIES **PER SERVING.** 4G PROTEIN | 5G CARBOHYDRATE | 10G TOTAL FAT (2G SATURATED) 1G FIBER | 6MG CHOLESTEROL | 380MG SODIUM 🔵

CHILLED TUSCAN-STYLE TOMATO SOUP

The lush summer flavors of Tuscany shine in this refreshing, easy-to-make cold tomato soup. We blend cubes of country bread in with the tomatoes to achieve a thicker body and a velvety mouthfeel.

TOTAL TIME: 15 MINUTES PLUS CHILLING
MAKES: 6 CUPS OR 4 FIRST-COURSE SERVINGS

In small skillet, heat **1 teaspoon olive oil** over medium heat until hot. Add **1 minced garlic clove** and cook 1 minute, stirring. Remove skillet from heat. In food processor with knife blade attached, pulse **2 cups 1-inch cubes country-style bread** until coarsely chopped. Add **3 pounds ripe tomatoes,** each cut into quarters, and sautéed garlic; pulse until soup is almost pureed. Pour soup into bowl; stir in **¼ cup loosely packed fresh basil leaves,** chopped, **1 teaspoon sugar,** and **½ teaspoon salt.** Cover and refrigerate until well chilled, at least 2 hours or overnight. Garnish each serving with **additional fresh basil leaves.**

145 CALORIES **PER SERVING.** 5G PROTEIN | 28G CARBOHYDRATE | 3G TOTAL FAT (1G SATURATED) 4G FIBER | 0MG CHOLESTEROL | 445MG SODIUM

145 **CALORIES**
Chilled Tuscan-Style
Tomato Soup
(opposite)

THE GOODNESS OF TOMATOES

Italian fare uses an abundance of tomatoes, both fresh and cooked. Not only do they add beautiful flavor and color, as in the Tuscan-style tomato soup shown above, they are loaded with nutrients, too. A single serving (1 cup) of uncooked tomatoes is an excellent source of vitamin C, which also enhances the body's ability to absorb iron. Tomatoes also contain lycopene and other substances associated with lowering the risk of certain cancers. However, lycopene is more readily absorbed by the body from cooked tomatoes, so make sure to prepare recipes that incorporate cooked or roasted tomatoes; our Homemade Marinara Sauce (page 16) and Braciole with Grape Tomatoes (page 81) are good choices.

TOMATO AND MOZZARELLA SALAD

Toss farm-stand tomatoes (we love to use red, yellow, and orange) with basil and extra-virgin olive oil for one of summer's simple pleasures. For the best flavor, don't refrigerate this salad.

TOTAL TIME: 20 MINUTES
MAKES: 4 SIDE-DISH SERVINGS

- 3 POUNDS TOMATOES, CUT INTO 1½-INCH CHUNKS
- 8 OUNCES LIGHTLY SALTED, SMALL FRESH MOZZARELLA BALLS, EACH CUT IN HALF, OR 1 PACKAGE (8 OUNCES) MOZZARELLA CHEESE, CUT INTO ½-INCH CHUNKS
- 1 CUP LOOSELY PACKED FRESH BASIL LEAVES, CHOPPED

- 3 TABLESPOONS EXTRA-VIRGIN OLIVE OIL
- ¾ TEASPOON SALT
- ¼ TEASPOON COARSELY GROUND BLACK PEPPER

In large bowl, toss tomatoes, mozzarella, basil, oil, salt, and pepper until evenly mixed.

160 CALORIES

PER SERVING. 7G PROTEIN | 9G CARBOHYDRATE | 12G TOTAL FAT (5G SATURATED) 1G FIBER | 22MG CHOLESTEROL | 255MG SODIUM 💙 ❤️

TOMATO AND RICOTTA SALATA BRUSCHETTA

Here's everyone's favorite Italian starter, two ways. Look for ricotta salata at Italian markets or specialty cheese shops. For photo, see page 112.

ACTIVE TIME: 20 MINUTES · **TOTAL TIME:** 25 MINUTES
MAKES: 16 BRUSCHETTA

1 LOAF (8 OUNCES) ITALIAN BREAD, CUT ON DIAGONAL INTO ½-INCH-THICK SLICES

8 GARLIC CLOVES, EACH CUT IN HALF

1 POUND RIPE PLUM TOMATOES (6 MEDIUM), SEEDED AND CUT INTO ½-INCH PIECES

1 TABLESPOON FINELY CHOPPED RED ONION

1 TABLESPOON CHOPPED FRESH BASIL

4 OUNCES RICOTTA SALATA OR GOAT CHEESE, CUT INTO ½-INCH PIECES

2 TABLESPOONS EXTRA-VIRGIN OLIVE OIL

2 TEASPOONS BALSAMIC VINEGAR

¼ TEASPOON SALT

¼ TEASPOON COARSELY GROUND BLACK PEPPER

1 Preheat oven to 400°F. Arrange bread on jelly-roll pan. Bake until lightly toasted, about 5 minutes. Rub one side of each slice with cut garlic.

2 Meanwhile, in medium bowl, gently toss tomatoes, onion, basil, cheese, oil, vinegar, salt, and pepper until combined.

3 To serve, spoon tomato mixture onto garlic-rubbed side of toast slices.

PER BRUSCHETTA. 2G PROTEIN | 9G CARBOHYDRATE | 4G TOTAL FAT (1G SATURATED) 1G FIBER | 6MG CHOLESTEROL | 236MG SODIUM 🔵 ❤️

TUSCAN WHITE BEAN BRUSCHETTA

Toast bread as directed. In bowl, with fork, lightly mash **1 can (15 to 19 ounces) white kidney beans** (cannellini), rinsed and drained, with **1 tablespoon fresh lemon juice.** Stir in **1 tablespoon olive oil, 2 teaspoons chopped fresh parsley, 1 teaspoon chopped fresh sage, ¼ teaspoon salt,** and **⅛ teaspoon ground black pepper.** Spoon mixture over garlic-rubbed side of toast. Sprinkle with **1 teaspoon chopped fresh parsley.**

PER BRUSCHETTA. 2G PROTEIN | 4G CARBOHYDRATE | 1G TOTAL FAT (0G SATURATED) 7G FIBER | 0MG CHOLESTEROL | 77MG SODIUM 🔵 ❤️ 🌾

ROMAN-STYLE ARTICHOKES

This stuffed vegetable recipe is best prepared in the springtime, when artichokes are in season.

ACTIVE TIME: 45 MINUTES · **TOTAL TIME:** 1 HOUR 35 MINUTES
MAKES: 8 FIRST-COURSE SERVINGS

2 TABLESPOONS FRESH LEMON JUICE

8 MEDIUM ARTICHOKES

1½ CUPS LOOSELY PACKED FRESH MINT LEAVES, CHOPPED

1 CUP FRESH BREAD CRUMBS (FROM 2 SLICES)

1 CUP PLAIN DRIED BREAD CRUMBS

½ CUP FRESHLY GRATED PECORINO-ROMANO CHEESE

3 TABLESPOONS EXTRA-VIRGIN OLIVE OIL

2 GARLIC CLOVES, FINELY CHOPPED

½ TEASPOON SALT

¼ TEASPOON GROUND BLACK PEPPER

1 Fill large bowl with *cold water* and 1 tablespoon lemon juice.

2 Prepare artichokes as described in "Artichoke Know-How," opposite, placing stems and trimmed artichokes in bowl of lemon water to prevent them from browning.

3 In deep 12-inch skillet or nonreactive 8-quart Dutch oven or saucepot, heat *1 inch water* to boiling over high heat. Stand artichokes in boiling water; add stems and return to boiling. Reduce heat to medium-low; cover and simmer 30 to 40 minutes or until knife inserted in bottom of artichoke goes in easily. Drain artichokes.

4 Meanwhile, in medium bowl, combine remaining 1 tablespoon lemon juice, mint, fresh and dried bread crumbs, Romano, olive oil, garlic, salt, and pepper.

5 Preheat oven to 400°F. When artichokes are cool enough to handle, pull out prickly center leaves from each artichoke; with teaspoon or melon baller, scrape out fuzzy choke (without cutting into heart) and discard. Finely chop stems; stir into mint mixture.

6 Stand artichokes on 15½" by 10½" jelly-roll pan, stem sides down. For each artichoke, pull leaves to open slightly; spoon scant ½ cup mint mixture into center cavity. Bake 20 to 25 minutes or until stuffing is golden and artichokes are heated through.

185 CALORIES

PER ¼-CUP SERVING. 7G PROTEIN | 24G CARBOHYDRATE | 8G TOTAL FAT (2G SATURATED) | 1G FIBER | 5MG CHOLESTEROL | 440MG SODIUM

ARTICHOKE KNOW-HOW

When shopping, look for artichokes that are compact, firm, and heavy for their size. They're at their peak in April and May. In spring and summer, choose those with an even green color. In fall and winter, it's okay to buy artichokes with touches of light brown or bronze on the outer leaves; this is caused by frost (and doesn't affect the flavor). Artichokes range in size from baby (2 ounces) to jumbo (20 ounces), but size is not a sign of maturity; they're all fully grown when picked. Cooked or raw, they keep for a week in the refrigerator.

To prepare artichokes for cooking:

STEP 1: With a sharp knife, cut 1 inch straight across the top. Cut off the stem so the artichoke can stand upright. Peel the stem.

STEP 2: Pull off the outer dark green leaves from the artichoke bottom. With kitchen shears, trim the thorny tips of the leaves.

STEP 3: Spread the artichoke open and carefully cut around the choke with a small knife, then scrape out the center petals and fuzzy center portion with a teaspoon and discard. Rinse the artichoke well. (You can remove the choke *after* cooking, but you have to wait till the artichoke cools a bit.)

ZUCCHINI CARPACCIO

This light summer salad features layers of zucchini and avocado drizzled with a lemon dressing and sprinkled with pine nuts.

TOTAL TIME: 35 MINUTES
MAKES: 4 SIDE-DISH SERVINGS

From **1 lemon,** finely grate ½ teaspoon peel and squeeze 2 tablespoons juice into small bowl. With wire whisk, stir in **2 tablespoons extra-virgin olive oil** and **⅛ teaspoon each salt and ground black pepper.** With sharp knife or adjustable blade slicer, cut **2 large zucchini** into paper-thin slices. On large serving plate, arrange zucchini in overlapping layers with thin slices from **1 ripe avocado.** Drizzle lemon dressing all over vegetables and top with **¼ cup toasted pine nuts.**

 205 CALORIES

PER SERVING. 4G PROTEIN | 8G CARBOHYDRATE | 19G TOTAL FAT (2G SATURATED) 5G FIBER | 0MG CHOLESTEROL | 110MG SODIUM 🌱 ❤️

SUPER-FAST ANTIPASTI

Here's an easy Italian antipasto platter that includes hummus, a Middle Eastern chickpea puree borrowed from Italy's Mediterranean neighbors.

TOTAL TIME: 15 MINUTES
MAKES: 6 FIRST-COURSE SERVINGS

1   CONTAINER (8 OUNCES) STORE-BOUGHT HUMMUS

8   OUNCES SMOKED MOZZARELLA CHEESE, THICKLY SLICED

4   OUNCES SALAMI, THINLY SLICED

2   BUNCHES RADISHES, TOPS TRIMMED

1   SMALL FENNEL BULB, CUT INTO THIN WEDGES

2   LARGE CARROTS, SLICED DIAGONALLY

½   CUP MIXED OLIVES

BREAD STICKS AND/OR CRACKERS

Spoon hummus into bowl and place on large tray or cutting board. Arrange mozzarella, salami, radishes, fennel, carrots, olives, and bread sticks around hummus.

280 CALORIES **PER SERVING.** 15G PROTEIN | 16G CARBOHYDRATE | 18G TOTAL FAT (8G SATURATED) 5G FIBER | 44MG CHOLESTEROL | 625MG SODIUM

65
CALORIES
Asparagus Gremolata
(page 127)

VEGETABLES & SIDES

Flavorful Italian ingredients like Parmesan, balsamic vinegar, and fresh herbs make everyday vegetables and grains extraordinary. To complement your 400-calorie (or less) main dish, choose from roasted baby carrots or grilled eggplant caponata, crumb-topped tomatoes, or asparagus sprinkled with gremolata, and other fresh, colorful veggie sides. If you're looking for something heartier, our polenta—with options to prepare it three different ways—fits the bill. *Mangia!*

KEY TO ICONS

⏱ 30 minutes or less   ❤ Heart healthy   🌾 High fiber   🍱 Make ahead   🍲 Slow cooker

BALSAMIC-GLAZED BABY CARROTS

This side dish is perfect for a family dinner or a large dinner party; the balsamic glaze adds a flavor burst to everyday carrots.

ACTIVE TIME: 15 MINUTES · **TOTAL TIME:** 45 MINUTES
MAKES: 8 SIDE-DISH SERVINGS

Preheat oven to 400°F. Trim **2 pounds baby carrots** (see Tip), leaving 1 inch green stems on. With vegetable brush, scrub carrots and rinse under cold water. Pat dry with paper towels. In 15½" by 10½" jelly-roll pan, toss carrots with **1 tablespoon olive oil, ¼ teaspoon salt,** and **½ teaspoon ground black pepper.** Roast 25 minutes. Stir in **2 tablespoons white or traditional balsamic vinegar** and **1 tablespoon sugar** until carrots are coated. Roast 6 to 8 minutes longer or until carrots are tender and sugar has dissolved.

 TIP In springtime, bunches of fresh baby carrots should be readily available at supermarkets and farmers' markets. If not, use 2 pounds medium carrots, quartered lengthwise then halved crosswise. For this recipe, we don't recommend using prepackaged "baby" carrots; they require a much longer roasting time, and we've found they don't caramelize as well.

65 CALORIES

PER SERVING. 1G PROTEIN | 11G CARBOHYDRATE | 2G TOTAL FAT (0G SATURATED) 2G FIBER | 0MG CHOLESTEROL | 110MG SODIUM ❤️

ASPARAGUS GREMOLATA

For this fresh-as-spring side dish, blanched asparagus is blanketed with a lemony, herbed bread crumb mix. For photo, see page 124.

ACTIVE TIME: 20 MINUTES · **TOTAL TIME:** 30 MINUTES
MAKES: 6 SIDE-DISH SERVINGS

1¼ TEASPOONS SALT

2 POUNDS JUMBO ASPARAGUS, TRIMMED AND PEELED

1 GARLIC CLOVE, FINELY CHOPPED

4 TEASPOONS EXTRA-VIRGIN OLIVE OIL

1 TEASPOON FRESHLY GRATED LEMON PEEL

¼ CUP PANKO (JAPANESE-STYLE BREAD CRUMBS)

1 TABLESPOON WATER

¼ CUP FINELY CHOPPED FRESH FLAT-LEAF PARSLEY LEAVES

¼ TEASPOON GROUND BLACK PEPPER

1 Heat large covered saucepot of *water* to boiling over high heat. Fill large bowl with ice and water.

2 Add 1 teaspoon salt, then asparagus, to boiling water. Cook uncovered 5 to 6 minutes or until spears are bright green and knife pierces stalks easily. With tongs, transfer directly to bowl of ice water. When asparagus is cool, drain well. Roll between paper towels to dry. Asparagus can be refrigerated in airtight container or zip-tight plastic bag up to overnight.

3 In 12-inch skillet, combine garlic, 1 tablespoon oil, and ½ teaspoon lemon peel. Cook over medium heat 2 minutes or until golden, stirring occasionally. Add panko and cook 1 to 2 minutes or until golden and toasted, stirring frequently. Transfer to small bowl; wipe out skillet.

4 In same skillet, combine asparagus, water, and remaining 1 teaspoon oil. Cook over medium heat 2 to 5 minutes or until heated through, turning frequently. Transfer to serving platter.

5 Stir chopped parsley, remaining ½ teaspoon lemon peel, remaining ¼ teaspoon salt, and pepper into panko mixture. Spoon seasoned panko over asparagus.

65 CALORIES

PER SERVING. 2G PROTEIN | 7G CARBOHYDRATE | 4G TOTAL FAT (1G SATURATED) 2G FIBER | 0MG CHOLESTEROL | 140MG SODIUM

GRILLED EGGPLANT CAPONATA SALAD

Eggplant simply inhales the smoky goodness from the grill. This delicious salad combines fresh tomatoes, sweet raisins, and briny capers with grilled onions, celery, and eggplant.

ACTIVE TIME: 25 MINUTES · **TOTAL TIME:** 35 MINUTES

MAKES: 6 SIDE-DISH SERVINGS

2	METAL SKEWERS (OPTIONAL)
2	SMALL RED ONIONS, CUT INTO ½-INCH-THICK SLICES
2	SMALL EGGPLANTS (1 TO 1¼ POUNDS EACH), CUT INTO ¾-INCH-THICK SLICES

NONSTICK COOKING SPRAY

4	MEDIUM STALKS CELERY
½	TEASPOON SALT
2	TABLESPOONS RED WINE VINEGAR
2	TABLESPOONS EXTRA-VIRGIN OLIVE OIL
1	TEASPOON SUGAR
¼	TEASPOON COARSELY GROUND BLACK PEPPER
1½	POUNDS RIPE PLUM TOMATOES, CUT INTO ½-INCH CHUNKS
1	CUP KALAMATA, GAETA, OR GREEN SICILIAN OLIVES, PITTED AND CHOPPED
¼	CUP GOLDEN RAISINS
3	TABLESPOONS DRAINED CAPERS
½	CUP LOOSELY PACKED FRESH ITALIAN PARSLEY LEAVES

1 Prepare outdoor grill for covered direct grilling over medium heat.

2 Meanwhile, for easier handling, insert metal skewers through onion slices, if you like. Lightly spray both sides of eggplant slices with cooking spray. Sprinkle onions, eggplants, and celery with salt.

3 Place onions, eggplants, and celery on hot grill rack. Cover grill and cook vegetables until tender and lightly browned, 8 to 10 minutes, turning over once and transferring to plate as they are done. Cool slightly until easy to handle.

4 Cut eggplants and celery into ¾-inch chunks; coarsely chop onions. In large bowl, mix vinegar, oil, sugar, and pepper until blended. Stir in tomatoes, olives, raisins, capers, and parsley. Add eggplant, onions, and celery, and gently toss to coat.

5 Serve salad at room temperature, or if not serving immediately, cover and refrigerate up to 1 day.

---

75 CALORIES

PER SERVING. 1G PROTEIN | 11G CARBOHYDRATE | 3G TOTAL FAT (1G SATURATED) 2G FIBER | 0MG CHOLESTEROL | 240MG SODIUM

SWISS CHARD SICILIAN STYLE

Vitamin-rich Swiss chard and onions gets a burst of salty-sweet flavor from raisins and toasted pine nuts (known as *pignoli* in Italy).

TOTAL TIME: 30 MINUTES

MAKES: 6 SIDE-DISH SERVINGS

1 LARGE BUNCH (1¼ POUNDS) SWISS CHARD, RINSED WELL, TOUGH STEM ENDS TRIMMED

1 TABLESPOON OLIVE OIL

1 SMALL ONION, CHOPPED

¼ CUP GOLDEN RAISINS

¼ TEASPOON SALT

2 TABLESPOONS PINE NUTS (PIGNOLI), TOASTED

1 Cut center ribs and stems from Swiss chard leaves. Cut ribs and stems into ½-inch pieces; set aside. Cut leaves into 2-inch pieces; transfer to colander to drain well.

2 In 7- to 8-quart Dutch oven, heat oil over medium heat until hot. Add onion and chard ribs and stems, and cook 7 to 9 minutes or until tender, stirring occasionally. Add drained chard leaves, raisins, and salt; cover and cook 2 to 3 minutes or until leaves are tender. Remove Dutch oven from heat; stir in pine nuts.

80 CALORIES

PER SERVING. 3G PROTEIN | 10G CARBOHYDRATE | 4G TOTAL FAT (1G SATURATED) 2G FIBER | 0MG CHOLESTEROL | 275MG SODIUM

GARLICKY ESCAROLE WITH WHITE BEANS

This Mediterranean-inspired side dish would also be delightful served on top of toasted Italian bread as an appetizer.

ACTIVE TIME: 5 MINUTES · **TOTAL TIME:** 15 MINUTES
MAKES: 8 SIDE-DISH SERVINGS

Heat **1 tablespoon extra-virgin olive oil** in 12-inch skillet over medium heat. Add **2 finely chopped garlic cloves** and **¼ teaspoon crushed red pepper.** Cook 1 minute, stirring. Add **2 heads chopped escarole** and **⅛ teaspoon each salt and ground black pepper.** Cook 3 to 4 minutes or until wilted, stirring and tossing. Stir in **1 can (14½ ounces) cannellini beans,** rinsed and drained, and **1 tablespoon capers,** drained and chopped. Cook 2 minutes.

80 CALORIES **PER SERVING.** 5G PROTEIN | 16G CARBOHYDRATE | 3G TOTAL FAT (0G SATURATED) 8G FIBER | 0MG CHOLESTEROL | 234MG SODIUM

GREEN BEANS WITH MINT

You'll love the flavor of these oven-roasted green beans tossed in a lemony vinaigrette. Serve them warm or at room temperature.

ACTIVE TIME: 20 MINUTES · **TOTAL TIME:** 45 MINUTES
MAKES: 8 SIDE-DISH SERVINGS

Preheat oven to 450°F. In large roasting pan (17" by 11½"), toss **1½ pounds trimmed green beans** with **1 tablespoon oil** and **½ teaspoon salt.** Roast beans, stirring twice, until tender and slightly browned, 25 to 30 minutes. Meanwhile, from **2 lemons,** grate 1 tablespoon peel and squeeze 2 tablespoons juice. Chop **½ cup loosely packed fresh mint leaves** and **2 tablespoons loosely packed fresh oregano leaves.** In large bowl, with wire whisk, mix lemon peel and juice, **¼ teaspoon ground black pepper, 2 tablespoons olive oil,** and **¼ teaspoon salt** until blended. When green beans are done, add to vinaigrette in bowl. Add chopped mint and oregano; toss until beans are evenly coated. Serve warm or cover and refrigerate up to 1 day.

90 CALORIES **PER SERVING.** 3G PROTEIN | 10G CARBOHYDRATE | 5G TOTAL FAT (1G SATURATED) 2G FIBER | 0MG CHOLESTEROL | 225MG SODIUM

CAULIFLOWER WITH RAISINS AND PINE NUTS

This Sicilian-inspired side dish has just a touch of anchovy for authentic flavor. If you prefer to omit the anchovy, add a little more salt.

ACTIVE TIME: 20 MINUTES · **TOTAL TIME:** 35 MINUTES
MAKES: 6 SIDE-DISH SERVINGS

8 CUPS WATER	1 TEASPOON ANCHOVY PASTE (OPTIONAL)
1 LARGE HEAD CAULIFLOWER (2½ POUNDS), CUT INTO 1½-INCH FLOWERETS	¼ TEASPOON CRUSHED RED PEPPER
2¼ TEASPOONS SALT	¼ CUP GOLDEN RAISINS
2 TABLESPOONS OLIVE OIL	2 TABLESPOONS PINE NUTS (PIGNOLI), LIGHTLY TOASTED
2 GARLIC CLOVES, CRUSHED WITH SIDE OF CHEF'S KNIFE	1 TABLESPOON CHOPPED FRESH PARSLEY

1   In 5-quart Dutch oven, heat water to boiling over high heat. Add cauliflower and 2 teaspoons salt; return to boiling. Cook until tender, 5 to 7 minutes; drain. Wipe Dutch oven dry.

2   In same Dutch oven, heat oil over medium heat. Add garlic and cook until golden. Add anchovy paste, if using, and crushed red pepper; cook 15 seconds. Add cauliflower, raisins, pine nuts, and remaining ¼ teaspoon salt; cook, stirring, until heated through, about 2 minutes. To serve, sprinkle with parsley.

PER SERVING. 2G PROTEIN | 9G CARBOHYDRATE | 6G TOTAL FAT (1G SATURATED)

CALORIES 2G FIBER | 0MG CHOLESTEROL | 401MG SODIUM

GARLIC-CRUMBED TOMATOES

Oven-roasted tomatoes are topped with bread crumbs seasoned with garlic, basil, and Parmesan for a simple but yummy side dish.

ACTIVE TIME: 20 MINUTES · **TOTAL TIME:** 35 MINUTES
MAKES: 4 SIDE-DISH SERVINGS

2	TABLESPOONS BUTTER OR MARGARINE	¼	CUP FRESHLY GRATED PARMESAN CHEESE
1	GARLIC CLOVE, CRUSHED WITH GARLIC PRESS	¼	TEASPOON SALT
½	CUP FRESH BREAD CRUMBS	⅛	TEASPOON GROUND BLACK PEPPER
¼	CUP LOOSELY PACKED FRESH BASIL OR PARSLEY LEAVES, CHOPPED	2	RIPE LARGE TOMATOES (12 OUNCES EACH), CORED AND CUT CROSSWISE IN HALF

1 Arrange oven rack in upper third of oven. Preheat oven to 425°F. Line cookie sheet with foil.

2 In 10-inch skillet, melt butter over medium heat. Add garlic and cook, stirring, until fragrant, about 1 minute. Remove skillet from heat; stir in bread crumbs, basil, Parmesan, salt, and pepper.

3 Place tomato halves, cut sides up, in prepared pan. Top with crumb mixture. Roast until tomatoes are heated through and topping is golden, about 15 minutes.

125 CALORIES

PER SERVING. 4G PROTEIN | 11G CARBOHYDRATE | 8G TOTAL FAT (4G SATURATED) 2G FIBER | 20MG CHOLESTEROL | 342MG SODIUM ❤

SPAGHETTI SQUASH WITH OLIVES AND PECORINO

Cook spaghetti squash the no-fuss way using the microwave—then just scrape it into strands, garnish, and serve.

ACTIVE TIME: 10 MINUTES · **TOTAL TIME:** 25 MINUTES
MAKES: 4 SIDE-DISH SERVINGS

Pierce **1 small spaghetti squash (2½ pounds)** all over. On plate, microwave squash on High for 14 minutes or until tender; let cool. Cut squash in half lengthwise; discard seeds. With fork, scrape squash lengthwise; place strands in medium bowl. Pit and chop **¼ cup Kalamata olives**; add to bowl along with **3 tablespoons freshly grated Pecorino-Romano, 2 tablespoons chopped fresh parsley, 1 tablespoon olive oil**, and **2 teaspoons red wine vinegar**.

125 CALORIES

PER SERVING. 4G PROTEIN | 12G CARBOHYDRATE | 8G TOTAL FAT (2G SATURATED) 3G FIBER | 8MG CHOLESTEROL | 252MG SODIUM 🔵 ❤️

PARMESAN BRUSSELS SPROUTS

Roasted Brussels sprouts are irresistible tossed with a little red wine vinegar and grated Parmesan cheese.

PREP TIME: 10 MINUTES · **TOTAL TIME:** 30 MINUTES
MAKES: 3 CUPS OR 4 SIDE-DISH SERVINGS

Preheat oven to 450°F. In large jelly-roll pan, toss **1¼ pounds thinly sliced Brussels sprouts, 2 tablespoons olive oil, 1 teaspoon fresh thyme leaves, 1 thinly sliced garlic clove, ⅛ teaspoon salt**, and **¼ teaspoon pepper**. Spread evenly to make a single layer. Roast for 20 minutes, stirring once, until sprouts are browned. In medium bowl, toss sprouts with **1 teaspoon red wine vinegar** and **¼ cup coarsely grated Parmesan**.

145 CALORIES

PER SERVING. 7G PROTEIN | 13G CARBOHYDRATE | 9G TOTAL FAT (2G SATURATED) 5G FIBER | 4MG CHOLESTEROL | 185MG SODIUM 🔵 🌾

125 CALORIES

Spaghetti Squash with Olives and Pecorino (opposite)

CREAMY POLENTA

Polenta has long been a popular staple in northern Italy. Our method for cooking it ensures lump-free results.

ACTIVE TIME: 5 MINUTES · **TOTAL TIME:** 30 MINUTES
MAKES: 8 SIDE-DISH SERVINGS

6½ CUPS COLD WATER

1 TEASPOON SALT

1½ CUPS YELLOW CORNMEAL

½ CUP FRESHLY GRATED PARMESAN CHEESE

4 TABLESPOONS BUTTER OR MARGARINE, CUT INTO PIECES

1 Bring 4½ cups water to a boil. In 5-quart Dutch oven, combine remaining 2 cups cold water and salt. With wire whisk, gradually beat in cornmeal until smooth. Whisk in boiling water. Return to boiling over high heat. Reduce heat to medium-low and cook, stirring frequently with wooden spoon, until mixture is very thick, 20 to 25 minutes.

2 Stir Parmesan and butter into polenta until butter has melted. Serve immediately.

175 CALORIES

PER SERVING. 5G PROTEIN | 20G CARBOHYDRATE | 8G TOTAL FAT (5G SATURATED) 0G FIBER | 20MG CHOLESTEROL | 464MG SODIUM

MICROWAVE POLENTA

In deep 4-quart microwave-safe bowl or casserole, combine **2 cups low-fat (1%) milk, 1½ cups cornmeal,** and **1 teaspoon salt** until blended. Stir in **4½ cups boiling water.** Cook in microwave oven on High for 12 to 15 minutes. After first 5 minutes of cooking, with wire whisk, stir vigorously until smooth (mixture will be lumpy at first). Stir two more times during cooking. When polenta is thick and creamy, stir in **4 tablespoons butter,** cut into pieces, and **½ cup freshly grated Parmesan cheese.** Makes 8 side-dish servings.

205 CALORIES

PER SERVING. 6G PROTEIN | 27G CARBOHYDRATE | 8G TOTAL FAT (5G SATURATED) 1G FIBER | 22MG CHOLESTEROL | 447MG SODIUM

BROILED ROSEMARY POLENTA WEDGES

Line 13" by 9" baking pan with foil, extending foil over rim. Prepare Creamy Polenta as directed but use only **3½ cups boiling water** and cook until mixture is very thick and indentation remains when spoon is dragged through polenta, 30 to 35 minutes. Stir in Parmesan and butter as directed. Spoon mixture into prepared pan, smoothing top. Refrigerate until very firm, at least 1 hour. Preheat broiler. Lift foil with polenta from baking pan; place on cookie sheet. Cut polenta into 16 triangles; separate triangles. Melt **1 tablespoon butter or margarine** and combine with **½ teaspoon chopped fresh rosemary or ¼ teaspoon dried rosemary;** brush onto polenta wedges. Broil 5 to 7 inches from heat source until lightly browned and heated through, about 10 minutes. Makes 16 side-dish servings.

100 CALORIES

PER SERVING. 2G PROTEIN | 12G CARBOHYDRATE | 5G TOTAL FAT (3G SATURATED)
1G FIBER | 12MG CHOLESTEROL | 216MG SODIUM

115 CALORIES
Buttermilk Panna Cotta with Blackberry Sauce (page 147)

DOLCI DESSERTS

Enjoy classic Italian desserts at home with our recipes for everything from biscotti (a twice-baked cookie) to panna cotta (a gelatin dessert made with cream, milk, and sugar) and tiramisu (a cake made from ladyfingers dipped in coffee then layered with a creamy filling). Our versions lighten up these treats with swaps like low-fat milk and reduced-fat cream cheese, so you can enjoy them without guilt. And calories range from 30 to 175, so you'll find a sweet match here for any main dish you choose.

KEY TO ICONS

🕐 30 minutes or less ❤ Heart healthy 🌾 High fiber 🍲 Make ahead 🍲 Slow cooker

ALMOND MACAROON FINGERS

It's hard to believe that cookies as chewy and rich as our chocolate-brushed macaroons are also low in fat, but it's the truth.

ACTIVE TIME: 1 HOUR 30 MINUTES PLUS STANDING · **BAKE TIME:** 17 MINUTES PER BATCH
MAKES: ABOUT 42 COOKIES

1 TUBE OR CAN (7 TO 8 OUNCES) ALMOND PASTE

½ CUP CONFECTIONERS' SUGAR

2 LARGE EGG WHITES

½ TEASPOON VANILLA EXTRACT

2 SQUARES (2 OUNCES) BITTERSWEET OR SEMISWEET CHOCOLATE, BROKEN INTO PIECES

1 Preheat oven to 300°F. Line two cookie sheets with parchment.

2 In food processor with knife blade attached, process almond paste and sugar until only occasional small lumps remain. Add egg whites and vanilla; pulse until well combined.

3 Spoon batter into decorating bag fitted with ½-inch star tip. Pipe batter into 3-inch-long fingers, 1 inch apart, onto prepared cookie sheets.

4 Bake macaroons until edges start to turn golden brown, 17 to 19 minutes, rotating sheets between upper and lower oven racks halfway through. Set cookie sheets on wire racks to cool. Repeat with remaining batter.

5 In microwave-safe cup, heat chocolate in microwave oven on High until soft and shiny, 1 minute. Stir until smooth. With pastry brush, brush chocolate on half of each macaroon. Let stand until set or refrigerate 5 minutes to set chocolate. Peel cookies from parchment.

6 Store macaroons, with waxed paper between layers, in tightly covered container up to 3 days or freeze up to 3 months.

30 CALORIES · **PER COOKIE.** 1G PROTEIN | 5G CARBOHYDRATE | 1G TOTAL FAT (0G SATURATED) 0G FIBER | 18MG CHOLESTEROL | 11MG SODIUM ♥ 🥗

CHOCOLATE-HAZELNUT MACARONS

Chocolate with hazelnuts is a beloved combo in desserts throughout Italy—and what a delectable duo it is! In Verona, these luscious indulgences are called *baci di Giulietta*, or "kisses of Juliet." Serve the cookies plain or make them into sandwiches with 1 teaspoon melted semisweet chocolate (115 calories per sandwich).

ACTIVE TIME: 15 MINUTES · **BAKE TIME:** 10 MINUTES PLUS TOASTING HAZELNUTS
MAKES: ABOUT 40 COOKIES

1 CUP HAZELNUTS, TOASTED (SEE TIP)
1 CUP SUGAR
¼ CUP UNSWEETENED COCOA
1 OUNCE UNSWEETENED CHOCOLATE, CHOPPED

⅛ TEASPOON SALT
2 LARGE EGG WHITES
1 TEASPOON VANILLA EXTRACT

1 Preheat oven to 350°F. Line two large cookie sheets with parchment paper.
2 In food processor with knife blade attached, pulse hazelnuts with sugar, cocoa, chocolate, and salt until ground. Add egg whites and vanilla; process until well blended. (Mixture will be tacky.)
3 Drop batter by rounded teaspoons, 2 inches apart, on cookie sheets. Bake 10 minutes or until tops look dry, rotating cookie sheets halfway through baking. Cool completely on cookie sheets on wire racks. Store in an airtight container up to 3 days or freeze up to 3 months.

TIP Toast hazelnuts in a 350°F oven for 15 minutes until they're golden and fragrant. Transfer the nuts to a clean, dry kitchen towel and rub them until the skins come off.

45 CALORIES

PER COOKIE. 1G PROTEIN | 6G CARBOHYDRATE | 3G TOTAL FAT (0G SATURATED)
1G FIBER | 0MG CHOLESTEROL | 10MG SODIUM ♥ 🗄

CRUNCHY CHOCOLATE BISCOTTI

We've given this biscotti recipe a healthy makeover, using egg whites instead of whole eggs and vegetable oil instead of butter.

ACTIVE TIME: 30 MINUTES PLUS COOLING · **BAKE TIME:** 50 MINUTES
MAKES: ABOUT 48 BISCOTTI

3 LARGE EGG WHITES	½ CUP UNSWEETENED COCOA
⅓ CUP VEGETABLE OIL	1 TEASPOON BAKING POWDER
2 TABLESPOONS STRONG BREWED COFFEE	¼ TEASPOON BAKING SODA
1 TEASPOON VANILLA EXTRACT	¼ TEASPOON SALT
1⅔ CUPS ALL-PURPOSE FLOUR	⅓ CUP CHOPPED HAZELNUTS OR OTHER NUTS, TOASTED (SEE TIP, PAGE 141)
¾ CUP SUGAR	⅓ CUP DRIED TART CHERRIES

1 Preheat oven to 350°F. Lightly grease large cookie sheet.

2 In small bowl, beat together egg whites, oil, coffee, and vanilla.

3 In large bowl, stir together flour, sugar, cocoa, baking powder, baking soda, salt, nuts, and cherries until well mixed. Pour egg mixture over dry ingredients and stir until combined. Shape dough into two 12" by 1" logs; place both on prepared cookie sheet and flatten slightly. Bake 30 minutes or until toothpick inserted in center comes out clean. Cool logs on cookie sheet on wire rack 10 minutes.

4 Transfer 1 log to cutting board. Cut diagonally into scant-½-inch-thick slices. Lay slices out flat on ungreased cookie sheet. Repeat with remaining log, using second cookie sheet if necessary. Bake until dry, 20 minutes, rotating cookie sheets between upper and lower oven racks halfway though baking if using two sheets. Using wide metal spatula, transfer biscotti to rack to cool.

5 Store biscotti in airtight container at room temperature up to 2 weeks or in freezer up to 3 months.

50 CALORIES **PER BISCOTTO.** 1G PROTEIN | 8G CARBOHYDRATE | 2G TOTAL FAT (1G SATURATED) 1G FIBER | 0MG CHOLESTEROL | 30MG SODIUM ❤

GRANITA KNOW-HOW

The heat-beating Italian ice known as granita doesn't require any special equipment—just a metal baking pan.

Cover and freeze the granita mixture until partially frozen, about 2 hours. Stir it with a fork to break up the chunks. Cover it again and return the pan to the freezer until the mixture is completely frozen, at least 3 hours or up to overnight.

To serve the granita, let it stand at room temperature until slightly softened, about 15 minutes. Use a metal spoon or fork to scrape across the surface, transferring the flavorful ice shards to chilled dessert dishes or wine goblets without packing them.

COFFEE GRANITA

A Neapolitan tradition. If you like, use decaffeinated espresso.

TOTAL TIME: 10 MINUTES PLUS COOLING AND FREEZING
MAKES: 6 SERVINGS

In medium bowl, stir ⅔ **cup sugar** and **2 cups hot espresso coffee** until sugar has completely dissolved. Pour into 9-inch square metal baking pan; cool. Cover, freeze, and scrape to serve as directed in box (opposite).

 55 CALORIES

PER ½-CUP SERVING. 0G PROTEIN | 14G CARBOHYDRATE | 0G TOTAL FAT (0G SATU-RATED) 0G FIBER | 0MG CHOLESTEROL | 1MG SODIUM ♥ ▤

BOLD BERRY GRANITA

Frosty, fruity, and fat-free, this ruby-red mix of pureed raspberries and strawberries is the ultimate summer dessert.

TOTAL TIME: 20 MINUTES PLUS FREEZING
MAKES: 10 SERVINGS

In 2-quart saucepan, **heat 1 cup water** and **½ cup sugar** to boiling over high heat, stirring until sugar dissolves. Reduce heat to low and simmer, un-covered, 5 minutes. Set aside to cool slightly, about 5 minutes. Meanwhile, from **1 or 2 lemons,** grate 2 teaspoons peel and squeeze ¼ cup juice. In food processor with knife blade attached, blend **1 pound hulled strawber-ries** and **1½ cups raspberries** until pureed. With back of spoon, press puree through sieve into medium bowl; discard seeds. Stir sugar syrup and lemon juice and peel into berry puree. Pour into 9-inch square metal baking pan. Cover, freeze, and scrape to serve, as directed in box (opposite).

 60 CALORIES

PER ½-CUP SERVING. 1G PROTEIN | 15G CARBOHYDRATE | 0G TOTAL FAT (0G SATU-RATED) 2G FIBER | 0MG CHOLESTEROL | 0MG SODIUM ♥ ▤

PIGNOLI COOKIES

Thanks to the food processor—and prepared almond paste—making these classic Italian cookies, with their topping of pine nuts, is a breeze. Use a pastry bag to form the rounds and keep your fingers from getting sticky.

ACTIVE TIME: 25 MINUTES · **BAKE TIME:** 10 MINUTES PER BATCH
MAKES: ABOUT 24 COOKIES

1 TUBE OR CAN (7 TO 8 OUNCES) ALMOND PASTE

¾ CUP CONFECTIONERS' SUGAR

1 LARGE EGG WHITE

4 TEASPOONS HONEY

½ CUP PINE NUTS (PIGNOLI; 3 OUNCES)

1 Preheat oven to 350°F. Line two large cookie sheets with parchment.

2 Crumble almond paste into food processor with knife blade attached. Add sugar and process until paste has texture of fine meal; transfer to large bowl. Add egg white and honey. With mixer at low speed, beat until dough is blended. Increase speed to medium-high and beat until very smooth, about 5 minutes.

3 Spoon batter into pastry bag fitted with ½-inch round tip. Pipe 1¼-inch rounds, 2 inches apart, onto prepared cookie sheets. Brush cookies lightly with *water* and cover completely with pine nuts, pressing gently to make nuts stick.

4 Bake until golden brown, 10 to 12 minutes, rotating sheets between upper and lower oven racks halfway through. Slide parchment paper onto wire racks and let cookies cool on parchment paper. Repeat with remaining dough and pine nuts.

5 Store pignoli in airtight container up to 5 days or freeze up to 3 months.

75 CALORIES **PER COOKIE.** 2G PROTEIN | 9G CARBOHYDRATE | 4G TOTAL FAT (0G SATURATED) 0G FIBER | 0MG CHOLESTEROL | 5MG SODIUM

BUTTERMILK PANNA COTTA WITH BLACKBERRY SAUCE

This luscious, creamy dessert features antioxidant-rich blackberries. For photo, see page 138.

TOTAL TIME: 25 MINUTES PLUS CHILLING
MAKES: 8 SERVINGS

1 ENVELOPE UNFLAVORED GELATIN

6 TABLESPOONS WATER

2¾ CUPS BUTTERMILK

½ CUP PLUS 4 TEASPOONS SUGAR

10 OUNCES FROZEN BLACKBERRIES, THAWED

1 TEASPOON FRESH LEMON JUICE

1 In cup, evenly sprinkle gelatin over ¼ cup water. Let stand 2 minutes to allow gelatin to absorb liquid and soften.

2 In 3-quart saucepan, heat ½ cup buttermilk and ½ cup sugar over medium heat 2 to 3 minutes or until sugar dissolves, stirring occasionally. Reduce heat to low; whisk in gelatin. Cook 1 to 2 minutes or until gelatin dissolves, stirring to assist. Remove saucepan from heat; stir in remaining 2¼ cups buttermilk.

3 Pour buttermilk mixture into eight 4-ounce ramekins or 6-ounce custard cups. Place ramekins in jelly-roll pan for easier handling. Cover pan with plastic wrap and refrigerate panna cotta at least 4 hours or overnight, until well chilled and set.

4 Set aside ⅓ cup blackberries for garnish. In blender, puree remaining blackberries with lemon juice and remaining 2 tablespoons water and 4 teaspoons sugar. Pour puree through sieve set over small bowl, stirring to press out fruit sauce; discard seeds. Cover and refrigerate sauce if not serving right away.

5 To unmold panna cottas, run tip of small knife around edge of ramekins. With hand, sharply tap side of each ramekin to break seal; invert onto dessert plates. Spoon sauce around each panna cotta. Garnish with reserved berries.

115 CALORIES **PER SERVING.** 4G PROTEIN | 24G CARBOHYDRATE | 1G TOTAL FAT (1G SATURATED) 1G FIBER | 3MG CHOLESTEROL | 90MG SODIUM ❤

CHIANTI-ROASTED PEARS

Bosc pears become tender and caramelized on the outside when baked with a butter-and-sugar coating and basted with red wine. This is a super-easy dessert to serve for company.

ACTIVE TIME: 25 MINUTES · **TOTAL TIME:** 1 HOUR PLUS COOLING
MAKES: 6 SERVINGS

1 LARGE NAVEL ORANGE	¼ CUP WATER
6 BOSC PEARS	¼ CUP SUGAR
½ CUP HEARTY RED WINE (SUCH AS CHIANTI)	1 TABLESPOON BUTTER OR MARGARINE, MELTED

1   Preheat oven to 450°F. With vegetable peeler, remove peel from orange in 2" by ½" strips. Reserve orange for another use.

2   With melon baller or small knife, remove cores and seeds from pears by cutting through blossom end (bottom) of pears; leave peels on and stems attached.

3   In shallow 1½- to 2-quart glass or ceramic baking dish, combine orange peel, wine, and water. Place sugar in medium bowl. Hold pears, one at a time, over bowl of sugar. Use pastry brush to brush pears with melted butter, then sprinkle with sugar until coated. Stand pears in baking dish. Sprinkle any remaining sugar into baking dish around pears.

4   Bake pears 35 to 40 minutes or until tender when pierced with tip of small knife, basting occasionally with syrup in baking dish.

5   Cool pears slightly, about 30 minutes, to serve warm. Or cool completely; cover and refrigerate up to 1 day. Reheat to serve warm if you like.

135 CALORIES

PER SERVING. 1G PROTEIN | 29G CARBOHYDRATE | 3 TOTAL FAT (1G SATURATED) 4G FIBER | 5MG CHOLESTEROL | 20MG SODIUM ♥ 🗑

SGROPPINO SORBET WITH PROSECCO AND MINT

Sgroppino is a classic after-dinner beverage from the Veneto region in northern Italy. It's usually made by whipping lemon sorbet and Prosecco together; a splash of vodka is sometimes added. Here we've left the sorbet intact as a light and refreshing float—a luscious and low-cal end to dinner.

TOTAL TIME: 5 MINUTES

MAKES: 6 SERVINGS

Divide **1 pint lemon sorbet** among 6 wineglasses or dessert bowls. Pour ⅓ **cup Prosecco** into each glass; garnish with **mint sprig.** Serve immediately.

PER SERVING. 0G PROTEIN | 22G CARBOHYDRATE | 0G TOTAL FAT (0G SATURATED) 0G FIBER | 0MG CHOLESTEROL | 10MG SODIUM ♥

HEALTHY MAKEOVER TIRAMISU

Tiramisu is a heavenly dessert made of ladyfingers dipped in coffee and liquor, traditionally layered with a whipped mixture of egg yolks and mascarpone cheese. Our cocoa-topped version has just 175 calories per serving, thanks to reduced-fat cream cheese and low-fat milk.

TOTAL TIME: 25 MINUTES PLUS CHILLING
MAKES: 9 SERVINGS

⅔ CUP HOT WATER

2 TABLESPOONS BRANDY

1 TABLESPOON INSTANT ESPRESSO POWDER

5 TABLESPOONS SUGAR

¼ CUP WHIPPING CREAM

1 PACKAGE (8 OUNCES) REDUCED-FAT CREAM CHEESE (NEUFCHATEL), SOFTENED

¼ CUP LOW-FAT (1%) MILK

½ TEASPOON VANILLA EXTRACT

30 SOFT (SPONGE-TYPE) LADYFINGERS (4 OUNCES)

1 TABLESPOON UNSWEETENED COCOA

CHOCOLATE CURLS (OPTIONAL)

1 In small bowl, combine water, brandy, espresso powder, and 1 tablespoon sugar until sugar dissolves.

2 In medium bowl, with mixer on medium speed, beat cream until soft peaks form when beaters are lifted.

3 In large bowl, with mixer on medium-high speed, beat cream cheese and remaining ¼ cup sugar until fluffy, about 4 minutes. Continue beating; add milk and vanilla in slow, steady stream. Beat until well mixed and fluffy, about 2 minutes.

4 With spatula, gently fold whipped cream into cream cheese mixture. In 8-inch square baking dish, arrange half of ladyfingers, flat sides up, in single layer. Pour half of brandy mixture evenly over; let stand until absorbed.

5 Spread half of cream cheese mixture evenly over ladyfingers. Top with remaining ladyfingers, flat sides up. Brush remaining brandy mixture over ladyfingers, allowing liquid to be absorbed before each addition. Spread evenly with remaining cream cheese mixture.

6 Sift cocoa evenly on top. Cover with plastic wrap and refrigerate at least 4 hours or overnight. Garnish with chocolate curls, if desired.

175 CALORIES

PER SERVING. 4G PROTEIN | 18G CARBOHYDRATE | 9G TOTAL FAT (5G SATURATED) 0G FIBER | 55MG CHOLESTEROL | 180MG SODIUM

400
CALORIE
VEGETARIAN

INTRODUCTION

Whether you're already following a vegetarian diet or are just beginning to explore what it means to eliminate meat from your meals, the health benefits are compelling. In study after study, it's been shown that a vegetarian diet rich in fruits, vegetables, whole grains, and legumes and low in fat results in numerous health benefits: It can reduce the risk of some cancers, lower the incidence of diabetes, decrease the possibility of stroke and heart disease, and have a positive effect on the health of those who already have heart disease. Furthermore, a balanced low-calorie vegetarian diet can help you lose weight or maintain a healthy weight.

A good vegetarian diet is filled with fresh vegetables and fruits and nutrient-rich, fiber-packed whole grains and beans, which makes it a natural subject for *Good Housekeeping 400 Calorie Meals*. In this section, we share more than 50 recipes for delicious meat-free mains, from yummy sandwiches to hearty soups and stews, playful stuffed, stacked, and stir-fried vegetable entrées and satisfying pastas, casseroles, and grain dishes, plus a chapter that invites you to enjoy breakfast favorites any time of day. You'll find low-cal, vegetarian takes on familiar dishes like burgers, pizza, burritos, and lasagna, plus tasty recipes that feature veggies, grains, and tofu in new ways.

As the title of the book promises, every main dish is 400 calories or less, and as a bonus, we've included chapters on vegetable and grain side dishes plus fruity desserts that will help you round out your meals in healthy vegetarian style. The 40 add-on recipes are organized by calorie count—from lowest to highest. Simply choose your entrée, then use your surplus calories to select an add-on (or two) that will make it a meal.

If you're watching your weight and limiting dinners to around 500 calories total, you could begin with Artichokes with Creamy Lemon Sauce for dipping (145 calories), enjoy our Stuffed Portobellos (290 calories, pictured opposite) as your main dish and finish with an orange: 145 + 290 + 60 = a 495-calorie meal. With this section, it's easy to build meat-free meals that are both satisfying *and* low calorie. See "Healthy Vegetarian Meal Planning," opposite, for examples.

HEALTHY VEGETARIAN MEAL PLANNING

Planning healthy, low-calorie vegetarian brunches, lunches, and dinners is a breeze with this section. Prepare the add-ons we've suggested under "Make It a Meal" with each main-dish recipe to make 500-calorie dinners, 400-calorie lunches, or 300-calorie breakfasts. Or get creative and choose from the veggie, grain, and dessert recipe lists on pages 253, 269, and 283 to make your own satisfying meal combos. Here are some tasty examples to get you started.

SAMPLE BRUNCH MENU

MAIN: Crustless Tomato-Ricotta Pie	190 calories
ADD-ON 1: Mesclun with Pears and Pumpkin Seeds	100 calories
ADD-ON 2: One cup coffee with 1½ tablespoons skim milk	10 calories
Total calories per meal	**300 calories**

SAMPLE LUNCH MENU

MAIN: Vegetarian Souvlaki	390 calories
ADD-ON: Kale Chips	15 calories
Total calories per meal	**405 calories**

SAMPLE DINNER MENU

MAIN: Stuffed Acorn Squash	250 calories
ADD-ON 1: Green Beans with Mixed Mushrooms	80 calories
ADD-ON 2: Stuffed Fresh Figs	170 calories
Total calories per meal	**500 calories**

STAYING SLIM THE VEGETARIAN WAY

You might think that a vegetarian diet is guaranteed to keep you skinny. But consider this: most French fries, cookies, and a lot of greasy takeout foods are vegetarian. To cultivate a low-calorie vegetarian diet that's wholesome, too, follow these guidelines.

• **Think seasonal.** When vegetables and fruits are in season, they're also at their most flavorful, abundant, and affordable—thus easy to transform into mouthwatering meals.

• **Bulk up.** Switching to a high-fiber diet can be a bit like taking a magic weight-loss pill: Fiber swells a little in your stomach, which quells hunger. Fiber is also low cal: Your body can't break it down, so it runs right through your system, providing only bulk. That's several good reasons to add fiber-rich, fill-you-up whole grains and legumes to your diet. Try some options that may be new to you like bulgur, wheat berries, or millet. Recipes containing all three—and many other wholesome whole grains—are sprinkled throughout this book.

• **Explore meat alternatives.** In addition to legumes, you can add protein to a vegetarian diet with tofu, tempeh, and textured vegetable protein (TVP). Our Fast Fried Rice (page 210) is an example of an easy way to use tofu. See pages 159–161 for information about meat alternatives made from soybeans.

• **Get technique-savvy:** Use high heat to alter a veggie's flavor. Grilling, roasting, and baking can take out the bite or boost the sweetness of vegetables. Our grilled Portobello Pesto Burger (page 178) and baked Vegetable Cobbler (page 228) are two flavorful examples.

• **Go for bold.** Tweak the taste of your dishes with zingy flavor boosters like chile peppers, mustard, or olives. It pays to get to know your spice cabinet and condiment options. Sweet-and-Sour Unstuffed Cabbage (page 211) is seasoned with fresh ginger, garlic, rice vinegar, and soy sauce, while Red Chili with Fire-Roasted Tomatoes (page 192) gets its zip from chipotle chiles, cumin, and oregano.

• **Eat fruit for dessert.** Berries, bananas, peaches, and citrus are naturally sweet and filled with vitamins and antioxidants. Instead of making chocolate cake a habit, sample the luscious fruit-based desserts in our Sweet & Fruity Treats chapter (page 283).

THE VEGETARIAN PANTRY

The following foods are essential to great vegetarian cooking. Get familiar with these nutritious ingredients, and you'll be well on your way to creating delicious, satisfying, low-calorie vegetarian meals.

Beans and other legumes: Whether you choose black beans, garbanzos, pintos, cannellini, lentils, or split peas, they are packed with protein and insoluble and soluble fiber. Insoluble fiber helps promote regularity and may stave off such digestive disorders as diverticulosis. Soluble fiber can reduce LDL cholesterol levels and help control blood-sugar levels in people with diabetes. Beans are also high in saponin, a cancer-fighting plant compound. We incorporate a wide variety of beans and legumes in recipes throughout this book, so you can easily get your daily dose of this energy-giving protein.

Barley: Barley is the oldest grain in cultivation. The fiber in barley is especially healthy; studies indicate it may be even more effective than oat fiber in lowering cholesterol. Our Peach, Cucumber, and Barley Salad (page 274) is a delicious way to get to know this grain.

Cornmeal: This is ground hulled yellow or white corn; the fine-grind type is used for cornbread, while medium-grind is used in polentas, like our easy Polenta Lasagna (page 223). Choose a water- or stone-ground cornmeal; both processes leave more of the bran and germ intact.

Couscous: Originally from North Africa, this grainlike pasta is made from semolina wheat flour. The packaged, precooked version is ready to eat in just five minutes and is widely available in supermarkets. Look for whole-wheat couscous, which is similar in taste and texture to regular couscous, but packs a whopping 8 grams of fiber per serving. And see Couscous Four Ways (page 279) for delicious ideas on how flavor it.

Millet: Although we typically cultivate this cereal grass for birdseed and fodder, it is a staple in Asia and Africa. It's best toasted, then prepared like rice to make seasoned pilafs, like our Southwestern-flavored Millet with Corn and Green Chiles (page 275) or hot cereal.

Quinoa: This is another grain that, botanically speaking, isn't a grain; rather, quinoa (pronounced KEEN-wah) is a relative of Swiss chard and beets. High in B vitamins, it is also a complete protein, containing all of the essential amino acids the body can't produce itself. Shaped a lot like a sesame seed, quinoa has a crunchy-melting quality. To remove any traces of bitterness, rub quinoa under cold running water, then rinse until the water is clear before cooking it.

Oats: Oats contain a type of fiber, beta-glucan, that studies have shown to help reduce cholesterol levels. Steel-cut oats are the whole oat kernels with only the inedible outer chaff removed, cut into pieces. They are chewy but have a wonderful nutty-sweet flavor. Rolled oats, or old-fashioned oats, are whole oats that have been rolled into flat flakes then steamed and lightly toasted.

Rice: Whenever possible, choose brown rice; it's processed to remove only its inedible outer husk, leaving its nutritive powers intact. It is rich in fiber, an excellent source of manganese (a mineral that helps produce energy from protein and carbohydrates), and a good source of magnesium (helps build bones) and selenium (key to a healthy immune system). Brown rice can be long-, medium-, or short-grain.

Wheat: Wheat is a nutritional powerhouse, containing thirteen B vitamins, vitamin E, protein, and essential fatty acids. Wheat berries, the unmilled kernels of wheat, are nutty tasting and very chewy. If you've never cooked them before, sample our Wheat-Berry Salad with Dried Cherries (page 272). Bulgur is quick-cooking cracked wheat that has been parboiled and dried. You can also enjoy the whole-grain goodness of wheat in the form of whole-wheat flour, which is made from whole hard wheat berries.

Tofu: Soybean curd that is drained and pressed in a process similar to cheese-making. The creamiest tofu (with the least liquid pressed out) is called soft or silken. Use it in shakes, dressings, and dips. Extracting still more liquid produces regular tofu, then firm, and finally extra-firm tofu, which are all excellent grilled or in stir-fries. Avoid bulk tofu, unpackaged blocks sold in water; it can be contaminated with bacteria. Sealed water-packed tofu and the aseptically packaged kind (unrefrigerated) are safer. To store tofu after opening the package, cover it with cool water and refrigerate it for up to 1 week, changing the water daily.

VEGAN DAIRY AND EGG SUBSTITUTES

If you've decided to follow a vegan diet (eliminating all animal foods from your diet) or just want to eat less dairy, here's a list of some of the dairy- and egg-alternative products available today. Once only sold at health-food stores and online, today you can find many of these items in large supermarkets. Take a look in your local grocery store—you may be surprised to see the vegan products they stock.

• Nondairy margarine, including soy margarine (try Earth Balance brand)

• Soy milk, rice milk, and nut milks (including almond and cashew milk)

• Nondairy soy sour cream and cream cheese

• Nondairy yogurts made with rice, soy, almond, or coconut milk

• Nondairy soy- or coconut-milk creamers

• Nondairy soy frozen yogurt

• Nondairy ice creams made with soy or coconut milk

• Nondairy chocolate (with the exception of unsweetened cocoa powder, chocolate usually contains milk solids)

• Egg-free soy mayonnaise (try Vegenaise brand)

• Egg replacements (check vegan and vegetarian websites for recommended substitutions)

To make it easy for vegans to cook from this section, we've included a vegan icon Ⓥ in the nutritional information for all recipes that do not contain any animal products. In addition, with a little practice, you can adapt many of the other recipes by swapping in the dairy and egg substitutes listed above. Experiment until you find the nondairy products you like best. Flavors and textures vary from brand to brand and also depend on what ingredient is used as the base. You may discover that you don't care much for soy-based products but adore anything made with nut or coconut milk. Or find that you love one type of nondairy yogurt for baking, while another is just the thing for a snack.

To prepare tofu for cooking, drain it and wrap it in a clean dish towel. Place the wrapped tofu on a pie plate, top it with a dinner plate, and weight it down to extract excess water. (One or two heavy cans make good weights for this purpose.) Let the tofu sit under weight for about 15 minutes.

Tempeh: A dense, chewy cake made from cooked, fermented soybeans. Like other soy products, tempeh absorbs the flavor of the ingredients it's cooked with, even though it has a smoky flavor of its own. Tempeh is sold refrigerated or frozen; try it in soups or stir-fries. Once only available in health-food stores, today you can find it in most supermarkets.

Textured vegetable protein (TVP): Also known as textured soy protein, these dried granules made from defatted soy flakes have to be rehydrated before cooking. Commercially, TVP is used to make soy veggie burgers, sausages, and hot dogs. You can find it in health-food stores and some supermarkets.

Vegetables and fruits: Eating a variety of fresh vegetables and fruits is an important part of any healthy vegetarian diet (and a good way to keep your meals skinny, too). A colorful diet filled with reds, yellows, oranges, and greens helps ensure that you get the widest range of vitamins and phytochemicals, the natural pigments in produce that help keep your body healthy. The recipes in this section offer dozens of fresh new ways to prepare veggies; see the Stuffed, Stacked & Stir-Fried chapter (page 199) for some particularly creative takes.

MEATLESS MAINS

To make skinny vegetarian meal planning a cinch, each main dish is paired with suggestions for add-on recipes that will make it a meal. Or to choose your own add-ons, see the complete recipe lists in the second half of the book, conveniently organized by calorie count, from lowest to highest: Snacks, Sides & Salads, page 253; Get Your Grains, page 269; and Sweet and Fruity Treats, page 283.

345 CALORIES

Portobello Pesto Burgers (page 178)

PIZZAS, BURGERS & SANDWICHES

If you're still new to a vegetarian diet, you may be wondering: What's pizza without pepperoni? Can my family give up burgers? The yummy, low-calorie recipes that follow are your answer. We offer three irresistible meat-free pizzas prepared on the grill for extra flavor. And our black bean and portobello burgers are so satisfying, no one will miss the meat. If you're hankering for Mexican, try our Vegetarian Tacos or Grilled Vegetable Burritos. For lovers of pulled chicken or pork sandwiches, we offer barbecued tofu sandwiches—so easy and delicious.

KEY TO ICONS

🔵 30 minutes or less   Ⓥ Vegan   ♥ Heart healthy   🌾 High fiber   🟩 Make ahead

GREEK SALAD PITAS

Making hummus—the Middle Eastern spread made with mashed garbanzo beans—is fast work when you use a food processor or blender.

TOTAL TIME: 20 MINUTES
MAKES: 4 SANDWICHES

---

1 CAN (15 TO 19 OUNCES) GARBANZO BEANS (CHICKPEAS), RINSED AND DRAINED

¼ CUP PLAIN NONFAT YOGURT

1 TABLESPOON OLIVE OIL

2 TABLESPOONS FRESH LEMON JUICE

½ TEASPOON SALT

¼ TEASPOON COARSELY GROUND BLACK PEPPER

¼ TEASPOON GROUND CUMIN

1 GARLIC CLOVE, PEELED

4 (6- TO 7-INCH) WHOLE-WHEAT PITAS

3 CUPS SLICED ROMAINE LETTUCE

2 MEDIUM TOMATOES (6 TO 8 OUNCES EACH), CUT INTO ¼-INCH PIECES

1 MEDIUM CUCUMBER, PEELED AND THINLY SLICED

1½ OUNCES FETA CHEESE, CRUMBLED (⅓ CUP)

2 TABLESPOONS CHOPPED FRESH MINT LEAVES, PLUS ADDITIONAL MINT LEAVES FOR GARNISH

---

1 In food processor with knife blade attached, or in blender, combine beans, yogurt, oil, lemon juice, salt, pepper, cumin, and garlic; puree until bean mixture is smooth.

2 Cut off top third of each pita to form a pocket and reserve tops for another use. Use half of bean mixture to spread inside pockets.

3 Combine lettuce, tomatoes, cucumber, feta, and chopped mint; fill pockets with mixture. Top with remaining bean mixture and garnish with mint leaves.

---

335 CALORIES

PER SERVING. 15G PROTEIN | 52G CARBOHYDRATE | 9G TOTAL FAT (2G SATURATED) 11G FIBER | 10MG CHOLESTEROL | 910MG SODIUM

MAKE IT A MEAL: Serve this sandwich with Spring Pea Dip with Veggies (page 255; 50 calories) for a fresh and healthy 385-calorie lunch.

VEGETARIAN SOUVLAKI

This vegetarian take on a traditionally meat-centered sandwich is just as satisfying as the original. Make the filling by cutting up your favorite veggie burgers. Swap in whole-wheat pitas for even more fiber.

ACTIVE TIME: 20 MINUTES · **TOTAL TIME:** 25 MINUTES
MAKES: 4 SANDWICHES

1 TABLESPOON OLIVE OIL

1 LARGE ONION (12 OUNCES), CUT IN HALF AND THINLY SLICED

4 FROZEN VEGETARIAN SOY BURGERS (10- TO 12-OUNCE PACKAGE), CUT INTO 1-INCH PIECES

¼ TEASPOON GROUND BLACK PEPPER

½ TEASPOON SALT

1 CONTAINER (8 OUNCES) PLAIN NONFAT YOGURT

1 SMALL ENGLISH (SEEDLESS) CUCUMBER (8 OUNCES), CUT INTO ¼-INCH DICE

1 TEASPOON DRIED MINT

1 SMALL GARLIC CLOVE, CRUSHED WITH GARLIC PRESS

4 (6- TO 7-INCH) PITA BREADS, WARMED

1 RIPE MEDIUM TOMATO (6 OUNCES), CUT INTO ½-INCH DICE

1 OUNCE FETA CHEESE, CRUMBLED (¼ CUP)

1 In nonstick 12-inch skillet, heat oil over medium heat until hot. Add onion and cook until tender and golden, 12 to 15 minutes, stirring occasionally. Add burger pieces, pepper, and ¼ teaspoon salt, and cook until heated through, about 5 minutes.

2 Meanwhile, in medium bowl, stir yogurt with cucumber, mint, garlic, and remaining ¼ teaspoon salt. Add burger mixture and toss gently to combine.

3 Cut 1-inch slice from each pita to make opening and reserve cut-off pita pieces for another use. Divide burger mixture evenly among pita pockets. Sprinkle with tomato and feta.

390 CALORIES

PER SANDWICH. 24G PROTEIN | 45G CARBOHYDRATE | 13G TOTAL FAT (3G SATURATED) 6G FIBER | 9MG CHOLESTEROL | 945MG SODIUM

MAKE IT A MEAL: What could be simpler than this sandwich made from your favorite store-bought veggie burgers? Serve with Kale Chips (15 calories; page 254) for a super-wholesome 390-calorie lunch.

LASAGNA TOASTS

These open-faced sandwiches topped with fresh tomato, zucchini, basil, and cheese invite you to enjoy all the flavors of lasagna in a flash—you bake them in your toaster oven!

ACTIVE TIME: 15 MINUTES · **TOTAL TIME:** 35 MINUTES
MAKES: 4 MAIN-DISH SERVINGS

4	SLICES (½ INCH THICK) ITALIAN BREAD
1	MEDIUM ZUCCHINI (8 OUNCES), CUT INTO ¼-INCH CHUNKS
1	GARLIC CLOVE, CRUSHED WITH GARLIC PRESS
1	TABLESPOON OLIVE OIL
4	RIPE PLUM TOMATOES (12 OUNCES), CHOPPED

⅜	TEASPOON SALT
½	TEASPOON GROUND BLACK PEPPER
¼	CUP PACKED FRESH BASIL LEAVES
1	CUP PART-SKIM RICOTTA CHEESE
¼	CUP FRESHLY GRATED PECORINO ROMANO CHEESE
4	OUNCES FRESH MOZZARELLA CHEESE, SLICED

1 Preheat toaster oven to 450°F. Toast bread 5 to 10 minutes or until golden.

2 In microwave-safe medium bowl, combine zucchini, garlic, and oil. Microwave on High for 4 minutes, stirring once. Add tomatoes and ¼ teaspoon each salt and pepper; cover with vented plastic wrap and microwave on High for 3 minutes.

3 Meanwhile, thinly slice basil leaves; reserve 2 tablespoons for garnish. In small bowl, combine basil, ricotta, Romano, and remaining ⅛ teaspoon salt and ¼ teaspoon pepper.

4 Divide ricotta mixture among bread slices and spread evenly. Using slotted spoon, divide tomato mixture among bread slices; top with mozzarella.

5 In single layer on foil-lined toaster-oven tray (working in batches if necessary), bake toasts 8 to 10 minutes or until tomato mixture is heated through and mozzarella is melted and lightly browned. Garnish with reserved basil.

320 CALORIES

PER SERVING. 18G PROTEIN | 24G CARBOHYDRATE | 17G TOTAL FAT (8G SATURATED) 3G FIBER | 46MG CHOLESTEROL | 550MG SODIUM

MAKE IT A MEAL: For a quick 390-calorie lunch with Italian flair, enjoy a lasagna toast along with two of our Chocolate-Almond Meringues (35 calories each; page 284).

VEGETARIAN TACOS

Beans make a hearty stand-in for ground beef in these vegetarian tacos—especially when they're gussied up with all your favorite toppings!

ACTIVE TIME: 10 MINUTES · **TOTAL TIME:** 20 MINUTES
MAKES: 4 MAIN-DISH SERVINGS

1 TABLESPOON OLIVE OIL

1 SMALL ONION, SLICED

1 MEDIUM RED PEPPER, SLICED

1 TEASPOON CHILI POWDER

¼ TEASPOON SALT

1 CAN (15 TO 19 OUNCES) BLACK BEANS OR OTHER FAVORITE BEANS, RINSED AND DRAINED

2 PLUM TOMATOES, COARSELY CHOPPED

¼ CUP LOOSELY PACKED FRESH CILANTRO LEAVES, CHOPPED

8 (6-INCH) FLOUR TORTILLAS

3 CUPS THINLY SLICED ROMAINE LETTUCE

2 OUNCES MONTEREY JACK OR MILD CHEDDAR CHEESE, SHREDDED (½ CUP)

1 In 12-inch nonstick skillet, heat oil over medium heat 1 minute. Add onion, pepper, chili powder, and salt; cook 10 minutes or until onion and pepper are tender, stirring occasionally. Stir in beans, tomatoes, and cilantro, and cook 3 to 4 minutes to heat through, stirring occasionally.

2 Just before serving tacos, place stack of tortillas between paper towels on microwave-safe plate; heat in microwave on High for 10 to 15 seconds to warm.

3 To serve, divide romaine lettuce and bean mixture among tortillas; top with Monterey Jack cheese, and fold over to eat out of hand.

400 CALORIES

PER SERVING. 16G PROTEIN | 61G CARBOHYDRATE | 13G TOTAL FAT (4G SATURATED) 11G FIBER | 15MG CHOLESTEROL | 840MG SODIUM ⌄ ✿

MAKE IT A MEAL: You can enjoy two of these bean and veggie tacos (one serving) for lunch without further embellishment. Or finish with our Sliced Citrus with Lime Syrup (95 calories; page 286) for a zippy 495-calorie dinner.

GRILLED VEGETABLE BURRITOS

Serve these burritos with your favorite bottled salsa and a dollop of reduced-fat or nondairy sour cream, if you like.

ACTIVE TIME: 25 MINUTES · **TOTAL TIME:** 40 MINUTES
MAKES: 4 MAIN-DISH SERVINGS

- 4 TEASPOONS VEGETABLE OIL
- 1 TEASPOON CHILI POWDER
- 1 TEASPOON GROUND CUMIN
- ½ TEASPOON SALT
- ¼ TEASPOON COARSELY GROUND BLACK PEPPER
- 2 MEDIUM ZUCCHINI (8 TO 10 OUNCES EACH), CUT LENGTHWISE INTO ¼-INCH-THICK SLICES
- 1 LARGE ONION (12 OUNCES), CUT INTO ½-INCH-THICK SLICES

- 1 MEDIUM RED PEPPER, CUT INTO QUARTERS
- 1 MEDIUM GREEN PEPPER, CUT INTO QUARTERS
- 4 BURRITO-SIZED (10-INCH) FLOUR TORTILLAS
- REDUCED-FAT OR NONDAIRY SOUR CREAM (OPTIONAL)
- ½ CUP LOOSELY PACKED FRESH CILANTRO LEAVES
- BOTTLED SALSA (OPTIONAL)

1 Prepare outdoor grill for direct grilling over medium heat.

2 In small bowl, mix oil, chili powder, cumin, salt, and black pepper. Brush one side of zucchini slices, onion slices, and red and green pepper pieces with oil mixture.

3 Place vegetables, oiled side down, on hot grill rack; grill until tender and golden, 15 to 20 minutes, turning over once and transferring vegetables to plate as they are done.

4 Arrange one-fourth of grilled vegetables down center of each tortilla and dollop with sour cream, if desired. Sprinkle with cilantro, then fold sides of tortillas over filling. Serve with salsa, if you like.

330 CALORIES **PER SERVING.** 11G PROTEIN | 43G CARBOHYDRATE | 14G TOTAL FAT (4G SATURATED) 7G FIBER | 15MG CHOLESTEROL | 655MG SODIUM ⓥ ❀

MAKE IT A MEAL: For a wholesome 500-calorie dinner, pair with a simple side of Lime Couscous (170 calories; page 279).

GRILLED MEXICAN PIZZA

For an easy weeknight dinner or a backyard barbecue, this Mexican pizza recipe puts a spin on a classic dish everyone loves.

TOTAL TIME: 15 MINUTES
MAKES: 4 MAIN-DISH SERVINGS

½ CUP PREPARED BLACK BEAN DIP

1 LARGE THIN PIZZA CRUST (10 OUNCES)

½ CUP SHREDDED MEXICAN CHEESE BLEND

1 RIPE AVOCADO, CUT INTO CHUNKS

2 TABLESPOONS FRESH LIME JUICE

2 CUPS SHREDDED ROMAINE LETTUCE

¼ TEASPOON GRATED LIME PEEL

1 RIPE MEDIUM TOMATO (6 TO 8 OUNCES), CHOPPED

1 Prepare outdoor grill for covered, direct grilling over medium heat. (Or preheat oven to 450°F.)

2 Spread black bean dip evenly on crust, leaving ½-inch border; sprinkle with cheese. Place crust on hot grill rack; cover and grill until grill marks appear, 8 to 9 minutes. (Or place crust on ungreased cookie sheet. Bake 8 to 10 minutes or until cheese melts.)

3 Meanwhile, gently stir avocado with 1 tablespoon lime juice. Toss romaine with lime peel and remaining juice.

4 Top cooked pizza with romaine mixture and tomato, then with avocado. Cut into slices.

310 CALORIES **PER SERVING.** 13G PROTEIN | 34G CARBOHYDRATE | 15G TOTAL FAT (4G SATURATED) 4G FIBER | 17MG CHOLESTEROL | 520MG SODIUM

MAKE IT A MEAL: Our pretty-in-pink Watermelon Slushie (170 calories; page 294) would make a refreshing match for this grilled pizza—and create a casual, fun 480-calorie dinner. Or pair a slice of this pizza with ten baby carrots and a dip of 2 tablespoons salsa for a 360-calorie lunch.

GRILLED WHOLE-WHEAT VEGGIE PIZZA

Everyone's favorite takeout gets a healthy makeover with a heap of veggies. You can purchase whole-wheat pizza dough, ready to roll out and bake, at some supermarkets and neighborhood pizza shops.

ACTIVE TIME: 25 MINUTES · **TOTAL TIME:** 30 MINUTES
MAKES: 4 MAIN-DISH SERVINGS

- 2   MEDIUM PORTOBELLO MUSHROOM CAPS (6 OUNCES), SLICED
- 1   SMALL RED ONION (4 TO 6 OUNCES), SLICED INTO ROUNDS
- 1   SMALL YELLOW SUMMER SQUASH, SLICED
- 1   TABLESPOON OLIVE OIL
- ¼   TEASPOON SALT
- ¼   TEASPOON PEPPER
- 1   POUND WHOLE-WHEAT PIZZA DOUGH
- 2   PLUM TOMATOES, THINLY SLICED
- ½   CUP SMOKED MOZZARELLA, SHREDDED (½ CUP)
- ¼   CUP PACKED FRESH BASIL LEAVES, SLICED

1   Prepare outdoor grill for covered direct grilling over medium heat. Brush mushrooms, onion, and squash with oil; sprinkle with salt and pepper.
2   If desired, place vegetables on grilling tray. Grill, covered, 6 minutes or until tender and browned, turning once. Separate onion rings; set aside. Reduce heat on grill to medium-low.
3   Cover large cookie sheet with foil; spray with cooking spray. Stretch dough into 10" by 14" rectangle. Place on cookie sheet.
4   Lift dough and foil; place, dough side down, on grill; gently peel off foil. Cover; cook 3 minutes or until bottom is crisp. Turn crust over. Quickly top with tomatoes, grilled vegetables, and cheese. Cover; cook 2 minutes longer or until bottom is crisp and cheese is melting. Slide onto cutting board; garnish with basil.

375 CALORIES   **PER SERVING.** 13G PROTEIN | 58G CARBOHYDRATE | 10G TOTAL FAT (2G SATURATED) 9G FIBER | 11MG CHOLESTEROL | 695MG SODIUM

MAKE IT A MEAL: Enjoy a slice of this pizza for a wholesome lunch or add our cooling Peachy Frozen Yogurt (130 calories; page 287) to create a yummy 505-calorie dinner.

SUMMER PHYLLO PIZZA

Using phyllo dough gives this pizza a whole different kind of crunch that you'll love. It's the perfect platform for thinly sliced sun-ripened tomatoes.

ACTIVE TIME: 15 MINUTES · **TOTAL TIME:** 35 MINUTES
MAKES: 6 MAIN-DISH SERVINGS

7   SHEETS (17" BY 12" EACH) FRESH OR THAWED FROZEN PHYLLO

5   TABLESPOONS UNSALTED BUTTER, MELTED

7   TABLESPOONS FRESHLY GRATED PARMESAN CHEESE

4   OUNCES COARSELY SHREDDED MOZZARELLA OR CRUMBLED GORGONZOLA CHEESE (1 CUP)

1   CUP VERY THINLY SLICED RED ONION

2   POUNDS RIPE TOMATOES (4 LARGE), PEELED, SEEDED, AND SLICED ¼ INCH THICK

1   TEASPOON FRESH THYME LEAVES OR ¼ TEASPOON DRIED, PLUS FRESH SPRIGS FOR GARNISH

½   TEASPOON DRIED OREGANO, CRUMBLED

1   Preheat oven to 375°F.

2   Place phyllo between two sheets waxed paper and cover with damp towel to prevent drying. Brush large cookie sheet with melted butter. Lay 1 sheet phyllo on buttered cookie sheet. Lightly brush top with butter. Sprinkle 1 tablespoon Parmesan on top of butter.

3   Place second sheet of phyllo on top and press so it adheres to first layer. Repeat brushing with butter and sprinkling with Parmesan. Continue layering phyllo sheets in same way, ending with sheet of phyllo and reserving last 1 tablespoon Parmesan.

4   Sprinkle top sheet of phyllo with mozzarella. Scatter onion evenly over cheese. Arrange tomatoes in single layer over onion. Sprinkle with thyme leaves, oregano, and remaining 1 tablespoon Parmesan.

5   Bake, making sure that phyllo browns but does not burn, 20 to 30 minutes. Garnish with thyme sprigs.

265 CALORIES

PER SERVING. 10G PROTEIN | 20G CARBOHYDRATE | 17G TOTAL FAT (10G SATURATED) 2G FIBER | 45MG CHOLESTEROL | 322MG SODIUM ❤

MAKE IT A MEAL: For a luscious Mediterranean meal, finish with our fresh figs stuffed with ricotta, honey, and toasted almonds (170 calories; page 295). The total meal is just 435 calories—and figs are a good source of dietary fiber and potassium, so you can feel virtuous as you indulge.

BLACK BEAN BURGERS

Spicy cumin and coriander flavor these savory black bean burgers, which can be prepared in a flash in a skillet.

ACTIVE TIME: 15 MINUTES · **TOTAL TIME:** 20 MINUTES
MAKES: 4 MAIN-DISH SERVINGS

¼ CUP DRIED BREAD CRUMBS

¼ TEASPOON GROUND CUMIN

¼ TEASPOON GROUND CORIANDER

2 CANS (15 TO 19 OUNCES EACH) LOW-SODIUM BLACK BEANS, RINSED AND DRAINED

¼ CUP LIGHT MAYONNAISE

¼ TEASPOON SALT

¼ TEASPOON GROUND BLACK PEPPER

2 LARGE STALKS CELERY, FINELY CHOPPED

1 CHIPOTLE CHILE IN ADOBO (SEE TIP), FINELY CHOPPED

4 GREEN-LEAF LETTUCE LEAVES

4 WHOLE-WHEAT HAMBURGER BUNS, TOASTED

4 SLICES RIPE TOMATO

1 In food processor with knife blade attached, pulse bread crumbs, cumin, coriander, two-thirds of beans, 2 tablespoons mayonnaise, salt, and pepper until well blended. Transfer to large bowl. Stir in celery and remaining whole beans until well combined. Divide into 4 portions and shape into patties.
2 Lightly coat 12-inch nonstick skillet with nonstick cooking spray. Heat over medium heat 1 minute, then add patties. Cook 10 to 12 minutes or until browned on both sides, carefully turning once.
3 Meanwhile, in small bowl, combine chipotle chile and remaining 2 tablespoons mayonnaise until well mixed. Place 1 lettuce leaf on bottom of each bun; top with patty, then tomato slice. Divide chipotle mayonnaise among burgers and replace tops of buns to serve.

TIP Chipotle chiles in adobo are dried, smoked jalapeño chiles canned in a thick puree. They are found in many supermarkets and Latin-American markets.

370 CALORIES | **PER SERVING.** 18G PROTEIN | 59G CARBOHYDRATE | 8G TOTAL FAT (1G SATURATED) 14G FIBER | 5MG CHOLESTEROL | 725MG SODIUM 🔵 🌾

> **MAKE IT A MEAL:** Make these Black Bean Burgers a 500-calorie dinner by adding our Wheat-Berry Salad with Dried Cherries (130 calories; page 272), and you'll get your grains along with your beans!

PORTOBELLO PESTO BURGERS

These hearty portobello burgers, topped with pesto and a carrot-fennel slaw, are satisfying and easy to prepare in the toaster oven (or traditional oven). For photo, see page 164.

ACTIVE TIME: 20 MINUTES · **TOTAL TIME:** 45 MINUTES
MAKES: 4 BURGERS

CARROT-FENNEL SLAW

- 2 CUPS SHREDDED CARROTS
- 1 SMALL FENNEL BULB (6 OUNCES), TRIMMED AND THINLY SLICED
- ½ CUP LOOSELY PACKED FRESH BASIL LEAVES, THINLY SLICED
- 2 TEASPOONS OLIVE OIL
- 1½ TEASPOONS CIDER VINEGAR
- ¼ TEASPOON SALT
- ¼ TEASPOON GROUND BLACK PEPPER

PORTOBELLO BURGERS

- 4 PORTOBELLO MUSHROOMS (1 POUND)
- ¼ CUP PREPARED SUN-DRIED-TOMATO PESTO
- 4 WHOLE-GRAIN HAMBURGER BUNS, SPLIT
- 1 LARGE RIPE TOMATO (10 TO 12 OUNCES), CUT INTO 8 SLICES
- 1 LOG (4 OUNCES) FRESH GOAT CHEESE, CUT CROSSWISE INTO 8 SLICES
- 8 LARGE FRESH BASIL LEAVES

1 Prepare slaw: In large bowl, mix carrots, fennel, basil, oil, vinegar, salt, and pepper until well combined. Set aside.

2 Prepare burgers: Preheat toaster oven to 425°F. Place portobellos on foil-lined toaster oven tray, rounded side up. Bake 14 minutes; turn mushrooms over and spread 1 tablespoon pesto evenly on each. Bake 10 minutes or until mushrooms are just tender.

3 Toast buns. Place 2 tomato slices on bottom of each bun. Top each with 1 portobello, 2 slices goat cheese, 2 basil leaves, and top of bun. Serve with Carrot-Fennel Slaw.

345 CALORIES **PER BURGER.** 15G PROTEIN | 38G CARBOHYDRATE | 16G TOTAL FAT (6G SATURATED) 8G FIBER | 13MG CHOLESTEROL | 635MG SODIUM 🌾

MAKE IT A MEAL: These easy portobello burgers will freshen up your lunchtime routine. Add a quick side of our Sun-Dried Tomato and Green Onion Couscous (180 calories; page 279) for a 525-calorie dinner.

BARBECUED TOFU SANDWICHES

Here's a quick and easy way to flavor tofu.

ACTIVE TIME: 20 MINUTES · **TOTAL TIME:** 25 MINUTES PLUS DRAINING TOFU
MAKES: 4 SANDWICHES

¼ CUP KETCHUP

2 TABLESPOONS DIJON MUSTARD

2 TABLESPOONS REDUCED-SODIUM SOY SAUCE

1 TABLESPOON MOLASSES

1 TABLESPOON GRATED, PEELED FRESH GINGER

⅛ TEASPOON CAYENNE (GROUND RED) PEPPER

2 GARLIC CLOVES, CRUSHED WITH GARLIC PRESS

1 PACKAGE (16 OUNCES) EXTRA-FIRM TOFU, DRAINED AND PRESSED (SEE PAGE 15)

2 TEASPOONS SESAME SEEDS

8 SLICES WHOLE-GRAIN BREAD, TOASTED

SLICED RIPE TOMATOES, SLICED RED ONION, AND LETTUCE LEAVES (OPTIONAL)

1 Preheat broiler. Coat rack in broiling pan with nonstick cooking spray.

2 In small bowl, combine ketchup, mustard, soy sauce, molasses, ginger, cayenne, and garlic, stirring until blended.

3 Cut tofu lengthwise into 8 slices.

4 Place slices on rack in broiling pan; brush with half of ketchup mixture. Place in broiler about 5 inches from source of heat and broil tofu until ketchup mixture looks dry, about 3 minutes. With metal spatula, turn slices over; brush with remaining ketchup mixture and sprinkle with sesame seeds. Broil tofu 3 minutes longer.

5 To serve, place 2 tofu slices on 1 slice toasted bread. Top with tomato, onion, and lettuce, if you like. Top with another slice of bread. Repeat with remaining tofu and bread to make remaining sandwiches.

230 CALORIES

PER SANDWICH. 14G PROTEIN | 35G CARBOHYDRATE | 5G TOTAL FAT (0G SATURATED) 2G FIBER | 0MG CHOLESTEROL | 975MG SODIUM Ⓥ 🌾

MAKE IT A MEAL: For a filling 380-calorie lunch, pair this quick vegetarian barbecue with our Healthy Makeover Potato Salad (150 calories; page 266).

205 CALORIES

Ginger Carrot Soup
(page 187)

SOUPS & STEWS

Beans and other legumes are an important part of the vegetarian diet, and the soup pot is where they really shine. Here you'll find a soul-satisfying selection of bean and lentil recipes made special with an exciting array of international flavors: Try a warming bowl of our Latin-style Black Bean Soup or our hearty chili recipe. Soup is also an easy, satisfying way to make sure you eat your vegetables: Enjoy our cooling Gazpacho with Cilantro Cream or our cozy Winter Vegetable Chowder. Want to get better acquainted with tofu? Our Hot and Sour Tofu Soup is simple to make and tastier than Chinese takeout.

KEY TO ICONS

 30 minutes or less   Vegan   ♥ Heart healthy   High fiber   Make ahead

RED LENTIL AND VEGETABLE SOUP

This meal-in-a-bowl brims with filling soluble fiber, thanks to the lentils. Translation: It may help keep weight down and also lower total and "bad" LDL cholesterol. The lentils, spinach, and tomatoes, all rich in potassium, work to keep blood pressure in check, too.

ACTIVE TIME: 20 MINUTES · **TOTAL TIME:** 30 MINUTES
MAKES: 4 MAIN-DISH SERVINGS

1 TABLESPOON OLIVE OIL

4 MEDIUM CARROTS, PEELED AND CHOPPED

1 SMALL ONION, CHOPPED

1 TEASPOON GROUND CUMIN

1 CAN (14½ OUNCES) DICED TOMATOES

1 CUP RED LENTILS, RINSED AND PICKED THROUGH

1 CAN (14½ OUNCES) VEGETABLE BROTH OR 1¾ CUPS HOMEMADE BROTH (OPPOSITE)

2 CUPS WATER

¼ TEASPOON SALT

⅛ TEASPOON GROUND BLACK PEPPER

1 BAG (5 OUNCES) BABY SPINACH

1 In 4-quart saucepan, heat oil over medium heat until hot. Add carrots and onion, and cook until tender and lightly browned, 6 to 8 minutes. Stir in cumin; cook 1 minute.

2 Add tomatoes with their juice, lentils, broth, water, salt, and pepper; cover and heat to boiling over high heat. Reduce heat to low; cover and simmer until lentils are tender, 8 to 10 minutes.

3 Just before serving, stir in spinach.

265 CALORIES

PER SERVING. 16G PROTEIN | 41G CARBOHYDRATE | 5G TOTAL FAT (1G SATURATED) 13G FIBER | 0MG CHOLESTEROL | 645MG SODIUM

MAKE IT A MEAL: One of our easy Whole-Wheat Sesame Biscuits (125 calories; page 271) is all you need to turn this soup into a wholesome 390-calorie lunch.

HOMEMADE VEGETABLE BROTH

It's great in soups, risottos, and sauces. The optional fennel and parsnip lend a natural sweetness and additional depth of flavor.

ACTIVE TIME: 25 MINUTES · **TOTAL TIME:** 2 HOURS 25 MINUTES
MAKES: ABOUT 6 CUPS

4 LARGE LEEKS

2 TO 4 GARLIC CLOVES, NOT PEELED

13 CUPS WATER

SALT

1 LARGE ALL-PURPOSE POTATO, PEELED, CUT LENGTHWISE IN HALF, AND THINLY SLICED

1 SMALL FENNEL BULB (6 OUNCES), TRIMMED AND CHOPPED (OPTIONAL)

3 PARSNIPS, PEELED AND THINLY SLICED (OPTIONAL)

2 LARGE CARROTS, PEELED AND THINLY SLICED

3 STALKS CELERY WITH LEAVES, THINLY SLICED

4 OUNCES MUSHROOMS, TRIMMED AND THINLY SLICED

10 PARSLEY SPRIGS

4 THYME SPRIGS

2 BAY LEAVES

1 TEASPOON WHOLE BLACK PEPPERCORNS

1 Trim and discard roots and dark green tops from leeks; thinly slice leeks. Rinse leeks in large bowl of cold water, swishing to remove sand. Lift out and place in colander, leaving sand in bowl.

2 In 6-quart saucepot, combine leeks, garlic, 1 cup water, and pinch salt; heat to boiling. Reduce heat to medium; cover and cook until leeks are tender, about 15 minutes.

3 Add potato, fennel if using, parsnips if using, carrots, celery, mushrooms, parsley and thyme sprigs, bay leaves, peppercorns, and remaining 12 cups water. Heat to boiling; reduce heat and simmer, uncovered, at least 1 hour 30 minutes.

4 Taste and continue cooking if flavor is not concentrated enough. Season with salt and pepper to taste. Strain broth through fine-mesh sieve into containers, pressing on solids with back of wooden spoon; cool. Cover and refrigerate to up to 3 days, or freeze up to 4 months.

20 CALORIES **PER CUP.** 1G PROTEIN | 4G CARBOHYDRATE | 0G TOTAL FAT (0G SATURATED) 0MG CHOLESTEROL | 0G FIBER | 9MG SODIUM ✅ ❤️ 🧺

GAZPACHO WITH CILANTRO CREAM

Recipes for gazpacho abound. This version is topped with a dollop of cilantro-spiked sour cream, a tasty combination.

TOTAL TIME: 30 MINUTES PLUS CHILLING

MAKES: 6 MAIN-DISH SERVINGS

4   MEDIUM CUCUMBERS (8 OUNCES EACH), PEELED

2   MEDIUM YELLOW PEPPERS (4 TO 6 OUNCES EACH)

4   POUNDS RIPE TOMATOES, PEELED, SEEDED, AND CHOPPED

1   TO 2 SMALL JALAPEÑO CHILES, SEEDED (TO TASTE)

6   TABLESPOONS FRESH LIME JUICE

¼   CUP EXTRA-VIRGIN OLIVE OIL

1¾ TEASPOONS SALT

½   SMALL RED ONION, COARSELY CHOPPED

½   CUP REDUCED-FAT SOUR CREAM OR PLAIN LOW-FAT YOGURT

2   TABLESPOONS MILK

2   TABLESPOONS PLUS 2 TEASPOONS CHOPPED FRESH CILANTRO

1   Coarsely chop 1 cucumber and 1 yellow pepper; set aside. Cut remaining cucumbers and yellow pepper into large pieces for pureeing.

2   In blender or food processor with knife blade attached, puree large pieces of cucumber and yellow pepper, tomatoes, jalapeño, lime juice, oil, and 1½ teaspoons salt until smooth. Pour puree into bowl; add coarsely chopped cucumber, yellow pepper, and onion. Cover and refrigerate until well chilled, at least 6 hours and up to overnight.

3   In small bowl, stir sour cream, milk, cilantro, and remaining ¼ teaspoon salt until smooth. Cover and refrigerate.

4   To serve, top soup with dollops of cilantro cream.

210 CALORIES

PER SERVING. 5G PROTEIN | 23G CARBOHYDRATE | 13G TOTAL FAT (3G SATURATED) | 5G FIBER | 8MG CHOLESTEROL | 727MG SODIUM 🌾 🧺

MAKE IT A MEAL: To create a summery 400-calorie lunch, pair this fresh and colorful soup with a salad of crisp greens and ½ cup cubed avocado; for dessert, have an orange (190 calories for salad and orange).

BLACK BEAN SOUP

This simple but hearty soup is sure to become a standby. The cilantro and fresh lime juice add Latin flavor.

ACTIVE TIME: 15 MINUTES · **TOTAL TIME:** 45 MINUTES PLUS COOLING
MAKES: 6½ CUPS OR 6 MAIN-DISH SERVINGS

1	TABLESPOON OLIVE OIL	½	TEASPOON SALT
2	MEDIUM CARROTS, PEELED AND CHOPPED	2	CUPS WATER
2	GARLIC CLOVES, FINELY CHOPPED	2	CANS BLACK BEANS (15 TO 19 OUNCES EACH), RINSED AND DRAINED
1	LARGE ONION (12 OUNCES), CHOPPED	1	CAN (14½ OUNCES) VEGETABLE BROTH OR 1¾ CUPS HOMEMADE BROTH (PAGE 183)
1	MEDIUM RED PEPPER (4 TO 6 OUNCES), CHOPPED	¼	CUP FRESH CILANTRO LEAVES, CHOPPED, PLUS SPRIGS FOR GARNISH
2	TEASPOONS GROUND CUMIN	1	TABLESPOON FRESH LIME JUICE
¼	TEASPOON CRUSHED RED PEPPER		

1 In 6-quart saucepot, heat oil over medium heat until hot. Add carrots, garlic, onion, and pepper; cook 12 to 15 minutes or until vegetables are lightly browned and tender, stirring occasionally. Add cumin, crushed red pepper, and salt; cook 1 minute.

2 Stir in water, beans, and broth; heat to boiling over medium-high heat. Reduce heat to low and simmer, uncovered, 15 minutes to blend flavors.

3 Ladle 3 cups soup into blender; remove center part of lid to allow steam to escape, cover soup, and blend until pureed. Stir puree into soup in saucepot; heat through over medium heat. Stir in cilantro and lime juice. Serve garnished with cilantro sprigs.

250 CALORIES   **PER SERVING.** 14G PROTEIN | 50G CARBOHYDRATE | 5G TOTAL FAT (0G SATURATED) 17G FIBER | 0MG CHOLESTEROL | 1,058MG SODIUM ✔ 🌾 🥬

MAKE IT A MEAL: For a 350-calorie lunch, add on half a mini pita stuffed with 2 tablespoons each mashed avocado and chopped tomato. For a 500-calorie dinner, finish this Latin-inspired meal with our Broiled Brown-Sugar Bananas (150 calories; page 280).

GINGER CARROT SOUP

This creamy-smooth soup is supercharged with vision-enhancing vitamin A. Subbing ginger-steeped green tea for stock slashes sodium. For photo, see page 180.

ACTIVE TIME: 25 MINUTES · **TOTAL TIME:** 55 MINUTES
MAKES: 4 MAIN-DISH SERVINGS

4 GREEN ONIONS	1½ POUNDS CARROTS, PEELED AND CUT INTO ¾-INCH-THICK PIECES
1 (1-INCH) PIECE FRESH GINGER	1 MEDIUM ALL-PURPOSE POTATO, PEELED AND CHOPPED
5 CUPS WATER	
3 TEA BAGS GREEN TEA	½ TEASPOON SALT
1 TABLESPOON OLIVE OIL	¼ TEASPOON GROUND BLACK PEPPER
1 MEDIUM ONION, FINELY CHOPPED	2 CUPS FROZEN PEAS

1 From green onions, cut off white and pale green parts and place in 5-quart saucepot. Thinly slice dark green onion parts; set aside. From ginger, cut 4 slices; set aside. Peel remaining piece of ginger and grate enough to make 1 teaspoon; set aside.

2 To saucepot, add sliced ginger and water. Heat to boiling over high heat. Add tea bags. Cover, remove from heat, and let stand 10 minutes.

3 While tea steeps, in 12-inch skillet, heat oil over medium-high heat. Add onion, carrots, potato, and ¼ teaspoon each salt and pepper. Cook, stirring, 6 minutes or until golden. Add grated ginger; cook 1 minute, stirring.

4 With slotted spoon, remove ginger, tea bags, and green onion pieces from pot and discard after squeezing excess liquid back into pot. Heat ginger tea to boiling over high heat; stir in carrot mixture. Reduce heat to maintain simmer. Cook 10 minutes or until vegetables are tender, stirring.

5 Transfer half of soup to blender; keep remaining soup simmering. Carefully puree until smooth, then return to pot. Stir in peas and remaining ¼ teaspoon salt. Cook 3 minutes or until peas are bright green and hot. Divide among soup bowls; garnish with sliced green onions.

205 CALORIES **PER SERVING.** 7G PROTEIN | 37G CARBOHYDRATE | 4G TOTAL FAT (1G SATURATED) 9G FIBER | 0MG CHOLESTEROL | 410MG SODIUM

MAKE IT A MEAL: For a nutrient-dense 365-calorie lunch, add on our Chunky Vegetable Bulgur Salad (160 calories; page 277) to throw some grains and legumes into the mix.

NOT YOUR GRANDMA'S VEGETABLE SOUP

It's impossible to peel beets without getting red all over your hands—unless you wear rubber gloves. For extra-easy cleanup, peel beets in the sink, too.

ACTIVE TIME: 15 MINUTES · **TOTAL TIME:** 1 HOUR 15 MINUTES
MAKES: 5 MAIN-DISH SERVINGS

1   TABLESPOON OLIVE OIL

1   ONION, CHOPPED

1   GARLIC CLOVE, CRUSHED WITH GARLIC PRESS

½   TEASPOON GROUND ALLSPICE

1   CAN (14½ OUNCES) DICED TOMATOES

1   POUND BEETS (NOT INCLUDING TOPS)

6   CUPS SLICED GREEN CABBAGE (1 POUND)

3   LARGE CARROTS, PEELED AND CUT INTO ½-INCH CHUNKS

4   CUPS WATER

1   CAN (14½ OUNCES) VEGETABLE BROTH OR 1¾ CUPS HOMEMADE BROTH (PAGE 183)

1   BAY LEAF

¾   TEASPOON SALT

2   TABLESPOONS RED WINE VINEGAR

¼   CUP LOOSELY PACKED FRESH DILL OR PARSLEY LEAVES, CHOPPED

REDUCED-FAT OR NONDAIRY SOUR CREAM (OPTIONAL)

1   In 5- to 6-quart saucepot, heat oil over medium heat until hot. Add onion and cook until tender, about 8 minutes. Stir in garlic and allspice; cook 30 seconds. Add tomatoes with their juice and cook 5 minutes.

2   Meanwhile, peel beets and shred in food processor (or using coarse side of box grater).

3   Add beets to onion mixture along with cabbage, carrots, water, broth, bay leaf, and salt; heat to boiling over high heat. Reduce heat to medium-low; cover and simmer until all vegetables are tender, about 30 minutes.

4   Remove bay leaf. Stir in vinegar and dill. Serve soup with sour cream, if you like.

200 CALORIES **PER SERVING.** 6G PROTEIN | 34G CARBOHYDRATE | 6G TOTAL FAT (1G SATURATED) 6G FIBER | 6MG CHOLESTEROL | 1,150MG SODIUM

MAKE IT A MEAL: Add creamy satisfaction with 1 tablespoon reduced-fat or nondairy sour cream (20 calories). Finish with warm Apple-Oat Crisp (175 calories; page 305) and you have a 395-calorie lunch.

WINTER VEGETABLE CHOWDER

We developed this slow-cooker recipe with leftovers in mind. Freeze any extra for a weekday meal that is ready whenever you are!

ACTIVE TIME: 40 MINUTES · **TOTAL TIME:** 1 HOUR 15 MINUTES
MAKES: 8 MAIN-DISH SERVINGS

6 MEDIUM LEEKS, TRIMMED	4 CUPS WATER
2 TABLESPOONS OLIVE OIL	½ TEASPOON CHOPPED FRESH THYME PLUS WHOLE SPRIGS FOR GARNISH
4 STALKS CELERY, CHOPPED	1 TEASPOON SALT
3 MEDIUM PARSNIPS, PEELED AND CHOPPED	¾ TEASPOON COARSELY GROUND BLACK PEPPER
2 MEDIUM RED POTATOES, CUT INTO ½-INCH PIECES	1 CUP HALF-AND-HALF OR LIGHT CREAM
2 POUNDS BUTTERNUT SQUASH, PEELED, SEEDED, AND CUT INTO ½-INCH PIECES	
2 CANS (14½ OUNCES EACH) VEGETABLE BROTH OR 3½ CUPS HOMEMADE BROTH (PAGE 183)	

1 Trim and discard roots and dark-green tops from leeks. Discard any tough outer leaves. Cut each leek lengthwise in half, then crosswise into ½-inch-thick slices. Rinse in large bowl of cold water; swish to remove sand. With hands, transfer leeks to colander, leaving sand in bottom of bowl. Repeat rinsing and draining several times, until all sand is removed. Drain well.
2 In 6-quart saucepot, heat oil over medium-high heat until hot. Add leeks, celery, and parsnips, and cook until all vegetables are tender, 10 to 12 minutes, stirring occasionally.
3 Add potatoes, squash, broth, water, chopped thyme, salt, and pepper; heat to boiling over medium-high heat. Reduce heat to medium-low; cover and simmer until potatoes and squash are tender, about 10 minutes.
4 Stir in half-and-half and heat through, about 13 minutes. Spoon soup into tureen and garnish with thyme sprigs.

5 To store leftovers, spoon soup into freezer-safe containers and freeze. Before serving, thaw overnight in refrigerator or follow manufacturer instructions for thawing in microwave. To heat thawed soup on stovetop, pour into saucepan, cover, and heat to boiling over medium, about 25 minutes, stirring often. To use microwave, pour into microwave-safe bowl, cover, and heat on Low (30 percent) 10 minutes, stirring once or twice, then on High for 15 to 20 minutes, stirring once.

215
CALORIES

PER SERVING. 5G PROTEIN | 35G CARBOHYDRATE | 8G TOTAL FAT (3G SATURATED) 5G FIBER | 11MG CHOLESTEROL | 560MG SODIUM

MAKE IT A MEAL: Serve this chowder with a fresh-from-the-oven popover (160 calories; page 278) and you'll have a thoroughly satisfying 375-calorie lunch. You can make the popovers ahead and reheat in a 400°F oven for 15 minutes.

RED CHILI WITH FIRE-ROASTED TOMATOES

Beets, chipotle chili powder, and fire-roasted tomatoes give this chili a beautiful color—it would be perfect for Valentine's Day.

ACTIVE TIME: 35 MINUTES · **TOTAL TIME:** 1 HOUR 30 MINUTES
MAKES: 9 CUPS OR 6 MAIN-DISH SERVINGS

---

2   TEASPOONS GROUND CUMIN

1   TEASPOON DRIED OREGANO

½   TEASPOON CHIPOTLE CHILE POWDER

2   TABLESPOONS VEGETABLE OIL

3   LARGE BEETS (6 TO 8 OUNCES EACH), TRIMMED, PEELED, AND CHOPPED

1   JUMBO RED ONION (1 POUND), FINELY CHOPPED

1   LARGE RED PEPPER (8 TO 10 OUNCES), CHOPPED

½   TEASPOON GROUND BLACK PEPPER

4   GARLIC CLOVES, CRUSHED WITH GARLIC PRESS

1   CAN (28 OUNCES) FIRE-ROASTED DICED TOMATOES

1   CAN (15 TO 19 OUNCES) LOW-SODIUM BLACK BEANS, RINSED AND DRAINED

1   CAN (15 TO 19 OUNCES) LOW-SODIUM RED KIDNEY BEANS, RINSED AND DRAINED

1   CAN (15 TO 19 OUNCES) LOW-SODIUM PINTO BEANS, RINSED AND DRAINED

1   CUP WATER

1   CUP REDUCED-FAT SOUR CREAM

¼   CUP FRESH CILANTRO LEAVES

1   In 7- to 8-quart Dutch oven or heavy saucepot, combine cumin, oregano, and chipotle powder. Cook over medium heat 1 to 2 minutes or until toasted and fragrant. Transfer to sheet of waxed paper; set aside. In same Dutch oven, heat oil over medium heat until hot. Add beets, onion, pepper, and ¼ teaspoon black pepper. Cook 15 minutes or until vegetables are tender, stirring occasionally.

2   Add garlic and reserved spice mixture. Cook 2 minutes, stirring constantly. Add tomatoes, all beans, and water. Heat to boiling over medium-high heat. Reduce heat to medium-low and simmer 30 minutes, stirring and mashing some beans occasionally. Season with remaining ¼ teaspoon black pepper. (Can be prepared up to this point up to 2 days ahead; transfer to airtight container and refrigerate. Reheat before serving.) Divide among serving bowls and top with sour cream and cilantro.

---

345 CALORIES   **PER SERVING.** 18G PROTEIN | 59G CARBOHYDRATE | 8G TOTAL FAT (1G SATURATED) 14G FIBER | 5MG CHOLESTEROL | 725MG SODIUM

MAKE IT A MEAL: For a hearty weeknight meal or casual dinner with friends, add our Double Cornbread (125 calories; page 270) and Sautéed Spinach with Garlic and Lemon (45 calories; page 255). You can enjoy it all for 515 calories per serving.

CAULIFLOWER-CURRY STEW

This easy-to-make vegetarian stew owes its complex flavor to spicy, fresh ginger and traditional Indian curry powder.

ACTIVE TIME: 25 MINUTES · **TOTAL TIME:** 50 MINUTES
MAKES: 8 MAIN-DISH SERVINGS

---

1   TABLESPOON OLIVE OIL

3   CARROTS, PEELED AND CHOPPED

1   ONION, CHOPPED

1½ CUPS BROWN RICE

1   TABLESPOON FINELY CHOPPED, PEELED FRESH GINGER

1   TABLESPOON CURRY POWDER

¾   TEASPOON SALT

2½ CUPS CANNED OR HOMEMADE VEGETABLE BROTH (PAGE 183)

1   MEDIUM (2-POUND) HEAD CAULIFLOWER, CUT INTO SMALL FLOWERETS

2   CANS (15 TO 19 OUNCES EACH) GARBANZO BEANS (CHICKPEAS), RINSED AND DRAINED

½   CUP LOOSELY PACKED FRESH CILANTRO LEAVES, CHOPPED

¼   CUP PLAIN LOW-FAT YOGURT PLUS ADDITIONAL FOR SERVING

1   In 6-quart Dutch oven, heat oil over medium-high heat until hot. Add carrots and onion, and cook 10 to 12 minutes or until vegetables are lightly browned and tender, stirring frequently.

2   Meanwhile, prepare rice as label directs; keep warm.

3   Stir ginger, curry, and salt into carrot mixture; cook 3 minutes, stirring constantly. Add broth; cover and heat to boiling on high. Stir in cauliflower and garbanzo beans; cover and cook over medium heat 15 to 20 minutes longer, gently stirring every 5 minutes until cauliflower is tender.

4   To serve, stir chopped cilantro and ¼ cup yogurt into cauliflower stew. Spoon rice into serving bowls; top with stew. Serve cauliflower stew with additional yogurt to dollop on top.

---

360 CALORIES   **PER SERVING.** 12G PROTEIN | 68G CARBOHYDRATE | 5G TOTAL FAT (1G SATURATED) 10G FIBER | 1MG CHOLESTEROL | 650MG SODIUM 🌱 🧺

MAKE IT A MEAL: Turn this stew into a hearty 460-calorie dinner: Start with one Ak-Mak Stone Ground Whole Wheat Cracker spread with 1 tablespoon mashed avocado (45 calories) and serve a side salad of Shredded Beets with Celery and Dates (50 calories; page 256).

HOT AND SOUR TOFU SOUP

We streamlined seasonings to help get this popular Asian soup on the table in record time—without sacrificing the great taste.

ACTIVE TIME: 15 MINUTES · **TOTAL TIME:** 30 MINUTES PLUS DRAINING TOFU
MAKES: 4 MAIN-DISH SERVINGS

1   TABLESPOON VEGETABLE OIL

4   OUNCES SHIITAKE MUSHROOMS, STEMS DISCARDED AND CAPS THINLY SLICED

3   TABLESPOONS REDUCED-SODIUM SOY SAUCE

1   PACKAGE (16 OUNCES) EXTRA-FIRM TOFU, DRAINED AND PRESSED (SEE PAGE 15), CUT INTO 1-INCH CUBES

2   TABLESPOONS CORNSTARCH

1   CUP WATER

1   CARTON (32 OUNCES) VEGETABLE BROTH OR 4 CUPS HOMEMADE BROTH (PAGE 183)

3   TABLESPOONS SEASONED RICE VINEGAR

2   TABLESPOONS GRATED, PEELED FRESH GINGER

1   TABLESPOON WORCESTERSHIRE SAUCE

½   TEASPOON ASIAN SESAME OIL

¼   TEASPOON CAYENNE (GROUND RED) PEPPER

2   LARGE EGGS, BEATEN

2   GREEN ONIONS, THINLY SLICED

1   In nonstick 5-quart saucepot, heat vegetable oil over medium-high heat until hot. Add mushrooms, soy sauce, and tofu, and cook until liquid evaporates, about 5 minutes, gently stirring often.

2   In cup, with fork, mix cornstarch with ¼ cup water until cornstarch is dissolved; set aside. Add broth and remaining ¾ cup water to tofu mixture; heat to boiling over high heat. Stir in cornstarch mixture and boil 30 seconds, stirring. Reduce heat to medium-low; stir in vinegar, ginger, Worcestershire, sesame oil, and cayenne, and simmer 5 minutes.

3   Remove saucepot from heat. Slowly pour beaten eggs into soup in a thin, steady stream around the edge of the saucepot. Carefully stir the soup once so eggs separate into strands. Serve sprinkled with green onions.

280 CALORIES

PER SERVING. 18G PROTEIN | 17G CARBOHYDRATE | 15G TOTAL FAT (3G SATURATED) 1G FIBER | 106MG CHOLESTEROL | 1,790MG SODIUM

MAKE IT A MEAL: Skip the Chinese takeout and serve this soup with ¾ cup basmati rice (150 calories) topped with our tasty Vegetables with Sesame Vinaigrette (80 calories; page 257) for an easy 510-calorie supper.

MOROCCAN SWEET POTATO STEW

With just 2 teaspoons of olive oil, this fragrant stew is both heart-healthy and satisfying.

ACTIVE TIME: 15 MINUTES · **TOTAL TIME:** 45 MINUTES
MAKES: 4 MAIN-DISH SERVINGS

2 TEASPOONS OLIVE OIL

1 MEDIUM YELLOW ONION, CHOPPED

3 GARLIC CLOVES, CRUSHED WITH GARLIC PRESS

1½ TEASPOONS CURRY POWDER

1½ TEASPOONS GROUND CUMIN

¼ TEASPOON GROUND ALLSPICE

1 CAN (14½ OUNCES) DICED TOMATOES

1 CAN (14½ OUNCES) REDUCED-SODIUM VEGETABLE BROTH OR 1¾ CUPS HOMEMADE BROTH (PAGE 183)

1 CUP NO-SALT-ADDED GARBANZO BEANS, RINSED AND DRAINED

1 LARGE SWEET POTATO (1 POUND), PEELED AND CUT INTO ¾-INCH CHUNKS

2 SMALL ZUCCHINI (6 OUNCES EACH), CUT INTO ¾-INCH CHUNKS

1 CUP WHOLE-GRAIN COUSCOUS (MOROCCAN PASTA)

¼ CUP LOOSELY PACKED FRESH MINT LEAVES, CHOPPED

1 In nonstick 12-inch skillet, heat oil over medium heat until hot. Add onion and cook until tender and lightly browned, 8 to 10 minutes, stirring occasionally. Stir in garlic, curry powder, cumin, and allspice; cook 30 seconds.
2 Add tomatoes and their juices, broth, beans, and sweet potato; cover and heat to boiling over medium-high heat. Reduce heat to medium and cook 10 minutes.
3 Stir in zucchini, cover, and cook until vegetables are tender, about 10 minutes. Meanwhile, prepare couscous as label directs.
4 Stir mint into stew. Serve stew with couscous.

360 CALORIES

PER SERVING. 14G PROTEIN | 70G CARBOHYDRATE | 5G TOTAL FAT (1G SATURATED)
13G FIBER | 0MG CHOLESTEROL | 670MG SODIUM Ⓥ 🌾 🍱

MAKE IT A MEAL: For authentic flavor, swap in our Moroccan-flavored couscous (adds 35 calories; page 279) and add a side of iron-rich Kale Chips (15 calories; page 254). You'll have a colorful, nutrient-dense meal for just 410 calories per serving.

285 CALORIES

Green Tomato Stacks
(page 200)

STUFFED, STACKED & STIR-FRIED

If you've been preparing vegetarian meals, you've probably steamed, sautéed, and roasted vegetables. But have you tried stuffing or stacking them? Here we offer lots of tempting recipes that do just that. Stuff chile peppers, artichokes, or acorn squash with veggies, whole grains, and seasonings to create satisfying vegetarian mains that are as wholesome as they are fun to eat. Or layer bread-crumb-crusted fried green tomatoes and top the stack with a luscious lemony chive and mayonnaise sauce. Tossing your veggies is a third quick and playful option: Check out the Fast Fried Rice and lo mein and our clever Sweet-and-Sour Unstuffed Cabbage.

KEY TO ICONS

🕐 30 minutes or less Ⓥ Vegan ♥ Heart healthy 🌾 High fiber ▮ Make ahead

GREEN TOMATO STACKS

Fried green tomatoes make a luscious summer meal. We top ours with chive-and-lemon-spiked mayo. Delish! For photo, see page 198.

TOTAL TIME: 25 MINUTES
MAKES: 4 MAIN-DISH SERVINGS

1	LARGE EGG WHITE	2	RIPE MEDIUM RED TOMATOES (6 TO 8 OUNCES EACH)
⅓	CUP CORNMEAL	3	TABLESPOONS OLIVE OIL
½	TEASPOON COARSELY GROUND BLACK PEPPER	1	LEMON
¼	TEASPOON SALT	⅓	CUP LIGHT MAYONNAISE
2	MEDIUM GREEN TOMATOES (6 TO 8 OUNCES EACH)	2	TABLESPOONS SNIPPED FRESH CHIVES
		8	SLICES MEATLESS CANADIAN BACON (SUCH AS YVES BRAND; OPTIONAL)

1 In pie plate, with fork, beat egg white. On waxed paper, mix cornmeal and ¼ teaspoon pepper. Cut each tomato into 4 slices and sprinkle with salt. Dip green tomato slices in egg white, then into cornmeal mixture to coat both sides. Place on waxed paper.

2 In 12-inch skillet, heat half of oil over medium-high heat until hot. Add 2 green tomato slices, and cook 4 to 5 minutes or until golden-brown on both sides and heated through, turning over once and reducing heat to medium if tomatoes brown too quickly. Transfer tomatoes to plate. Repeat with remaining oil and green tomato slices.

3 Meanwhile, from lemon, grate 1 teaspoon peel and squeeze 2 tablespoons juice. In small bowl, mix lemon peel and juice with mayonnaise, chives, and remaining ¼ teaspoon pepper; set aside.

4 If using meatless bacon, add to same skillet and cook over medium-high heat 2 to 3 minutes or until lightly browned on both sides and heated through, turning slices over once. Cut slices in half.

5 To serve, on each dinner plate, alternately stack slices of red tomato and fried green tomatoes and bacon; drizzle with lemon-chive mayonnaise.

285 CALORIES

PER SERVING. 15G PROTEIN | 22G CARBOHYDRATE | 16G TOTAL FAT (2G SATURATED) 3G FIBER | 7MG CHOLESTEROL | 654MG SODIUM

MAKE IT A MEAL: Pair these with Millet with Corn and Green Chiles (150 calories; page 275) and finish with 1 cup cubed watermelon (45 calories). A light and refreshing dinner for just 480 calories per serving.

STUFFED ACORN SQUASH

Preparation of this dish is easy and efficient, because the beans cook on the stovetop while the squash steams in the microwave.

ACTIVE TIME: 30 MINUTES · **TOTAL TIME:** 35 MINUTES
MAKES: 4 MAIN-DISH SERVINGS

1   TABLESPOON OLIVE OIL

1   JUMBO ONION (1 POUND),
    CUT INTO ¼-INCH DICE

1   MEDIUM CARROT, PEELED AND
    CUT INTO ¼-INCH DICE

2   GARLIC CLOVES, CRUSHED
    WITH GARLIC PRESS

1   CAN (15 TO 19 OUNCES) WHITE
    KIDNEY BEANS (CANNELLINI), RINSED
    AND DRAINED

¾   CUP CANNED OR HOMEMADE
    VEGETABLE BROTH (PAGE 183)

¼   TEASPOON SALT

¼   TEASPOON COARSELY
    GROUND BLACK PEPPER

1   TABLESPOON CHOPPED FRESH SAGE
    PLUS SAGE SPRIGS FOR GARNISH

2   VERY SMALL ACORN SQUASHES
    (12 OUNCES EACH)

1   RIPE MEDIUM TOMATO (6 TO 8
    OUNCES), CUT INTO ¼-INCH DICE

FRESHLY GRATED PARMESAN CHEESE
(OPTIONAL)

1   In nonstick 12-inch skillet, heat oil over medium-high heat until hot. Add onion, carrot, and garlic, and cook until vegetables are tender and golden, about 15 minutes, stirring occasionally. Add beans, broth, salt, pepper, and 2 teaspoons chopped sage; heat to boiling. Cover skillet and keep warm.

2   Meanwhile, cut each squash lengthwise in half and remove seeds and strings. Place squash halves in 3-quart microwave-safe baking dish. Cover and cook in microwave oven on High for 6 to 8 minutes, until squash is fork-tender.

3   Place squash halves, cut sides up, on platter. Fill each half with one-fourth of warm bean mixture; sprinkle with tomato and remaining 1 teaspoon chopped sage. Garnish with sage sprigs. Serve with Parmesan, if you like.

250 CALORIES

PER SERVING. 9G PROTEIN | 47G CARBOHYDRATE | 5G TOTAL FAT (1G SATURATED)
11G FIBER | 0MG CHOLESTEROL | 520MG SODIUM 🅥 🌾

MAKE IT A MEAL: These protein-packed "casseroles" make a cozy 455-calorie dinner when matched with Double Cornbread (125 calories; page 270) and a side of Green Beans with Mixed Mushrooms (80 calories; page 259).

MEXICAN VEGGIE STACKS

These Mexican-style stacks deliver a heaping helping of chili-spiced grilled vegetables, including fresh corn, tomatoes, onions, and zucchini.

ACTIVE TIME: 35 MINUTES · **TOTAL TIME:** 50 MINUTES
MAKES: 4 MAIN-DISH SERVINGS

2	TEASPOONS HOT MEXICAN-STYLE CHILI POWDER, OR 1 TABLESPOON REGULAR CHILI POWDER	1	METAL SKEWER
3	TABLESPOONS OLIVE OIL	1	LARGE RED ONION (12 OUNCES), CUT CROSSWISE INTO SLICES
¾	TEASPOON SALT	1	MEDIUM ZUCCHINI (8 OUNCES), CUT DIAGONALLY INTO ½-INCH-THICK SLICES
¼	CUP CHOPPED FRESH CILANTRO	2	LARGE RIPE TOMATOES (10 TO 12 OUNCES EACH), EACH CUT HORIZONTALLY IN HALF
2	TABLESPOONS FRESH LIME JUICE		
1	LARGE POBLANO CHILE (6 OUNCES)	4	OUNCES MONTEREY JACK CHEESE, SHREDDED (1 CUP)
2	EARS CORN, HUSKS AND SILKS REMOVED		

1 Prepare outdoor grill for direct grilling over medium-high heat.

2 In cup, combine chili powder, 2 tablespoons oil, and ½ teaspoon salt; set aside. In bowl, combine cilantro, lime juice, remaining ¼ teaspoon salt, and remaining 1 tablespoon oil; set aside.

3 Place poblano and corn on hot grill rack. Grill until poblano is blistered on all sides and corn is charred in spots, 10 to 15 minutes, turning occasionally.

4 Remove poblano from grill; wrap in foil, sealing tightly, and set aside to steam until cool enough to handle, about 15 minutes. Transfer corn to cutting board.

5 Push metal skewer horizontally through each onion slice to hold slice together. Brush both sides of onion and zucchini slices and cut sides of tomatoes with reserved chili oil; place on hot grill rack and cook until tender, about 10 minutes, turning over once. Place tomatoes on grill and cook until slightly softened, 6 to 8 minutes, turning over once. As vegetables are done, remove to platter and keep warm.

6 Unwrap poblano; remove stem and cut poblano lengthwise in half. Peel off skin and discard seeds, then cut into ¼-inch-wide strips. Cut corn from cobs; add to cilantro mixture.

7 Remove skewers from onion slices. On each plate, place 1 tomato half, cut side up. Place one-quarter of zucchini on top of each tomato; arrange half of cheese over zucchini. Arrange onion on top, separating into rings; sprinkle with remaining cheese, then poblano. Top with corn.

340
CALORIES

PER SERVING. 13G PROTEIN | 31G CARBOHYDRATE | 21G TOTAL FAT (8G SATURATED) 6G FIBER | 30MG CHOLESTEROL | 670MG SODIUM

MAKE IT A MEAL: These stacks are so pretty and colorful. Pair them with our equally lovely Peach, Cucumber, and Barley Salad (145 calories; page 274) and you'll have a summery buffet for just 485 calories per serving.

RICOTTA-STUFFED PEPPERS

Jarred piquillo peppers—roasted, peeled, and ready to serve—are the time-saving secret behind this meatless main dish. Stuff with ricotta, then top with a simple basil pesto and toasted pine nuts.

ACTIVE TIME: 25 MINUTES · **TOTAL TIME:** 35 MINUTES
MAKES: 4 MAIN-DISH SERVINGS

1½ CUPS PART-SKIM RICOTTA CHEESE

¼ CUP FINELY GRATED PECORINO ROMANO CHEESE

1 GREEN ONION, GREEN PART ONLY, FINELY CHOPPED

⅜ TEASPOON SALT

⅜ TEASPOON GROUND BLACK PEPPER

12 WHOLE ROASTED RED PIQUILLO PEPPERS, PATTED DRY

½ CUP PACKED FRESH BASIL LEAVES

½ CUP PACKED FRESH FLAT-LEAF PARSLEY LEAVES

1 TABLESPOON WATER

3 TABLESPOONS EXTRA-VIRGIN OLIVE OIL

2 YELLOW SUMMER SQUASHES, THINLY SLICED INTO ROUNDS

2 TABLESPOONS PINE NUTS (PIGNOLI), TOASTED

1 In large bowl, using wire whisk, beat ricotta until smooth and fluffy. Gently stir in Pecorino, onion, and ¼ teaspoon each salt and pepper. Transfer filling to zip-tight plastic bag.

2 Snip off one corner of bag to make ½-inch hole. Into opening of 1 pepper, squeeze filling until pepper is full. Repeat with remaining peppers and filling. If making ahead, cover and refrigerate up to overnight.

3 In food processor, with knife blade attached, pulse basil, parsley, water, and remaining ⅛ teaspoon each salt and pepper until herbs are finely chopped. With machine running, add oil in steady stream; process until herb mixture forms smooth puree. If making ahead, cover and refrigerate up to overnight.

4 To serve, on large serving platter, arrange squash; place stuffed peppers on top. Stir sauce and spoon over peppers. Garnish with pine nuts.

320 CALORIES

PER SERVING. 15G PROTEIN | 17G CARBOHYDRATE | 22G TOTAL FAT (8G SATURATED) 3G FIBER | 36MG CHOLESTEROL | 615MG SODIUM

MAKE IT A MEAL: These stuffed peppers create an impressive platter. For an equally impressive finish, serve our individual Meyer Lemon Pudding Cakes (170 calories; page 292) for dessert. The complete meal costs just 490 calories.

COUSCOUS-STUFFED ARTICHOKES

Instead of topping your grains with veggies, why not fill your veggies with whole-grain goodness?

ACTIVE TIME: 1 HOUR · **TOTAL TIME:** 1 HOUR 15 MINUTES
MAKES: 4 MAIN-DISH SERVINGS

4   LARGE ARTICHOKES

1   TABLESPOON FRESH LEMON JUICE

3   TABLESPOONS OLIVE OIL

2   MEDIUM CARROTS,
     PEELED AND DICED

2   GARLIC CLOVES, MINCED

¼   CUP CHOPPED FRESH MINT

3   TABLESPOONS CHOPPED
     FRESH PARSLEY

1   CUP WHOLE-WHEAT COUSCOUS
     (MOROCCAN PASTA)

1½   CUPS CANNED OR HOMEMADE
     VEGETABLE BROTH (PAGE 183)

½   TEASPOON SALT

¼   TEASPOON COARSELY
     GROUND BLACK PEPPER

1   LEMON, CUT INTO WEDGES

PARSLEY SPRIGS FOR GARNISH

1   With sharp knife, cut 1 inch straight across tops of artichokes. Cut off stems so artichokes can stand upright. Reserve and peel stems. Pull off outer dark green leaves from artichoke bottoms. Using kitchen shears, trim thorny leaf tips.

2   Spread artichokes open and carefully cut around chokes with small knife; scrape out center petals and fuzzy center portions with teaspoon and discard. Rinse artichokes well.

3   In 5-quart saucepot, heat lemon juice and *1 inch water* to boiling over high heat. Set artichokes on stem ends in boiling water, along with peeled stems; return to boiling. Reduce heat to low; cover and simmer until knife inserted in center goes through bottom easily, 30 to 40 minutes. Drain.

4   Meanwhile, preheat oven to 400°F.

5   In nonstick 10-inch skillet, heat 1 tablespoon oil over medium heat until hot. Add carrots and cook until tender, about 10 minutes, stirring occasionally. Stir in garlic; cook 1 minute longer. Remove to medium bowl. When artichoke stems are cooked through, dice and add to carrot mixture with mint and parsley.

6   Prepare couscous as label directs but use 1 cup broth in place of equal amount water. When couscous is done, stir in salt, pepper, carrot mixture, and remaining 2 tablespoons oil.

7 Pour remaining ½ cup broth into shallow baking dish large enough to hold all artichokes (13" by 9"); arrange cooked artichokes in dish. Spoon couscous mixture between artichoke leaves and into center cavities. Bake until artichokes are heated through, 15 to 20 minutes.

8 Serve artichokes with lemon wedges and garnish with parsley sprigs.

 PER SERVING. 11G PROTEIN | 54G CARBOHYDRATE | 11G TOTAL FAT (2G SATURATED) 12G FIBER | 4MG CHOLESTEROL | 600MG SODIUM Ⓥ ✿

MAKE IT A MEAL: For a Mediterranean-style dinner, nibble on three or four Kalamata olives (30 calories) as a starter, then serve these grain-stuffed artichokes with a hearty side of Roasted Cauliflower (70 calories; page 256) or Root Vegetable Gratin (145 calories; page 263).

STUFFED PORTOBELLOS

This healthy meal is low in calories, yet hearty enough to serve as a main course. Meaty portobello mushrooms combine with protein-rich quinoa, creamy feta, and vitamin-dense Brussels sprouts to create a flavorful dish packed with nutrients. Quinoa, which has a mild, slightly nutty flavor, packs more protein than any other grain.

TOTAL TIME: 30 MINUTES
MAKES: 4 MAIN-DISH SERVINGS

½ CUP QUINOA, RINSED

¾ CUP WATER

1¼ POUNDS BRUSSELS SPROUTS

4 TEASPOONS EXTRA-VIRGIN OLIVE OIL

⅜ TEASPOON SALT

¼ TEASPOON GROUND BLACK PEPPER

4 LARGE PORTOBELLO MUSHROOM CAPS (1 POUND)

1 TEASPOON FRESH THYME LEAVES, FINELY CHOPPED

⅔ CUP FROZEN CORN

3 OUNCES FETA CHEESE, CRUMBLED (¾ CUP)

½ TEASPOON GROUND CUMIN

1 Preheat oven to 450°F. In 2-quart saucepan, combine quinoa and water. Heat to boiling over high heat; reduce heat to medium-low. Cover and cook 15 minutes or until liquid is absorbed.

2 Meanwhile, trim and halve sprouts. In 18" by 12" jelly-roll pan, toss sprouts, 2 teaspoons oil, and ¼ teaspoon each salt and pepper. Roast 10 minutes.

3 Meanwhile, brush mushrooms with remaining 2 teaspoons oil and sprinkle with remaining ⅛ teaspoon salt. Combine thyme, corn, feta, cumin, and cooked quinoa in medium bowl.

4 When sprouts have roasted 10 minutes, push to one side of pan and arrange mushrooms, gill sides up, on other side. Divide quinoa mixture among mushrooms; roast 10 minutes or until mushrooms are tender.

290 CALORIES

PER SERVING. 14G PROTEIN | 38G CARBOHYDRATE | 11G TOTAL FAT (4G SATURATED) 9G FIBER | 19MG CHOLESTEROL | 500MG SODIUM

MAKE IT A MEAL: You can't go wrong with this protein- and vitamin-packed plate. For a fresh, pretty first course, add on our Mesclun with Pears and Pumpkin Seeds (100 calories; page 260) to create a 390-calorie meal.

FAST FRIED RICE

Who needs Chinese takeout when you can make a low-cal veggie fried rice at home with such ease? The secrets to this easy weeknight dish are quick-cooking brown rice, precut frozen vegetables, and ready-to-use stir-fry sauce.

TOTAL TIME: 20 MINUTES
MAKES: 4 MAIN-DISH SERVINGS

1½ CUPS INSTANT (10-MINUTE) BROWN RICE

1 PACKAGE (16 OUNCES) FIRM TOFU, DRAINED AND CUT INTO 1-INCH CUBES

6 TEASPOONS OLIVE OIL

1 PACKAGE (16 OUNCES) FROZEN VEGETABLES FOR STIR-FRY

2 LARGE EGGS, LIGHTLY BEATEN

½ CUP STIR-FRY SAUCE

¼ CUP WATER

1 In medium saucepan, prepare rice as label directs.
2 Meanwhile, place three layers of paper towels in medium bowl. Place tofu on towels and top with three more layers paper towels. Gently press tofu with hands to extract excess moisture.
3 In 12-inch skillet, heat 2 teaspoons oil over medium-high heat until hot. Add frozen vegetables; cover and cook 5 minutes, stirring occasionally. Transfer vegetables to bowl; keep warm.
4 In same skillet, heat remaining 4 teaspoons oil until hot. Add tofu and cook 5 minutes, gently stirring. Stir in rice and cook 4 minutes longer.
5 With spatula, push rice mixture around edge of skillet, leaving space in center. Add eggs to center of skillet; cook 1 minute, stirring eggs until scrambled. Add stir-fry sauce, vegetables, and water; cook 1 minute, stirring. Serve immediately.

360 **PER SERVING.** 17G PROTEIN | 41G CARBOHYDRATE | 15G TOTAL FAT (2G SATURATED)
CALORIES 5G FIBER | 106MG CHOLESTEROL | 760MG SODIUM

MAKE IT A MEAL: Add a side of our Crunchy Peanut Broccoli (150 calories; page 265) to create a yummy 510-calorie dinner.

SWEET-AND-SOUR UNSTUFFED CABBAGE

These cabbage wedges are microwaved, then topped with a sweet-and-sour tomato sauce—a simplified version of classic stuffed cabbage.

ACTIVE TIME: 20 MINUTES · **TOTAL TIME:** 40 MINUTES
MAKES: 4 MAIN-DISH SERVINGS

1 SMALL HEAD SAVOY CABBAGE (1½ POUNDS)	3 GREEN ONIONS, THINLY SLICED
¼ CUP WATER	1 TABLESPOON MINCED, PEELED FRESH GINGER
1 TABLESPOON OLIVE OIL	1 CAN (14½ OUNCES) DICED TOMATOES
2 MEDIUM CARROTS, PEELED AND CHOPPED	2 TABLESPOONS SOY SAUCE
2 STALKS CELERY, CHOPPED	2 TABLESPOONS SEASONED RICE VINEGAR
1 MEDIUM RED PEPPER (4 TO 6 OUNCES), CHOPPED	1 TABLESPOON PACKED LIGHT BROWN SUGAR
3 GARLIC CLOVES, CRUSHED WITH GARLIC PRESS	

1 Discard tough outer leaves from cabbage; core and cut cabbage into 4 wedges. Place wedges and water in 3-quart microwave-safe dish; cover and cook in microwave oven on High for 12 to 14 minutes, until fork-tender.
2 Meanwhile, in nonstick 12-inch skillet, heat oil over medium-high heat until hot. Add carrots, celery, and red pepper; cook until vegetables are tender and golden, about 12 minutes. Add garlic, green onions, and ginger; cook 2 minutes, stirring. Add tomatoes with their juice, soy sauce, vinegar, and brown sugar; heat to boiling over medium-high heat. Reduce heat to medium-low and simmer 5 minutes, stirring occasionally.
3 Spoon tomato mixture over cabbage in baking dish; cover and cook in microwave on High for 2 minutes to blend flavors.

145 CALORIES
PER SERVING. 6G PROTEIN | 26G CARBOHYDRATE | 4G TOTAL FAT (1G SATURATED) 7G FIBER | 0MG CHOLESTEROL | 1,200MG SODIUM

MAKE IT A MEAL: Brown rice seasoned with lemon juice and parsley (215 calories per serving) makes the perfect base for this sweet-and-sour cabbage. Finish with one of our oatmeal-raisin cookies (65 calories; page 305) for a comforting meal that's just 425 calories per serving.

LO MEIN WITH TOFU, SNOW PEAS, AND CARROTS

Packaged ramen noodles can be a great short-cut ingredient. Here they're combined with tofu, snow peas, carrots, and bean sprouts for a tasty homemade lo mein.

TOTAL TIME: 15 MINUTES PLUS DRAINING TOFU

MAKES: 4 MAIN-DISH SERVINGS

2   PACKAGES (3 OUNCES EACH) ORIENTAL-FLAVOR RAMEN NOODLES

2   TEASPOONS VEGETABLE OIL

1   PACKAGE (16 OUNCES) EXTRA-FIRM TOFU, DRAINED AND PRESSED (SEE PAGE 161), DICED

6   OUNCES (2 CUPS) SNOW PEAS, STRINGS REMOVED AND EACH CUT DIAGONALLY IN HALF

3   GREEN ONIONS, CUT INTO 2-INCH PIECES

1   PACKAGE (5 OUNCES) SHREDDED CARROTS (1½ CUPS)

½   CUP BOTTLED STIR-FRY SAUCE

3   OUNCES FRESH BEAN SPROUTS (1 CUP), RINSED AND DRAINED

1 Heat 4-quart covered saucepot of *water* to boiling over high heat. Add ramen noodles (reserve flavor packets) and cook 2 minutes. Drain noodles, reserving ¼ *cup cooking water*.

2 Meanwhile, in nonstick 12-inch skillet, heat oil over medium heat until hot. Add tofu and cook until lightly browned, 6 to 8 minutes, gently stirring a few times. Add snow peas and green onions; cook until vegetables are tender-crisp, 3 to 5 minutes, stirring frequently. Stir in carrots, stir-fry sauce, and contents of 1 ramen flavor packet to taste (depending on salt level of sauce); cook until carrots are tender, 2 to 3 minutes. (Discard remaining flavor packet or save for another use.)

3 Reserve some bean sprouts for garnish. Add noodles, reserved noodle cooking water, and remaining bean sprouts to skillet; cook 1 minute to blend flavors, stirring. Sprinkle with reserved bean sprouts to serve.

375 CALORIES **PER SERVING.** 18G PROTEIN | 47G CARBOHYDRATE | 12G TOTAL FAT (3G SATURATED) 4G FIBER | 0MG CHOLESTEROL | 1,485MG SODIUM

MAKE IT A MEAL: For a super-fast takeout-style meal that comes in under 500 calories, nibble on some steamed edamame (100 calories for 1 cup) before digging into the yummy noodle dish.

310 CALORIES
*Vegetable Lasagna
(page 222)*

PASTAS, GRAINS & CASSEROLES

If you associate pasta and casseroles with a growing bulge around your middle, try these low-calorie recipes on for size. Pasta dishes like Farfalle with Baby Artichokes and Mushrooms and Spaghetti with Beets and Greens are bursting with vitamin-packed seasonal vegetables; you can swap in wholesome whole-wheat noodles, if you like. Even our trio of lasagnas contain loads of vegetables, plus cheese for added richness. If you've only enjoyed risotto in a restaurant, try our super-easy Summer Tomato Risotto: This pretty, company-worthy dish is prepared in the microwave for maximum ease.

KEY TO ICONS

🕐 30 minutes or less   Ⓥ Vegan   ❤ Heart healthy   🌾 High fiber   🍲 Make ahead

FARFALLE WITH BABY ARTICHOKES AND MUSHROOMS

These baby artichokes harness the sweet, rich flavor of their full-grown counterparts, without requiring you to remove the inedible center thistle, or "choke." When cut, uncooked artichokes discolor quickly—be sure to rub lemon on any exposed surfaces.

ACTIVE TIME: 30 MINUTES · **TOTAL TIME:** 1 HOUR
MAKES: 6 MAIN-DISH SERVINGS

- 1 POUND FARFALLE OR ORECHIETTE PASTA
- 1 LEMON, CUT IN HALF
- 1 POUND (ABOUT 14) BABY ARTICHOKES
- 2 TABLESPOONS OLIVE OIL
- 1 PACKAGE (10 OUNCES) SLICED MUSHROOMS
- ½ TEASPOON SALT
- ¼ TEASPOON GROUND BLACK PEPPER
- 2 GARLIC CLOVES, CRUSHED WITH GARLIC PRESS
- 1 CUP CANNED OR HOMEMADE VEGETABLE BROTH (PAGE 183)
- ½ CUP DRY WHITE WINE
- 1 TABLESPOON CHOPPED FRESH THYME LEAVES
- 2 TABLESPOONS CHOPPED FRESH PARSLEY LEAVES
- FRESHLY GRATED PARMESAN CHEESE (OPTIONAL)

1 Cook pasta as label directs and reserve ¼ cup *cooking water* before draining.

2 Meanwhile, in covered nonstick 12-inch skillet, heat *1 inch water* to boiling over high heat. Fill medium bowl with cold water and add juice of 1 lemon half.

3 Trim artichokes: Bend back outer green leaves and snap off at base until remaining leaves are green on top and yellow on bottom. Cut off top half of each artichoke and discard. Rub cut surfaces with remaining lemon half to prevent browning. With vegetable peeler, peel stems. Cut off stems level with bottom of artichoke and coarsely chop stems; add to bowl of lemon water. Cut each artichoke into quarters; add to lemon water.

4 Drain artichokes and stems and place in boiling water in skillet. Cook, covered, 8 to 10 minutes or until artichokes are tender when pierced with tip of small knife. Drain well and set aside.

5 Dry skillet with paper towel. Add oil to skillet and heat over medium-high heat until hot. Add mushrooms, salt, and pepper, and cook about 3 minutes or until mushrooms begin to soften, stirring occasionally. Add artichoke pieces and garlic, and cook about 5 minutes longer or until mushrooms are lightly browned and artichokes are very tender. Stir broth, wine, and thyme into skillet, and heat to boiling; boil 1 minute. Stir in parsley.
6 When pasta is done, add to skillet with artichokes and mushrooms. Cook 1 minute to blend flavors, tossing to combine. Stir in reserved cooking water if pasta is dry. Serve with grated Parmesan, if you like.

360 **CALORIES** — **PER SERVING.** 13G PROTEIN | 63G CARBOHYDRATE | 6G TOTAL FAT (1G SATURATED) 4G FIBER | 0MG CHOLESTEROL | 495MG SODIUM Ⓥ

MAKE IT A MEAL: For a colorful finish to a 485-calorie Italian dinner, serve Berries in Red Wine (125 calories; page 287) for dessert.

MIDDLE-EASTERN GARBANZO BEANS AND MACARONI

Here's a flavorful entrée based on pantry staples—canned chickpeas and crushed tomatoes—tossed with pasta.

ACTIVE TIME: 10 MINUTES · **TOTAL TIME:** 35 MINUTES
MAKES: 6 MAIN-DISH SERVINGS

12 OUNCES MACARONI TWISTS OR ELBOW MACARONI

1 TABLESPOON OLIVE OIL

1 TABLESPOON BUTTER OR MARGARINE

1 LARGE ONION (12 OUNCES), CUT INTO ¼-INCH PIECES

2 GARLIC CLOVES, CRUSHED WITH GARLIC PRESS

1 TEASPOON SALT

1 TEASPOON GROUND CUMIN

¾ TEASPOON GROUND CORIANDER

¼ TEASPOON GROUND ALLSPICE

¼ TEASPOON COARSELY GROUND BLACK PEPPER

1 CAN (28 OUNCES) CRUSHED TOMATOES

1 CAN (15 TO 19 OUNCES) GARBANZO BEANS, RINSED AND DRAINED

¼ CUP LOOSELY PACKED FRESH PARSLEY LEAVES, CHOPPED

PARSLEY SPRIGS FOR GARNISH

1 In large saucepot, cook pasta as label directs.

2 Meanwhile, in nonstick 12-inch skillet, heat oil with butter over medium heat until hot and melted. Add onion and cook, stirring occasionally, until tender and golden, about 20 minutes. Stir in garlic, salt, cumin, coriander, allspice, and pepper; cook 1 minute.

3 Add tomatoes and garbanzos to skillet; heat to boiling over medium-high heat. Reduce heat to medium-low; simmer, stirring occasionally, 5 minutes.

4 Drain pasta; return to saucepot. Toss garbanzo-bean mixture with pasta; heat through. Toss with chopped parsley just before serving. Garnish with parsley sprigs.

400 CALORIES **PER SERVING.** 14G PROTEIN | 73G CARBOHYDRATE | 7G TOTAL FAT (2G SATURATED) 5G FIBER | 5MG CHOLESTEROL | 1,039MG SODIUM

MAKE IT A MEAL: Add on a side of Sautéed Spinach with Garlic and Lemon (45 calories; page 255) to round out this hearty 445-calorie dinner.

PASTA WITH SPINACH-CHIVE PESTO

We're all familiar with the classic pesto made from fresh basil leaves, olive-oil, pine nuts, and Parmesan cheese. But did you know you can make pesto sauce from other fresh herbs and even tender greens like baby spinach? This garden-fresh recipe teaches you how.

ACTIVE TIME: 10 MINUTES · **TOTAL TIME:** 40 MINUTES
MAKES: 4 MAIN-DISH SERVINGS

1   PACKAGE (16 OUNCES) RIGATONI OR PENNE

2   CUPS BABY SPINACH LEAVES

1½ CUPS FRESH FLAT-LEAF PARSLEY LEAVES

¼   CUP CHOPPED FRESH CHIVES

3   TABLESPOONS EXTRA-VIRGIN OLIVE OIL

¼   CUP PINE NUTS (PIGNOLI), PLUS ADDITIONAL FOR GARNISH

¼   TEASPOON SALT

¼   CUP FRESHLY GRATED PARMESAN CHEESE, PLUS FRESHLY SHAVED PARMESAN FOR GARNISH

1   Cook pasta as label directs, then drain and return to cooking pot.
2   Meanwhile, in blender, combine spinach, parsley, chives, oil, pine nuts, and salt. Puree pesto until smooth. Stir in grated Parmesan (see Tip).
3   Transfer pasta to large serving bowl. Add pesto to pasta; toss to combine. Top with shaved Parmesan and additional pine nuts.

TIP If you aren't serving the pesto immediately, don't add the grated Parmesan. Refrigerate the pesto in an airtight container for up to two days or freeze it for up to two months and stir in the cheese before serving.

395 CALORIES

PER SERVING. 12G PROTEIN | 48G CARBOHYDRATE | 18G TOTAL FAT (3G SATURATED) 4G FIBER | 4MG CHOLESTEROL | 282MG SODIUM ❤ 🥗

MAKE IT A MEAL: For a light summer supper, pair this delicate pasta with a wedge of cantaloupe dressed with a squeeze of lime (25 calories). Enjoy the whole meal for just 420 calories.

SPAGHETTI WITH BEETS AND GREENS

In this innovative dish, garlicky beets and their greens are tossed with spaghetti, tinting the pasta a beautiful pinkish-red! If you're not going to use beets immediately, trim the tops ahead of time, since the leaves leach moisture and color from the beets. Refrigerate the greens and the beets in separate plastic bags and use them within two days.

ACTIVE TIME: 20 MINUTES · **TOTAL TIME:** 35 MINUTES
MAKES: 6 MAIN-DISH SERVINGS

2 BUNCHES BEETS WITH TOPS (ABOUT 3 POUNDS TOTAL)	2 GARLIC CLOVES, CRUSHED WITH GARLIC PRESS
½ CUP WATER	⅛ TEASPOON CRUSHED RED PEPPER
1 PACKAGE (16 OUNCES) SPAGHETTI	1 TEASPOON SALT
3 TABLESPOONS OLIVE OIL	

1 Cut tops from beets and set greens aside. If beets are not uniform in size, cut larger beets in half. Place beets and water in deep 3-quart microwave-safe baking dish; cover and cook in microwave oven on High for 15 to 20 minutes, or until beets are tender when pierced with tip of knife. Rinse beets under cold running water until cool enough to handle. Peel beets; cut into ½-inch pieces.

2 Meanwhile, in large saucepot, cook spaghetti as label directs. Trim and discard stems from beet greens. Coarsely chop beet greens; set aside.

3 In nonstick 12-inch skillet, heat oil, garlic, and crushed red pepper over medium heat 5 minutes or until garlic is lightly golden. Increase heat to medium-high; add beet greens and cook 3 minutes, stirring. Add beets and salt and cook 1 to 2 minutes or until mixture is hot.

4 When spaghetti is done, reserve ¾ *cup pasta cooking water*, then drain and return pasta to pot. Add beet mixture and reserved water; toss.

375 CALORIES

PER SERVING. 11G PROTEIN | 64G CARBOHYDRATE | 8G TOTAL FAT (1G SATURATED) 5G FIBER | 0MG CHOLESTEROL | 570MG SODIUM

MAKE IT A MEAL: To keep the red theme, finish the meal with Berries in Red Wine (125 calories; page 287) for a jewel-like 500-calorie dinner.

VEGETABLE LASAGNA

This lasagna is loaded with veggies. For photo, see page 214.

ACTIVE TIME: 25 MINUTES · **TOTAL TIME:** 1 HOUR 15 MINUTES
MAKES: 4 MAIN-DISH SERVINGS

2 MEDIUM ZUCCHINI OR YELLOW SUMMER SQUASHES (8 OUNCES EACH), THINLY SLICED	1 TEASPOON FRESH THYME LEAVES, CHOPPED
1 TABLESPOON OLIVE OIL	1 POUND PLUM TOMATOES, CORED AND THINLY SLICED
¼ TEASPOON SALT	4 NO-BOIL LASAGNA NOODLES, RINSED WITH COLD WATER
1 BUNCH SWISS CHARD, TOUGH STEMS DISCARDED, THINLY SLICED	2 CARROTS, PEELED AND SHREDDED
1 SMALL ONION, FINELY CHOPPED	1 CUP PART-SKIM RICOTTA CHEESE
2 GARLIC CLOVES, CRUSHED WITH GARLIC PRESS	2 OUNCES PROVOLONE CHEESE, FINELY SHREDDED (½ CUP)

1 Arrange one oven rack 4 inches from broiler heat source and place second rack in center. Preheat broiler.

2 In large bowl, toss zucchini with 1 teaspoon oil and ⅛ teaspoon salt. Arrange on 18" by 12" jelly-roll pan in single layer. Broil 6 minutes or until golden brown, turning over once. Set aside. Reset oven control to 425°F.

3 Rinse chard in cold water; drain, leaving some water clinging to leaves.

4 In 12-inch skillet, heat remaining 2 teaspoons oil over medium heat. Add onion; cook 3 minutes or until soft, stirring occasionally. Add chard, garlic, thyme, and remaining ⅛ teaspoon salt. Cook 6 to 7 minutes or until chard is very soft, stirring frequently. Remove from heat and set aside.

5 In 8-inch square baking dish, layer half of tomatoes, lasagna noodles, Swiss chard, shredded carrots, zucchini slices, and ricotta, in that order. Repeat layering once. Top with provolone. Cover with foil. (Lasagna can be prepared to this point and refrigerated up to overnight.) Bake 30 minutes, covered (if refrigerated, bake 10 minutes longer). Uncover and bake 20 minutes longer or until golden brown and bubbling.

310 CALORIES

PER SERVING. 17G PROTEIN | 33G CARBOHYDRATE | 13G TOTAL FAT (6G SATURATED) 6G FIBER | 29MG CHOLESTEROL | 520MG SODIUM

MAKE IT A MEAL: Artichokes with Creamy Lemon Sauce (145 calories; page 264) are just the thing to complete a 455-calorie lasagna dinner.

POLENTA LASAGNA

This stress-free casserole is perfect for a last-minute dinner party.

ACTIVE TIME: 45 MINUTES · **TOTAL TIME:** 1 HOUR 15 MINUTES PLUS STANDING
MAKES: 6 MAIN-DISH SERVINGS

1 TABLESPOON OLIVE OIL

1 SMALL ONION, FINELY CHOPPED

1 GARLIC CLOVE, MINCED

1 CAN (28 OUNCES) TOMATOES

2 TABLESPOONS TOMATO PASTE

2 TABLESPOONS CHOPPED FRESH BASIL

1 TEASPOON SALT

1 PACKAGE (10 OUNCES) FROZEN CHOPPED SPINACH, THAWED AND SQUEEZED DRY

1 CUP PART-SKIM RICOTTA CHEESE

2 TABLESPOONS FRESHLY GRATED PARMESAN CHEESE

¼ TEASPOON COARSELY GROUND BLACK PEPPER

1 LOG (24 OUNCES) PRECOOKED PLAIN POLENTA, CUT INTO 16 SLICES

4 OUNCES PART-SKIM MOZZARELLA CHEESE, SHREDDED (1 CUP)

1 In 3-quart saucepan, heat oil over medium heat. Add onion and cook until tender, about 8 minutes, stirring occasionally. Add garlic and cook 30 seconds longer. Stir in tomatoes with their juice, tomato paste, basil, and ½ teaspoon salt; heat to boiling over high heat. Reduce heat to low and simmer, uncovered, 20 minutes, stirring occasionally and breaking up tomatoes with side of spoon. Set sauce aside.

2 Meanwhile, in medium bowl, mix spinach, ricotta, Parmesan, pepper, and remaining ½ teaspoon salt until blended.

3 Preheat oven to 350°F. Grease 8-inch square glass baking dish.

4 Arrange half of polenta slices, overlapping, in baking dish. Drop half of spinach mixture, by rounded tablespoons, on top of polenta (mixture will not completely cover slices). Spread half of sauce on top to form an even layer. Sprinkle with half of mozzarella. Repeat layering.

5 Bake casserole until hot and bubbling, about 30 minutes. Let stand 10 minutes for easier serving.

270 CALORIES **PER SERVING.** 16G PROTEIN | 3G CARBOHYDRATE | 10G TOTAL FAT (15G SATURATED) 4G FIBER | 28MG CHOLESTEROL | 1,210MG SODIUM

MAKE IT A MEAL: For a perfect autumn meal, serve with our Mesclun with Pears and Pumpkin Seeds (100 calories; page 260). You can enjoy it all for just 370 calories!

BUTTERNUT SQUASH AND SAGE LASAGNA

With our freeze-now, serve-later dishes, you can serve a comfy meal on even the busiest weeknight. The light, minty flavor of fresh sage pairs beautifully with sweet butternut squash in this special entrée.

ACTIVE TIME: 50 MINUTES · **TOTAL TIME:** 2 HOURS
MAKES: 2 CASSEROLES OR 12 MAIN-DISH SERVINGS

2   LARGE ONIONS (12 OUNCES EACH), EACH CUT IN HALF, THEN CUT CROSSWISE INTO ¼-INCH SLICES

2   TABLESPOONS OLIVE OIL

1½ TEASPOONS SALT

¾   TEASPOON COARSELY GROUND BLACK PEPPER

2   MEDIUM BUTTERNUT SQUASHES (1¾ POUNDS EACH), EACH CUT IN HALF AND SEEDED

7   CUPS LOW-FAT MILK (1%)

½   CUP CORNSTARCH

¼   CUP PACKED FRESH SAGE LEAVES, CHOPPED

¼   TEASPOON GROUND NUTMEG

2   CUPS FRESHLY GRATED PARMESAN CHEESE

12 NO-BOIL LASAGNA NOODLES

3   PACKAGES (10 OUNCES EACH) FROZEN CHOPPED SPINACH, THAWED AND SQUEEZED DRY

1 Preheat oven to 450°F. In large bowl, toss onions with oil, ¼ teaspoon salt, and ¼ teaspoon pepper. Place onions in one 15½" by 10½" jelly-roll pan. Line a second jelly-roll pan with foil; arrange squash in pan, cut sides up. Sprinkle with ¼ teaspoon salt and ¼ teaspoon pepper. Cover squash pan tightly with aluminum foil. (Do not cover onions.) Roast both pans 45 minutes or until squash is tender and onions are browned, stirring onions halfway through cooking. Reset oven control to 375°F.

2 Meanwhile, in 5-quart saucepot (do not use smaller pot; milk mixture may boil over), heat 6 cups milk over medium-high heat just to simmering, stirring occasionally. In small bowl, whisk cornstarch into remaining 1 cup milk. Add cornstarch mixture to simmering milk; heat to full rolling boil and cook 1 minute, stirring constantly and scraping bottom of pot to prevent scorching. Remove from heat; stir in sage, nutmeg, 1½ cups Parmesan, and remaining 1 teaspoon salt and ¼ teaspoon pepper.

3 When vegetables are done, scrape squash flesh out of skins and into food processor with knife blade attached; discard skins. Add onions; puree until smooth. Makes about 4 cups puree.

4 Into each of two 8-inch square glass or ceramic baking dishes, spoon ½ cup white sauce to cover bottoms. Arrange 2 lasagna noodles over sauce in each casserole. Evenly spread 1 cup squash puree, then ¾ cup chopped spinach over noodles in each casserole. Top each with 1 cup sauce. Repeat layering one time, starting with noodles. Top each with 2 more noodles. Spread remaining sauce on top; sprinkle with remaining Parmesan.

5 Cover one casserole with aluminum foil. Place on cookie sheet (to catch any spills) and bake 30 minutes. Uncover and bake 15 minutes longer or until hot and bubbly. Let stand 10 minutes for easier serving. Wrap second casserole in plastic and freeze until solid; then remove from dish, wrap tightly with heavy-duty foil, label, and freeze for up to 3 months.

335 CALORIES **PER SERVING.** 17G PROTEIN | 46G CARBOHYDRATE | 10G TOTAL FAT (4G SATURATED) 5G FIBER | 17MG CHOLESTEROL | 730MG SODIUM 🌻 🧺

MAKE IT A MEAL: Make the lasagna ahead of time and reheat when you're ready to serve. Our Greens with Goat Cheese and Tangerine Vinaigrette (165 calories; page 267) is all you need to round out a quick 500-calorie dinner.

BULGUR PILAF WITH APRICOTS

A hint of curry transforms this simple grain and bean pilaf.

ACTIVE TIME: 10 MINUTES · **TOTAL TIME:** 30 MINUTES
MAKES: 4 MAIN-DISH SERVINGS

¾ CUP WATER

1 CAN (14½ OUNCES) VEGETABLE BROTH OR 1¾ CUPS HOMEMADE BROTH (PAGE 183)

1 CUP BULGUR

1 TABLESPOON OLIVE OIL

1 SMALL ONION, CHOPPED

2 TEASPOONS CURRY POWDER

1 GARLIC CLOVE, CRUSHED WITH GARLIC PRESS

1 CAN (15 TO 19 OUNCES) GARBANZO BEANS (CHICKPEAS), RINSED AND DRAINED

½ CUP DRIED APRICOTS, CHOPPED

½ TEASPOON SALT

¼ CUP LOOSELY PACKED FRESH PARSLEY LEAVES, CHOPPED

1 In 2-quart covered saucepan, heat water and 1¼ cups vegetable broth to boiling on high. Stir in bulgur; heat to boiling. Reduce heat to medium-low; cover and simmer 12 to 15 minutes or until liquid is absorbed. Remove saucepan from heat. Uncover and fluff with fork to separate grains.
2 Meanwhile, in nonstick 12-inch skillet, heat oil over medium heat. Add onion and cook 10 minutes, stirring occasionally. Stir in curry powder and garlic; cook 1 minute.
3 Stir in garbanzo beans, apricots, salt, and remaining ½ cup vegetable broth; heat to boiling. Remove saucepan from heat; stir in bulgur and parsley.

370
CALORIES

PER SERVING. 13G PROTEIN | 71G CARBOHYDRATE | 6G TOTAL FAT (1G SATURATED)
15G FIBER | 0MG CHOLESTEROL | 815MG SODIUM

MAKE IT A MEAL: For a sweet and fruity finish to this tasty pilaf, try our Three-Fruit Salad with Vanilla Syrup (140 calories; page 289).

VEGETABLE COBBLER

What a satisfying, savory twist on fruit cobbler! Here winter vegetables are roasted until tender, then bathed in a lightened cream sauce (no cream here, though—it's made with low-fat milk) and topped with biscuit dough baked to golden-brown goodness.

ACTIVE TIME: 15 MINUTES · **TOTAL TIME:** 1 HOUR 30 MINUTES
MAKES: 6 MAIN-DISH SERVINGS

1 MEDIUM BUTTERNUT SQUASH (1¾ POUNDS), PEELED, SEEDED, AND CUT INTO 1½-INCH CHUNKS

1 POUND RED POTATOES (3 LARGE), CUT INTO 1½-INCH CHUNKS (SEE TIP)

3 MEDIUM PARSNIPS, PEELED AND CUT INTO 1-INCH PIECES

1 MEDIUM RED ONION, CUT INTO 6 WEDGES

¾ TEASPOON SALT

½ TEASPOON DRIED TARRAGON

2 TABLESPOONS OLIVE OIL

1 CAN (14½ OUNCES) VEGETABLE BROTH OR 1¾ CUPS HOMEMADE BROTH (PAGE 183)

½ TEASPOON FRESHLY GRATED LEMON PEEL

1 SMALL BUNCH (12 OUNCES) BROCCOLI, CUT INTO 2" BY 1" PIECES

½ CUP PLUS ⅔ CUP LOW-FAT MILK (1%)

1 TABLESPOON CORNSTARCH

1¾ CUPS ALL-PURPOSE BAKING MIX

½ CUP CORNMEAL

¾ TEASPOON COARSELY GROUND BLACK PEPPER

1 Preheat oven to 450°F. In shallow 3½- to 4-quart casserole or 13" by 9" glass baking dish, toss squash, potatoes, parsnips, onion, salt, and tarragon with oil until well coated. Bake until vegetables are fork-tender and lightly browned, about 1 hour, stirring once.

2 After vegetables have cooked 45 minutes, in 3-quart saucepan, heat broth and lemon peel to boiling over high heat. Add broccoli; return to boiling. Reduce heat to low; cover and simmer broccoli 1 minute.

3 In cup, with fork or wire whisk, stir ½ cup milk with cornstarch until blended. Combine milk and broccoli mixtures, stirring constantly, until liquid boils and thickens slightly; boil 1 minute. Pour broccoli mixture over vegetables; stir until brown bits are loosened from bottom of casserole.

4 In medium bowl, stir together baking mix, cornmeal, pepper, and remaining ⅔ cup milk until just combined. Drop 12 heaping spoonfuls biscuit dough on top of vegetable mixture. Continue baking cobbler until biscuits are browned, about 15 minutes.

TIP You can peel the potatoes, but leaving the skin on during cooking is the best way to conserve their nutrients. If you do peel them, keep the peelings as thin as possible.

 395 CALORIES **PER SERVING.** 11G PROTEIN | 67G CARBOHYDRATE | 11G TOTAL FAT (2G SATURATED) 8G FIBER | 5MG CHOLESTEROL | 940MG SODIUM 🌾 🧺

MAKE IT A MEAL: Serve with a crunchy salad of Romaine hearts, sliced, three Bosc pears, sliced, tossed with 3 tablespoons each olive oil and lemon juice, and ¼ teaspoon each salt and pepper. Top with 2 tablespoons toasted walnuts. The salad is 130 calories per serving; enjoy it with the cobbler for a 525-calorie meal.

SUMMER TOMATO RISOTTO

Heat-beating and hands-off, this risotto, featuring the summer bounty of corn and tomatoes, is simmered in the microwave from beginning to end, so there's no endless toiling over a steamy stove.

ACTIVE TIME: 30 MINUTES · **TOTAL TIME:** 40 MINUTES
MAKES: 6 MAIN-DISH SERVINGS

- 1 BAG (12 OUNCES) MICROWAVE-IN-BAG GREEN BEANS
- 1 CAN (14½ OUNCES) REDUCED-SODIUM VEGETABLE BROTH OR 1¾ CUPS HOMEMADE BROTH (PAGE 183)
- 2 CUPS WATER
- 2 TABLESPOONS BUTTER
- 1 SMALL ONION, CHOPPED
- 2 CUPS ARBORIO RICE
- 2 POUNDS RIPE TOMATOES
- 2 CUPS FRESH CORN KERNELS
- 2 OUNCES FINELY GRATED PARMESAN CHEESE
- ½ TEASPOON SALT
- ¼ TEASPOON GROUND BLACK PEPPER
- 2 TABLESPOONS CHOPPED BASIL

1 Cook beans as label directs. Cool slightly; cut into 1 inch pieces.

2 In 2-quart saucepan, heat broth and water to boiling.

3 Meanwhile, in 4-quart microwave-safe bowl, microwave butter and onion, uncovered, on High for 3 minutes. Stir in rice. Cook on High for 1 minute. Stir in broth. Cover with vented plastic wrap; microwave on Medium (50% power) 10 minutes.

4 Meanwhile, in food processor, puree half of tomatoes; strain juice through sieve into measuring cup, pressing on solids. Discard solids. Chop remaining tomatoes.

5 Stir 1½ cups tomato juice into rice mixture. Re-cover with vented plastic wrap; microwave on Medium for 5 minutes or until most liquid is absorbed.

6 Stir corn into rice mixture, cover again with vented plastic wrap; microwave on Medium for 3 minutes or until corn is heated through.

7 Stir Parmesan, green beans, chopped tomatoes, salt, pepper, and half of basil into risotto. Sprinkle with remaining basil before serving.

390 CALORIES

PER SERVING. 12G PROTEIN | 70G CARBOHYDRATE | 8G TOTAL FAT (5G SATURATED) 6G FIBER | 8MG CHOLESTEROL | 485MG SODIUM 🌱

MAKE IT A MEAL: Serve with Sliced Citrus with Lime Syrup (95 calories; page 286). In summer, make the syrup and use on unpeeled nectarines or peaches.

330 CALORIES

*California Breakfast Wrap
(page 237)*

BREAKFAST AROUND THE CLOCK

You've heard it before, and we'll say it again: A good breakfast is the foundation of any healthy diet. So why not enjoy the light and healthy vegetarian breakfasts that follow morning, noon, or night? Our egg-based frittatas, tarts, wraps, and scrambles are not only perfect for brunch; they make stellar vegetarian dinners, too. (See "The Nutritional Benefits of Eggs" on page 242). If you're hankering for something sweet, you can tuck into our pancakes and French toast without guilt because they're pre-pared with whole grains. Or, for something different, sample our savory take on pancakes; they are enriched with a little reduced-fat ricotta and topped with a delectable tomato and Swiss chard sauce.

KEY TO ICONS

 30 minutes or less Vegan ♥ Heart healthy  High fiber ▮ Make ahead

FIVE-MINUTE MULTIGRAIN CEREAL

Get a great-grains start to your day with a hot and tasty serving of three kinds of grains—it cooks up in five minutes flat. Serve it with your choice of low-fat or nondairy milk.

ACTIVE TIME: 5 MINUTES · **TOTAL TIME:** 10 MINUTES

MAKES: 1 SERVING

2   TABLESPOONS QUICK-COOKING BARLEY

2   TABLESPOONS BULGUR

2   TABLESPOONS OLD-FASHIONED OATS, UNCOOKED

⅔   CUP WATER

2   TABLESPOONS DARK SEEDLESS RAISINS

PINCH GROUND CINNAMON

1   TABLESPOON CHOPPED WALNUTS OR PECANS

In microwave-safe 1-quart bowl, combine barley, bulgur, oats, and water. Microwave on High for 2 minutes. Stir in raisins and cinnamon; microwave 3 minutes longer. Stir, then top with walnuts.

265 CALORIES

PER SERVING. 8G PROTEIN | 50G CARBOHYDRATE | 6G TOTAL FAT (1G SATURATED) 7G FIBER | 0MG CHOLESTEROL | 5MG SODIUM 🔵 🟢 ❤️ 🌼

MAKE IT A MEAL: For a wholesome start to your day, pour on ½ cup low-fat (2%) milk or soy milk (60 or 65 calories). If you want to add some protein to keep you going, serve with one hard-boiled egg (80 calories).

SCRAMBLED EGGS WITH FRESH HERBS

Scrambled eggs are the perfect quick and easy protein-filled dish to start your morning off right. The Dijon mustard and herbs add flavor, so there's no need to add cheese.

TOTAL TIME: 10 MINUTES
MAKES: 4 MAIN-DISH SERVINGS

8   LARGE EGGS, BEATEN
2   TABLESPOONS BUTTER OR MARGARINE
⅛   TEASPOON SALT
⅛   TEASPOON GROUND BLACK PEPPER
1½ TEASPOONS DIJON MUSTARD

¼   CUP PACKED FRESH FLAT-LEAF PARSLEY LEAVES, FINELY CHOPPED, PLUS ADDITIONAL FOR GARNISH
¼   CUP FINELY CHOPPED FRESH CHIVES, PLUS ADDITIONAL WHOLE CHIVES FOR GARNISH

1 In 12-inch skillet, combine eggs, butter, salt, and pepper. Turn heat to medium-low. With wire whisk, gently and constantly whisk 3 to 5 minutes or until soft curds form but eggs are still wet.

2 Whisk in Dijon mustard, then chopped parsley and chives. Continue whisking 1 to 2 minutes or until eggs are almost set and very creamy. Immediately remove skillet from heat and spoon eggs into warmed large serving bowl. Garnish with additional herbs.

205 CALORIES **PER SERVING.** 13G PROTEIN | 2G CARBOHYDRATE | 16G TOTAL FAT (4G SATURATED) 0G FIBER | 425MG CHOLESTEROL | 285MG SODIUM 🔵

MAKE IT A MEAL: The possibilities are endless: Keep it simple and add on a slice of toast spread with 1 teaspoon trans-fat-free margarine (115 calories). Or serve the eggs with a Whole-Grain Blueberry Muffin (170 calories; page 280) and ½ grapefruit (40 calories); it's just 415 calories for the whole meal.

CALIFORNIA BREAKFAST WRAP

Filling and filled with good-for-you-ingredients, this wrap is the perfect way to start your morning. It's packed with protein from the eggs and cheese, healthy fats from the avocado, and cancer-fighting antioxidants and lycopene from the spinach and tomato. For photo, see page 232.

TOTAL TIME: 25 MINUTES
MAKES: 4 MAIN-DISH SERVINGS

4 LARGE EGGS	1 TEASPOON CANOLA OIL
2 LARGE EGG WHITES	1 RIPE MEDIUM TOMATO, SEEDED AND FINELY CHOPPED (1 CUP)
⅜ TEASPOON SALT	1 HASS AVOCADO, FINELY CHOPPED
⅛ TEASPOON GROUND BLACK PEPPER	1 TABLESPOON CHOPPED FRESH DILL LEAVES
4 (8-INCH) WHOLE-WHEAT TORTILLAS	
4 TABLESPOONS GOAT CHEESE	
3½ OUNCES BABY SPINACH (7 CUPS)	

1 In medium bowl, beat eggs, egg whites, and ⅛ teaspoon each salt and pepper.

2 On microwave-safe plate, cover tortillas with damp paper towel. Microwave on High for 30 seconds or until just warm and pliable.

3 Spread 1 tablespoon goat cheese on each tortilla; divide spinach evenly on top of cheese.

4 In 12-inch nonstick skillet, heat oil over medium heat. Add egg mixture. Cook 2 minutes or until almost set, stirring gently. Remove from heat; fold in tomato, avocado, and remaining ¼ teaspoon salt.

5 Divide hot egg mixture among tortillas. Top with dill; fold in half.

330 CALORIES

PER SERVING. 16G PROTEIN | 29G CARBOHYDRATE | 16G TOTAL FAT (4G SATURATED) 6G FIBER | 191MG CHOLESTEROL | 565MG SODIUM

MAKE IT A MEAL: You don't need more than a fruit salad to complete this meal: Pair it with ½ cup cubed melon and 1 sliced kiwi fruit per person to create a 395-calorie breakfast or brunch.

TOSTADA STACKS

Try this new spin on tostadas served with a tomato-zucchini salsa and fried eggs on top. It's a hit at brunches.

ACTIVE TIME: 30 MINUTES · **TOTAL TIME:** 35 MINUTES
MAKES: 4 MAIN-DISH SERVINGS

4   (6-INCH) CORN TORTILLAS

4   TEASPOONS VEGETABLE OIL

1   MEDIUM WHITE ONION, FINELY CHOPPED

3   GARLIC CLOVES, CHOPPED

¾   TEASPOON SALT

¼   TEASPOON GROUND BLACK PEPPER

1   CAN (15 TO 19 OUNCES) LOW-SODIUM BLACK BEANS, RINSED AND DRAINED

1   MEDIUM ZUCCHINI (8 OUNCES), FINELY CHOPPED

1   MEDIUM ORANGE PEPPER, FINELY CHOPPED

2   CUPS FRESH CORN KERNELS

2   RIPE PLUM TOMATOES, FINELY CHOPPED

1   TEASPOON CHIPOTLE HOT SAUCE

2   TABLESPOONS FRESH LIME JUICE

2   TABLESPOONS CHOPPED FRESH CILANTRO

4   LARGE EGGS

1 Place tortillas between two paper towels on large plate. Microwave on High for 3 minutes or until crisp.

2 In nonstick 12-inch skillet, heat 1 tablespoon oil over medium heat. Add onion, garlic, and ⅛ teaspoon each salt and pepper. Cook 8 minutes or until golden, stirring.

3 Meanwhile, place beans and ¼ teaspoon salt in medium bowl. In large bowl, combine zucchini, orange pepper, corn, tomatoes, hot sauce, lime juice, 1 tablespoon cilantro, and ¼ teaspoon salt. Add half of onion mixture to beans; mash well. Stir remaining onion mixture into vegetables.

4 Wipe pan. Heat remaining 1 teaspoon oil over medium heat. Fry eggs 6 minutes or until whites are set. Sprinkle with remaining ⅛ teaspoon salt.

5 Meanwhile, spread bean mixture on tortillas. Top each with fried egg; serve with zucchini mix. Sprinkle with remaining 1 tablespoon cilantro.

375 CALORIES

PER SERVING. 19G PROTEIN | 53G CARBOHYDRATE | 11G TOTAL FAT (2G SATURATED) 10G FIBER | 186MG CHOLESTEROL | 605MG SODIUM 🌾

MAKE IT A MEAL: This brunch favorite can stand on its own. But if you want, serve with ½ cup frozen grapes (50 calories) to make it a 425-calorie meal.

CRUSTLESS TOMATO-RICOTTA PIE

This delicious cross between a frittata and a quiche makes a great vegetarian dinner or brunch option. Try this simple cheese-and-tomato pie with 2 tablespoons chopped fresh oregano or ¼ cup chopped fresh dill in place of the basil.

ACTIVE TIME: 20 MINUTES · **TOTAL TIME:** 55 MINUTES PLUS STANDING
MAKES: 4 MAIN-DISH SERVINGS

1 CONTAINER (15 OUNCES) PART-SKIM RICOTTA CHEESE	1 TABLESPOON CORNSTARCH
4 LARGE EGGS	½ CUP LOOSELY PACKED FRESH BASIL LEAVES, CHOPPED
¼ CUP FRESHLY GRATED PECORINO ROMANO CHEESE	½ CUP LOOSELY PACKED FRESH MINT LEAVES, CHOPPED
½ TEASPOON SALT	1 POUND RIPE TOMATOES, THINLY SLICED
⅛ TEASPOON COARSELY GROUND BLACK PEPPER	
¼ CUP LOW-FAT MILK (1%)	

1 Preheat oven to 375°F. In large bowl, whisk ricotta, eggs, Romano, salt, and pepper until blended.

2 In measuring cup, stir milk and cornstarch until smooth; whisk into cheese mixture. Stir in basil and mint.

3 Pour mixture into 10-inch nonstick skillet with oven-safe handle. Arrange tomato slices on top, overlapping if necessary. Bake pie 35 to 40 minutes or until edge is lightly browned and set and center is puffed. Let stand 5 minutes before serving.

 190 CALORIES

PER SERVING. 15G PROTEIN | 10G CARBOHYDRATE | 10G TOTAL FAT (5G SATURATED) 2G FIBER | 165MG CHOLESTEROL | 380MG SODIUM

MAKE IT A MEAL: If you want to serve this for dinner or brunch, pair with Greens with Goat Cheese and Tangerine Vinaigrette (165 calories; page 267) for a 355-calorie meal.

TOMATO TARTE TATIN

Frozen puff pastry is the shortcut secret to this skillet dish.

ACTIVE TIME: 30 MINUTES · **TOTAL TIME:** 1 HOUR PLUS COOLING
MAKES: 6 MAIN-DISH SERVINGS

1   FROZEN SHEET PUFF PASTRY
(HALF 17⅓-OUNCE PACKAGE), THAWED

1   TABLESPOON OLIVE OIL

1   MEDIUM ONION, CHOPPED

1   LARGE YELLOW PEPPER, CHOPPED

½   TEASPOON SALT

¼   TEASPOON GROUND BLACK PEPPER

1   TEASPOON FRESH THYME

2   TABLESPOONS BUTTER
(NO SUBSTITUTIONS)

2   TABLESPOONS SUGAR

1½ POUNDS FIRM RIPE PLUM TOMATOES,
SEEDED, CUT IN HALF LENGTHWISE

3   OUNCES GOAT CHEESE, CRUMBLED

8   SMALL FRESH BASIL LEAVES

1   Preheat oven to 400°F. On lightly floured surface, with floured rolling pin, roll pastry into 12-inch square; cut into 12-inch round. Place on waxed-paper-lined cookie sheet; refrigerate.

2   In 12-inch heavy ovenproof skillet, heat oil over medium heat. Add onion, yellow pepper, and ⅛ teaspoon each salt and pepper. Cook 6 minutes or just until tender, stirring. Stir in thyme; cook 1 minute. Transfer to bowl.

3   To same pan, add butter and sugar; cook 1 to 2 minutes, stirring. Add tomatoes, cut sides down, in single layer; cover, cook 2 minutes, then uncover. Cook 3 to 4 minutes or until most of pan juices are reduced, swirling pan frequently. Turn tomatoes over; sprinkle with ¼ teaspoon salt and ⅛ teaspoon pepper. Cook 2 minutes or until softened, swirling pan frequently; any remaining liquid should be thick and glossy. Remove pan from heat.

4   Sprinkle onion mixture over tomatoes. Carefully invert dough from waxed paper into mixture in pan. Cut six small slits in dough. Bake 30 to 35 minutes or until crust is dark golden brown. Cool in pan 10 minutes.

5   To unmold, place platter over top of tart. Quickly and carefully turn platter with skillet upside down to invert tart; remove skillet. Sprinkle tart with ⅛ teaspoon salt, goat cheese, and basil. Serve immediately.

290 CALORIES

PER SERVING. 7G PROTEIN | 27G CARBOHYDRATE | 18G TOTAL FAT (7G SATURATED)
3G FIBER | 17MG CHOLESTEROL | 440MG SODIUM

MAKE IT A MEAL: Serve with Spring Pea Dip with Veggies (50 calories; page 255) for a delightful 340-calorie brunch.

ASPARAGUS TART

This spring tart is an elegant addition to any brunch table.

ACTIVE TIME: 25 MINUTES · **TOTAL TIME:** 1 HOUR PLUS COOLING
MAKES: 8 MAIN-DISH SERVINGS

1⅜ TEASPOONS SALT

1¾ CUPS ALL-PURPOSE FLOUR

1 TEASPOON BAKING POWDER

¼ TEASPOON GROUND BLACK PEPPER

6 TABLESPOONS COLD BUTTER OR MARGARINE, CUT UP

6 TO 8 TABLESPOONS ICE WATER

1 POUND THIN ASPARAGUS, TRIMMED

3 LARGE EGGS

1⅓ CUPS MILK

1 TEASPOON DIJON MUSTARD

2 TEASPOONS GRATED FRESH LEMON PEEL

1 Preheat oven to 425°F. In covered 10-inch skillet over high heat, bring about 1 *inch water* and 1 teaspoon salt to boiling. Spray removable bottom of 11-inch tart pan with cooking spray.

2 In food processor with knife blade attached, combine flour, baking powder, ⅛ teaspoon salt, and ¼ teaspoon pepper; pulse until blended. Add butter and pulse until mixture resembles coarse meal. Add ice water, 1 tablespoon at a time, pulsing until moist clumps form. Gather dough together and flatten into disk. On lightly floured surface, with floured rolling pin, roll dough into 13-inch round. Gently ease dough into prepared tart pan. Fold overhang inward and press against dough on side of pan to reinforce edge (dough can be covered and refrigerated up to 4 hours before baking). Place pan on cookie sheet; bake 15 minutes. Cool slightly on wire rack.

3 Meanwhile, add asparagus to boiling water in skillet and cook 5 minutes. Drain and rinse under cold running water; drain well. In medium bowl, with wire whisk or fork, mix eggs, milk, Dijon, and remaining ¼ teaspoon salt until well blended.

THE NUTRITIONAL BENEFITS OF EGGS

Eggs got a bum rap for years. Yes, the yolk of an egg does contain cholesterol, but as hundreds of studies can attest, if eaten in moderation, eggs won't raise a person's overall cholesterol level. And eggs have so much to offer nutritionally. A single egg is a good source of selenium, which provides antioxidant protection; iodine, vital to thyroid function; energy-producing vitamin B_2; and protein.

4 Arrange asparagus spears in spoke fashion in baked tart shell with tips pointing outward. Sprinkle lemon peel evenly over asparagus in tart shell. Carefully pour egg mixture over asparagus.

5 Bake tart, on cookie sheet, 20 to 25 minutes or until tart puffs and custard jiggles only slightly in center. Cool on wire rack 15 minutes to serve warm or cool completely to serve at room temperature. Remove side of pan before serving.

245 CALORIES — **PER SERVING.** 8G PROTEIN | 24G CARBOHYDRATE | 13G TOTAL FAT (7G SATURATED) 1G FIBER | 110MG CHOLESTEROL | 340MG SODIUM

MAKE IT A MEAL: To create a memorable brunch spread, add a basket of our Bran Muffins (140 calories; page 273) and a bowl of fresh strawberries, halved (25 calories for ½ cup). A slice of Asparagus Tart, a muffin, and one serving strawberries comes in at just 410 calories.

SOUTHWESTERN FRITTATA

Frittatas are a great choice for breakfast, brunch, or a light dinner.

ACTIVE TIME: 25 MINUTES · **TOTAL TIME:** 50 MINUTES PLUS STANDING
MAKES: 6 MAIN-DISH SERVINGS

1 PACKAGE (8 TO 9 OUNCES) PRECOOKED BROWN RICE (SCANT 2 CUPS)	8 LARGE EGGS
4 TEASPOONS OLIVE OIL	¼ CUP MILK
1 SMALL ONION, CHOPPED	¼ CUP LOOSELY PACKED FRESH CILANTRO LEAVES, CHOPPED
1 JALAPEÑO CHILE, SEEDED AND FINELY CHOPPED	½ TEASPOON SALT
1 GARLIC CLOVE, FINELY CHOPPED	½ CUP SHREDDED MEXICAN CHEESE BLEND
1 CUP FROZEN CORN KERNELS	PREPARED SALSA (OPTIONAL)

1 Prepare brown rice as label directs. Preheat oven to 400°F.

2 In nonstick 10-inch skillet with oven-safe handle, heat 2 teaspoons olive oil over medium-high heat until hot. Add onion and cook until lightly browned, 2 to 3 minutes, stirring occasionally. Stir in jalapeño and garlic; cook 30 seconds, stirring. Add frozen corn and cook until thawed, about 1 minute, stirring a few times. Transfer corn mixture to bowl.

3 In large bowl, with wire whisk, beat eggs, milk, cilantro, and salt until well blended. Stir in rice, corn mixture, and cheese.

4 In same skillet, heat remaining 2 teaspoons oil over medium heat until hot. Pour in egg mixture; cover and cook until egg mixture starts to set around edge, about 3 minutes.

5 Remove cover and place skillet in oven; bake until knife inserted 2 inches from edge comes out clean, about 20 minutes. Remove frittata from oven; let stand 5 minutes.

6 To serve, loosen frittata from skillet; slide onto warm platter. Cut into wedges; serve with salsa if you like.

245
CALORIES

PER SERVING. 13G PROTEIN | 19G CARBOHYDRATE | 14G TOTAL FAT (5G SATURATED) 2G FIBER | 293MG CHOLESTEROL | 355MG SODIUM

MAKE IT A MEAL: For a fun 390-calorie meal, pair this mildly spicy frittata with our cooling Banana Berry Parfait (145 calories; page 289).

CHILES RELLEÑOS CASSEROLE

Green chiles and Cheddar cheese are baked into eggs for a healthy take on a classic dish.

ACTIVE TIME: 15 MINUTES · **TOTAL TIME:** 50 MINUTES PLUS COOLING
MAKES: 4 MAIN-DISH SERVINGS

6 LARGE EGGS	1 LARGE RED PEPPER, CUT INTO ¼-INCH PIECES
1 CUP REDUCED-FAT MILK (2%)	
2 TABLESPOONS ALL-PURPOSE FLOUR	4 OUNCES EXTRA-SHARP CHEDDAR CHEESE, SHREDDED (1 CUP)
¼ TEASPOON SWEET PAPRIKA	½ CUP PACKED FRESH CILANTRO LEAVES, FINELY CHOPPED
¼ TEASPOON SALT	
½ TEASPOON GROUND BLACK PEPPER	
2 CANS (5¾ OUNCES EACH) WHOLE GREEN CHILES, DRAINED AND THINLY SLICED	

1 Preheat oven to 350°F. Grease shallow 2-quart ceramic or glass baking dish well.

2 In large bowl, with wire whisk, mix eggs, milk, flour, paprika, salt, and black pepper until well blended. Stir in chiles, red pepper, Cheddar, and half of cilantro; pour into prepared dish.

3 Bake casserole 35 to 40 minutes or until surface is puffed and golden brown and center still jiggles slightly.

4 Cool in dish on wire rack 10 minutes. Garnish with remaining chopped cilantro and cut into squares or wedges to serve.

305 CALORIES

PER SERVING. 20G PROTEIN | 14G CARBOHYDRATE | 18G TOTAL FAT (9G SATURATED) 3G FIBER | 353MG CHOLESTEROL | 825MG SODIUM

MAKE IT A MEAL: This is an egg dish that easily translates to lunch or dinner. Serve with a side of baked tortilla chips (15 chips for 125 calories) and dip them into the casserole for a casual 430-calorie meal your whole family will enjoy.

SAVORY RICOTTA PANCAKES

Pancakes transcend breakfast when they're made with ricotta cheese and topped with an Italian tomato and Swiss chard sauce.

ACTIVE TIME: 55 MINUTES · **TOTAL TIME:** 1 HOUR 10 MINUTES
MAKES: 16 PANCAKES OR 4 MAIN-DISH SERVINGS

1 SMALL BUNCH (8 OUNCES) SWISS CHARD, TOUGH ENDS TRIMMED	3 LARGE EGGS, SEPARATED
1 TABLESPOON OLIVE OIL	1 CUP PART-SKIM RICOTTA CHEESE
1 MEDIUM ONION, CHOPPED	⅓ CUP REDUCED-FAT MILK (2%)
1 GARLIC CLOVE, CRUSHED WITH GARLIC PRESS	½ CUP ALL-PURPOSE FLOUR
1 TABLESPOON TOMATO PASTE	¼ TEASPOON BAKING POWDER
1 CAN (28 OUNCES) WHOLE TOMATOES IN PUREE, CHOPPED	1 TABLESPOON BUTTER OR MARGARINE, CUT INTO 3 PIECES
½ TEASPOON SALT	¼ CUP FRESHLY GRATED PECORINO ROMANO CHEESE

1 Cut ribs and stems from Swiss chard leaves. Cut ribs and stems into 1-inch pieces; cut leaves into 2-inch pieces. Rinse chard thoroughly in large bowl of cold water; swish to remove any dirt. With hands, transfer chard to colander, leaving dirt in bottom of bowl. Repeat process, changing water until all dirt is removed.

2 In 4-quart saucepan, heat olive oil over medium heat until hot. Add onion and garlic, and cook 6 to 8 minutes or until tender. Add tomato paste; cook 1 minute, stirring. Add tomatoes with their puree and ¼ teaspoon salt; heat to boiling over medium-high heat. Stir in Swiss chard; reduce heat to medium-low and simmer, covered, 10 minutes. Remove cover and cook 8 to 10 minutes longer or until chard is tender and sauce is thickened slightly, stirring occasionally. Remove saucepan from heat; cover to keep sauce warm.

3 Meanwhile, preheat oven to 200°F. In blender or food processor with knife blade attached, blend egg yolks, ricotta, and milk until smooth. Add flour, baking powder, and remaining ¼ teaspoon salt, and blend until smooth; transfer batter to 8-cup glass measure or medium bowl.

4 In small bowl, with mixer on high speed, beat egg whites just until stiff peaks form when beaters are lifted. With rubber spatula, fold beaten whites into batter.

5 In nonstick 12-inch skillet, melt 1 piece butter over medium heat. Drop batter by ¼ cups into skillet, making 4 to 5 pancakes per batch. Cook 3 to 4 minutes or until edges look dry and bottoms are browned. Turn pancakes over and cook 2 to 3 minutes or until bottoms are browned. Transfer pancakes to platter; keep warm in oven.

6 Repeat with remaining butter and batter. Serve pancakes with warm sauce; sprinkle with Romano.

350 CALORIES **PER SERVING.** 19G PROTEIN | 31G CARBOHYDRATE | 17G TOTAL FAT (6G SATURATED) 3G FIBER | 185MG CHOLESTEROL | 1,155MG SODIUM

MAKE IT A MEAL: Pair these savory pancakes with a Morningstar veggie sausage patty to make it a 430-calorie brunch. Or add a small micro-baked apple (55 calories).

TEMPTING PANCAKE TOPPERS

Maple syrup will always be a classic, but here are some other wholesome and delicious topping options.

- Drizzle ¼ cup low-fat vanilla yogurt (50 calories per ¼ cup) over the raspberries and chopped peaches called for in the recipe.

- Dollop with part-skim ricotta (80 calories for ¼ cup) and fresh orange pieces (40 calories for ¼ cup).

- Spread with 2 tablespoons apple butter or other favorite fruit puree (40 calories) and sprinkle with 1 tablespoon roasted pumpkin seeds (35 calories).

- Drizzle with 1 tablespoon maple syrup (50 calories) and sprinkle with 1 tablespoon toasted chopped pecans (45 calories) plus 1 tablespoon sweetened coconut flakes (30 calories).

WHOLE-GRAIN PANCAKES

Have a stack of pancakes without a side of guilt. These flapjacks contain oats and whole-wheat flour. They're topped with delicious fresh fruit.

TOTAL TIME: 30 MINUTES

MAKES: 12 PANCAKES OR 4 MAIN-DISH SERVINGS

2 RIPE PEACHES, PITTED AND CHOPPED	2 TEASPOONS BAKING POWDER
½ PINT RASPBERRIES (1½ CUPS)	½ TEASPOON SALT
1 TABLESPOON SUGAR	1¼ CUPS SKIM MILK
½ CUP ALL-PURPOSE FLOUR	1 LARGE EGG, LIGHTLY BEATEN
½ CUP WHOLE-WHEAT FLOUR	1 TABLESPOON VEGETABLE OIL
½ CUP QUICK-COOKING OATS, UNCOOKED	

1 Preheat oven to 200°F. In medium bowl, combine peaches, raspberries, and sugar. Stir to coat; set fruit mixture aside.

2 In large bowl, combine flours, oats, baking powder, and salt. Add milk, egg, and oil; stir just until flour mixture is moistened; batter will be lumpy.

3 Spray 12-inch nonstick skillet with cooking spray; heat over medium heat 1 minute. Pour batter by scant ¼ cups into skillet, making about 4 pancakes at a time. Cook until tops are bubbly, some bubbles burst, and edges look dry. With wide spatula, turn pancakes over and cook until undersides are golden. Transfer pancakes to platter. Cover; keep warm in oven.

4 Repeat with remaining batter, using more nonstick cooking spray if necessary. To serve, top with fruit mixture.

275 CALORIES

PER SERVING. 10G PROTEIN | 46G CARBOHYDRATE | 6G TOTAL FAT (1G SATURATED) 6G FIBER | 55MG CHOLESTEROL | 545MG SODIUM

MAKE IT A MEAL: What are pancakes without maple syrup? Add 1 tablespoon to make this a 325-calorie breakfast.

EASY ADD-ONS

To make your meal planning a breeze, we've organized the add-on recipes in the following chapters by calorie count—from lowest to highest. Choose your main dish from the preceding chapters, then select one or more of these tempting veggie or grain sides or desserts to round out your meal. So, if you're preparing our Vegetable Lasagna, a 310-calorie main dish, you could serve Artichokes with Creamy Lemon Sauce (145 calories) as a starter, or you could enjoy two lower-calorie add-ons instead: Mesclun with Pears and Pumpkin Seeds (100 calories) plus Sliced Citrus with Lime Syrup (95 calories) for dessert—and your dinner still adds up to approximately 500 calories total. It's that easy!

50 CALORIES

Spring Pea Dip
With Veggies
(page 255)

SNACKS, SIDES & SALADS

For generations, the mealtime mantra of mothers everywhere has been "Eat your vegetables!" As usual, Mom was right. In study after study, it's been shown that eating a diet rich in vegetables, fruits, and whole grains results in numerous health benefits, from reducing the risk of some cancers to maintaining a healthy weight. In this chapter, we provide delicious and original recipes for broccoli and peas, dark greens and artichokes, mixed vegetables and side salads. Add these colorful sides onto your meals—and make your mother proud.

KEY TO ICONS

 30 minutes or less  Vegan   Heart healthy   High fiber   Make ahead

KALE CHIPS

Our crisp kale "chips" are virtually fat free—perfect for guilt-free snacking.

ACTIVE TIME: 10 MINUTES · TOTAL TIME: 20 MINUTES
MAKES: 6 SIDE-DISH SERVINGS

Preheat oven to 350°F. From **1 bunch kale** (10 ounces), remove and discard thick stems, and tear leaves into large pieces. Spread leaves in single layer on two large cookie sheets. Coat leaves lightly with nonstick cooking spray and sprinkle with ½ **teaspoon salt**. Bake 12 to 15 minutes or just until crisp but not browned. Cool on cookie sheets on wire racks.

 15 CALORIES **PER 1-CUP SERVING.** 1G PROTEIN | 3G CARBOHYDRATE | 0G TOTAL FAT | 1G FIBER 0MG CHOLESTEROL | 175MG SODIUM 💙 🅥 ❤️ 🍱

SAUTÉED SPINACH WITH GARLIC AND LEMON

This lemon-kissed sautéed spinach is packed with folate, iron, calcium, and vitamins A and C.

ACTIVE TIME: 5 MINUTES · **TOTAL TIME:** 10 MINUTES
MAKES: 4 SIDE-DISH SERVINGS

In 6-quart saucepot, heat **1 tablespoon olive oil** over medium-high heat. Add **2 crushed garlic cloves** and cook 1 minute or until golden, stirring. Rinse **2 bags (10 ounces each) spinach** and add to pot, with water still clinging to leaves, in 3 batches; cook 2 minutes or until spinach fits in pot. Cover and cook 2 minutes longer or just until spinach wilts, stirring once. Stir in **1 tablespoon lemon juice** and **¼ teaspoon salt** and serve.

45 CALORIES

PER SERVING. 4G PROTEIN | 1G CARBOHYDRATE | 4G TOTAL FAT (1G SATURATED) 12G FIBER | 0MG CHOLESTEROL | 305MG SODIUM 🔵 🟢 ❤️ 🌾

SPRING PEA DIP

Serve this vibrant green dip with assorted spring vegetables for dipping, such as cucumber strips, yellow and red pepper strips, and baby carrots, or with homemade pita chips. For photo, see page 252.

ACTIVE TIME: 15 MINUTES · **TOTAL TIME:** 20 MINUTES
MAKES: 1 CUP

In food processor with knife blade attached, puree **1 cup thawed frozen peas,** with **¼ cup loosely packed mint leaves,** chopped; and **¼ teaspoon each salt and pepper.** Transfer to small bowl; stir in **⅓ cup part-skim ricotta cheese** and **2 tablespoons freshly grated Parmesan cheese.** Serve dip, with **½ cup assorted raw vegetables,** or cover and refrigerate to serve later.

50 CALORIES

PER SERVING. 4G PROTEIN | 7G CARBOHYDRATE | 1G TOTAL FAT (1G SATURATED) 2G FIBER | 4MG CHOLESTEROL | 120MG SODIUM 🔵 ❤️ 🟩

GREENS WITH GOAT CHEESE AND TANGERINE VINAIGRETTE

Savory goat cheese is the perfect companion to our sweet and tangy citrus vinaigrette. If you crave something other than raisins as a garnish, try dried cranberries or apricots.

TOTAL TIME: 15 MINUTES
MAKES: 4 SIDE-DISH SERVINGS

2 TANGERINES	8 CUPS LOOSELY PACKED MIXED BABY GREENS SUCH AS ROMAINE, ARUGULA, AND/OR SPINACH
2 TEASPOONS CIDER VINEGAR	
½ TEASPOON DIJON MUSTARD	½ CUP CRUMBLED GOAT CHEESE (2 OUNCES)
¼ TEASPOON SALT	
⅛ TEASPOON GROUND BLACK PEPPER	¼ CUP GOLDEN RAISINS
2 TABLESPOONS OLIVE OIL	
1 TABLESPOON CHOPPED FRESH CHIVES	

1 From tangerines, grate 1 teaspoon peel; place in small bowl. Cut remaining peel and pith from fruit. Hold tangerine over second small bowl and cut on either side of membranes to remove each segment, allowing fruit and juice to drop into bowl. Repeat with remaining tangerine. Squeeze 3 tablespoons juice from membranes; add to bowl with peel, then whisk in vinegar, Dijon, salt, and pepper. In thin, steady stream, whisk in oil until vinaigrette is blended. Stir in tangerine segments and chives.

2 Place greens on salad plates; sprinkle each with goat cheese and raisins. Drizzle with vinaigrette.

---

165 CALORIES

PER SERVING. 3G PROTEIN | 15G CARBOHYDRATE | 10G TOTAL FAT (3G SATURATED) 2G FIBER | 10MG CHOLESTEROL | 335MG SODIUM 💙 ❤️

VEGETABLES WITH SESAME VINAIGRETTE

This lively mix of green vegetables, cooked just until crisp-tender and tossed with the rich roasted flavor of sesame oil, will have you and your family eating your vegetables every chance you get.

ACTIVE TIME: 25 MINUTES · **TOTAL TIME:** 30 MINUTES
MAKES: MAKES 10 SIDE-DISH SERVINGS

1 MEDIUM BUNCH BROCCOLI, CUT INTO 2½-INCH PIECES	1 POUND ASPARAGUS, TRIMMED AND CUT INTO 2-INCH PIECES
2 TABLESPOONS OLIVE OR VEGETABLE OIL	8 OUNCES SUGAR SNAP PEAS OR SNOW PEAS, STEMS AND STRINGS ALONG BOTH EDGES REMOVED
2 MEDIUM ZUCCHINI (8 OUNCES EACH), CUT INTO 1½-INCH CHUNKS	
1 BUNCH GREEN ONIONS, CUT INTO 1-INCH PIECES	3 TABLESPOONS SEASONED RICE VINEGAR
1½ TEASPOONS SALT	1 TABLESPOON ASIAN SESAME OIL
	½ TEASPOON SUGAR

1 In 3-quart saucepan over high heat, bring 1 *inch water* to boil. Add broccoli and return to boiling. Reduce heat to low; cover and simmer until broccoli is just tender-crisp, 4 to 5 minutes. Drain.

2 In nonstick 12-inch skillet, place 1 tablespoon olive oil over medium-high heat, until hot. Add zucchini, green onions, and ¼ teaspoon salt and cook until vegetables are golden and tender-crisp, stirring frequently; with slotted spoon, remove to bowl.

3 Add remaining 1 tablespoon olive oil to skillet and heat until hot. Add asparagus, snap peas, and ¼ teaspoon salt and cook until vegetables are golden and tender-crisp, stirring frequently.

4 In cup, mix vinegar, sesame oil, sugar, and remaining 1 teaspoon salt. Add zucchini, green onions, and broccoli to vegetables in skillet. Stir in sesame vinaigrette, tossing to coat vegetables well; heat through. Serve warm. Or cover and refrigerate to serve cold later.

PER SERVING. 3G PROTEIN | 10G CARBOHYDRATE | 4G TOTAL FAT (0G SATURATED) 3G FIBER | 0MG CHOLESTEROL | 465MG SODIUM

GREEN BEANS WITH MIXED MUSHROOMS

This simple side borrows the basic flavors of a casserole, but features the grabbed-from-the-garden goodness of field-picked beans, thin-sliced onions, and earthy creminis and shiitakes.

ACTIVE TIME: 30 MINUTES · **TOTAL TIME:** 45 MINUTES
MAKES: 6 SIDE-DISH SERVINGS

---

1 TABLESPOON OLIVE OIL

2 SPRIGS FRESH THYME

1 LARGE ONION (12 OUNCES), THINLY SLICED

1 GARLIC CLOVE, CRUSHED WITH GARLIC PRESS

4 OUNCES CREMINI MUSHROOMS, THINLY SLICED

4 OUNCES SHIITAKE MUSHROOMS, STEMS DISCARDED, THINLY SLICED

1¼ TEASPOONS SALT

¼ TEASPOON GROUND BLACK PEPPER

1½ POUNDS GREEN BEANS, TRIMMED

1 Heat covered 5- to 6-quart saucepot of *water* to boiling over high heat.

2 Meanwhile, in 12-inch skillet, heat oil over medium-high heat. Add thyme and onion; cook 10 to 12 minutes or until browned and very tender, stirring occasionally. Stir in garlic and cook 1 minute. Add all mushrooms and cook 5 minutes or until tender, stirring occasionally. Stir in ¼ teaspoon each salt and pepper. Remove and discard thyme.

3 Add green beans and remaining 1 teaspoon salt to boiling water. Cook, uncovered, 8 to 9 minutes or until tender, stirring occasionally. Drain and rinse with cold water. If making ahead, transfer mushroom mixture to medium bowl. Cover; refrigerate up to overnight. Transfer beans to zip-tight plastic bag; refrigerate up to overnight.

4 When ready to serve, return green beans to saucepot and add mushroom mixture, stirring to combine. Cook over medium heat until beans are heated through, stirring occasionally.

80
CALORIES

PER SERVING. 3G PROTEIN | 14G CARBOHYDRATE | 3G TOTAL FAT (0G SATURATED) 4G FIBER | 0MG CHOLESTEROL | 125MG SODIUM 🔵 Ⓥ ❤️ 🟩

MESCLUN WITH PEARS AND PUMPKIN SEEDS

We love slicing pears into autumn salads: The fruit's honeyed juiciness partners perfectly with greens. Instead of the more classic pecans, here we've swapped in toasted pumpkin seeds, or pepitas, which have become a supermarket staple in recent years.

TOTAL TIME: 10 MINUTES

MAKES: 6 SIDE-DISH SERVINGS

2   TABLESPOONS PUMPKIN SEEDS (PEPITAS)

1½ TABLESPOONS APPLE CIDER VINEGAR

½   TABLESPOON DIJON MUSTARD

1   TEASPOON HONEY OR AGAVE NECTAR (SEE TIP)

2   TABLESPOONS EXTRA-VIRGIN OLIVE OIL

2   RIPE RED PEARS, CORED AND THINLY SLICED

1   PACKAGE (5 OUNCES) MIXED BABY GREENS

⅛   TEASPOON SALT

⅛   TEASPOON GROUND BLACK PEPPER

1 In skillet, heat pumpkin seeds over medium heat 2 to 3 minutes or until all are toasted and some start to pop. Cool completely. Toasted seeds can be stored in airtight container up to 1 week.

2 In small bowl, with wire whisk, combine vinegar, Dijon, and honey until blended. Continue whisking and add oil in slow, steady stream. Whisk until well blended and emulsified. Dressing can be made ahead; cover tightly and refrigerate up to 3 days.

3 In large bowl, combine sliced pears, greens, pumpkin seeds, dressing, salt, and pepper. Toss until evenly coated (see Tip).

TIP Agave nectar is a delicious vegan sweetener derived from the agave, a desert plant. You can combine the dressing and pears up to 1 hour before serving to prevent the pears from turning brown. When you're ready to serve, toss in the greens, pumpkin seeds, and seasonings.

100 CALORIES — **PER SERVING.** 1G PROTEIN | 9G CARBOHYDRATE | 7G TOTAL FAT (1G SATURATED) 2G FIBER | 0MG CHOLESTEROL | 85MG SODIUM 🔵 Ⓥ ❤️ 🧺

ROOT VEGETABLE GRATIN

Potatoes and vegetables fuse together and can be served as a satisfying meal or side dish in this recipe. This is delicious left over, but you also can easily cut the recipe in half.

ACTIVE TIME: 35 MINUTES · **TOTAL TIME:** 2 HOURS PLUS STANDING
MAKES: 16 SIDE-DISH SERVINGS

¾ CUP CANNED OR HOMEMADE VEGETABLE BROTH (PAGE 183)

2 TABLESPOONS BUTTER OR MARGARINE

1½ POUNDS RUSSET (BAKING) POTATOES (3 MEDIUM), PEELED AND THINLY SLICED

1½ POUNDS SWEET POTATOES (3 SMALL), PEELED AND THINLY SLICED

1 POUND CELERY ROOT (1 LARGE OR 2 SMALL), TRIMMED, PEELED, QUARTERED, AND THINLY SLICED

1 POUND PARSNIPS (6 MEDIUM), PEELED AND THINLY SLICED

1¼ TEASPOONS SALT

½ TEASPOON GROUND BLACK PEPPER

1 CUP HEAVY OR WHIPPING CREAM

2 TABLESPOONS SNIPPED FRESH CHIVES

1 Preheat oven to 400°F. In shallow 3½- to 4-quart baking pan or casserole, combine broth and butter; place in oven during preheating to melt butter, about 5 minutes.

2 Meanwhile, in large bowl, toss all potatoes, celery root, and parsnips with salt and pepper until well mixed.

3 Remove baking pan from oven. Add broth mixture to vegetables and stir to coat. Spoon vegetable mixture into baking pan; cover with foil and bake 40 minutes.

4 In 1-cup liquid measuring cup, warm cream in microwave on High for 45 seconds. Pour cream evenly over vegetables. (If making ahead, see Tip.)

5 Return baking pan to oven and bake, uncovered, 30 to 35 minutes longer or until top is golden and vegetables are fork-tender. Let stand 10 minutes, then sprinkle with chives to serve.

TIP To make the gratin ahead, prepare and bake the recipe through step 4; refrigerate it for up to two days. When you're ready to continue, bake it, uncovered, as described in step 5, on the bottom rack of the oven, increasing the final baking time to 55 minutes. Snip the chives for garnish a day ahead and store them in the fridge in plastic wrap.

145 CALORIES

PER SERVING. 2G PROTEIN | 19G CARBOHYDRATE | 7G TOTAL FAT (4G SATURATED) 3G FIBER | 21MG CHOLESTEROL | 255MG SODIUM ❤️ 🍱

ARTICHOKES WITH CREAMY LEMON SAUCE

Artichokes and lemon are a classic combination—enjoy them in this light and easy side dish.

ACTIVE TIME: 10 MINUTES · **TOTAL TIME:** 45 MINUTES
MAKES: 4 SIDE-DISH SERVINGS

Fill 6-quart saucepot with *1 inch water* and place steamer insert in pot. Heat to boiling over high heat; reduce heat to medium. Place **4 artichokes,** stems trimmed, stem side down in saucepot. Cover and steam 35 minutes or until knife pierces easily through base. Stir together ⅓ **cup each light mayonnaise and plain low-fat yogurt, ¼ cup snipped chives, 2 tablespoons each lemon juice and water, 1 tablespoon Dijon mustard,** and **¼ teaspoon salt.** Serve artichokes with sauce.

145
CALORIES

PER SERVING. 5G PROTEIN | 19G CARBOHYDRATE | 7G TOTAL FAT (1G SATURATED)
10G FIBER | 8MG CHOLESTEROL | 475MG SODIUM 🌱

CRUNCHY PEANUT BROCCOLI

This dish takes simple steamed broccoli to a gourmet level.

ACTIVE TIME: 20 MINUTES · **TOTAL TIME:** 30 MINUTES
MAKES: 4 SIDE-DISH SERVINGS

Heat large covered saucepot of **water** to boiling. Fill large bowl with **ice and water.** Add **1 teaspoon salt,** then **1 pound broccoli flowerets,** to boiling water. Cook uncovered 3 to 4 minutes or until crisp-tender. Drain and transfer to ice water. When cool, drain well and place between paper towels to dry. Broccoli can be refrigerated in airtight container up to overnight.

In 12-inch skillet, combine **2 tablespoons vegetable oil** and ¼ **cup chopped roasted unsalted peanuts.** Cook over medium heat 4 minutes or until nuts are golden, stirring occasionally. Stir in **1 small chopped shallot** and cook 1 minute. Stir in **1 teaspoon reduced-sodium soy sauce,** then broccoli. Sprinkle with ¼ **teaspoon each salt and ground black pepper.** Cook 2 minutes or until broccoli is heated through and evenly coated with nut mixture, stirring and tossing. Garnish with the thinly sliced green parts of **1 green onion.**

PER SERVING. 6G PROTEIN | 9G CARBOHYDRATE | 12G TOTAL FAT (1G SATURATED) 4G FIBER | 0MG CHOLESTEROL | 300MG SODIUM

HEALTHY MAKEOVER POTATO SALAD

Our healthy take on classic potato salad just might become your favorite summertime-picnic recipe. This slimmed-down salad (minus 50 calories and 7 fat grams per serving) has just the right level of tangy flavor and no gloppiness. We used light mayo (and less of it than in our traditional recipe) and swapped whole milk with low-fat buttermilk to keep it moist.

ACTIVE TIME: 10 MINUTES · **TOTAL TIME:** 35 MINUTES PLUS CHILLING
MAKES: 6 CUPS OR 10 SIDE-DISH SERVINGS

- 3 POUNDS YUKON GOLD POTATOES, PEELED AND CUT INTO 1-INCH CHUNKS
- 1¼ TEASPOONS SALT
- ¾ CUP BUTTERMILK
- ¼ CUP LIGHT MAYONNAISE
- 2 TABLESPOONS SNIPPED FRESH DILL
- 2 TABLESPOONS CIDER VINEGAR
- 1 TABLESPOON DIJON MUSTARD
- 2 GREEN ONIONS, THINLY SLICED
- ¼ TEASPOON COARSELY GROUND BLACK PEPPER

1 In 4-quart saucepan, combine potatoes, 1 teaspoon salt, and enough *water to cover*; heat to boiling over high heat. Reduce heat to medium-low; cover and simmer 10 minutes or until potatoes are just fork-tender.
2 Meanwhile, in large bowl, whisk buttermilk with mayonnaise, dill, vinegar, Dijon, green onions, remaining ¼ teaspoon salt, and pepper.
3 Drain potatoes well. Toss hot potatoes with buttermilk dressing until coated; mixture will look very loose before chilling. Cover and refrigerate potato salad at least 2 hours or overnight to blend flavors and cool slightly, stirring gently after 1 hour.

150 CALORIES

PER SERVING. 3G PROTEIN | 29G CARBOHYDRATE | 2G TOTAL FAT (0G SATURATED) 2G FIBER | 3MG CHOLESTEROL | 200MG SODIUM ❤️

BROCCOLI MAC AND CHEESE

A classic mac and cheese is made healthier—and more colorful—with broccoli florets and a sprinkling of whole-wheat breadcrumbs. You can also double the recipe and serve it as a main dish.

ACTIVE TIME: 26 MINUTES · **TOTAL TIME:** 40 MINUTES

MAKES: 8 SIDE-DISH SERVINGS

1 SLICE WHOLE-WHEAT BREAD	½ BOX (8 OUNCES) ELBOW MACARONI
4 OUNCES REDUCED-FAT EXTRA-SHARP CHEDDAR CHEESE, SHREDDED (1¼ CUPS)	⅛ TEASPOON SALT
	¼ TEASPOON FRESHLY GROUND PEPPER
1 TABLESPOON CORNSTARCH	½ POUND SMALL BROCCOLI FLORETS
1⅔ CUP LOW-FAT MILK (1%)	PINCH FRESHLY GRATED NUTMEG
3 OUNCES GOUDA CHEESE, SHREDDED (1 CUP)	

1 Heat covered 8-quart saucepot with 6 *quarts water* to boiling on high.

2 Arrange oven rack 6 inches from broiler heat source. Preheat broiler. Tear bread into large chunks. In food processor with knife blade attached, pulse bread until crumbs form. In small bowl, combine breadcrumbs and ¼ cup shredded Cheddar.

3 Meanwhile, in 3½- to 4-quart saucepot, whisk together cornstarch and 2 tablespoons milk. Heat on medium-high, gradually adding remaining milk in a slow, steady stream, whisking constantly. Heat to boiling, whisking frequently, then cook 2 minutes longer, whisking constantly. Remove saucepot from heat and add Gouda and remaining Cheddar, stirring until cheeses are melted and sauce is smooth.

4 Add macaroni and ½ teaspoon salt to boiling water. Cook 1 minute, stirring occasionally, then add the broccoli. Cook 4 to 5 minutes longer or until pasta is just tender but firm and broccoli is bright green and crisp-tender, stirring occasionally. Drain well, then immediately return to saucepot. Add sauce, nutmeg, remaining ⅛ teaspoon salt, and ¼ teaspoon pepper, stir over medium-low heat until well mixed.

5 Transfer mixture to 3-quart shallow baking dish. Sprinkle breadcrumb mixture evenly over top. Broil 1 to 2 minutes or until topping is golden brown.

180 CALORIES

PER SERVING. 11G PROTEIN | 28G CARBOHYDRATE | 6G TOTAL FAT (3G SATURATED) 3G FIBER | 18MG CHOLESTEROL | 245MG SODIUM

145
CALORIES

Peach, Cucumber, and
Barley Salad
(page 274)

GET YOUR GRAINS

We've all heard about the health benefits of whole grains—how eating three servings a day of these "good carbs" can reduce our chances of stroke, heart disease, and type 2 diabetes. But if you're unsure how to incorporate their heart-healthy goodness into your daily meals, we provide plenty of easy, delicious possibilities. From salads featuring barley, wheat-berries, and bulgur to cornbread, whole-wheat biscuits, and two kinds of whole-grain muffins, these sides will help ensure that you and your family get your daily grains. To familiarize yourself with the many whole grains now available in most supermarkets, see "The Vegetarian Pantry" on page 158 for a glossary of grains.

KEY TO ICONS

🔵 30 minutes or less 🟢 Vegan ❤️ Heart healthy 🌾 High fiber 🟩 Make ahead

DOUBLE CORNBREAD

Adding whole corn kernels enhances the texture and flavor of hearty cornbread, which is a terrific item to make ahead. You can freeze the baked cornbread, tightly wrapped, for up to 1 month. When you're ready to serve it, thaw it completely, then reheat it, covered, at 450°F for 15 minutes—it'll come out tasting as fresh as the day you first made it.

ACTIVE TIME: 20 MINUTES · **TOTAL TIME:** 40 MINUTES
MAKES: 24 SIDE-DISH SERVINGS

1½ CUPS ALL-PURPOSE FLOUR

1½ CUPS YELLOW CORNMEAL

¼ CUP SUGAR

4 TEASPOONS BAKING POWDER

½ TEASPOON BAKING SODA

1 TEASPOON SALT

2½ CUPS BUTTERMILK

3 LARGE EGGS

1 PACKAGE (10 OUNCES) FROZEN CORN, THAWED

6 TABLESPOONS BUTTER OR MARGARINE, MELTED

2 JALAPEÑO CHILES, SEEDS AND MEMBRANES DISCARDED, FINELY CHOPPED

1 Preheat oven to 450°F. Grease 13" by 9" metal baking pan.

2 In large bowl, combine flour, cornmeal, sugar, baking powder, baking soda, and salt. In medium bowl, with wire whisk or fork, beat buttermilk and eggs until blended.

3 Add corn, melted butter, and jalapeños to buttermilk mixture; then add to flour mixture. Stir until ingredients are just mixed.

4 Pour batter into prepared pan. Bake 22 to 25 minutes or until golden at edges and toothpick inserted in center comes out clean. Cut lengthwise into 4 strips, then cut each strip crosswise into 6 pieces. Serve warm.

125 CALORIES

PER SERVING. 4G PROTEIN | 19G CARBOHYDRATE | 4G TOTAL FAT (2G SATURATED) 1G FIBER | 36MG CHOLESTEROL | 255MG SODIUM ♥ 🗑

WHOLE-WHEAT SESAME BISCUITS

We blended whole-wheat flour with toasted sesame seeds to make these light golden rounds.

ACTIVE TIME: 15 MINUTES · **TOTAL TIME:** 30 MINUTES
MAKES: 12 BISCUITS

2   TABLESPOONS SESAME SEEDS

1   CUP WHOLE-WHEAT FLOUR

1   CUP ALL-PURPOSE FLOUR

1   TABLESPOON BAKING POWDER

¾   TEASPOON SALT

4   TABLESPOONS COLD BUTTER OR MARGARINE

¾   CUP PLUS 3 TABLESPOONS MILK

1 In small skillet, toast sesame seeds over medium heat until lightly browned, about 5 minutes, stirring occasionally.

2 Preheat oven to 425°F. Lightly grease large cookie sheet.

3 In large bowl, mix whole-wheat and all-purpose flours, baking powder, salt, and 5 teaspoons toasted sesame seeds. With pastry blender or two knives used scissor-fashion, cut in butter until mixture resembles coarse crumbs. Stir in ¾ cup plus 2 tablespoons milk, stirring just until mixture forms a soft dough that leaves sides of bowl.

4 Turn dough onto lightly floured surface; knead 8 to 10 strokes to mix thoroughly. With floured rolling pin, roll dough ½ inch thick

5 With floured 2½-inch round biscuit cutter, cut out biscuits. Place biscuits about 2 inches apart on cookie sheet. Press trimmings together; roll out and cut again.

6 Brush tops of biscuits with remaining 1 tablespoon milk; sprinkle with remaining 1 teaspoon sesame seeds. Bake until golden, 12 to 15 minutes.

125 CALORIES

PER BISCUIT. 3G PROTEIN | 17G CARBOHYDRATE | 6G TOTAL FAT (1G SATURATED) 2G FIBER | 3MG CHOLESTEROL | 285MG SODIUM ❤️ 🍱

WHEAT-BERRY SALAD WITH DRIED CHERRIES

This salad is a wonderful mix of textures and flavors: Chewy, nutty wheat berries, tart dried cherries, and crunchy celery are dressed with a sweet and tangy vinaigrette.

ACTIVE TIME: 15 MINUTES · **TOTAL TIME:** 1 HOUR 45 MINUTES
MAKES: 12 SIDE-DISH SERVINGS

2 CUPS WHEAT BERRIES (WHOLE-WHEAT KERNELS)

8 CUPS WATER

1 LARGE SHALLOT, MINCED

3 TABLESPOONS FRESH LEMON JUICE

1 TABLESPOON DIJON MUSTARD

1 TABLESPOON OLIVE OIL

2 TEASPOONS HONEY OR AGAVE NECTAR (SEE TIP, PAGE 260)

1½ TEASPOONS SALT

½ TEASPOON COARSELY GROUND BLACK PEPPER

3 STALKS CELERY, CUT INTO ¼-INCH DICE

¾ CUP DRIED TART CHERRIES, CHOPPED

½ CUP CHOPPED FRESH FLAT-LEAF PARSLEY PLUS ADDITIONAL SPRIGS FOR GARNISH

LETTUCE LEAVES

1 In 4-quart saucepan, heat wheat berries and water to boiling over high heat. Reduce heat to low; cover and simmer until wheat berries are just tender but still firm to the bite, about 1½ hours.

2 Meanwhile, in large bowl, with wire whisk or fork, mix shallot, lemon juice, mustard, oil, honey, salt, and pepper.

3 When wheat berries are cooked, drain well. Add warm wheat berries to dressing with celery, cherries, and chopped parsley; toss well. Serve salad on lettuce leaves at room temperature, or cover and refrigerate until ready to serve. Garnish with parsley sprigs.

130 CALORIES

PER SERVING. 4G PROTEIN | 26G CARBOHYDRATE | 2G TOTAL FAT (0G SATURATED) 6G FIBER | 0MG CHOLESTEROL | 310MG SODIUM

BRAN MUFFINS

These healthful fiber-packed muffins are sweetly flavored with a hint of molasses. Try our tasty banana and toasted wheat germ variation.

ACTIVE TIME: 15 MINUTES · **TOTAL TIME:** 35 MINUTES
MAKES: 12 MUFFINS

1½ CUPS ORIGINAL WHOLE-BRAN CEREAL (NOT BRAN FLAKES)
1 CUP LOW-FAT MILK (1%)
¼ CUP VEGETABLE OIL
¼ CUP LIGHT (MILD) MOLASSES
1 LARGE EGG

1 CUP ALL-PURPOSE FLOUR
¼ CUP SUGAR
2 TEASPOONS BAKING POWDER
½ TEASPOON SALT
¼ TEASPOON BAKING SODA

1 Preheat oven to 400°F. Grease twelve 2½-inch muffin-pan cups.
2 In medium bowl, with fork, mix bran cereal with milk, oil, molasses, and egg until blended; let stand 10 minutes.
3 Meanwhile, in large bowl, combine flour, sugar, baking powder, salt, and baking soda.
4 Add liquid mixture to flour mixture; stir just until flour is evenly moistened. Spoon batter into prepared muffin-pan cups.
5 Bake until toothpick inserted in center of muffin comes out clean, 18 to 20 minutes. Immediately remove muffins from pan. Serve warm, or cool on wire rack to serve later.

 140 CALORIES

PER MUFFIN. 3G PROTEIN | 22G CARBOHYDRATE | 6G TOTAL FAT (1G SATURATED) 3G FIBER | 19MG CHOLESTEROL | 205MG SODIUM ♥ 🍱

BANANA–WHEAT GERM BRAN MUFFINS

Prepare Bran Muffins as instructed above but use only **¾ cup milk,** add **¼ teaspoon ground cinnamon** to flour mixture, and fold **1 mashed medium banana (about ½ cup)** and **2 tablespoons honey-toasted wheat germ** into batter before spooning into muffin cups.

 150 CALORIES

PER MUFFIN. 4G PROTEIN | 25G CARBOHYDRATE | 6G TOTAL FAT (1G SATURATED) 4G FIBER | 18MG CHOLESTEROL | 205MG SODIUM ♥ 🍱

PEACH, CUCUMBER, AND BARLEY SALAD

Juicy, just-picked peaches play off the pearl barley, garbanzo beans, and cucumbers in this filling, supper-worthy salad. Double the portion and serve over a bed of Boston lettuce leaves for a colorful and cooling meal. For photo, see page 268.

ACTIVE TIME: 20 MINUTES · **TOTAL TIME:** 50 MINUTES
MAKES: 10 FIRST-COURSE SERVINGS

1 CUP PEARL BARLEY	2 RIPE PEACHES, CHOPPED INTO ¼-INCH PIECES
1 CAN (14½ OUNCES) REDUCED-SODIUM VEGETABLE BROTH OR 1¾ CUPS HOMEMADE BROTH (PAGE 183)	2 PINTS CHERRY TOMATOES, CUT INTO QUARTERS
1¼ CUPS WATER	½ CUP PACKED FRESH BASIL LEAVES, VERY FINELY CHOPPED
2 TABLESPOONS CIDER VINEGAR	
1 TABLESPOON VEGETABLE OIL	1 CAN (15-OUNCE) CHICKPEAS (GARBANZO BEANS), RINSED AND DRAINED
¼ TEASPOON SALT	
1 ENGLISH (SEEDLESS) CUCUMBER, CHOPPED INTO ¼-INCH PIECES	1 HEAD BOSTON LETTUCE, LEAVES SEPARATED

1   Place barley in 4-quart saucepan. Cook over medium heat 5 minutes or until toasted, stirring. Stir in broth and water. Heat to boiling over high heat. Cover, reduce heat to low, and simmer 35 minutes or until tender. Drain if necessary and cool slightly.

2   Meanwhile, in large bowl, whisk vinegar, oil, and salt. Add barley and toss until well coated. Cool until no longer hot, then add cucumber, peaches, tomatoes, basil, and chickpeas, tossing until well combined. Serve over lettuce leaves.

145 CALORIES

PER SERVING. 5G PROTEIN | 28G CARBOHYDRATE | 2G TOTAL FAT (0G SATURATED) 6G FIBER | 0MG CHOLESTEROL | 206MG SODIUM

MILLET WITH CORN AND GREEN CHILES

Millet has a mild flavor that is greatly enhanced by pan-toasting it first. For an extra shot of flavor, serve this topped with a dollop of nonfat Greek yogurt and your favorite salsa.

ACTIVE TIME: 15 MINUTES · **TOTAL TIME:** 50 MINUTES PLUS STANDING
MAKES: 8 SIDE-DISH SERVINGS

1 CUP MILLET	1 TEASPOON GROUND CUMIN
2 CUPS FRESH CORN KERNELS (CUT FROM 4 EARS) OR FROZEN CORN KERNELS	3½ CUPS WATER
	1 CAN (4½ OUNCES) DICED GREEN CHILES, DRAINED
2 TEASPOONS VEGETABLE OIL	½ TEASPOON SALT
1 MEDIUM ONION, CHOPPED	¼ CUP LIGHTLY PACKED FRESH CILANTRO LEAVES, CHOPPED (OPTIONAL)
1 GARLIC CLOVE, CRUSHED WITH GARLIC PRESS	

1 In large skillet, toast millet over medium heat, about 5 minutes, stirring frequently. Pour millet into bowl and set aside.

2 Add corn to dry skillet and cook over high heat until corn browns, about 5 minutes, stirring frequently. Transfer corn to plate.

3 In same skillet, heat oil over medium heat. Add onion; cook until softened, about 5 minutes. Stir in garlic and cumin and cook until fragrant, about 1 minute. Add water, green chiles, and salt. Heat to boiling. Stir in millet. Reduce heat; cover and simmer until millet is tender and water is absorbed, 25 to 30 minutes.

4 Remove skillet from heat, stir in corn; cover and let stand 5 minutes to heat through. Stir in cilantro if using.

150 CALORIES

PER SERVING. 4G PROTEIN | 29G CARBOHYDRATE | 3G TOTAL FAT (0G SATURATED) 4G FIBER | 0MG CHOLESTEROL | 200MG SODIUM

CHUNKY VEGETABLE BULGUR SALAD

Reminiscent of tabbouleh, this healthy whole-grain salad also contains cherry tomatoes and two kinds of summer squash.

ACTIVE TIME: 20 MINUTES · **TOTAL TIME:** 20 MINUTES PLUS STANDING
MAKES: 8 SIDE-DISH SERVINGS

2   CUPS BULGUR

2½ CUPS BOILING WATER

2   LEMONS

1   TABLESPOON OLIVE OIL

1   SMALL RED ONION, FINELY CHOPPED

1   CUP CHERRY TOMATOES, EACH CUT IN HALF

1   MEDIUM ZUCCHINI (8 TO 10 OUNCES), CHOPPED

1   MEDIUM YELLOW SUMMER SQUASH (8 TO 10 OUNCES), CHOPPED

½   CUP LOOSELY PACKED FRESH MINT LEAVES, CHOPPED

½   CUP LOOSELY PACKED FRESH PARSLEY LEAVES, CHOPPED

½   TEASPOON SALT

¼   TEASPOON COARSELY GROUND BLACK PEPPER

1 In large bowl, stir together bulgur and boiling water. Cover and let stand until liquid is absorbed, about 30 minutes.

2 Meanwhile, from lemons, grate 1 teaspoon peel and squeeze ¼ cup juice; set aside.

3 In 12-inch skillet, heat oil over medium-high heat until hot. Add onion and cook until it begins to soften, 3 to 4 minutes. Add tomatoes, zucchini, and squash, and cook until vegetables are tender, 6 to 8 minutes, stirring occasionally.

4 Stir vegetables into bulgur with lemon peel and juice, mint, parsley, salt, and pepper. If not serving right away, refrigerate in airtight container up to 1 day.

160 CALORIES | **PER SERVING.** 6G PROTEIN | 32G CARBOHYDRATE | 2G TOTAL FAT (0G SATURATED) 8G FIBER | 0MG CHOLESTEROL | 160MG SODIUM

POPOVERS

These irresistible rolls are crispy on the outside and hollow on the inside. Serve them fresh from the oven as an accompaniment or fill with one of our grain or green salads. You can make them ahead and reheat in a 400°F oven for 15 minutes.

ACTIVE TIME: 10 MINUTES · **TOTAL TIME:** 1 HOUR 10 MINUTES
MAKES: 8 POPOVERS

3   LARGE EGGS

1   CUP MILK

3   TABLESPOONS BUTTER OR
    MARGARINE, MELTED

1   CUP ALL-PURPOSE FLOUR

½   TEASPOON SALT

1   Preheat oven to 375°F. Generously grease eight 6-ounce custard cups or twelve 2½" by 1¼" muffin-pan cups with butter or vegetable oil. Place custard cups in jelly-roll pan for easier handling.

2   In blender, combine eggs, milk, butter, flour, and salt; blend until smooth.

3   Pour about ⅓ cup batter into each prepared custard cup, or fill muffin-pan cups half full. Bake 50 minutes, then, with tip of knife, quickly cut small slit in top of each popover to release steam; bake 10 minutes longer. Immediately remove popovers from cups, loosening with spatula if necessary. Serve hot.

160
CALORIES   **EACH POPOVER.** 5G PROTEIN | 14G CARBOHYDRATE | 9G TOTAL FAT (5G SATURATED) 0G FIBER | 101MG CHOLESTEROL | 247MG SODIUM

COUSCOUS FOUR WAYS

Couscous, or Moroccan pasta, is the perfect side for a busy weekday meal, taking all of ten minutes to put together from start to finish. It's satisfying as is, but it only takes another couple of minutes to put your own personal spin on it. Try one of our three flavor variations, then let your own imagination guide you. Start with 1 cup of whole-wheat couscous and prepare it according to package instructions, but omit any added butter. Makes 4 side-dish servings.

 170 CALORIES   **PER SERVING.** 7G PROTEIN | 37G CARBOHYDRATE | 0G TOTAL FAT | 6G FIBER 0MG CHOLESTEROL | 290MG SODIUM 🔵 Ⓥ ❤️ 🌾

LIME COUSCOUS

Add **1 tablespoon fresh lime juice** and **1 teaspoon freshly grated lime peel** to water when preparing couscous.

 170 CALORIES   **PER SERVING.** 7G PROTEIN | 37G CARBOHYDRATE | 0G TOTAL FAT | 6G FIBER 0MG CHOLESTEROL | 290MG SODIUM 🔵 Ⓥ ❤️ 🌾

SUN-DRIED TOMATO AND GREEN ONION COUSCOUS

Add **1 sliced medium green onion** and **5 chopped sun-dried tomato halves** to water when preparing couscous.

 180 CALORIES   **PER SERVING.** 7G PROTEIN | 38G CARBOHYDRATE | 1G TOTAL FAT (0G SATURATED) | 6G FIBER | 0MG CHOLESTEROL | 300MG SODIUM 🔵 Ⓥ ❤️ 🌾

MOROCCAN COUSCOUS

Add ¼ **cup golden raisins,** ¼ **teaspoon ground cinnamon,** ¼ **teaspoon ground turmeric,** and ¼ **teaspoon ground cumin** to water when preparing couscous.

 205 CALORIES   **PER SERVING.** 7G PROTEIN | 45G CARBOHYDRATE | 1G TOTAL FAT (0G SATURATED) | 7G FIBER | 0MG CHOLESTEROL | 290MG SODIUM 🔵 Ⓥ ❤️ 🌾

WHOLE-GRAIN BLUEBERRY MUFFINS

Deliciously dense, these muffins are made with a combination of regular all-purpose flour, whole-wheat flour, and old-fashioned oats for the optimum blend of flavor and healthful benefits.

ACTIVE TIME: 20 MINUTES · **TOTAL TIME:** 40 MINUTES

MAKES: 12 MUFFINS

1   CUP OLD-FASHIONED OATS, UNCOOKED

1   CUP WHOLE-WHEAT FLOUR

½   CUP ALL-PURPOSE FLOUR

2   TEASPOONS BAKING POWDER

½   TEASPOON BAKING SODA

½   TEASPOON SALT

5   TABLESPOONS PACKED BROWN SUGAR

1   CUP LOW-FAT BUTTERMILK

¼   CUP FRESH ORANGE JUICE

2   TABLESPOONS CANOLA OIL

1   LARGE EGG

1   TEASPOON VANILLA EXTRACT

2   CUPS BLUEBERRIES

¼   CUP NATURAL ALMONDS, CHOPPED

1   Preheat oven to 400°F. Line 12-cup muffin pan with paper liners.

2   Grind oats in blender. In bowl, whisk oats, flours, baking powder and soda, salt, and ¼ cup sugar. In small bowl, whisk buttermilk, juice, oil, egg, and vanilla. Stir into flour mixture; fold in blueberries.

3   Combine nuts and remaining 1 tablespoon sugar. Spoon batter into pan; sprinkle with almond sugar. Bake 22 minutes or until toothpick inserted in center of muffin comes out clean. Cool in pan on wire rack 5 minutes. Remove from pan; cool completely.

170 CALORIES **PER MUFFIN.** 5G PROTEIN | 28G CARBOHYDRATE | 5G TOTAL FAT (1G SATURATED) 3G FIBER | 16MG CHOLESTEROL | 270MG SODIUM ❤ 🧺

130 CALORIES

*Peachy Frozen Yogurt
(page 287)*

SWEET & FRUITY TREATS

We've decided to put the spotlight on fruit because, in general, fruit is high in vitamin C and a good source of dietary fiber. And, if you eat fruits in season throughout the year, you'll get a rotating roster of nutritional highs—including a range of vitamins and antioxidants—and satisfy your sweet tooth, too. For your dessert add-ons, enjoy fresh fruit sliced in a parfait or fruit salad, dried fruit mixed into cookies, or apples and bananas broiled or baked. Or for something new, sample our pretty-in-pink Watermelon Slushie or our delectable Stuffed Fresh Figs.

KEY TO ICONS

🔵 30 minutes or less   🟢 Vegan   ❤️ Heart healthy   🌾 High fiber   🟩 Make ahead

CHOCOLATE-ALMOND MERINGUES

These dainty meringues are dipped first in bittersweet chocolate, then in roasted salted almonds. The results? Heavenly.

ACTIVE TIME: 40 MINUTES · **TOTAL TIME:** 2 HOURS 10 MINUTES PLUS STANDING
MAKES: ABOUT 54 COOKIES

3	LARGE EGG WHITES	½	CUP SUGAR
¼	TEASPOON ALMOND EXTRACT	¾	CUP ROASTED SALTED ALMONDS
⅛	TEASPOON CREAM OF TARTAR	5	SQUARES (5 OUNCES) BITTERSWEET CHOCOLATE, CHOPPED
PINCH SALT			

1 Preheat oven to 200°F. Line two cookie sheets with parchment paper.

2 In medium bowl, with mixer on high speed, beat egg whites, almond extract, cream of tartar, and salt until soft peaks form. With mixer running, sprinkle in sugar, 2 tablespoons at a time, beating until sugar dissolves and meringue stands in stiff, glossy peaks when beaters are lifted.

3 Spoon meringue into large decorating bag fitted with ¾-inch round tip, or into large zip-tight plastic bag with small hole cut in one corner. Pipe meringue into 1-inch rounds, about 1 inch apart, on prepared cookie sheets.

4 Bake until crisp but not brown, 1 hour 30 minutes to 1 hour 40 minutes, rotating cookie sheets between upper and lower oven racks halfway through.

5 Cool meringues completely on cookie sheets on wire racks.

6 Meanwhile, in food processor, pulse almonds until chopped; place on plate. In small microwave-safe bowl, microwave chocolate on Medium for 1 minute 30 seconds or until melted, stirring every 30 seconds.

7 Line large jelly-roll pan with parchment paper. Dip bottom third of each meringue in chocolate, then almonds. Place meringues on prepared pan; let stand until set, about 1 hour.

8 Store cookies, with waxed paper between layers, in airtight container at room temperature up to 3 days or in freezer up to 1 month.

---

35 CALORIES

PER COOKIE. 1G PROTEIN | 4G CARBOHYDRATE | 2G TOTAL FAT (1G SATURATED) 0G FIBER | 0MG CHOLESTEROL | 10MG SODIUM ❤️ 🧺

HEALTHY MAKEOVER OATMEAL-RAISIN COOKIES

If you thought the words "delicious" and "low-fat" could never be used to describe the same cookie, think again. This one's chewy and sweet, yet it has only 2 grams of fat per cookie.

ACTIVE TIME: 15 MINUTES · **TOTAL TIME:** 10 MINUTES PER BATCH
MAKES: ABOUT 48 COOKIES

2	CUPS ALL-PURPOSE FLOUR	2	LARGE EGG WHITES
1	TEASPOON BAKING SODA	1	LARGE EGG
½	TEASPOON SALT	2	TEASPOONS VANILLA EXTRACT
½	CUP (1 STICK) LIGHT CORN-OIL SPREAD (56 TO 60% FAT)	1	CUP QUICK-COOKING OATS, UNCOOKED
¾	CUP PACKED DARK BROWN SUGAR	½	CUP DARK SEEDLESS RAISINS
½	CUP GRANULATED SUGAR		

1 Preheat oven to 375°F. Grease two large cookie sheets. In medium bowl, combine flour, baking soda, and salt.

2 In large bowl, with mixer at low speed, beat corn-oil spread and both sugars until well combined. Increase speed to high; beat until mixture is light and fluffy. Add egg whites, whole egg, and vanilla; beat until blended. With wooden spoon, stir in flour mixture, oats, and raisins until combined.

3 Drop dough by level tablespoons, 2 inches apart, on prepared cookie sheets. Bake until golden, 10 to 12 minutes, rotating cookie sheets between upper and lower oven racks halfway through. With wide spatula, transfer cookies to wire racks to cool completely.

4 Repeat with remaining dough.

65 CALORIES **PER COOKIE.** 1G PROTEIN | 12G CARBOHYDRATE | 2G TOTAL FAT (0G SATURATED) 0G FIBER | 4MG CHOLESTEROL | 72MG SODIUM ❤️ 🥗

SLICED CITRUS WITH LIME SYRUP

Served on top of plain or vanilla yogurt, this versatile fruit dish is fabulous for breakfast or dessert. It's also a fun addition to a brunch buffet.

ACTIVE TIME: 20 MINUTES · **TOTAL TIME:** 25 MINUTES PLUS CHILLING
MAKES: 6 SERVINGS

From **1 or 2 lemons,** grate 1 teaspoon peel and squeeze 3 tablespoons juice. From **1 lime,** grate ½ teaspoon peel and squeeze 1 tablespoon juice. In 1-quart saucepan, combine juices and **½ cup sugar**; heat to boiling over medium-high heat. Reduce heat to low; simmer 1 minute. Stir in lemon and lime peels, cover, and refrigerate until cold. Meanwhile, cut peel and white pith from **2 navel oranges, 2 clementines,** and **2 red or white grape-fruit.** Slice all fruit crosswise into ¼-inch-thick rounds. Arrange slices on deep large platter. Spoon syrup over fruit. If not serving right away, cover and refrigerate up to 2 days.

 95 CALORIES **PER SERVING.** 1G PROTEIN | 24G CARBOHYDRATE | 0G TOTAL FAT | 3G FIBER | 0MG CHOLESTEROL | 1MG SODIUM ♥ Ⓥ 🥡

BERRIES IN RED WINE

A delectable summer dessert—mixed berries steeped in a sweet, cinnamon-scented red-wine syrup.

TOTAL TIME: 15 MINUTES PLUS CHILLING
MAKES: 5 CUPS OR 6 SERVINGS

In 1-quart saucepan, heat **⅓ cup sugar, 1 (3-inch-long) stick cinnamon,** and **½ cup red wine** such as Shiraz or Zinfandel to boiling over medium-high heat. Boil 2 minutes. Place **1 pound hulled strawberries** and **1 pint raspberries** in medium bowl. Pour **1½ cups wine** and wine mixture over berries. Cover mixture and refrigerate 1 to 3 hours to blend flavors. To serve, ladle berries with syrup into wine goblets or dessert bowls.

125 CALORIES

PER SERVING. 1G PROTEIN | 22G CARBOHYDRATE | 1G TOTAL FAT (0G SATURATED) 4G FIBER | 0MG CHOLESTEROL | 5MG SODIUM

PEACHY FROZEN YOGURT

Served as a fruity dessert or snack, our creamy Peachy Frozen Yogurt delivers a double dose of peach flavor and only 1 gram of fat per serving. For photo, see page 282. This formula works with other frozen fruit and fruit yogurt combos too—try cherry, raspberry, or strawberry.

TOTAL TIME: 5 MINUTES
MAKES: 2½ CUPS OR 4 SERVINGS

In food processor with knife blade attached, process **1 bag frozen sliced peaches (10 to 12 ounces)** until finely shaved. Add **2 containers (6 ounces each) low-fat peach yogurt** and **1 tablespoon sugar.** Process just until smooth. Serve immediately or, if not serving right away, pour into 9-inch square baking pan; cover and freeze no longer than 1 hour for best texture.

130 CALORIES

PER SERVING. 4G PROTEIN | 28G CARBOHYDRATE | 1G TOTAL FAT (1G SATURATED) 2G FIBER | 6MG CHOLESTEROL | 50MG SODIUM

140
CALORIES

Banana Berry
Parfaits
(opposite)

BANANA BERRY PARFAITS

This quick dessert looks sensational in an old-fashioned sundae glass.

TOTAL TIME: 10 MINUTES

MAKES: 4 SERVINGS

1¼ CUPS UNSWEETENED FROZEN RASPBERRIES, PARTIALLY THAWED

1 TABLESPOON SUGAR

2⅔ CUPS FAT-FREE VANILLA YOGURT

2 RIPE BANANAS, PEELED AND THINLY SLICED

FRESH RASPBERRIES FOR GARNISH (OPTIONAL)

1 In food processor with knife blade attached, pulse thawed raspberries and sugar until almost smooth.

2 Into four 10-ounce glasses or goblets, layer about half of berry puree, half of yogurt, and half of banana slices; repeat layering. Top with fresh raspberries, if you like.

140 CALORIES

PER SERVING. 6G PROTEIN | 30G CARBOHYDRATE | 0G TOTAL FAT (0G SATURATED) 2G FIBER | 3MG CHOLESTEROL | 95MG SODIUM

THREE-FRUIT SALAD WITH VANILLA SYRUP

Perfect alone or alongside pound cake. If you don't have a vanilla bean, stir ½ teaspoon vanilla extract into the chilled syrup.

ACTIVE TIME: 30 MINUTES · **TOTAL TIME:** 40 MINUTES PLUS CHILLING

MAKES: 12 SERVINGS

Use vegetable peeler to remove 1-inch-wide continuous strip of peel from **1 lemon,** then squeeze ¼ cup juice (**another lemon** may be needed). Cut **1 vanilla bean** lengthwise in half. With small knife, scrape seeds into 1-quart saucepan; drop pod into pan. Add lemon peel and ¾ **cup each water and sugar**; heat to boiling over high heat. Reduce heat to medium and cook until syrup thickens slightly, about 5 minutes. Pour mixture through sieve into small bowl; stir in lemon juice. Cover and refrigerate until chilled, about 2 hours. Peel and seed **3 ripe mangoes** and **1 medium honeydew** and cut into 1-inch pieces; hull **2 pints strawberries** and cut each in half or into quarters if large. Place fruit in large bowl, add syrup, and toss.

140 CALORIES

PER SERVING. 1G PROTEIN | 35G CARBOHYDRATE | 0G TOTAL FAT | 3G FIBER 0MG CHOLESTEROL | 13MG SODIUM

BROILED BROWN-SUGAR BANANAS

A sweet, satisfying dessert with just four basic ingredients.

ACTIVE TIME: 5 MINUTES · **TOTAL TIME:** 10 MINUTES
MAKES: 4 SERVINGS

Preheat broiler and place rack close to heat source. Cut **4 bananas,** with peels still on, almost in half lengthwise, taking care not to cut all the way through and leaving 1 inch uncut at ends. In cup, with fork, blend **2 tablespoons packed brown sugar, 1 tablespoon reduced-fat margarine,** and ⅛ **teaspoon ground cinnamon.** Place bananas, cut side up, on rack in broiling pan. Spoon sugar mixture over split bananas. Broil until browned, about 5 minutes. Serve in skins and use spoon to scoop out fruit.

150 CALORIES **PER SERVING.** 1G PROTEIN | 34G CARBOHYDRATE | 2G TOTAL FAT (1G SATURATED) 3G FIBER | 0MG CHOLESTEROL | 20MG SODIUM

STUFFED FRESH FIGS

Figs are a good source of dietary fiber and potassium, as well as being one of the best sources of phytosterols, plant nutrients that have been shown to help reduce cholesterol levels. And did we mention that they're delicious? When you're lucky enough to find ripe figs in your market, be sure to try this recipe.

TOTAL TIME: 25 MINUTES
MAKES: 6 SERVINGS

19 SMALL FRESH RIPE FIGS
(1¼ POUNDS; SEE TIP)

¼ CUP HONEY

½ CUP PART-SKIM RICOTTA CHEESE

¼ CUP NATURAL ALMONDS,
TOASTED AND CHOPPED

1   On plate, with fork, mash ripest fig with honey; set aside.
2   With sharp knife, trim stems from remaining figs, then cut a deep X in top of each, making sure not to cut through to bottom. With fingertips, gently spread each fig apart to make "petals."
3   In small bowl, combine ricotta and almonds. With back of spoon, press mashed fig-and-honey mixture through sieve into 1-cup measure.
4   To serve, spoon ricotta mixture into figs. Arrange figs on platter. Drizzle with fig honey.

TIP The season for fresh figs is short, and they're expensive, so if you indulge in them, be sure to get your money's worth. Buy fruit that is heavy, smells fresh (not musty), and is soft to the touch. Use promptly; figs will keep, refrigerated, for only a day or two. Rinse figs gently before using them. The entire fruit is edible, skin and all—just discard the stem.

 PER SERVING. 4G PROTEIN | 32G CARBOHYDRATE | 4G TOTAL FAT (1G SATURATED)
4G FIBER | 6MG CHOLESTEROL | 25MG SODIUM

MEYER LEMON PUDDING CAKES

Meyer lemons, now available in most supermarkets, give this dessert its sweet-tart taste. The lemons also help create the light layers—since the acid in the juice can't bind with the egg whites, the dish divides into a citrusy cake and a creamy custard.

ACTIVE TIME: 25 MINUTES · **TOTAL TIME:** 1 HOUR PLUS COOLING
MAKES: 8 CAKES

¾ CUP SUGAR

¼ CUP ALL-PURPOSE FLOUR

¼ TEASPOON SALT

2 MEYER LEMONS OR 3 REGULAR LEMONS

3 LARGE EGGS, SEPARATED

2 TABLESPOONS BUTTER OR MARGARINE, MELTED AND COOLED

1 CUP WHOLE MILK

1 PINT RASPBERRIES FOR GARNISH

8 FRESH MINT SPRIGS FOR GARNISH

1 Preheat oven to 350°F. Grease eight 4- to 5-ounce ramekins; using 1 teaspoon sugar per ramekin, coat bottom and sides; shake out excess.

2 On sheet of waxed paper, with fork, combine flour, ⅓ cup sugar, and salt. From lemons, grate 1½ tablespoons peel and squeeze ½ cup juice. In large bowl, with wire whisk, beat egg yolks and lemon peel and juice. Whisk in butter and milk. Gradually whisk in flour mixture.

3 In another large bowl, with mixer on medium speed, beat egg whites until foamy. Gradually beat in remaining ¼ cup sugar until soft peaks form when beaters are lifted, 2 to 3 minutes.

4 Add one-third beaten whites to yolk mixture and, with rubber spatula, stir gently until incorporated. Gently fold in remaining whites until just incorporated. With ladle, divide batter evenly among prepared ramekins.

5 Arrange ramekins 1 inch apart in large (17" by 13") roasting pan. Fill pan with enough *hot water* to come halfway up sides of ramekins. Carefully transfer pan to oven and bake 30 to 35 minutes or until cakes are golden brown and tops rise ½ inch above rims.

6   Cool cakes in pan on wire rack 5 minutes. With sturdy metal spatula, carefully remove ramekins from pan with water and transfer to wire rack to cool 15 minutes longer.

7   Run thin knife around edge of 1 ramekin. Place small serving plate on top of ramekin and invert plate and ramekin together; remove ramekin. Repeat with remaining ramekins. Garnish each cake with a few raspberries and a mint sprig; serve warm.

170 CALORIES

PER SERVING. 4G PROTEIN | 25G CARBOHYDRATE | 6G TOTAL FAT (3G SATURATED) 3G FIBER | 92MG CHOLESTEROL | 145MG SODIUM ♥ 🍱

WATERMELON SLUSHIE

We combined antioxidant-rich pomegranate juice with fresh watermelon and ice to create this ruby-red summer cooler.

TOTAL TIME: 5 MINUTES
MAKES: 1 SERVING

In blender, combine **2 cups 1-inch pieces seedless watermelon, ½ cup pomegranate juice**, and **½ cup ice cubes**. Blend until smooth. Pour into tall glass.

170 CALORIES **PER 2-CUP SERVING.** 2G PROTEIN | 40G CARBOHYDRATE | 1G TOTAL FAT | 2G FIBER 0MG CHOLESTEROL | 10MG SODIUM

APPLE-OAT CRISP

This crisp works beautifully with either tart Granny Smith apples or the sweeter Golden Delicious variety; both hold their shape nicely when baked. Our test kitchen staff prefers a combination of the two.

ACTIVE TIME: 15 MINUTES · **TOTAL TIME:** 45 MINUTES
MAKES: 12 SERVINGS

- 1 LEMON
- 3 POUNDS GRANNY SMITH AND/OR GOLDEN DELICIOUS APPLES, PEELED, CORED, AND CUT INTO 1-INCH WEDGES
- ⅓ CUP PLUS ¼ CUP PACKED LIGHT BROWN SUGAR
- 2 TABLESPOONS PLUS ⅓ CUP ALL-PURPOSE FLOUR
- 1 TEASPOON GROUND CINNAMON
- ½ TEASPOON SALT
- 1 CUP OLD-FASHIONED OATS, UNCOOKED
- 4 TABLESPOONS BUTTER OR MARGARINE, SOFTENED

1 Preheat oven to 425°F. From lemon, grate ½ teaspoon peel and squeeze 2 tablespoons juice. In 13" by 9" glass or ceramic baking dish, toss lemon peel and juice with apple wedges, ⅓ cup brown sugar, 2 tablespoons flour, cinnamon, and salt until apples are evenly coated.

2 In medium bowl, mix oats with remaining ¼ cup sugar and ⅓ cup flour. With fingertips, blend in butter until mixture resembles coarse crumbs. Press crumb mixture into clumps and sprinkle over apple mixture.

3 Bake apple crisp 30 to 35 minutes or until apples are tender and topping is lightly browned. Cool crisp on wire rack for 10 minutes to serve warm, or cool completely (1 hour) on rack to serve later. Reheat if desired.

175 CALORIES

PER ½-CUP SERVING. 2G PROTEIN | 33G CARBOHYDRATE | 5G TOTAL FAT (3G SATURATED) | 3G FIBER | 11MG CHOLESTEROL | 145MG SODIUM

400 CALORIE CHICKEN

INTRODUCTION

Like many family cooks, you may already be preparing chicken a couple of nights a week and looking for new inspiration. Whether you want to stir-fry chicken tenders, braise bone-in parts, or roast the whole bird, chicken provides a succulent canvas for just about any mix of ethnic flavors, herbs, and spices. All this and a great nutrition profile, too—it's no wonder that chicken has become the most frequently served main dish on American dinner tables.

This versatility and widespread popularity makes chicken a natural subject for *Good Housekeeping 400 Calorie Meals*. In this section, we share 60 delicious recipes for chicken entrées, from quick stir-fries, sautés, grills, and salads to slow-cooked soups, stews, roasts, and casseroles. You'll find low-cal takes on satisfyingly familiar dishes like chicken potpie, barbecue, and even "fried" chicken (we oven-bake it rather than deep-fry it to keep it skinny), along with tasty traditional recipes from a wide variety of cultures—Jerk Chicken Kabobs, Chicken Bruschetta, and Chicken, Bouillabaisse-Style.

As the title of the book promises, every single main dish is 400 calories or less, and as a bonus, we've included chapters on sides (and even skinny desserts!) that will help you round out your meals. From veggies and side salads like Corn on the Cob with Molasses Butter and Tricolor Slaw to potato and whole-grain dishes like Warm Dijon Potato Salad and Polenta and Spinach Gratin to sweet bites like Apricot Oatmeal Cookies and Summer Fruit in Spiced Syrup, the more than 30 add-on recipes are organized by calorie count—from lowest to highest. Simply choose your chicken main dish, then use your surplus calories to select an add-on (or two!) that will make it a meal.

For example, if you're watching your weight and limiting dinners to 500 calories maximum, enjoy BBQ Chicken Cutlets with Citrus Slaw (265 calories) with a side of our Light Mashed Potatoes (145 calories), and finish with one of our Healthy Makeover Brownies (95 calories): 265 + 145 + 95 = 505 calories. With this book, it's easy to build a satisfying low-calorie meal. See "Skinny Meal Planning," opposite, for tips on how to create fabulous low-cal meals with chicken playing the starring role.

SKINNY MEAL PLANNING

Planning low-calorie brunches, lunches, and dinners is easy with this setion. Prepare the add-ons we've suggested under "Make It a Meal" with each main-dish recipe to make 500-calorie dinners or 400-calorie lunches and brunches. Or get creative and choose from the sides and dessert recipe lists on pages 401, 415, and 429 to make your own meal combos. Here are examples of flavorful (and skinny!) chicken meals to get you started.

SAMPLE BRUNCH MENU

MAIN: Asian Chicken Salad	285 calories
ADD-ON: Summer Fruit in Spiced Syrup	125 calories
Total calories per meal	**410 calories**

SAMPLE LUNCH MENU

MAIN: Pan-Seared Chicken Thighs with Pear Slaw	230 calories
ADD-ON: Sweet-Potato Corn Sticks	170 calories
Total calories per meal	**400 calories**

SAMPLE DINNER MENU

MAIN: Almond-Crusted Chicken	350 calories
ADD-ON: Roasted Acorn Squash	150 calories
Total calories per meal	**500 calories**

CHOOSING CHICKEN

Chicken's versatility and affordability make it hugely popular, and the poultry industry has responded to consumer demand for more convenient cuts and high-quality options. Take the following pointers into account when you buy and cook chicken.

• **Take advantage of lean, quick-cooking cuts.** Many of our recipes call for skinless chicken breast halves, which may include the tenderloin, a long, narrow muscle attached to the underside of the breast. Tenderloins, or chicken tenders, are great for finger food, salads, and stir-fries because they are already bite-size and super fast to cook. For even faster cooking, use chicken cutlets: breasts with the tenderloin removed and cut in half horizontally.

• **Serve chicken skinless.** Chicken skin gets 80 percent of its calories from fat, so it makes sense to serve your bird without it. You don't have to remove the skin before cooking, though. According to the USDA, it makes little nutritional difference in the fat content whether the skin is removed before or after cooking. But it does make a difference in taste. Especially when roasting whole chicken, you'll get a moister, more tender result if you cook it with the skin intact.

• **Weigh the pros and cons of white meat versus dark.** The breast is the tenderest part of the bird—and the leanest. A 3½-ounce portion of the breast meat without skin has about 4 grams of fat, while the same amount of dark meat has about 10 grams. However, removing the skin from dark meat slashes the amount of fat almost in half.

White meat is ideal for quick, moist cooking methods like stir-frying and sautéing; it also works well with dry-heat methods such as grilling. Dark meat comes into its own in long-simmered casseroles and stews. While it's true that poultry cooked on the bone has the best flavor and tends to be juicier, seasonings and marinades add flavor and moisture to boneless thighs and breasts, which are convenient and cook quickly.

• **Buy the best-quality chicken you can afford.** If you are looking for a good-quality bird for your family, you have more options than ever, including natural, organic, and free-range chickens. This trio of options typically deliver a healthier bird with better flavor (organic chicken is free of added hormones and antibiotics), so experiment if your budget allows.

LIGHT AND HEALTHY TECHNIQUES

We use high-flavor, low-fat cooking techniques in the chicken recipes throughout this book. Some are slow, others fast, but all can be a low-maintenance part of your light and healthy cooking repertoire.

Stir-frying: This fast cooking method yields quick, tasty results and requires only a small amount of oil. Small pieces of food are cooked over high heat in a wok or skillet, stirred constantly to keep the food from sticking or burning. Vegetables and pieces of chicken should be sliced or chopped to roughly the same size to ensure even cooking; the fastest-cooking ingredients should be the last items you add to the pan. Our Basil Chile Chicken Stir-Fry and Tangerine Chicken Stir-Fry (pages 310 and 314) use this fast and flavorful method. Tip: When a recipe calls for soy sauce, use the reduced-sodium kind or dilute regular soy sauce with water, using a 2:1 ratio.

Sautéing: The cousin of stir-frying, sautéing is used to quickly cook larger pieces of food like whole boneless, skinless chicken breasts in a small amount of oil. We include lots of recipes for this easy, skinny cooking method; for starters, see Chicken Dill Sauté and Skillet Chicken with Two Sauces (pages 312 and 316). Tip: Nonstick skillets are perfect for sautéing (see "Safe Nonstick Cooking," opposite).

Braising and Stewing: Few dishes satisfy as much as braised chicken pieces or a long-simmered stew. Braising is usually done in a Dutch oven or pot with a heavy bottom and tight-fitting lid. For the richest flavor, brown the poultry (first cut into chunks if you're making stew), add vegetables and a small amount of stock or water, cover tightly, and simmer. Chicken will become meltingly tender through this moist-heat method in under an hour.

Tip: A slow cooker makes braising and stewing especially easy. Brown the chicken in a skillet before adding it to the slow cooker, if you like. Then add the rest of the ingredients, set the heat level as recipe specifies, and go about your business until dinnertime.

SAFE NONSTICK COOKING

Nonstick pans will help you prepare chicken dishes in a flash, with little added oil. However, they've recently come under fire over concerns about dangerous chemical emissions. Just be aware that the cookware is safe as long as it's not overheated. (At temperatures above 500°F, the coating may begin to break down, releasing toxic particles and gases.) Any food that cooks quickly over low or medium heat and coats most of the pan's surface (which lowers the pan's temperature) is unlikely to cause problems. Follow these cook-safe guidelines:

Never preheat an empty nonstick pan, even one with oil in it.

Don't cook over high heat. Most nonstick manufacturers now advise consumers not to go above medium.

Ventilate your kitchen. When cooking, turn on the exhaust fan to help clear away any fumes.

Don't broil or sear chicken. Those techniques require temperatures above what a nonstick pan can usually handle.

Choose a heavier nonstick pan. Lightweight pans generally heat up fastest and may scorch more quickly too.

Avoid scratching or chipping the pan. Use wooden spoons for stirring, don't use steel wool for cleaning, and don't stack the pans when you store them. (If you do, place a paper towel between them.)

Grilling: Whether you grill outdoors on a gas or charcoal grill or indoors in a ridged grill pan, the intense heat caramelizes the crust and lends delicious smoky flavor to any cut of chicken. Much of the fat drips away during the process, making this quick and easy method an excellent choice for those looking to lighten up. Because this method is so simple and popular, we've included an entire chapter of grilled chicken recipes; turn to page 347 and get grilling. Tip: To intensify flavor, use a dry rub or marinade.

LOW-CAL BBQ SAUCE

Meet your newest license to grill: a low-cal, but still sweet, barbecue sauce.

In 2-quart saucepan, combine **one 14½-ounce can no-salt-added tomatoes, 2 tablespoons balsamic vinegar, 2 teaspoons spicy brown mustard, 1 crushed garlic clove, ½ teaspoon smoked paprika, ½ teaspoon salt,** and **1 chopped medium Gala apple.** Heat for 3 minutes over high heat; reduce heat to medium; simmer for 30 minutes. Puree until smooth. Makes 2 cups sauce. Refrigerate in airtight container for up to 1 week.

15
CALORIES

PER 2 TABLESPOONS. 0G PROTEIN | 3G CARBOHYDRATE | 0G TOTAL FAT | 1G FIBER | 0MG CHOLESTEROL | 99MG SODIUM ♥ 🛒

Baking: Chicken can be baked in the oven in covered cookware with a little liquid, which ensures that it won't dry out. Baked Honey-Lime Drumsticks and Rosemary-Apricot Chicken (pages 374 and 375) are two delicious examples of this low-maintenance technique. Tip: Baking also can be used as a low-cal alternative to deep-frying. When chicken is breaded and baked, you get a similarly crispy coating without so much added fat. Our Finger Food Feast (page 372) coats chicken drumsticks in light panko-style bread crumbs with gratifyingly crispy results.

Roasting: Slow-cooking chicken and vegetables in the oven intensifies their natural flavors. The interior of the food becomes succulent and tender, while the exterior develops a delightfully caramelized crust. You'll need a heavy, shallow roasting pan; place chicken, uncovered, on a rack in the center of the oven so the hot air can circulate freely. When your roast chicken recipe includes vegetables, spread them out in a single layer, or they will steam instead of caramelizing. Maple-Roasted Chicken Thighs and Roast Chicken Béarnaise (pages 377 and 378) are just two of our succulent roast chicken recipes.

Tip: The only way to guarantee that chicken is roasted to the desired doneness is to use an instant-read thermometer. To ensure an accurate reading, always insert the thermometer into the center or thickest part of the roast or chicken pieces without touching any bone or fatty sections. The thermometer should register a minimum temperature of 165°F before you remove the poultry from the oven.

OUR GO-TO MAINS

To make skinny meal planning a cinch, each chicken main dish is paired with suggestions for add-on recipes that will make it a meal. Or to choose your own add-ons, see the complete recipe lists in the second part of this section, conveniently organized by calorie count, from lowest to highest: Veggies & Side Salads, page 401; Potatoes, Beans & Grains, page 415; and Sweet Bites, page 429.

230 CALORIES

Chicken Dill Sauté
(page 312)

STIR-FRIES & SKILLETS

We kick off the recipes with quick and delicious chicken-in-a-skillet mains, a go-to category for family meals on busy weeknights. Many of these stir-fries and skillet dishes incorporate veggies and grains, so you can enjoy a full meal for 400 calories or less! Our colorful Basil-Chile Chicken Stir-Fry and Tangerine Chicken Stir-Fry are just two of the mains that include fiber-rich brown rice. And several of these dishes are so pretty, they could be company fare: Try the Mediterranean-style Chicken Sauté with Artichokes, Pan-Seared Chicken Thighs with Pear Slaw, or Tarragon Chicken with Grapes.

KEY TO ICONS

 30 minutes or less   Heart healthy   High fiber    Make ahead   Slow cooker

BASIL-CHILE CHICKEN STIR-FRY

Whip up this simple dinner in half an hour—in a single skillet. If you like things a bit spicier, leave the seeds in the chile.

ACTIVE TIME: 25 MINUTES · **TOTAL TIME:** 30 MINUTES
MAKES: 4 MAIN-DISH SERVINGS

1 CUP QUICK-COOKING SHORT-GRAIN BROWN RICE	1¼ POUNDS CHICKEN BREAST TENDERS, VERY THINLY SLICED CROSSWISE
4 GARLIC CLOVES	2 TABLESPOONS REDUCED-SODIUM FISH SAUCE
4 TEASPOONS VEGETABLE OIL	
1 POUND GREEN BEANS, TRIMMED AND CUT INTO 1-INCH PIECES	1 TEASPOON REDUCED-SODIUM SOY SAUCE
6 TABLESPOONS WATER	2 TEASPOONS SUGAR
¼ TEASPOON SALT	1 CUP PACKED FRESH BASIL LEAVES PLUS ADDITIONAL BASIL LEAVES FOR GARNISH
¼ TEASPOON GROUND BLACK PEPPER	
1 FRESH THAI OR SERRANO CHILE, STEM AND SEEDS DISCARDED, FINELY CHOPPED	

1 Prepare rice as label directs, but do not add any salt.

2 Very thinly slice 2 garlic cloves; finely chop remaining 2 garlic cloves.

3 In 12-inch skillet, heat 1 teaspoon oil over medium-high heat until hot. Add thinly sliced garlic and cook 10 seconds or until garlic is golden. Add green beans, ¼ cup water, salt, and black pepper. Cook 4 to 5 minutes or until beans are crisp-tender and water has evaporated, stirring frequently. Transfer bean mixture to large plate or bowl.

4 In same skillet, heat remaining 1 tablespoon oil over medium-high heat until hot. Add chile and chopped garlic and cook, stirring, 10 seconds or until garlic is golden. Add chicken tenders in single layer and cook 2 to 3 minutes or until chicken just loses pink color throughout, stirring occasionally. (Instant-read thermometer inserted horizontally into chicken tender should register 165°F.)

5 Add fish sauce, soy sauce, sugar, and remaining 2 tablespoons water. Cook 1 minute or until chicken is just cooked through, stirring. Stir in basil and cook 15 to 20 seconds or until just wilted.

6 To serve, divide cooked rice, green beans, and chicken with sauce among serving plates. Garnish with 2 or 3 fresh basil leaves.

325 **PER SERVING.** 35G PROTEIN | 28G CARBOHYDRATE | 9G TOTAL FAT (1G SATURATED)
CALORIES 4G FIBER | 91MG CHOLESTEROL | 815MG SODIUM

MAKE IT A MEAL: This Thai-style dish includes brown rice, making it a wholesome meal. If you want a sweet finish, add Summer Fruit in Spiced Syrup (125 calories; page 435) to create a skinny 450-calorie lunch or dinner.

CHICKEN DILL SAUTÉ

To keep this lemony spring chicken dish lean and luscious, we sear the meat in a little oil first, then add water. This prevents the meat and vegetables from sticking to the pan—and helps make a flavorful sauce. For photo, see page 308.

ACTIVE TIME: 30 MINUTES · **TOTAL TIME:** 40 MINUTES
MAKES: 4 MAIN-DISH SERVINGS

---

1 LEMON	½ CUP WATER
1 POUND SKINLESS, BONELESS CHICKEN BREAST HALVES, CUT INTO ½-INCH CHUNKS	⅝ TEASPOON SALT
	⅜ TEASPOON GROUND BLACK PEPPER
3 TEASPOONS EXTRA-VIRGIN OLIVE OIL	8 OUNCES SUGAR SNAP PEAS, STRINGS REMOVED, CUT IN HALF
1 SMALL ONION, THINLY SLICED	⅓ CUP FRESH DILL, CHOPPED
1 LARGE ORANGE PEPPER, SLICED	
1 LARGE YELLOW PEPPER, SLICED	

1 From lemon, grate 1 teaspoon peel; set aside. Squeeze 1 tablespoon juice and pour into pie plate. Add chicken; turn to coat.

2 In 12-inch skillet, heat 1 teaspoon oil over medium-high heat. Add onion, sliced peppers, 2 tablespoons water, and ¼ teaspoon each salt and black pepper. Cook 3 minutes or until softened, stirring. Transfer to large plate.

3 In same skillet, heat 1 teaspoon oil over medium-high heat. Add peas, 2 tablespoons water, ⅛ teaspoon salt, and remaining ⅛ teaspoon black pepper. Cook, stirring occasionally, 2 to 3 minutes or until beginning to brown. Add to onion mixture.

4 In same skillet, heat remaining 1 teaspoon oil over medium-high heat. Add chicken; sprinkle with ¼ teaspoon salt. Cook 3 minutes or until golden and cooked through, stirring once. Return vegetables to pan; add remaining ¼ cup water. Cook 1 minute or until saucy, stirring. Stir in dill, remaining ¼ teaspoon salt, and reserved peel.

---

 230 CALORIES **PER SERVING.** 27G PROTEIN | 14G CARBOHYDRATE | 7G TOTAL FAT (1G SATURATED) 3G FIBER | 73MG CHOLESTEROL | 650MG SODIUM

MAKE IT A MEAL: For a light, 335-calorie lunch, serve this colorful stir-fry over whole-wheat couscous (105 calories per serving).

CHICKEN WITH SHALLOTS

Shallot-infused red wine vinegar sauce is as luscious with chicken as it is with red meat.

ACTIVE TIME: 15 MINUTES · **TOTAL TIME:** 30 MINUTES
MAKES: 4 MAIN-DISH SERVINGS

4   SKINLESS, BONELESS CHICKEN
    BREAST HALVES (1½ POUNDS)

⅜   TEASPOON SALT

¼   TEASPOON GROUND BLACK PEPPER

4   TEASPOONS OLIVE OIL

1   POUND SUGAR SNAP PEAS,
    STRINGS REMOVED

2   MEDIUM SHALLOTS, THINLY SLICED

¼   CUP RED WINE VINEGAR

¾   CUP CANNED OR HOMEMADE
    CHICKEN BROTH (PAGE 330)

1   TEASPOON FRESH THYME LEAVES,
    CHOPPED, PLUS ADDITIONAL LEAVES
    FOR GARNISH

1   TEASPOON BUTTER
    (NO SUBSTITUTIONS)

1   Place chicken between two sheets plastic wrap and, with meat mallet, pound to even ½-inch thickness; sprinkle with ¼ teaspoon salt and ⅛ pepper to season both sides.

2   In 12-inch skillet, heat 2 teaspoons oil over medium heat until hot. Add chicken and cook 12 to 14 minutes, turning over once, until breasts are browned on both sides and instant-read thermometer inserted horizontally into thickest part registers 165°F. Transfer to platter; cover with foil.

3   Meanwhile, in 4-quart saucepot, place steamer basket and 1 *inch water*; cover and heat to boiling over high heat. Place snap peas in steamer basket; cover and steam over medium heat 5 to 6 minutes or until peas are tender-crisp. Toss with remaining ⅛ teaspoon each salt and pepper.

4   To skillet, add remaining 2 teaspoons oil. Add shallots and cook 3 to 4 minutes or until tender, stirring often. Stir in vinegar and cook 30 seconds. Add broth and chopped thyme. Heat to boiling over medium-high; boil 1 minute to reduce slightly. Off heat, stir butter into sauce. Makes 1 cup.

5   Thinly slice chicken breasts and top with shallot sauce; serve with snap peas. Garnish with thyme.

 295 CALORIES   **PER SERVING.** 43G PROTEIN | 13G CARBOHYDRATE | 8G TOTAL FAT (2G SATURATED) 3G FIBER | 101MG CHOLESTEROL | 470MG SODIUM

MAKE IT A MEAL: Add Light Mashed Potatoes (145 calories; page 417) and three Lemon Meringue Drops (5 calories each; page 430) for a 455-calorie dinner.

TANGERINE CHICKEN STIR-FRY

Toss stir-fried chicken and vegetables with a citrus-infused sauce for a quick and colorful meal.

ACTIVE TIME: 20 MINUTES · **TOTAL TIME:** 30 MINUTES
MAKES: 4 MAIN-DISH SERVINGS

3 TANGERINES	1 CUP QUICK-COOKING (10-MINUTE) BROWN RICE
¼ CUP DRY SHERRY	
1 TABLESPOON GRATED, PEELED FRESH GINGER	4 TEASPOONS VEGETABLE OIL
1 TEASPOON ASIAN SESAME OIL	1 BAG (12 OUNCES) BROCCOLI FLOWERETS
4 TEASPOONS CORNSTARCH	2 CARROTS, PEELED AND THINLY SLICED DIAGONALLY
2 TABLESPOONS REDUCED-SODIUM SOY SAUCE	3 GREEN ONIONS, CUT INTO 1-INCH PIECES
1½ POUNDS SKINLESS, BONELESS CHICKEN BREAST HALVES, CUT INTO ½-INCH-WIDE STRIPS	⅓ CUP WATER

1 From 1 tangerine, with vegetable peeler, remove peel in strips. Using small knife, remove and discard any white pith from peel; set peel aside. Into 1-cup liquid measuring cup, squeeze ½ cup juice from tangerines. Stir in sherry, ginger, sesame oil, and 1 teaspoon cornstarch; set juice mixture aside.

2 In medium bowl, combine soy sauce and remaining 1 tablespoon cornstarch. Add chicken and toss to coat; set chicken mixture aside.

3 Cook rice as label directs. Meanwhile, in 12-inch skillet, heat 2 teaspoons vegetable oil on medium-high until hot. Add citrus peel and cook 1 minute or until lightly browned. With tongs or slotted spoon, transfer to large bowl.

4 To same skillet, add broccoli, carrots, and green onions; stir to coat with oil. Add water; cover and cook 4 minutes, stirring once. Uncover and cook 1 minute longer or until vegetables are tender-crisp, stirring frequently. Transfer vegetables to bowl with peel.

5 To same skillet, add remaining 2 teaspoons vegetable oil; reduce heat to medium. Add chicken mixture and cook 6 to 7 minutes or until chicken is golden on the outside and no longer pink inside, stirring frequently. Transfer to bowl with cooked vegetables.

6 Add juice mixture to skillet and bring to boil over medium-high heat; boil 1 minute, stirring to loosen browned bits. Return chicken and vegetables to skillet and cook 1 minute to heat through, stirring. To serve, spoon brown rice into shallow dinner bowls; top with chicken and vegetables.

390 PER SERVING. 45G PROTEIN | 32G CARBOHYDRATE | 9G TOTAL FAT (1G SATURATED)

CALORIES   5G FIBER | 99MG CHOLESTEROL | 420MG SODIUM

MAKE IT A MEAL: This stir-fry on brown rice makes a pretty (and whole-some) lunch for guests. Finish with Frozen Fruit Yogurt (100 calories per serving; page 434) for a 490-calorie meal.

SKILLET CHICKEN WITH TWO SAUCES

Here's a pair of speedy—and delicious—sauces to serve with sautéed chicken breasts. For best results, use chicken breasts of uniform size.

TOTAL TIME: 20 MINUTES
MAKES: 4 MAIN-DISH SERVINGS

4	MEDIUM SKINLESS, BONELESS CHICKEN BREAST HALVES (1¼ POUNDS)
¼	TEASPOON SALT
⅛	TEASPOON GROUND BLACK PEPPER

1 TABLESPOON OLIVE OIL

CHOICE OF SAUCE: PLUM-BALSAMIC OR LEMON-SAGE

1 Place chicken pieces between two sheets of plastic wrap. With meat mallet or rolling pin, pound to even ½-inch thickness; sprinkle with salt and pepper.
2 In nonstick 12-inch skillet, heat oil over medium heat. Add breasts and cook 6 to 8 minutes, turning over once, until browned on both sides and instant-read thermometer inserted horizontally into thickest part registers 165°F. Transfer to platter; cover with foil to keep warm.
3 In same skillet, prepare choice of sauce; spoon over breasts.

PLUM-BALSAMIC

Chop ½ **medium red onion** and cook in skillet over medium heat 3 minutes or until softened, stirring frequently. Pit **3 small plums,** cut each into 8 wedges, and add to skillet; cook 3 minutes or until lightly browned, turning occasionally. Increase heat to medium-high; stir in ½ **cup canned reduced-sodium chicken broth or Homemade Chicken Broth (page 330), 2 tablespoons balsamic vinegar, 1 tablespoon honey, ¼ teaspoon salt,** and **juices from chicken** on platter. Cook 2 to 3 minutes to reduce sauce slightly, stirring occasionally.

 PER SERVING. 34G PROTEIN | 13G CARBOHYDRATE | 6G TOTAL FAT (1G SATURATED) 1G FIBER | 82MG CHOLESTEROL | 440MG SODIUM

LEMON-SAGE

To skillet, add **½ cup canned reduced-sodium chicken broth or Home-made Chicken Broth (page 330)** and **⅓ cup white wine.** Cook 2 minutes on medium-high to reduce by half. Stir in **1 teaspoon grated lemon peel, 2 tablespoons lemon juice, 2 tablespoons chopped fresh parsley, 1 teaspoon chopped fresh sage,** and **juices from chicken** on platter. Remove skillet from heat; stir in **1 tablespoon cold butter or margarine.**

 220 CALORIES | **PER SERVING.** 33G PROTEIN | 1G CARBOHYDRATE | 8G TOTAL FAT (1G SATURATED) 0G FIBER | 82MG CHOLESTEROL | 335MG SODIUM ❤

MAKE IT A MEAL: Pair either of these skillet variations with ten spears steamed asparagus and one small baked potato topped with 1 teaspoon olive oil (255 calories).

CHICKEN AND MUSHROOM SAUTÉ

Earthy mushrooms and whole grains make this chicken and rice dish a satisfying and healthful dinner option.

ACTIVE TIME: 10 MINUTES · **TOTAL TIME:** 45 MINUTES
MAKES: 4 MAIN-DISH SERVINGS

---

2   TABLESPOONS OLIVE OIL

1¼ POUNDS SKINLESS, BONELESS
     CHICKEN THIGHS

1   PACKAGE (10 OUNCES) SLICED
     CREMINI MUSHROOMS

2   STALKS CELERY, THINLY SLICED

1   TEASPOON CHOPPED
     FRESH THYME LEAVES

1   CAN (14½ OUNCES) CHICKEN BROTH,
     OR 1¾ CUPS HOMEMADE BROTH
     (PAGE 330)

1   CUP INSTANT BROWN RICE

½   CUP DRY WHITE WINE

¼   TEASPOON SALT

¼   TEASPOON COARSELY GROUND BLACK
     PEPPER

1 In 12-inch skillet, heat oil over medium-high heat until hot. Add chicken and cook, covered, 5 minutes. Reduce heat to medium; turn chicken and cook, covered, 5 more minutes. Transfer to plate.

2 To same skillet, add mushrooms, celery, and thyme; cook 5 minutes or until vegetables are softened, stirring occasionally. Add broth, rice, wine, salt, and pepper; heat to boiling.

3 Return chicken to skillet. Reduce heat to low; cover and simmer 12 minutes or until instant-read thermometer inserted into thickest part of thighs registers 165°F.

340
CALORIES

PER SERVING. 35G PROTEIN | 21G CARBOHYDRATE | 13G TOTAL FAT (2G SATURATED)
3G FIBER | 118MG CHOLESTEROL | 595MG SODIUM

MAKE IT A MEAL: Pair with Oven-Roasted Brussels Sprouts (95 calories; page 407) for a 435-calorie lunch. Add on 1 small sliced pear (80 calories) for a 515-calorie dinner.

SWEET AND SAVORY CHICKEN

Prunes provide the sweet while olives deliver the savory in this easy chicken and whole-grain dinner recipe.

TOTAL TIME: 30 MINUTES

MAKES: 4 MAIN-DISH SERVINGS

1 CAN (14½ OUNCES) REDUCED-SODIUM CHICKEN BROTH, OR 1¾ CUPS HOMEMADE BROTH (PAGE 330)	1 TABLESPOON OLIVE OIL
1 CUP WATER	1 SMALL ONION, CHOPPED
1 CUP BULGUR	¼ CUP CHOPPED PIMIENTO-STUFFED OLIVES
1½ POUNDS CHICKEN BREAST TENDERS	¼ CUP CHOPPED PRUNES
¼ TEASPOON SALT	1 TEASPOON CAPERS, DRAINED AND CHOPPED
¼ TEASPOON GROUND BLACK PEPPER	

1 In 2-quart saucepan, heat 1 cup broth and water to boiling. Stir in bulgur. Cover and simmer over low heat 15 minutes or until liquid is absorbed.

2 Meanwhile, place chicken tenders between two sheets plastic wrap. With meat mallet, pound each to ¼-inch thickness. Sprinkle chicken with salt and pepper.

3 In 12-inch skillet, heat oil over medium-high heat. Add chicken and cook 4 minutes or until no longer pink throughout, turning over once. Transfer to plate; cover and keep warm.

4 Add onion to skillet; cook over medium heat 5 minutes or until beginning to soften, stirring occasionally. Add olives, prunes, capers, remaining broth, and juices from chicken on plate; heat to boiling, stirring. Boil 1 minute. Serve chicken and sauce over bulgur.

385 CALORIES

PER SERVING. 45G PROTEIN | 35G CARBOHYDRATE | 7G TOTAL FAT (1G SATURATED) 8G FIBER | 99MG CHOLESTEROL | 670MG SODIUM

MAKE IT A MEAL: Add on Green Beans with Shallots (90 calories; page 406) to create a 475-calorie dinner.

CHICKEN SAUTÉ WITH ARTICHOKES

Frozen, ready-to-serve artichoke hearts are the secret to this streamlined, Greek-style favorite, with its light and zesty add-ins.

TOTAL TIME: 30 MINUTES

MAKES: 4 MAIN-DISH SERVINGS

4 MEDIUM SKINLESS, BONELESS CHICKEN BREAST HALVES (1½ POUNDS)

¼ TEASPOON SALT

⅛ TEASPOON GROUND BLACK PEPPER

4 TEASPOONS OLIVE OIL

1 PACKAGE (8 TO 10 OUNCES) FROZEN ARTICHOKE HEARTS, THAWED

¾ CUP CANNED OR HOMEMADE CHICKEN BROTH (PAGE 330)

¼ CUP MINT LEAVES, CHOPPED, PLUS MORE FOR GARNISH

1 TABLESPOON FRESH LEMON JUICE

1 OUNCE FETA CHEESE, CRUMBLED (¼ CUP)

1 Place chicken between two sheets plastic wrap and, with meat mallet or bottom of skillet, pound to even ½-inch thickness; sprinkle salt and pepper on both sides.

2 In 12-inch skillet, heat 2 teaspoons oil over medium heat. Add chicken and cook 12 to 14 minutes, turning over once, until breasts are browned on both sides and instant-read thermometer inserted horizontally into thickest part registers 165°F. Transfer to shallow serving bowl; cover with foil to keep warm.

3 In same skillet, heat remaining 2 teaspoons oil until hot. Add artichokes and cook 3 minutes or until browned, stirring occasionally. Stir in broth and heat to boiling over medium-high; boil 2 to 3 minutes or until reduced by half. Remove skillet from heat; stir in mint and lemon juice.

4 To serve, spoon artichoke sauce over chicken; top with feta. Garnish with additional chopped mint leaves.

285 CALORIES

PER SERVING. 43G PROTEIN | 7G CARBOHYDRATE | 9G TOTAL FAT (3G SATURATED) 3G FIBER | 107MG CHOLESTEROL | 515MG SODIUM

MAKE IT A MEAL: Enjoy a glass of crisp white wine (120 calories) while nibbling on three cheese sticks (110 calories) before moving on to this flavorful Mediterranean entrée. Total calories: 515.

CHICKEN AND VEGGIES ON POLENTA

Sliced precooked polenta forms the base for a delectable sautéed chicken and mixed pepper topping.

ACTIVE TIME: 20 MINUTES · **TOTAL TIME:** 30 MINUTES
MAKES: 4 MAIN-DISH SERVINGS

---

1 LOG (16 OUNCES) PRECOOKED PLAIN POLENTA, CUT INTO 8 SLICES

2 TABLESPOONS OLIVE OIL

½ TEASPOON SALT

¾ TEASPOON GROUND BLACK PEPPER

1½ POUNDS SKINLESS, BONELESS CHICKEN BREAST HALVES, CUT INTO ½-INCH-WIDE STRIPS

2 RED, ORANGE, AND/OR YELLOW PEPPERS, SLICED

1 ONION, SLICED

½ CUP DRY VERMOUTH OR DRY WHITE WINE

1 TABLESPOON CAPERS, DRAINED AND CHOPPED

1 Preheat broiler and place rack 6 inches from heat source. Place polenta slices on cookie sheet and brush with 1 teaspoon oil on both sides; sprinkle with ¼ teaspoon salt and ½ teaspoon pepper on both sides. Broil polenta 18 to 20 minutes or until golden. Set aside.

2 Meanwhile, in 12-inch skillet, heat 2 teaspoons oil over medium heat until hot. Sprinkle chicken with remaining ¼ teaspoon each salt and pepper. Add to skillet and cook 5 to 6 minutes or until chicken is golden and no longer pink throughout, stirring occasionally. (Instant-read thermometer inserted horizontally into chicken strip should register 165°F.) Transfer to bowl.

3 To same skillet, add remaining 1 tablespoon oil; reduce heat to medium. Add peppers and onion; cook 8 minutes or until vegetables are tender, stirring occasionally. Stir in vermouth and capers; increase heat to medium-high and cook 2 minutes. Return chicken to skillet; cook 1 minute or until heated through, stirring. Serve chicken and vegetables over polenta slices.

365 CALORIES

PER SERVING. 43G PROTEIN | 43G CARBOHYDRATE | 9G TOTAL FAT (2G SATURATED) 3G FIBER | 99MG CHOLESTEROL | 820MG SODIUM

MAKE IT A MEAL: Pair with our Green Beans with Garlic (50 calories; page 406) for a thoroughly satisfying 415-calorie dinner!

COUNTRY HASH

This down-home hash takes full advantage of leftover chicken.

ACTIVE TIME: 20 MINUTES · **TOTAL TIME:** 55 MINUTES
MAKES: 4 MAIN-DISH SERVINGS

3 LARGE ALL-PURPOSE POTATOES (1¾ POUNDS), PEELED AND CUT INTO ¾-INCH CHUNKS

2 CARROTS, PEELED AND CUT INTO ¾-INCH PIECES

1 TABLESPOON BUTTER OR MARGARINE

1 TABLESPOON VEGETABLE OIL

1 ONION, CHOPPED

1 LARGE STALK CELERY, CUT INTO ¾-INCH PIECES

½ TEASPOON SALT

¼ TEASPOON GROUND BLACK PEPPER

10 OUNCES LEFTOVER COOKED CHICKEN, CUT INTO ½-INCH PIECES (2 CUPS)

2 OUNCES FONTINA OR SWISS CHEESE, SHREDDED (½ CUP)

1 TABLESPOON CHOPPED FRESH PARSLEY LEAVES

1 In 2-quart saucepan, place potatoes and *water* to cover; heat to boiling over high heat. Add carrots; reduce heat to low. Cover; simmer 5 minutes or until vegetables are almost fork-tender. Drain.

2 Meanwhile, in heavy 12-inch skillet, heat butter with oil over medium heat until hot. Add onion and celery; cook, stirring occasionally, 15 minutes or until lightly browned and tender.

3 Increase heat to medium-high; add potatoes and carrots, salt, and pepper, and cook 10 to 15 minutes or until browned, stirring occasionally.

4 Stir in chicken and cook 1 minute. Sprinkle top with cheese; cover skillet and cook 1 minute or until cheese melts. Sprinkle with parsley to serve.

370 CALORIES · **PER SERVING.** 25G PROTEIN | 38G CARBOHYDRATE | 14G TOTAL FAT (5G SATURATED) 4G FIBER | 60MG CHOLESTEROL | 490MG SODIUM

MAKE IT A MEAL: For a country-style brunch at 425 calories per serving, stir in 2 cups steamed broccoli florets (15 calories per ½-cup serving). Or serve the hash with half a grapefruit (40 calories).

PAN-SEARED CHICKEN THIGHS WITH PEAR SLAW

This pretty dish, which pairs chicken thighs with a warm pear and celery slaw, can be prepared on the fly in just 20 minutes!

TOTAL TIME: 20 MINUTES
MAKES: 4 MAIN-DISH SERVINGS

1   TEASPOON OLIVE OIL

1   POUND SKINLESS, BONELESS CHICKEN THIGHS, CUT INTO 1-INCH-WIDE STRIPS

½   TEASPOON SALT

¼   TEASPOON GROUND BLACK PEPPER

2   BARTLETT PEARS

2   STALKS CELERY

2   TABLESPOONS LEMON JUICE

1   SHALLOT, MINCED

¾   CUP APPLE CIDER

1   TABLESPOON DIJON MUSTARD

1   TABLESPOON CHOPPED FRESH PARSLEY LEAVES

1 In nonstick 12-inch skillet, heat oil over medium heat until hot. Add chicken strips to skillet and sprinkle with salt and pepper. Cook 8 to 10 minutes, turning occasionally, until chicken loses pink color throughout. (Instant-read thermometer inserted horizontally into chicken strip should register 165°F.) Transfer to warm plate.

2 Meanwhile, cut each pear lengthwise in half (do not peel); discard core. Cut halves lengthwise into matchstick-thin strips (a mandoline or V-slicer makes this easy). Thinly slice celery on diagonal. In large bowl, toss pear and celery slices with lemon juice; set aside.

3 To same skillet, add shallot and cook 30 seconds to 1 minute or until it begins to brown, stirring constantly. Add cider and heat to boiling over high heat; whisk in mustard. Pour cider dressing over pear mixture and toss to coat. Serve slaw with chicken. Sprinkle with parsley.

230
CALORIES

PER SERVING. 23G PROTEIN | 21G CARBOHYDRATE | 6G TOTAL FAT (1G SATURATED)
3G FIBER | 94MG CHOLESTEROL | 430MG SODIUM

MAKE IT A MEAL: Pair this warm chicken salad with our Sweet-Potato Corn Sticks (170 calories; page 424).

PLUM-GLAZED CHICKEN THIGHS

Chinese five-spice powder and yummy plum jam give this fast Asian chicken recipe a burst of sweet, sour, and spicy flavor.

ACTIVE TIME: 10 MINUTES · **TOTAL TIME:** 25 MINUTES
MAKES: 4 MAIN-DISH SERVINGS

1¼ POUNDS SKINLESS, BONELESS CHICKEN THIGHS

½ TEASPOON CHINESE FIVE-SPICE POWDER

½ TEASPOON SALT

3 GREEN ONIONS

1 TABLESPOON OLIVE OIL

½ CUP CANNED OR HOMEMADE CHICKEN BROTH (PAGE 330)

½ CUP PLUM JAM

2 TABLESPOONS BALSAMIC VINEGAR

1 BAG (12 OUNCES) MICROWAVE-IN-THE-BAG TRIMMED GREEN BEANS

1 PACKAGE (8 TO 9 OUNCES) HEAT-AND-SERVE PRECOOKED BROWN RICE

1 In bowl, toss thighs with five-spice powder and salt. From dark-green end of onions, finely chop enough to equal 2 tablespoons; reserve for garnish. Cut remainder of onions into 1-inch pieces; set aside.

2 In 12-inch skillet, heat oil over medium-high heat until hot. Add thighs and cook 10 minutes, turning once, until chicken is browned and instant-read thermometer inserted into thickest part registers 165°F. Transfer to plate; cover to keep warm.

3 Leaving drippings in skillet, add 1-inch onion pieces and cook over medium heat 4 minutes or until lightly browned. Stir in broth, jam, and vinegar; heat to boiling. Reduce heat to medium and cook 3 to 4 minutes or until sauce is syrupy. Return chicken to skillet and turn to coat with sauce.

4 Meanwhile, cook beans and rice as labels direct; serve with chicken; sprinkle with reserved chopped green onions.

400 CALORIES

PER SERVING. 26G PROTEIN | 52G CARBOHYDRATE | 7G TOTAL FAT (1G SATURATED) 4G FIBER | 94MG CHOLESTEROL | 465MG SODIUM

> **MAKE IT A MEAL:** Glazed chicken thighs, brown rice, and green beans—this dish is already a complete meal. For a refreshing start or finale, add on our Cantaloupe and Cucumber Salad (45 calories; page 402), if you like.

TARRAGON CHICKEN WITH GRAPES

Seedless grapes are an unusual but delicious addition to savory dishes. Their mild sweetness complements the flavor of these chicken breasts.

ACTIVE TIME: 15 MINUTES · **TOTAL TIME:** 30 MINUTES
MAKES: 4 MAIN-DISH SERVINGS

1 CUP QUICK-COOKING (10-MINUTE) BROWN RICE	¼ TEASPOON GROUND BLACK PEPPER
	4 TEASPOONS OLIVE OIL
4 MEDIUM SKINLESS, BONELESS CHICKEN BREAST HALVES (1½ POUNDS)	1 SMALL ONION (4 TO 6 OUNCES)
	½ CUP DRY WHITE WINE
1 TABLESPOON CHOPPED FRESH TARRAGON LEAVES, PLUS ADDITIONAL SPRIGS FOR GARNISH	2 CUPS SEEDLESS RED GRAPES
	1 CUP CANNED OR HOMEMADE CHICKEN BROTH (PAGE 330)
¼ TEASPOON SALT	

1 Prepare rice as label directs.

2 Meanwhile, place chicken between two sheets plastic wrap and, using meat mallet, pound to even ½-inch thickness; season with 2 teaspoons chopped tarragon, salt, and pepper.

3 In 12-inch skillet, heat 2 teaspoons oil over medium heat until hot. Add chicken and cook 12 to 14 minutes, turning over once, until chicken breasts are browned on both sides and instant-read thermometer inserted horizontally into thickest part registers 165°F. Transfer chicken to platter; cover with foil to keep warm.

4 To same skillet, add remaining 2 teaspoons oil and heat over medium heat until hot. Add onion and cook 6 minutes or until tender, stirring occasionally. Stir in wine and cook over medium-high heat 1 minute. Add grapes, broth, and remaining 1 teaspoon tarragon and heat to boiling. Cook 5 minutes or until grapes are tender, stirring occasionally.

5 To serve, divide rice evenly among dinner plates; place chicken breast on rice and spoon grape sauce on top; garnish with tarragon sprigs.

380 CALORIES

PER SERVING. 43G PROTEIN | 34G CARBOHYDRATE | 8G TOTAL FAT (1G SATURATED) 2G FIBER | 99MG CHOLESTEROL | 420MG SODIUM ♥

MAKE IT A MEAL: Add some green to the plate with 1 cup steamed green beans (45 calories).

235 CALORIES

Chicken, Bouillabaisse-Style (page 343)

SOUPS & STEWS

There's nothing more nurturing than a bowl of chicken noodle soup. We share our classic recipe, along with globally inspired variations like Chicken Tortilla Soup and Poule au Pot, a comforting chicken soup that hails from France. We also encourage you to take advantage of the convenience that only a slow cooker can provide: Try Latin Chicken Stew; Chicken, Bouillabaisse-Style; and our tangy Slow-Cooker Barbecue Chicken. For ease, you can use canned chicken broth, but we've also provided a recipe for homemade broth. Make a batch, freeze it in ice cube trays, then transfer to a zip-tight bag in your freezer so you have chicken stock whenever you need it.

KEY TO ICONS

 30 minutes or less   Heart healthy   High fiber   Make ahead   Slow cooker

HOMEMADE CHICKEN BROTH

Nothing beats the rich flavor of homemade chicken broth. Make it in large batches and freeze it in air-tight containers for up to four months. Our recipe has an added bonus: The cooked chicken can be used in casseroles and salads.

ACTIVE TIME: 30 MINUTES · **TOTAL TIME:** 4 HOURS 40 MINUTES PLUS COOLING
MAKES: 5½ CUPS

1	CHICKEN (3½ POUNDS), INCLUDING NECK (RESERVE GIBLETS FOR ANOTHER USE)	5	PARSLEY SPRIGS
2	CARROTS, PEELED AND CUT INTO 2-INCH PIECES	1	GARLIC CLOVE, NOT PEELED
1	STALK CELERY, CUT INTO 2-INCH PIECES	½	TEASPOON DRIED THYME
1	ONION, NOT PEELED, CUT INTO QUARTERS	½	BAY LEAF
		3	QUARTS WATER PLUS MORE IF NEEDED

1 In 6-quart saucepot, combine chicken, chicken neck, carrots, celery, onion, parsley, garlic, thyme, bay leaf, and water. If necessary, add more water to cover broth ingredients; heat to boiling over high heat. With slotted spoon, skim foam from surface. Reduce heat to low; cover and simmer, turning chicken once and skimming foam occasionally, 1 hour.

2 Remove pot from heat; transfer chicken to large bowl. When chicken is cool enough to handle, remove skin and bones; reserve meat for another use. Return skin and bones to pot and heat to boiling over high heat. Skim foam; reduce heat to low and simmer, uncovered, 3 hours.

3 Strain broth through colander into large bowl; discard solids. Strain again though sieve into containers; cool. Cover and refrigerate to use within 3 days, or freeze up to 4 months.

4 Skim and discard fat from surface of broth before use.

35 CALORIES **PER CUP.** 3G PROTEIN | 4G CARBOHYDRATE | 1G TOTAL FAT (1G SATURATED) 0G FIBER | 3MG CHOLESTEROL | 91MG SODIUM ❤

CHICKEN TORTILLA SOUP

This simple, spicy soup will instantly warm you up on a chilly day.

ACTIVE TIME: 25 MINUTES · **TOTAL TIME:** 45 MINUTES
MAKES: 4 MAIN-DISH SERVINGS

6 CORN TORTILLAS	1¾ CUPS WATER
3 TABLESPOONS VEGETABLE OIL	1 POUND SKINLESS, BONELESS CHICKEN BREASTS
1 JAR (15½ OUNCES) MILD CHUNKY TOMATO SALSA	¼ CUP REDUCED-FAT SOUR CREAM
1 CAN (14½ OUNCES) REDUCED-SODIUM CHICKEN BROTH, OR 1¾ CUPS HOMEMADE BROTH (PAGE 330)	1 AVOCADO, PITTED, PEELED, AND CHOPPED

1 Cut tortillas in half, then cut crosswise into ¼-inch-wide strips. In 4-quart saucepan, heat oil over medium heat until shimmering. Add one-third of strips. (Frying in batches makes for crunchy tortilla strips.) Cook 3 to 4 minutes or until golden, stirring and adjusting the heat, if needed, to maintain steady sizzle. With slotted spoon, transfer to paper towels to drain. Repeat with remaining tortillas in two batches. Discard oil.

2 To same saucepan, add salsa. Cook 3 minutes or until thickened. Stir in broth and water and heat to boiling. Reduce heat to maintain gentle simmer. Submerge chicken and half of tortilla strips in liquid. Cover and cook 12 minutes or until chicken is no longer pink in center and instant-read thermometer registers 165°F when inserted horizontally into thickest part of breast. Transfer chicken to plate and use two forks to shred into bite-size pieces. Transfer liquid in pot to blender and puree until smooth. If necessary, return to pot and reheat.

3 Divide soup and chicken among bowls. Top with sour cream, avocado, and remaining tortilla strips.

350 CALORIES

PER SERVING. 28G PROTEIN | 27G CARBOHYDRATE | 15G TOTAL FAT (3G SATURATED) 7G FIBER | 80MG CHOLESTEROL | 1,175MG SODIUM

MAKE IT A MEAL: Pair this south-of-the-border soup with our Corn and Barley Salad (155 calories; page 421). The bright, fresh flavors of both dishes come in at just over 500 calories. Want soup for lunch? Add on ten baby carrots with 2 tablespoons salsa for dipping (50 calories) for a 400-calorie meal.

CHICKEN NOODLE SOUP

For old-fashioned flavor with a minimum of fuss, try this hearty version of the cozy classic.

ACTIVE TIME: 10 MINUTES · **TOTAL TIME:** 25 MINUTES
MAKES: 5 MAIN-DISH SERVINGS

- 1 CARTON (32 OUNCES) CHICKEN BROTH, OR 4 CUPS HOMEMADE BROTH (PAGE 330)
- 4 CUPS WATER
- 1 TABLESPOON OLIVE OIL
- 1 SMALL ONION, CHOPPED
- 2 STALKS CELERY, THINLY SLICED
- 2 CARROTS, PEELED AND THINLY SLICED
- ¼ TEASPOON GROUND BLACK PEPPER
- 1 POUND SKINLESS, BONELESS CHICKEN BREAST HALVES
- 3 CUPS MEDIUM EGG NOODLES, UNCOOKED (6 OUNCES)
- 1 CUP FROZEN PEAS, THAWED

1 In covered 3-quart saucepan, heat chicken broth and water over high heat.
2 Meanwhile, in 5- to 6-quart saucepot, heat oil over medium heat. Add onion and cook, stirring occasionally, until lightly browned, about 5 minutes. Add celery, carrots, hot broth mixture, and pepper; cover saucepot and heat to boiling over high heat.
3 While vegetables are cooking, cut chicken into ¾-inch pieces.
4 Uncover saucepot and stir in egg noodles; cover and cook 3 minutes. Stir in peas and chicken; cover and heat to boiling, 3 to 4 minutes, or until chicken is cooked through.

305 CALORIES

PER SERVING. 30G PROTEIN | 33G CARBOHYDRATE | 6G TOTAL FAT (1G SATURATED) 3G FIBER | 85MG CHOLESTEROL | 615MG SODIUM

MAKE IT A MEAL: To add some crunch and make a 350-calorie lunch, crumble two Saltine crackers (25 calories) into your soup and munch on five baby carrots (20 calories). For a 500-calorie dinner, add one of our Jam Crumble Bars (150 calories; page 437) or a whole-grain roll (100 calories).

THAI CHICKEN-BASIL SOUP

Fresh basil and lime juice give this easy Thai noodle soup its perky personality.

ACTIVE TIME: 20 MINUTES · **TOTAL TIME:** 1 HOUR
MAKES: 4 MAIN-DISH SERVINGS

1½ TEASPOONS VEGETABLE OIL

1   SMALL ONION, CHOPPED

1   SMALL POBLANO CHILE (2 OUNCES), SEEDED AND CHOPPED

2   TEASPOONS FINELY CHOPPED, PEELED FRESH GINGER

2   GARLIC CLOVES, THINLY SLICED

⅛   TEASPOON CRUSHED RED PEPPER

1   CARTON (32 OUNCES) REDUCED-SODIUM CHICKEN BROTH, OR 4 CUPS HOMEMADE BROTH (PAGE 330)

1½ CUPS WATER

¼   CUP PACKED FRESH BASIL LEAVES, THINLY SLICED, PLUS BASIL SPRIGS FOR GARNISH

¾   POUND SKINLESS, BONELESS CHICKEN THIGHS, TRIMMED OF FAT, THINLY SLICED CROSSWISE

½   PACKAGE (7 OUNCES) LINGUINE-STYLE (¼-INCH-WIDE) RICE NOODLES

2   TABLESPOONS FRESH LIME JUICE

1   TABLESPOON REDUCED-SODIUM FISH SAUCE, PLUS ADDITIONAL FOR SERVING (OPTIONAL)

1   In 4- to 5-quart Dutch oven, heat oil over medium heat until hot. Add onion and poblano, and cook 10 minutes or until lightly browned and tender, stirring occasionally. Add ginger, garlic, and crushed red pepper; cook 1 minute.

2   Add broth, water, and half of basil; heat to boiling over high heat. Reduce heat to low; cover and simmer 20 minutes. Uncover; increase heat to medium-high. Stir in chicken and uncooked noodles; heat to boiling. Boil 1 minute, or until chicken is cooked through.

3   Remove Dutch oven from heat. Skim off fat. To serve, stir in lime juice, fish sauce, and remaining basil. Garnish each serving with basil sprigs. Serve with additional fish sauce if you like.

315 **PER SERVING.** 19G PROTEIN | 70G CARBOHYDRATE | 6G TOTAL FAT (1G SATURATED)
CALORIES 1G FIBER | 70MG CHOLESTEROL | 925MG SODIUM

MAKE IT A MEAL: For a fresh and flavorful 465-calorie dinner, start with 45 steamed edamame pods (100 calories). After your soup, enjoy ½ cup ripe, sliced mango (50 calories).

POULE AU POT

This traditional French country chicken soup is light but flavorful, thanks to the addition of fresh tarragon, parsley, and thyme.

ACTIVE TIME: 25 MINUTES · **TOTAL TIME:** 1 HOUR 25 MINUTES
MAKES: 6 MAIN-DISH SERVINGS

2	LARGE LEEKS	1	POUND RED POTATOES, SCRUBBED AND CUT INTO 2-INCH CHUNKS
1	CHICKEN (3 POUNDS), CUT INTO QUARTERS	4	SPRIGS FRESH TARRAGON
4	LARGE CARROTS, PEELED AND CUT INTO 3-INCH SPEARS	4	SPRIGS FRESH FLAT-LEAF PARSLEY
2	LARGE STALKS CELERY, CUT INTO 2-INCH PIECES	3	SPRIGS FRESH THYME
		½	TEASPOON PLUS PINCH SALT
2	LARGE TURNIPS, PEELED AND CUT INTO ½-INCH WEDGES	½	TEASPOON PLUS PINCH GROUND BLACK PEPPER

1 Trim and discard roots and dark green tops from leeks. Discard tough outer leaves. Cut leeks lengthwise in half down to middle of white part, keeping bottom 1 to 2 inches intact. Rinse leeks thoroughly under cold running water, gently fanning cut portion to allow water to remove all sand.
2 In 7½- to 8-quart Dutch oven, arrange chicken in single layer. Top with carrots, celery, turnips, potatoes, and leeks. Add *cold water* to just cover.
3 Strip leaves from tarragon and parsley stems; reserve for garnish. With kitchen string, tie thyme sprigs and tarragon and parsley stems together. Add to Dutch oven, along with ½ teaspoon each salt and pepper; heat to boiling over high heat.
4 Skim and discard foam from surface of water. Partially cover, reduce heat to low, and simmer 30 to 45 minutes or until vegetables are tender and chicken is no longer pink. Finely chop tarragon and parsley leaves.
5 Discard chicken skin and herb stems. Divide chicken and vegetables among serving bowls. Ladle 1 *cup cooking liquid* into each bowl (refrigerating the rest for another use), then season with pinch salt and pepper. Garnish with chopped tarragon and parsley.

345 CALORIES

PER SERVING. 29G PROTEIN | 27G CARBOHYDRATE | 13G TOTAL FAT (4G SATURATED) 5G FIBER | 79MG CHOLESTEROL | 380MG SODIUM ♥ ❂ 🍱

MAKE IT A MEAL: In France, this dish is often served with a toasted baguette, cornichons, Dijon mustard, and fleur de sel or other flaky sea salt. (A slice of baguette is 100 calories; the calories for pickles, Dijon, and salt are negligible.)

CHICKEN AND DUMPLINGS

For a stick-to-your-ribs supper, nothing beats chicken and dumplings. Our low-sodium, lean-chicken version is rich in flavor, but includes only 2 grams of saturated fat and a relatively slim 385 calories. Simmering the skim-milk dumplings in stock makes them as fluffy and delicious as buttery ones and transforms the broth into a silky sauce.

ACTIVE TIME: 30 MINUTES · **TOTAL TIME:** 45 MINUTES
MAKES: 4 MAIN-DISH SERVINGS

1¼ POUNDS BONELESS CHICKEN BREASTS, CUT INTO 1-INCH CHUNKS

¾ TEASPOON SALT

¼ TEASPOON GROUND BLACK PEPPER

2 TABLESPOONS VEGETABLE OIL

4 LARGE CARROTS, PEELED AND THINLY SLICED

3 LARGE STALKS CELERY, THINLY SLICED

1 ONION, CHOPPED

1 CAN (14½ OUNCES) REDUCED-SODIUM CHICKEN BROTH, OR 1¾ CUPS HOMEMADE BROTH (PAGE 330)

1 SPRIG FRESH ROSEMARY

2 CUPS WATER

½ CUP ALL-PURPOSE FLOUR

½ TEASPOON BAKING SODA

2 TEASPOONS TRANS-FAT-FREE SHORTENING

¼ CUP NONFAT MILK

1 CUP FROZEN PEAS

2 TABLESPOONS CHOPPED FRESH PARSLEY

1 Heat 6-quart Dutch oven over medium-high heat until hot. Season chicken with ¼ teaspoon each salt and pepper. To pot, add 1 tablespoon oil, then chicken. Cook 2 to 3 minutes or until no longer pink on outside, stirring. Transfer chicken to bowl; reduce heat to medium.

2 To same pot, add remaining 1 tablespoon oil; stir in carrots, celery, and onion. Cook 5 to 7 minutes or until onion is translucent, stirring occasionally. Add broth, rosemary, and water; heat to simmering.

3 In small bowl, whisk flour, baking soda, and remaining ½ teaspoon salt. With fork, cut in shortening until mixture forms coarse crumbs. Stir in milk just until dough forms.

4 Stir chicken into simmering broth; cook 2 minutes. Stir in peas; cook 1 minute longer. With slotted spoon, transfer chicken and vegetables to large bowl. Do not remove pot from heat.

5 Drop dough into Dutch oven by teaspoons. Simmer 5 minutes, covered, then uncover and simmer 3 to 5 minutes longer or until dumplings are cooked through.
6 Spoon dumplings and broth over chicken mixture. Divide among bowls and garnish with parsley.

385 **PER SERVING.** 39G PROTEIN | 31G CARBOHYDRATE | 11G TOTAL FAT (2G SATURATED)
CALORIES 6G FIBER | 83MG CHOLESTEROL | 780MG SODIUM

MAKE IT A MEAL: Finish this comfort food dinner with an Apricot Oatmeal Cookie (130 calories; page 436)—just 515 calories in all.

CHICKEN AND WHITE BEAN CHILI

Chili is one of the easiest meals to make. We keep this hot and spicy version in the good-for-you category by using heart-healthy white beans and lower-fat ground chicken.

ACTIVE TIME: 20 MINUTES · **TOTAL TIME:** 40 MINUTES
MAKES: 8½ CUPS OR 8 MAIN-DISH SERVINGS

4 TEASPOONS OLIVE OIL	1 JAR (16 OUNCES) MILD SALSA VERDE
2 POUNDS GROUND CHICKEN	2 CANS (15 TO 19 OUNCES EACH) WHITE KIDNEY BEANS (CANNELLINI), RINSED AND DRAINED
1 TEASPOON SALT	
1 ONION, CHOPPED	1 CAN (14½ OUNCES) REDUCED-SODIUM CHICKEN BROTH, OR 1¾ CUPS HOMEMADE BROTH (PAGE 330)
1 GARLIC CLOVE, CRUSHED WITH PRESS	
1 TEASPOON GROUND CUMIN	
½ TEASPOON DRIED OREGANO	2 TABLESPOONS FRESH CILANTRO LEAVES
¼ TEASPOON GROUND CINNAMON	
¼ TEASPOON CAYENNE (GROUND RED) PEPPER	

1 In 6-quart Dutch oven, heat 1 teaspoon oil over medium-high heat until very hot. Sprinkle chicken with salt. Add chicken to Dutch oven in two batches, and cook 6 minutes per batch or until chicken is no longer pink, stirring occasionally and adding 1 teaspoon more oil for second batch. With slotted spoon, transfer chicken to medium bowl once done.

2 After all chicken is cooked, add remaining 2 teaspoons oil with onion and garlic to Dutch oven, and cook over medium heat 5 to 6 minutes or until browned, stirring occasionally. Stir in cumin, oregano, cinnamon, and cayenne; cook 1 minute. Add salsa, beans, broth, and browned chicken; heat to boiling over high heat. Reduce heat to medium; cover and cook chili 15 minutes to blend flavors. To serve, garnish with cilantro.

370 CALORIES

PER SERVING. 25G PROTEIN | 25G CARBOHYDRATE | 18G TOTAL FAT (0G SATURATED) 6G FIBER | 0MG CHOLESTEROL | 815MG SODIUM 🌱 🗂

MAKE IT A MEAL: Pair this zippy chili with our crunchy Tricolor Slaw (40 calories; page 402) for a 410-calorie lunch or casual dinner.

CHICKEN RAGOUT IN SQUASH BOWLS

This warming main-dish stew is cleverly served in acorn squash bowls. Once you've finished the stew, you can nibble on your bowl.

TOTAL TIME: 25 MINUTES
MAKES: 4 MAIN-DISH SERVINGS

2   SMALL ACORN SQUASHES
    (1 POUND EACH), EACH CUT
    CROSSWISE IN HALF AND SEEDED

¼   TEASPOON COARSELY GROUND
    BLACK PEPPER

½   TEASPOON SALT

1   SLICE BACON, CUT INTO
    ¼-INCH PIECES

1   ONION, CUT IN HALF
    AND THINLY SLICED

1½ CUPS APPLE CIDER

1   TEASPOON CORNSTARCH

1   GRANNY SMITH APPLE,
    CUT INTO THIN WEDGES

½   TEASPOON DRIED SAGE

8   OUNCES SKINLESS, BONELESS
    COOKED CHICKEN BREAST, CUT
    INTO ½-INCH PIECES (2 CUPS)

1 Sprinkle insides of squash halves with pepper and ¼ teaspoon salt. Place halves, cut sides down, on microwave-safe plate. Cook in microwave oven on High for 8 minutes or until fork-tender. Keep warm.

2 Meanwhile, in 12-inch skillet, cook bacon and onion over medium heat 8 to 10 minutes or until browned. In small bowl, with wire whisk, mix cider and cornstarch until blended. Add cider mixture and apple to skillet; increase heat to medium-high. Cook 3 minutes or until mixture thickens slightly, stirring occasionally.

3 Add sage, chicken, and remaining ¼ teaspoon salt to skillet; cover and cook 3 minutes or until apple is tender and chicken is no longer pink and heated through. Spoon chicken mixture into centers of squash halves to serve.

300 CALORIES **PER SERVING.** 20G PROTEIN | 39G CARBOHYDRATE | 8G TOTAL FAT (3G SATURATED)
5G FIBER | 55MG CHOLESTEROL | 410MG SODIUM

MAKE IT A MEAL: Pair with a corn muffin made from store-bought mix (150 calories) for a 450-calorie meal.

QUICK CHICKEN MOLE

Our speedy version of mole, a richly-flavored sauce with spices, nuts, and raisins, is authentic enough to satisfy any Mexican-food aficionado.

ACTIVE TIME: 10 MINUTES · **TOTAL TIME:** 15 MINUTES
MAKES: 4 MAIN-DISH SERVINGS

---

2   TEASPOONS OLIVE OIL

1   ONION, CHOPPED

2   GARLIC CLOVES,
    CRUSHED WITH PRESS

2   TEASPOONS CHILI POWDER

2   TEASPOONS UNSWEETENED COCOA

¼   TEASPOON GROUND CINNAMON

1¼ CUPS CANNED OR HOMEMADE
    BROTH (PAGE 330)

1   TABLESPOON CREAMY
    PEANUT BUTTER

1   TABLESPOON TOMATO PASTE

¼   CUP GOLDEN OR DARK
    SEEDLESS RAISINS

1   ROTISSERIE CHICKEN (2 TO 2½
    POUNDS), CUT INTO 8 PIECES, SKIN
    REMOVED

¼   CUP LOOSELY PACKED FRESH
    CILANTRO LEAVES, CHOPPED

COOKED RICE (OPTIONAL)

LIME WEDGES FOR GARNISH

1 In nonstick 12-inch skillet, heat oil over medium heat until hot. Add onion and cook 5 minutes, stirring occasionally. Add garlic, chili powder, cocoa, and cinnamon; cook 1 minute, stirring constantly.

2 Stir in chicken broth, peanut butter, and tomato paste. Add raisins; heat to boiling. Add chicken pieces to skillet. Reduce heat to medium-low; cover and simmer about 5 minutes (10 minutes if chicken has been refrigerated) to blend flavors, turning chicken pieces over halfway through cooking to coat all sides with sauce. (Instant-read thermometer inserted into chicken should register 165°F.)

3 Sprinkle chicken with cilantro. Serve chicken and sauce over rice if you like. Garnish with lime wedges.

400 CALORIES **PER SERVING.** 44G PROTEIN | 15G CARBOHYDRATE | 18G TOTAL FAT (4G SATURATED) 2G FIBER | 126MG CHOLESTEROL | 475MG SODIUM 💙 ❤️

MAKE IT A MEAL: One-half cup cooked white rice (100 calories) makes this a 500-calorie dinner. Or, for a 465-calorie meal, skip the rice and pair the mole with our zippy Bloody Mary Tomato Salad (65 calories; page 403).

LATIN CHICKEN STEW

This spicy, smoky slow-cooker dish provides a good portion of your daily fiber and beta carotene, thanks to black beans and sweet potatoes.

ACTIVE TIME: 15 MINUTES · **SLOW-COOK TIME:** 8 HOURS ON LOW OR 4 HOURS ON HIGH
MAKES: 6 MAIN-DISH SERVINGS

---

3   POUNDS BONE-IN SKINLESS
    CHICKEN THIGHS

2   TEASPOONS GROUND CUMIN

¼   TEASPOON SALT

¼   TEASPOON GROUND BLACK PEPPER

1   TEASPOON SMOKED PAPRIKA, OR
    ½ TEASPOON CHOPPED CHIPOTLE
    CHILES IN ADOBO SAUCE

½   TEASPOON GROUND ALLSPICE

1   CUP CANNED OR HOMEMADE
    CHICKEN BROTH (PAGE 330)

½   CUP PREPARED SALSA

3   LARGE GARLIC CLOVES,
    CRUSHED WITH PRESS

2   CANS (15 TO 19 OUNCES EACH) BLACK
    BEANS, RINSED AND DRAINED

2   POUNDS SWEET POTATOES, PEELED
    CUT INTO 2-INCH CHUNKS

1   JARRED ROASTED RED PEPPER, CUT
    INTO STRIPS (1 CUP)

⅓   CUP LOOSELY PACKED FRESH
    CILANTRO LEAVES, CHOPPED

LIME WEDGES

1   Sprinkle chicken thighs with ½ teaspoon ground cumin, salt, and pepper. Heat nonstick 12-inch skillet over medium heat; add chicken thighs and cook until well browned on all sides, about 12 minutes. Transfer to plate. Remove skillet from heat.

2   In same skillet, combine smoked paprika, allspice, chicken broth, salsa, garlic, and remaining 1½ teaspoons cumin.

3   In 6-quart slow cooker, combine beans and sweet potatoes. Place chicken on top of potato mixture in slow cooker; pour broth mixture over chicken. Cover slow cooker with lid and cook as manufacturer directs, on Low 8 hours or on High 4 hours.

4   With tongs or slotted spoon, remove chicken pieces to large platter. Gently stir roasted red pepper strips into potato mixture. Spoon mixture over chicken. Sprinkle with cilantro and serve with lime wedges.

---

400 CALORIES   **PER SERVING.** 35G PROTEIN | 54G CARBOHYDRATE | 5G TOTAL FAT (1G SATURATED) 16G FIBER | 93MG CHOLESTEROL | 954MG SODIUM 🌾 🥗 🍱

MAKE IT A MEAL: Wrap up dinner with a strawberry and kiwi fruit salad (50 calories for 1 cup halved berries plus 1 sliced kiwi). The entire meal—and it's substantial—is just 450 calories.

CHICKEN, BOUILLABAISSE-STYLE

Instead of seafood, this delectable bouillabaisse boasts easy-to-prepare chicken thighs simmered in a traditional saffron broth.

ACTIVE TIME: 30 MINUTES · **SLOW-COOK TIME:** 8 HOURS ON LOW OR 4 HOURS ON HIGH
MAKES: 6 MAIN-DISH SERVINGS

1 TABLESPOON OLIVE OIL PLUS ADDITIONAL IF NEEDED

3 POUNDS BONE-IN CHICKEN THIGHS, SKIN AND FAT REMOVED

1 TEASPOON SALT

¼ TEASPOON GROUND BLACK PEPPER

½ CUP DRY WHITE WINE

1 LARGE BULB FENNEL (1½ POUNDS)

1 ONION, CHOPPED

2 GARLIC CLOVES, FINELY CHOPPED

1 CAN (14½ OUNCES) CHICKEN BROTH, OR 1¾ CUPS HOMEMADE BROTH (PAGE 330)

1 CAN (14½ OUNCES) DICED TOMATOES IN JUICE

1 BAY LEAF

½ TEASPOON DRIED THYME

¼ TEASPOON SAFFRON THREADS, CRUMBLED

1 In 12-inch skillet, heat oil over medium-high heat. Sprinkle chicken with salt and pepper. Add to skillet in two batches and cook, turning once and adding more oil if necessary, until lightly browned on both sides, 7 to 8 minutes per batch. With tongs, transfer chicken to bowl when browned. Then add wine to skillet and heat to boiling, stirring to loosen any browned bits. Boil 1 minute.

2 Trim stems and tough outer layers from fennel bulb. Cut bulb into quarters, then thinly slice crosswise.

3 In 4¼- to 6-quart slow-cooker bowl, combine fennel, onion, garlic, broth, tomatoes with their juice, bay leaf, thyme, and saffron. Top with browned chicken, any juices in bowl, and wine mixture from skillet; do not stir. Cover slow cooker and cook on Low 8 hours or on High 4 hours.

4 With tongs, transfer chicken to serving bowls. Discard bay leaf. Skim and discard fat from sauce. Pour sauce over chicken. Serve with bread, if desired.

235 CALORIES **PER SERVING.** 29G PROTEIN | 12G CARBOHYDRATE | 8G TOTAL FAT (1G SATURATED) 4G FIBER | 113MG CHOLESTEROL | 770MG SODIUM 🥗 🍲

MAKE IT A MEAL: Add a small slice of French bread (115 calories) to soak up the broth and a glass of white wine (120 calories). Total calories: 470.

SLOW-COOKER BARBECUE CHICKEN

Who knew you could make barbecue chicken in a slow cooker? This recipe yields more than enough for one family meal. Use the leftovers to make our salad with apples and cheddar (opposite) the next day.

ACTIVE TIME: 15 MINUTES · **SLOW-COOK TIME:** 4 HOURS ON HIGH
MAKES: 4 MAIN-DISH SERVINGS

1	CUP KETCHUP	⅜	TEASPOON GROUND BLACK PEPPER
2	TABLESPOONS SPICY BROWN MUSTARD	½	TEASPOON SALT
2	TABLESPOONS BALSAMIC VINEGAR	4	BONE-IN CHICKEN BREAST HALVES (3 TO 3½ POUNDS), SKIN REMOVED
2	TEASPOONS WORCESTERSHIRE SAUCE	4	CHICKEN DRUMSTICKS (1½ POUNDS), SKIN REMOVED
1	GARLIC CLOVE, CRUSHED WITH PRESS		COLESLAW, FOR SERVING (OPTIONAL)
¼	TEASPOON SMOKED PAPRIKA		

1 Spray 6-quart slow-cooker bowl with nonstick cooking spray.

2 In medium mixing bowl, with wire whisk, stir together ketchup, mustard, vinegar, Worcestershire, garlic, paprika, and ⅛ teaspoon pepper; transfer half of sauce to slow-cooker bowl.

3 Sprinkle chicken with salt and remaining ¼ teaspoon pepper; add to slow-cooker bowl. Spoon remaining sauce over and around chicken to coat. Cover with lid and cook on High 4 hours, or until chicken is no longer pink.

4 Transfer 2 chicken breasts to container; refrigerate up to 3 days. Transfer remaining chicken to serving platter. Whisk cooking liquid until well mixed; drizzle over chicken. (If you prefer thicker sauce, boil liquid in saucepan until reduced to desired consistency.) Serve chicken with coleslaw, if you like, and any remaining sauce.

320 CALORIES | **PER SERVING.** 44G PROTEIN | 18G CARBOHYDRATE | 7G TOTAL FAT (2G SATURATED) 0G FIBER | 144MG CHOLESTEROL | 1,275MG SODIUM

MAKE IT A MEAL: Our recipe suggests a side of coleslaw, as shown in the photo. Try our Tricolor Slaw (40 calories; page 402) for a 360-calorie lunch. For a festive barbecue dinner for less than 500 calories, pair the chicken with our Three-Bean and Corn Salad (160 calories; page 422).

CHICKEN SALAD WITH APPLES AND CHEDDAR

Remove and discard bones from leftover Slow-Cooker Barbecue Chicken; shred meat. In large bowl, whisk **3 tablespoons olive oil, 2 tablespoons cider vinegar, 2 teaspoons Dijon mustard, and ¼ teaspoon each salt and ground black pepper.** To same bowl, add **1 chopped head red leaf lettuce** and **1 very thinly sliced small red pepper**; toss until well combined. Divide among serving plates; top with chicken, **1 thinly sliced Granny Smith apple, ¼ cup toasted and chopped walnuts,** and **2 ounces shredded extra-sharp Cheddar cheese**. Makes 4 main-dish servings.

400 **CALORIES** — **PER SERVING.** 36G PROTEIN | 12G CARBOHYDRATE | 23G TOTAL FAT (6G SATURATED) 3G FIBER | 95MG CHOLESTEROL | 415MG SODIUM

210 CALORIES

Tandoori Chicken with Chutney (page 360)

HOT OFF THE GRILL

Chicken skewers, cutlets, bone-in breasts, and thighs are all spectacular grilled outdoors on the patio or in a grill pan in the kitchen. Savor this tasty selection of quick options for both methods. Skinless, boneless chicken breasts or cutlets are the fastest—and skinniest!—choice. You'll love Chicken and Veggies with Avocado Salsa, Barbecue Chicken Cutlets with Citrus Slaw, and Basil-Orange Chicken served on a bed of whole-wheat couscous. Each can be made in a grill pan for a fast weeknight meal. Entertaining outdoors? Our 400-calorie (or less) Mojito Chicken with Pineapple or Tandoori Chicken with Chutney will be sure to impress your guests.

KEY TO ICONS

● 30 minutes or less   ♥ Heart healthy   ❀ High fiber   ▤ Make ahead   ▥ Slow cooker

JERK CHICKEN KABOBS

Originally, jerk seasoning was used to season pork shoulder, which was "jerked" apart into shreds before serving. Nowadays, this very popular power-packed seasoning rub is enjoyed on chicken and fish as well.

ACTIVE TIME: 15 MINUTES · **TOTAL TIME:** 25 MINUTES PLUS MARINATING
MAKES: 4 MAIN-DISH SERVINGS

2 GREEN ONIONS, CHOPPED	3 TEASPOONS VEGETABLE OIL
1 JALAPEÑO CHILE, SEEDED AND MINCED	⅝ TEASPOON SALT
1 TABLESPOON MINCED, PEELED FRESH GINGER	1 POUND SKINLESS, BONELESS CHICKEN BREAST HALVES, CUT INTO 12 PIECES
2 TABLESPOONS WHITE WINE VINEGAR	1 RED PEPPER, CUT INTO 1-INCH PIECES
2 TABLESPOONS WORCESTERSHIRE SAUCE	1 GREEN PEPPER, CUT INTO 1-INCH PIECES
1 TEASPOON GROUND ALLSPICE	4 (12-INCH) METAL SKEWERS
1 TEASPOON DRIED THYME	

1 In blender or in food processor with knife blade attached, process green onions, jalapeño, ginger, vinegar, Worcestershire, allspice, thyme, 2 teaspoons oil, and ½ teaspoon salt until paste forms.
2 Place chicken in small bowl or zip-tight plastic bag and add paste, turning to coat chicken. Cover bowl or seal bag and refrigerate 1 hour to marinate.
3 Meanwhile, in small bowl, toss red and green peppers with remaining 1 teaspoon oil and ⅛ teaspoon salt.
4 Prepare outdoor grill for direct grilling over medium heat. Alternately thread chicken and pepper pieces on each skewer.
5 Place kabobs on hot grill rack. Brush kabobs with any remaining marinade. Cook kabobs 5 minutes; turn over and cook until instant-read thermometer inserted in chicken reaches 165°F, about 5 minutes longer.

200 CALORIES

PER SERVING. 27G PROTEIN | 6G CARBOHYDRATE | 5G TOTAL FAT (1G SATURATED) 2G FIBER | 66MG CHOLESTEROL | 525MG SODIUM

MAKE IT A MEAL: Pair with Confetti Rice Pilaf (165 calories; page 423) for a 365-calorie lunch. For dinner, add Corn on the Cob with Molasses Butter (105 calories; page 409) to make a 470-calorie meal.

SPICED CHICKEN SKEWERS

Spice up your meal with this quick and healthy recipe seasoned with chili powder and fresh lemon and served on top of fiber-packed bulgur.

ACTIVE TIME: 20 MINUTES · **TOTAL TIME:** 30 MINUTES
MAKES: 4 MAIN-DISH SERVINGS

8	BAMBOO SKEWERS	½	TEASPOON SALT
1	CUP BULGUR	½	TEASPOON GROUND BLACK PEPPER
1¾	CUPS WATER	2	PINTS CHERRY TOMATOES
1	POUND BONELESS SKINLESS CHICKEN BREASTS, CUT INTO 1-INCH CHUNKS	2	LEMONS
2	TEASPOONS CHILI POWDER	1	GARLIC CLOVE, CRUSHED WITH PRESS
2	TEASPOONS EXTRA-VIRGIN OLIVE OIL	1	CUP CHOPPED FLAT-LEAF PARSLEY LEAVES

1 Soak skewers in cold water at least 30 minutes. Prepare outdoor grill for direct grilling or preheat large grill pan over medium-high heat.

2 In large microwave-safe bowl, combine bulgur and water. Microwave on High for 10 minutes or until bulgur is tender and water is absorbed, stirring once.

3 In medium bowl, toss chicken with chili powder, 1 teaspoon oil, and ¼ teaspoon each salt and pepper until well coated. Thread chicken and tomatoes alternately onto skewers, spacing ¼ inch apart.

4 Place chicken skewers on hot grill grate or pan and grill 7 to 8 minutes or until chicken just loses pink color throughout, turning occasionally.

5 Meanwhile, from 1 lemon, finely grate 1 teaspoon peel and squeeze 3 tablespoons juice and place in bowl with bulgur. Add garlic, parsley, remaining ¼ teaspoon each salt and pepper, and remaining 1 teaspoon oil. Stir well.

6 Divide bulgur mixture and chicken skewers among serving plates. Serve with remaining lemon, cut into wedges.

305 CALORIES

PER SERVING. 29G PROTEIN | 37G CARBOHYDRATE | 6G TOTAL FAT (1G SATURATED) 10G FIBER | 63MG CHOLESTEROL | 390MG SODIUM

MAKE IT A MEAL: Pair this spicy kabob and whole-grains combo with a green salad topped with ½ cup ripe avocado cubes and enjoy an orange for dessert (190 calories for add-ons). The complete meal is 495 calories.

CHINESE FIVE-SPICE CHICKEN

This glazed chicken dish is a cinch for outdoor or indoor grilling—just a few ingredients provide so much flavor.

ACTIVE TIME: 10 MINUTES · **TOTAL TIME:** 35 MINUTES PLUS MARINATING
MAKES: 4 MAIN-DISH SERVINGS

¼   CUP DRY SHERRY

1   TABLESPOON ASIAN SESAME OIL

1   TEASPOON CHINESE
    FIVE-SPICE POWDER

¼   TEASPOON CAYENNE
    (GROUND RED) PEPPER

1   CHICKEN (3½ POUNDS), CUT INTO
    8 PIECES, SKIN REMOVED FROM
    ALL BUT WINGS

⅓   CUP HOISIN SAUCE

1   TABLESPOON SOY SAUCE

1   TEASPOON SESAME SEEDS

1 In large bowl, stir sherry, sesame oil, five-spice powder, and cayenne. Add chicken and toss until evenly coated. Cover bowl and let stand 15 minutes at room temperature, turning chicken occasionally.

2 Prepare outdoor grill for direct grilling over medium heat.

3 Place chicken on hot grill rack. Cover and cook 20 to 25 minutes, turning pieces over once. As pieces finish cooking, remove to platter.

4 In small bowl, mix hoisin sauce and soy sauce. Brush all over chicken and return to grill. Cook 4 to 5 minutes longer or until glazed, turning once. Chicken is done when instant-read thermometer inserted into thickest part registers 165°F. Return chicken to platter; sprinkle with sesame seeds.

350
CALORIES
PER SERVING. 41G PROTEIN | 10G CARBOHYDRATE | 15G TOTAL FAT (4G SATURATED) 1G FIBER | 121MG CHOLESTEROL | 595MG SODIUM

MAKE IT A MEAL: Serve the chicken over ¾ cup aromatic jasmine or basmati rice (150 calories) alongside 2 cups steamed spinach (15 calories). The complete meal is just 515 calories.

BASIL-ORANGE CHICKEN

Marinating chicken in orange and basil gives it a bright, fresh flavor. This light dish is perfect for warmer weather.

ACTIVE TIME: 20 MINUTES · **TOTAL TIME:** 30 MINUTES
MAKES: 4 MAIN-DISH SERVINGS

2	LARGE NAVEL ORANGES	4	SKINLESS, BONELESS CHICKEN BREAST HALVES (1½ POUNDS)
3	LEMONS		
½	CUP PACKED FRESH BASIL LEAVES, CHOPPED	½	TEASPOON SUGAR
		1	CUP WHOLE-WHEAT COUSCOUS
2	TABLESPOONS OLIVE OIL	1	PACKAGE (8 OUNCES) STRINGLESS SUGAR SNAP PEAS
⅜	TEASPOON SALT		
⅜	TEASPOON GROUND BLACK PEPPER		

1 From 1 orange, grate 1½ teaspoons peel and squeeze ¼ cup juice. From 2 lemons, grate 1½ teaspoons peel and squeeze ⅓ cup juice. Cut remaining orange and lemon into slices and set aside.

2 In medium bowl, combine 1 teaspoon each orange and lemon peel and 1 tablespoon orange juice with half of basil, 1 tablespoon olive oil, and ¼ teaspoon each salt and pepper.

3 Place chicken breasts between two sheets plastic wrap and, using flat side of meat mallet, pound to even ½-inch thickness. Add chicken to citrus mixture, turning to coat; set aside.

4 In small pitcher or bowl, combine sugar along with remaining ⅛ teaspoon each salt and pepper, citrus peels, and orange juice; add remaining lemon juice, basil, and oil; set aside. (Can be made to this point up to 8 hours ahead. Cover chicken and citrus sauce and refrigerate.)

5 Preheat large ridged grill pan or prepare outdoor grill for direct grilling over medium-high heat.

6 Meanwhile, prepare couscous as label directs. Fill 4-quart saucepan with ½ inch *water* and set vegetable steamer inside. Heat to boiling over high heat.

7 Grill chicken 4 minutes. Turn chicken over and cook 3 to 4 minutes longer or until no longer pink in center. Instant-read thermometer inserted horizontally into thickest part should register 165°F. During last 2 to 3 minutes while chicken cooks, place citrus slices on grill.

8 While chicken is cooking on second side, add snap peas to steamer; cook 2 to 3 minutes or until tender-crisp. Fluff couscous and spoon onto large platter; top with chicken and snap peas. Drizzle sauce over all. Garnish with grilled citrus slices.

400 **PER SERVING.** 46G PROTEIN | 33G CARBOHYDRATE | 9G TOTAL FAT (1G SATURATED)
CALORIES 6G FIBER | 99MG CHOLESTEROL | 365MG SODIUM

MAKE IT A MEAL: Grilled chicken, whole-wheat couscous, and snap peas are a meal on their own. If you want to add a refreshing finish, scoop ½ cup lemon sorbet and top with ¼ cup blueberries (100 calories). The total meal is 500 calories.

GRILLED CHICKEN AND GREENS

Lighten up with seasonal watercress and asparagus, served with easy flash-grilled chicken breasts. The greens deliver disease-fighting antioxidants and fiber—and almost no calories.

TOTAL TIME: 30 MINUTES

MAKES: 4 MAIN-DISH SERVINGS

1   CUP FRESH MINT LEAVES, PACKED

1 TO 2 LEMONS

2   GARLIC CLOVES, CRUSHED WITH PRESS

5   TEASPOONS EXTRA-VIRGIN OLIVE OIL

¼   TEASPOON PLUS PINCH SALT

¼   TEASPOON PLUS PINCH GROUND BLACK PEPPER

1   POUND SKINLESS, BONELESS CHICKEN BREAST HALVES, POUNDED TO EVEN ⅓-INCH THICKNESS

1   POUND ASPARAGUS, ENDS TRIMMED

1   POUND RADISHES, TRIMMED AND VERY THINLY SLICED

2   PACKAGES (4 OUNCES EACH) WATERCRESS

1 Preheat large ridged grill pan or prepare outdoor grill for direct grilling over medium-high heat.

2 Finely chop half of mint. From lemons, finely grate 1 teaspoon peel and squeeze ¼ cup juice. In 9-inch pie plate, combine chopped mint, lemon peel, 1 tablespoon lemon juice, half of garlic, 1 teaspoon oil, and ⅛ teaspoon each salt and pepper. Add chicken and rub to evenly coat.

3 On jelly-roll pan, toss asparagus with 1 teaspoon oil, pinch each salt and pepper, and remaining garlic. Grill 4 to 6 minutes, turning occasionally.

4 Meanwhile, in large bowl, toss radishes, watercress, and remaining 3 tablespoons lemon juice, 1 tablespoon oil, and ⅛ teaspoon each salt and pepper, and mint leaves. Divide among plates.

5 Place asparagus on greens. Grill chicken 2 to 3 minutes per side, until instant-read thermometer inserted horizontally into center registers 165°F. Divide among plates with greens; serve immediately.

225 CALORIES **PER SERVING.** 27G PROTEIN | 10G CARBOHYDRATE | 9G TOTAL FAT (2G SATURATED) 5G FIBER | 63MG CHOLESTEROL | 315MG SODIUM

MAKE IT A MEAL: Pair with Red Quinoa Pilaf (250 calories; page 427) for a nutrient-packed 475-calorie dinner.

CHICKEN BRUSCHETTA

Add grilled chicken breasts to this popular appetizer, and you have a lean, fiber- and vitamin C-rich dinner that's good for your heart—and your taste buds.

ACTIVE TIME: 20 MINUTES · **TOTAL TIME:** 25 MINUTES
MAKES: 4 MAIN-DISH SERVINGS

---

3   GARLIC CLOVES

1   TABLESPOON EXTRA-VIRGIN OLIVE OIL

⅜   TEASPOON SALT

⅜   TEASPOON GROUND BLACK PEPPER

4   SKINLESS, BONELESS CHICKEN BREAST HALVES (1½ POUNDS)

1¾ POUNDS TOMATOES, CHOPPED

1   SMALL SHALLOT, FINELY CHOPPED

¼   CUP PACKED FRESH BASIL LEAVES, FINELY CHOPPED

2   TABLESPOONS RED WINE VINEGAR

1   LOAF ROUND CRUSTY WHOLE WHEAT BREAD (8 OUNCES), SLICED

1   Prepare outdoor grill for direct grilling over medium heat. Crush 2 garlic cloves with garlic press.

2   In 9-inch pie plate, mix crushed garlic cloves, 1 teaspoon oil, and ¼ teaspoon each salt and pepper, then rub all over chicken.

3   In large bowl, combine tomatoes, shallot, basil, vinegar, 1 teaspoon oil, and remaining ⅛ teaspoon each salt and pepper. Let stand.

4   Grill chicken breasts, covered, 10 to 13 minutes, until instant-read thermometer inserted horizontally into thickest part registers 165°F. Transfer to cutting board. Let rest 10 minutes; slice.

5   Cut remaining garlic clove in half. Rub cut sides all over bread slices, then brush bread with remaining 1 teaspoon oil. Grill 1 minute, turning once. Divide bread and chicken among serving plates; top with tomato mixture.

365 CALORIES

PER SERVING. 45G PROTEIN | 31G CARBOHYDRATE | 7G TOTAL FAT (1G SATURATED)
5G FIBER | 99MG CHOLESTEROL | 325MG SODIUM 💙 ❤️ 🌾

MAKE IT A MEAL: Grilled chicken, garlic-rubbed toast, and grilled tomatoes make a lovely lunch. If you'd like to serve this main dish for dinner, add a simple salad of 2 cups mixed greens tossed with 1 tablespoon balsamic vinaigrette (120 calories)—that's 485 calories in all.

CHICKEN AND VEGGIES WITH AVOCADO SALSA

Whip up the easy salsa while the chicken and veggies are on the grill.

TOTAL TIME: 30 MINUTES
MAKES: 4 MAIN-DISH SERVINGS

4 MEDIUM SKINLESS, BONELESS CHICKEN BREAST HALVES (1½ POUNDS)

¾ TEASPOON SALT

¼ TEASPOON GROUND BLACK PEPPER

1 TO 2 LIMES

2 TABLESPOONS OLIVE OIL

2 LARGE TOMATOES (10 TO 12 OUNCES EACH), CUT CROSSWISE INTO ½-INCH-THICK SLICES

2 RED, ORANGE, AND/OR YELLOW PEPPERS, EACH CUT INTO QUARTERS

1 RIPE AVOCADO, CUT INTO ½-INCH CHUNKS

1 CUP CHOPPED JICAMA (10 TO 12 OUNCES)

¼ CUP LOOSELY PACKED FRESH CILANTRO LEAVES, CHOPPED, PLUS ADDITIONAL LEAVES FOR GARNISH

⅛ TEASPOON CAYENNE (GROUND RED) PEPPER

1 Preheat large ridged grill pan or prepare outdoor grill for direct grilling over medium heat.

2 Place chicken between two sheets plastic wrap and, using meat mallet, pound to even ½-inch thickness; season with ¼ teaspoon salt and ⅛ teaspoon pepper.

3 From limes, grate 1½ teaspoons peel and squeeze 3 tablespoons juice. In small bowl, combine peel, 1 tablespoon juice, oil, ¼ teaspoon salt, and remaining ⅛ teaspoon pepper.

4 Brush tomatoes and peppers with oil mixture and place on hot grill pan or rack. Place chicken on pan or rack. Cook chicken and vegetables 8 to 9 minutes, turning over once. Vegetables should be browned and tender. Chicken breasts should be browned on both sides and no longer pink throughout; instant-read thermometer inserted horizontally into thickest part should register 165°F.

5 While vegetables and chicken are grilling, in medium bowl, stir together avocado, jicama, cilantro, cayenne, and remaining ¼ teaspoon salt and 2 tablespoons lime juice. Makes 2½ cups salsa.

6 Serve chicken and vegetables with avocado salsa; garnish with fresh cilantro leaves.

380
CALORIES

PER SERVING. 42G PROTEIN | 17G CARBOHYDRATE | 17G TOTAL FAT (3G SATURATED)
7G FIBER | 99MG CHOLESTEROL | 545MG SODIUM

MAKE IT A MEAL: Serve with two corn tortillas (100 calories) warmed on
the grill.

BBQ CHICKEN CUTLETS WITH CITRUS SLAW

This quick and easy grill-pan dish is sure to become a weeknight fave.

TOTAL TIME: 30 MINUTES
MAKES: 4 MAIN-DISH SERVINGS

1 LARGE NAVEL ORANGE

4 MEDIUM SKINLESS, BONELESS CHICKEN BREAST HALVES

¾ CUP BOTTLED BARBECUE SAUCE

1 TEASPOON DIJON MUSTARD

8 OUNCES SHREDDED CABBAGE MIX FOR COLESLAW

1 SMALL BULB FENNEL, THINLY SLICED, SOME FRONDS RESERVED FOR GARNISH

1 TABLESPOON WHITE WINE VINEGAR

¼ TEASPOON SALT

¼ TEASPOON GROUND BLACK PEPPER

1 From orange, grate 1½ teaspoons peel; set aside. With knife, cut remaining peel and white pith from orange and discard. Holding orange over small bowl to catch juice, cut out segments between membranes; drop segments into bowl. With slotted spoon, transfer segments to cutting board; coarsely chop. Reserve 2 tablespoons orange juice.

2 Place chicken between two sheets plastic wrap and, using meat mallet, pound to even ½-inch thickness. Spray large ridged grill pan with cooking spray and heat over medium-high until hot. Combine barbecue sauce, Dijon, and 1 teaspoon orange peel; reserve ¼ cup sauce for serving.

3 Grill chicken 4 minutes, turning over once. Generously brush with remaining barbecue-sauce mixture; cook 3 to 4 minutes longer, turning over often and brushing with sauce frequently, until instant-read thermometer inserted horizontally into thickest of part of breast registers 165°F.

4 While chicken is cooking, make citrus slaw. In large bowl, mix orange pieces, reserved 2 tablespoons juice, cabbage mix, fennel, vinegar, salt, pepper, and remaining ½ teaspoon orange peel; toss. Makes 4½ cups.

5 Serve slaw with chicken; garnish with fennel fronds and drizzle with reserved barbecue sauce.

265 CALORIES **PER SERVING.** 42G PROTEIN | 17G CARBOHYDRATE | 3G TOTAL FAT (1G SATURATED) 4G FIBER | 99MG CHOLESTEROL | 600MG SODIUM

MAKE IT A MEAL: Pair Garden Macaroni Salad (135 calories; page 412) with barbecued chicken and slaw.

TANDOORI CHICKEN WITH CHUTNEY

Make an Indian classic on your home grill. For photo, see page 346.

ACTIVE TIME: 20 MINUTES · **TOTAL TIME:** 50 MINUTES PLUS MARINATING
MAKES: 4 MAIN-DISH SERVINGS

3 TABLESPOONS PLAIN LOW-FAT YOGURT	¾ TEASPOON SALT
1 TABLESPOON PAPRIKA	4 MEDIUM BONE-IN CHICKEN BREAST HALVES (2 POUNDS TOTAL), SKIN REMOVED
1½ TEASPOONS GROUND CUMIN	
1½ TEASPOONS GROUND CORIANDER	2 FIRM, RIPE MANGOES, PEELED, SEEDED, AND CUT INTO SLICES
½ TEASPOON CAYENNE (GROUND RED) PEPPER	1 TABLESPOON LIGHT BROWN SUGAR
1 GARLIC CLOVE, CRUSHED WITH PRESS	1 TABLESPOON CIDER VINEGAR
4½ TEASPOONS GRATED, PEELED FRESH GINGER	1 SMALL GREEN ONION, THINLY SLICED
	COOKED BASMATI RICE (OPTIONAL)

1 In small bowl, mix yogurt, paprika, cumin, coriander, cayenne, garlic, 4 teaspoons ginger, and ½ teaspoon salt; pour into large zip-tight plastic bag. Add chicken, turning to coat; refrigerate at least 1 hour or up to 4 hours.
2 Meanwhile, prepare outdoor grill for direct grilling over medium heat.
3 Grill mango until lightly charred, about 8 minutes, turning over once. Transfer to cutting board to cool slightly.
4 Coarsely chop mangoes and place in medium bowl. Add brown sugar, vinegar, green onion, and remaining ¼ teaspoon salt and ½ teaspoon ginger; stir to combine. Makes about 2 cups chutney.
5 Remove chicken from marinade; discard marinade. Grill chicken breasts, covered, 20 to 25 minutes, turning over once, until instant-read thermometer inserted into thickest part registers 165°F. Transfer chicken to platter and serve with mango chutney and, if you like, basmati rice.

210 CALORIES **PER SERVING.** 35G PROTEIN | 13G CARBOHYDRATE | 3G TOTAL FAT (1G SATURATED) 1G FIBER | 85MG CHOLESTEROL | 450MG SODIUM

MAKE IT A MEAL: Serve with the optional basmati rice (150 calories for ¾ cup cooked rice). Or pair the chicken with Grilled Vegetables with Thai Pesto (205 calories; page 413) instead to create a 415-calorie meal. Grill the vegetables during the last 12 minutes the chicken is on the grill.

MOJITO CHICKEN WITH PINEAPPLE

Serve a taste of summer with mojito-infused chicken and tasty grilled pineapple. This recipe will quickly end up on your list of grilling favorites.

ACTIVE TIME: 10 MINUTES · **TOTAL TIME:** 30 MINUTES
MAKES: 4 MAIN-DISH SERVINGS

4 MEDIUM SKINLESS, BONELESS CHICKEN BREAST HALVES (1½ POUNDS)

2 LIMES

1 TABLESPOON OLIVE OIL

1 MEDIUM PINEAPPLE (3½ POUNDS), PEELED AND CUT INTO ½-INCH SLICES

¼ CUP LOOSELY PACKED FRESH MINT LEAVES, CHOPPED

½ TEASPOON SALT

¼ TEASPOON GROUND BLACK PEPPER

1 Preheat large ridged grill pan or prepare outdoor grill for direct grilling over medium heat.

2 Meanwhile, place chicken between two sheets plastic wrap and, using meat mallet, pound to even ½-inch thickness.

3 From 1 lime, grate 1 teaspoon peel and squeeze 2 tablespoons juice. Cut remaining lime into 4 wedges; set aside. In small bowl, combine oil, lime peel, and lime juice. Lightly brush pineapple on both sides with lime mixture; set aside remaining mixture in bowl. Place pineapple slices on hot grill pan or rack and cook 10 minutes or until browned on both sides, turning over once.

4 Stir mint into remaining lime mixture and pat onto both sides of chicken. Sprinkle both sides of chicken with salt and pepper. Place on hot grill pan or rack and cook 5 minutes, turning over once, until breasts are browned on both sides and instant-read thermometer inserted horizontally into thickest part registers 165°F. Serve chicken with pineapple and lime wedges.

320 CALORIES **PER SERVING.** 40G PROTEIN | 27G CARBOHYDRATE | 6G TOTAL FAT (1G SATURATED) 3G FIBER | 99MG CHOLESTEROL | 385MG SODIUM

MAKE IT A MEAL: This taste-of-the-tropics main dish pairs beautifully with our Creamy Banana Sorbet (115 calories; page 434).

CHICKEN PARM STACKS

Chicken Parmesan goes healthy with grilled—rather than breaded and fried—chicken and fresh veggies.

ACTIVE TIME: 20 MINUTES · **TOTAL TIME:** 30 MINUTES

MAKES: 4 MAIN-DISH SERVINGS

1 SLICE WHOLE-WHEAT BREAD	1 POUND CHICKEN BREAST CUTLETS
4 TEASPOONS OLIVE OIL	1 POUND YELLOW SQUASH, CUT INTO ½-INCH-THICK SLICES
¼ CUP PACKED FRESH FLAT-LEAF PARSLEY LEAVES	1 POUND RIPE TOMATOES, CUT INTO ½-INCH-THICK SLICES
1 GARLIC CLOVE	1 OUNCE PARMESAN CHEESE
⅜ TEASPOON SALT	BASIL LEAVES FOR GARNISH
⅜ TEASPOON GROUND BLACK PEPPER	

1 Set oven rack 6 inches from broiler heat source and preheat broiler. Line 18" by 12" jelly-roll pan with foil. Preheat large ridged grill pan or prepare outdoor grill for direct grilling over medium-high heat.

2 Tear bread into large chunks. In food processor with knife blade attached, pulse bread into fine crumbs. In small bowl, combine bread crumbs with 1 teaspoon oil.

3 To food processor, add parsley, garlic, ¼ teaspoon each salt and pepper, and remaining 1 tablespoon oil. Pulse until very finely chopped.

4 On large plate, rub half of parsley mixture all over chicken cutlets. Add chicken to hot grill pan or place on hot grill grate; cook 4 minutes. Turn chicken over and cook 3 to 4 minutes longer, until instant-read thermometer inserted horizontally into center registers 165°F.

5 Meanwhile, arrange squash slices in single layer in prepared pan. Toss with remaining parsley mixture. Broil 7 to 9 minutes or until squash is tender and browned. Transfer squash slices to serving platter in single layer. Place chicken on top.

6 In same baking pan, arrange tomato slices in single layer. Divide crumb mixture evenly among tomatoes. Sprinkle with remaining ⅛ teaspoon each salt and pepper. Broil 30 seconds or until crumbs are golden brown.

7 Arrange crumb-topped tomato slices on top of chicken. With vegetable peeler, shave paper-thin slices of Parmesan directly over tomatoes. Garnish with fresh basil leaves.

250 **PER SERVING.** 29G PROTEIN | 12G CARBOHYDRATE | 10G TOTAL FAT (3G SATURATED)

CALORIES 3G FIBER | 69MG CHOLESTEROL | 415MG SODIUM 💙 ❤️

MAKE IT A MEAL: Finish this delightful chicken and veggie grill with 1 cup mixed berries topped with ½ cup nonfat Greek yogurt and 1 tablespoon honey (175 calories). You can enjoy the entire meal for just 425 calories!

365
CALORIES

King Ranch Chicken
(page 370)

ROASTS & BAKES

When the weather gets chilly, roasted chicken dishes and comforting casseroles are what we crave. Here, we provide irresistible 400-calorie or less options guaranteed to please your family or a crowd. Our easy Chicken Potpie is made in a store-bought phyllo crust; King Ranch Chicken is a deliciously cheesy chicken casserole with a chile pepper kick. If you love roast chicken, savor our Maple-Roasted Chicken Thighs—the sweet potatoes roast alongside the poultry—or Roast Chicken Béarnaise, a French classic. For an anything but ordinary meal, try Chicken and Apple Meat Loaves or our ingenious Chicken-Stuffed Spuds.

KEY TO ICONS

● 30 minutes or less ♥ Heart healthy ✻ High fiber ▮ Make ahead ▮ Slow cooker

CHICKEN POTPIE WITH PHYLLO CRUST

We updated this timeless classic by using a crispy phyllo crust instead of a traditional piecrust.

ACTIVE TIME: 15 MINUTES · **TOTAL TIME:** 1 HOUR 5 MINUTES
MAKES: 8 MAIN-DISH SERVINGS

- 7 TABLESPOONS BUTTER OR MARGARINE
- 2 POUNDS SKINLESS, BONELESS CHICKEN BREAST HALVES
- ¾ TEASPOON SALT
- 8 SHEETS (16" BY 12" EACH) FRESH OR THAWED FROZEN PHYLLO
- ½ CUP FRESH PARSLEY LEAVES
- 1 ONION, CHOPPED
- 1 PACKAGE (8 OUNCES) WHOLE WHITE MUSHROOMS, EACH CUT INTO QUARTERS (OR INTO EIGHTHS IF LARGE)
- 1 PACKAGE (4 OUNCES) SLICED MIXED WILD MUSHROOMS

- ¼ CUP DRY WHITE WINE
- 1 PACKAGE (10 OUNCES) FROZEN PEAS
- 1 TABLESPOON CHOPPED FRESH TARRAGON LEAVES
- ¼ CUP ALL-PURPOSE FLOUR
- 1 CAN (14½ OUNCES) CHICKEN BROTH, OR 1¾ CUPS HOMEMADE BROTH (PAGE 330)
- 1 CUP WHOLE MILK
- ¼ TEASPOON GROUND BLACK PEPPER

1 In nonstick 12-inch skillet, melt 1 tablespoon butter over medium-high heat. Add chicken; sprinkle with ¼ teaspoon salt. Cook 5 minutes. Reduce heat to medium; turn breasts over and cook chicken 5 to 7 minutes longer, until instant-read thermometer inserted horizontally into thickest part registers 165°F. Transfer chicken to cutting board, leaving drippings in skillet. Preheat oven to 375°F.

2 Meanwhile, in small microwave-safe bowl, heat 3 tablespoons butter in microwave oven on High, stirring once, until melted, about 30 seconds. Remove phyllo from package; cover with plastic wrap to keep moist. Place 1 phyllo sheet on large cookie sheet, leaving other sheets covered; lightly brush with melted butter. Repeat layering with 6 more phyllo sheets and melted butter. Arrange parsley leaves on top. Cover parsley with remaining phyllo sheet and butter. Cut phyllo stack lengthwise in half, then crosswise into 8 equal rectangles. Bake until deep golden, 10 to 12 minutes. Place cookie sheet on wire rack; set aside.

3 Cut chicken breasts into ¾-inch chunks. Transfer with any juices to large bowl; keep warm.

4 Add onion to drippings in skillet; cook over medium heat, stirring frequently, 5 minutes. Add all mushrooms and cook until tender, 5 minutes. Add wine; heat to boiling. Boil 1 minute. Stir in peas and tarragon; cook just until peas are heated through. Transfer mixture to bowl with chicken; keep warm.

5 In same skillet, melt remaining 3 tablespoons butter over medium-high heat. With wire whisk, stir in flour and cook, stirring frequently, 2 minutes. Gradually whisk in broth and milk; heat to boiling. Boil until mixture has thickened, about 1 minute. Stir in pepper and remaining ½ teaspoon salt.

6 Stir sauce into chicken mixture, then divide mixture among shallow soup bowls. With wide metal spatula, top each with 1 phyllo rectangle.

360
CALORIES

PER SERVING. 33G PROTEIN | 23G CARBOHYDRATE | 14G TOTAL FAT (8G SATURATED)
3G FIBER | 97MG CHOLESTEROL | 769MG SODIUM

MAKE IT A MEAL: Serve with Carrot and Parsnip Coins (115 calories; page 409) for a yummy 475-calorie dinner.

CHICKEN AND APPLE MEAT LOAVES

Easy to prepare mini meat loaves brushed with an apple jelly and mustard glaze make for a scrumptious and calorie-saving main dish.

ACTIVE TIME: 25 MINUTES · **TOTAL TIME:** 1 HOUR
MAKES: 4 MAIN-DISH SERVINGS

---

1 SLICE WHOLE-WHEAT BREAD	1½ TEASPOONS FENNEL SEEDS
¼ CUP LOW-FAT MILK (1%)	½ TEASPOON SALT
4 GOLDEN DELICIOUS APPLES	½ TEASPOON GROUND BLACK PEPPER
1 POUND GROUND DARK-MEAT CHICKEN	1 TABLESPOON VEGETABLE OIL
½ CUP FINELY CHOPPED ONION	¼ CUP APPLE JELLY
¼ CUP PACKED FRESH FLAT-LEAF PARSLEY LEAVES, FINELY CHOPPED	1 TABLESPOON DIJON MUSTARD WITH SEEDS
1 LARGE EGG, LIGHTLY BEATEN	

1 Preheat oven to 450°F. In food processor with knife blade attached, pulse bread into fine crumbs. Transfer to large bowl and stir in milk. While crumbs soak, remove and discard cores from apples. Grate half of 1 apple on large holes of box grater. Cut remaining 3½ apples into wedges; set aside.

2 To bowl with crumbs, add chicken, onion, parsley, egg, grated apple, ½ teaspoon fennel seeds, salt, and pepper. With hands, mix until well combined. Divide mixture into quarters. On 18" by 12" jelly-roll pan, form each piece into 4½" by 2½" loaf, spacing 3 inches apart.

3 In large bowl, toss apple wedges, oil, and remaining 1 teaspoon fennel seeds to coat; scatter evenly around meat loaves. Roast 10 minutes.

4 Meanwhile, stir together apple jelly and mustard until well blended. Brush thick layer of mixture onto loaves. Roast 10 minutes or until tops are browned and instant-read thermometer inserted into center of meat loaves registers 165°F. Transfer apples and meat loaves to serving plates.

380 CALORIES

PER SERVING. 27G PROTEIN | 44G CARBOHYDRATE | 11G TOTAL FAT (2G SATURATED) 6G FIBER | 145MG CHOLESTEROL | 515MG SODIUM 🌾 🟩

MAKE IT A MEAL: Add on Green Beans with Garlic (50 calories; page 406) for a 430-calorie dinner. Or instead serve the meat loaves with Light Mashed Potatoes (145 calories; page 417) for a 525-calorie meal.

KING RANCH CHICKEN

With the slightly spicy kick of poblano and jalapeño chiles, this cheesy chicken casserole is anything but ordinary. For photo, see page 364.

ACTIVE TIME: 30 MINUTES · **TOTAL TIME:** 1 HOUR
MAKES: 6 MAIN-DISH SERVINGS

- 2 CUPS LOW-FAT MILK (1%)
- 2 TABLESPOONS VEGETABLE OIL
- 1 SMALL ONION (4 TO 6 OUNCES), FINELY CHOPPED
- 1 LARGE RED PEPPER, FINELY CHOPPED
- 1 LARGE POBLANO CHILE, SEEDS DISCARDED, FINELY CHOPPED
- 1 JALAPEÑO CHILE, SEEDS DISCARDED, FINELY CHOPPED
- 2 GARLIC CLOVES, CRUSHED WITH PRESS
- 3 TABLESPOONS ALL-PURPOSE FLOUR
- 1 CUP CANNED REDUCED-SODIUM CHICKEN BROTH OR HOMEMADE BROTH (PAGE 330)
- 1 CAN (14½ OUNCES) NO-SALT-ADDED DICED TOMATOES, DRAINED
- ¼ TEASPOON SALT
- ¼ TEASPOON GROUND BLACK PEPPER
- 3½ OUNCES BAKED TORTILLA CHIPS, CRUSHED (1¼ CUPS)
- 10 OUNCES COOKED SHREDDED CHICKEN BREAST MEAT (2 CUPS)
- 4 OUNCES PEPPER JACK OR MONTEREY JACK CHEESE, SHREDDED (2 CUPS)
- 1 GREEN ONION, THINLY SLICED, FOR GARNISH

1 Preheat oven to 350°F. Grease shallow 3-quart baking dish. Microwave milk on High for 2 minutes or until warm.

2 Meanwhile, in 12-inch skillet, heat oil over medium-high heat. Add onion, red pepper, poblano, and jalapeño. Cook 4 minutes or until vegetables are just tender, stirring occasionally. Add garlic and cook 1 minute, stirring.

3 Add flour and cook 1 minute, stirring. Stir in broth, then warm milk, in a steady stream. Heat to boiling, stirring; cook 3 minutes or until thickened, stirring constantly. Stir in tomatoes, salt, and pepper.

4 Spread thin, even layer of sauce on bottom of prepared dish. Top with half of chips, sauce, chicken, and cheese. Repeat layering once.

5 Bake 30 minutes or until bubbling. Garnish with green onions.

365 CALORIES

PER SERVING. 22G PROTEIN | 30G CARBOHYDRATE | 18G TOTAL FAT (6G SATURATED) 3G FIBER | 60MG CHOLESTEROL | 535MG SODIUM

MAKE IT A MEAL: Add a serving of baked tortilla chips (about 15 chips; 120 calories) to dip into the casserole. It's a 485-calorie dinner that's likely to become a family favorite.

CHICKEN-STUFFED SPUDS

This quick recipe takes advantage of the microwave and toaster oven for baking potatoes, then spices things up with a zesty chicken filling.

TOTAL TIME: 25 MINUTES

MAKES: 4 MAIN-DISH SERVINGS

4 BAKING POTATOES, NOT PEELED	1 LARGE RED PEPPER, CHOPPED
1 TABLESPOON OLIVE OIL	2 TEASPOONS ASIAN CHILI SAUCE (SRIRACHA)
1 BUNCH GREEN ONIONS, SLICED (¼ CUP), DARK-GREEN TOPS RESERVED	½ TEASPOON SALT
1 TEASPOON FENNEL SEEDS	¼ CUP REDUCED-FAT SOUR CREAM
1 POUND GROUND CHICKEN	

1 Preheat toaster oven to 425°F. Pierce potatoes with fork and place on microwave-safe plate; microwave on High for 14 to 16 minutes or until tender, turning once. Transfer potatoes to toaster oven; cook 5 to 7 minutes or until skin is crisp.

2 Meanwhile, in nonstick 12-inch skillet, heat oil over medium heat 1 minute. Add green onions and fennel seeds; cook 2 minutes, stirring frequently. Add chicken, red pepper, chili sauce, and salt. Cook 8 minutes or until chicken loses pink color throughout, stirring occasionally.

3 To serve, cut a slit in each potato and fill with chicken mixture. Top with sour cream and green onion tops.

PER SERVING. 25G PROTEIN | 41G CARBOHYDRATE | 14G TOTAL FAT (4G SATURATED) 5G FIBER | 105MG CHOLESTEROL | 437MG SODIUM

MAKE IT A MEAL: Complete this playful meal with a chocolate fix: One of our Healthy Makeover Brownies (just 95 calories each; page 332). You can enjoy it all for 480 calories.

FINGER FOOD FEAST

Dipping food is fun for kids and adults alike. In this recipe, we pair panko-breaded chicken drumsticks and healthy veggies with a lemon and basil yogurt dip.

ACTIVE TIME: 35 MINUTES · **TOTAL TIME:** 55 MINUTES
MAKES: 6 MAIN-DISH SERVINGS

- 3 TABLESPOONS DIJON MUSTARD
- 3 TABLESPOONS LIGHT MAYONNAISE
- 12 LARGE CHICKEN DRUMSTICKS (3½ POUNDS), SKIN REMOVED
- 1 LEMON
- 1 CUP PANKO (JAPANESE-STYLE BREAD CRUMBS)
- ½ CUP FINELY GRATED PARMESAN CHEESE
- 2 TABLESPOONS OLIVE OIL
- ⅛ TEASPOON CAYENNE (GROUND RED) PEPPER
- ⅞ TEASPOON SALT
- ⅜ TEASPOON GROUND BLACK PEPPER
- ⅓ CUP PLAIN NONFAT YOGURT
- ¼ CUP PACKED FRESH BASIL LEAVES, FINELY CHOPPED
- 1 POUND ASPARAGUS, TRIMMED
- CARROTS, CELERY STICKS, GREEN BEANS, AND SLICED PEPPERS, FOR SERVING

1 Arrange oven rack in top third of oven. Preheat oven to 450°F. Line 18" by 12" jelly-roll pan with foil.

2 In large bowl, stir mustard and mayonnaise until well combined; add chicken pieces and toss until evenly coated. Set aside.

3 From lemon, grate 1 teaspoon peel into 9-inch pie plate and squeeze 1 tablespoon juice into small bowl. In pie plate with lemon peel, combine panko, grated Parmesan, oil, cayenne, and ⅛ teaspoon each salt and pepper. Dredge each drumstick in crumb mixture until well coated, shake off excess, and place on prepared pan. Bake 30 minutes or until crust is golden brown and juices run clear when chicken is pierced with tip of knife. (Instant-read thermometer inserted into thickest part of drumstick should register 165°F.)

4 Meanwhile, to small bowl with lemon juice, add yogurt, and ¼ teaspoon each salt and pepper; stir until smooth. Stir in basil.

5 Fill 12-inch skillet with 1 inch water. Cover and heat to boiling over high heat. Add asparagus and remaining ½ teaspoon salt (see Tip). Cook, uncovered, 4 to 5 minutes or until bright green and crisp-tender, turning occasionally for even cooking. Rinse under cold running water; drain.

6 Serve chicken with asparagus and assorted raw vegetables, with dipping sauce alongside.

TIP Kids love carrots that have been boiled for 3 to 4 minutes; they're extra sweet, but still crunchy. If you want to do this, just cook them in the same water used for the asparagus.

335 CALORIES **PER SERVING.** 37G PROTEIN | 11G CARBOHYDRATE | 15G TOTAL FAT (4G SATURATED) 1G FIBER | 122MG CHOLESTEROL | 560MG SODIUM

MAKE IT A MEAL: Enjoy the chicken and dipping veggies on their own, for lunch. For a 500-calorie dinner, add our Confetti Rice Pilaf (165 calories; page 423).

HONEY-LIME DRUMSTICKS

We removed the skin from these drumsticks, then baked them with a sweet and tangy lime glaze.

ACTIVE TIME: 20 MINUTES · **TOTAL TIME:** 50 MINUTES
MAKES: 12 DRUMSTICKS

2   LIMES

2   TABLESPOONS HONEY

1   GARLIC CLOVE, CRUSHED WITH PRESS

½   TEASPOON GROUND CORIANDER

½   TEASPOON SALT

¼   TEASPOON COARSELY GROUND BLACK PEPPER

12   MEDIUM CHICKEN DRUMSTICKS (3 POUNDS), SKIN REMOVED

¼   CUP LOOSELY PACKED FRESH PARSLEY OR CILANTRO LEAVES, CHOPPED

1   Preheat oven to 450°F. From 1 or 2 limes, grate 1 teaspoon peel and squeeze 2 tablespoons juice. Cut any remaining lime into wedges and set aside to use as garnish.

2   In small bowl, with fork, mix honey, garlic, coriander, salt, pepper, lime juice, and ½ teaspoon lime peel.

3   Arrange drumsticks on 15½" by 10½" jelly-roll pan. Drizzle lime mixture over chicken; toss to coat evenly. Bake, occasionally brushing chicken with glaze in pan, 30 to 35 minutes, until instant-read thermometer inserted into thickest part of drumstick registers 165°F.

4   Transfer to serving dish. Drizzle with pan juices. Sprinkle with parsley or cilantro and remaining ½ teaspoon lime peel. Serve with lime wedges.

180 CALORIES

PER SERVING. 26G PROTEIN | 6G CARBOHYDRATE | 6G TOTAL FAT (2G SATURATED) 0G FIBER | 82MG CHOLESTEROL | 160MG SODIUM ♥

MAKE IT A MEAL: Prep some Herbed Roasted Potatoes (125 calories; page 416) and roast alongside the drumsticks. Add Green Beans with Shallots (90 calories; page 406). This kid-pleasing supper is only 395 calories.

ROSEMARY-APRICOT CHICKEN

A crowd-pleaser to serve hot or cold, this dish is perfect for a picnic or a potluck. If you'll have access to a grill, bake the marinated chicken at home for 45 minutes without the glaze, then reheat it on the grill, brushing it with the apricot mixture just before removing it from the heat.

ACTIVE TIME: 20 MINUTES · **TOTAL TIME:** 1 HOUR 5 MINUTES PLUS MARINATING
MAKES: 12 MAIN-DISH SERVINGS

2	TEASPOONS SALT	3	CHICKENS (3 POUNDS EACH), EACH CUT INTO QUARTERS, SKIN REMOVED
1	TEASPOON DRIED ROSEMARY, CRUMBLED	½	CUP APRICOT JAM
½	TEASPOON COARSELY GROUND BLACK PEPPER	2	TABLESPOONS FRESH LEMON JUICE
4	GARLIC CLOVES, CRUSHED WITH PRESS	2	TEASPOONS DIJON MUSTARD

1 In cup, mix salt, rosemary, pepper, and garlic. Rub mixture over chicken quarters; cover and refrigerate in large bowl about 2 hours.

2 Preheat oven to 350°F and position two racks in upper and lower thirds of oven. Place chicken quarters, skinned side up, in two large roasting pans (17" by 11½" each) or jelly-roll pans (15½" by 10½" each). Bake 25 minutes, rotating pans between upper and lower racks halfway through.

3 Meanwhile, in small bowl, with fork, mix apricot jam, lemon juice, and mustard. Brush apricot mixture over chicken; continue baking about 20 minutes longer, rotating pans after 10 minutes. Chicken is done when instant-read thermometer inserted into thickest part registers 165°F. Serve hot, or cover and refrigerate to serve cold later.

230
CALORIES
PER SERVING. 35G PROTEIN | 9G CARBOHYDRATE | 5G TOTAL FAT (1G SATURATED)
0G FIBER | 114MG CHOLESTEROL | 540MG SODIUM

MAKE IT A MEAL: Our Warm Dijon Potato Salad (150 calories; page 418) is just the thing to complete the party. Add our grilled Corn on the Cob with Molasses Butter (105 calories; page 409) to make it a fun 485-calorie meal.

MAPLE-ROASTED CHICKEN THIGHS

There's nothing simpler than roasted chicken and vegetables; a tasty glaze makes this rustic dish really special.

ACTIVE TIME: 15 MINUTES · **TOTAL TIME:** 55 MINUTES

MAKES: 4 MAIN-DISH SERVINGS

4 LARGE SKINLESS BONE-IN CHICKEN THIGHS (1½ POUNDS)	8 OUNCES BABY CARROTS OR PARSNIPS, CUT INTO 1-INCH CHUNKS
1 POUND SWEET POTATOES, PEELED AND CUT INTO 1-INCH CHUNKS	¼ CUP MAPLE SYRUP
	1 TEASPOON SALT
1 SMALL ONION, CUT INTO 1-INCH PIECES	½ TEASPOON GROUND BLACK PEPPER

1 Preheat oven to 450°F.

2 In 15½" by 10½" jelly-roll pan or large shallow roasting pan, combine chicken, sweet potatoes, onion, carrots, maple syrup, salt, and pepper; toss to coat.

3 Roast chicken mixture 40 to 45 minutes or until juices run clear when thickest part of thigh is pierced with tip of knife and liquid in pan thickens slightly, stirring vegetables once and turning chicken over halfway through. Instant-read thermometer inserted into thickest part of thigh will register 165°F when chicken is done.

290 CALORIES **PER SERVING.** 21G PROTEIN | 41G CARBOHYDRATE | 4G TOTAL FAT (1G SATURATED) 4G FIBER | 80MG CHOLESTEROL | 695MG SODIUM

MAKE IT A MEAL: For a hearty, 445-calorie dinner, pair these maple-glazed thighs and root vegetables with our Polenta and Spinach Gratin (155 calories; page 420). You can bake both dishes in the oven at the same time at 450°F.

ROAST CHICKEN BÉARNAISE

The classic but easy French sauce is made right in the roasting pan.

ACTIVE TIME: 15 MINUTES · **TOTAL TIME:** 1 HOUR 25 MINUTES
MAKES: 4 MAIN-DISH SERVINGS

1	CHICKEN (3½ POUNDS)	3	MEDIUM SHALLOTS (2 OUNCES EACH)
1	TEASPOON SALT	¼	CUP DRY WHITE WINE
½	TEASPOON COARSELY GROUND BLACK PEPPER	1	TEASPOON TARRAGON VINEGAR OR WHITE WINE VINEGAR
1	LARGE LEMON, CUT IN HALF	1	TABLESPOON BUTTER OR MARGARINE
4	SPRIGS FRESH TARRAGON PLUS 1 TABLESPOON CHOPPED FRESH TARRAGON LEAVES		

1 Preheat oven to 450°F. Remove giblets and neck from chicken; reserve for another use. Sprinkle ½ teaspoon salt and ¼ teaspoon pepper inside cavity. Squeeze juice from lemon into cavity, then place lemon halves inside cavity along with tarragon sprigs. Coarsely chop 2 shallots; add to cavity.

2 With chicken breast side up, lift wings up toward neck, then fold tips under back of chicken to hold in place. Tie legs together with string. Place chicken, breast side up, on rack in small roasting pan (13" by 9"). Sprinkle outside of chicken with remaining ½ teaspoon salt and ¼ teaspoon pepper.

3 Roast chicken about 1 hour, until instant-read thermometer inserted into thickest part of thigh registers 165°F.

4 Finely chop remaining shallot. With tongs, tilt chicken to allow juices from cavity to run into roasting pan. Transfer chicken to warm platter; let stand 10 minutes to set juices for easier carving.

5 Meanwhile, remove rack from roasting pan. Skim and discard fat from drippings in pan. Add wine, vinegar, and chopped shallot to pan; heat to boiling over high heat. Remove pan from heat; stir in butter and chopped tarragon. Serve chicken with sauce.

---

375 CALORIES

PER SERVING. 40G PROTEIN | 1G CARBOHYDRATE | 22G TOTAL FAT (7G SATURATED) 0G FIBER | 164MG CHOLESTEROL | 726MG SODIUM

MAKE IT A MEAL: Serve with our Savory Pear Stuffing (110 calories; page 416) for a 485-calorie meal.

CHICKEN WITH ORANGE RELISH

Incredibly healthy and full of flavor, this quick main dish is so refreshingly tasty, you'll forget that it's good for you! Can't find whole-wheat couscous? Use quick-cooking bulgur.

TOTAL TIME: 25 MINUTES
MAKES: 4 MAIN-DISH SERVINGS

---

4 CHICKEN BREAST CUTLETS (4 OUNCES EACH)	3 STALKS CELERY, FINELY CHOPPED
¾ TEASPOON GRATED, PEELED FRESH GINGER	2 GREEN ONIONS, SLICED
¼ TEASPOON GROUND BLACK PEPPER	1 TABLESPOON RED WINE VINEGAR
¼ TEASPOON SALT	¼ CUP PACKED FRESH CILANTRO LEAVES, FINELY CHOPPED
1 LARGE ORANGE	1 CUP WHOLE-WHEAT COUSCOUS

1 Preheat oven to 425°F. Spray jelly-roll pan with nonstick cooking spray. Arrange chicken on pan. Rub chicken with ½ teaspoon ginger; sprinkle with pepper and ⅛ teaspoon salt. Roast chicken 10 to 12 minutes, until instant-read thermometer inserted horizontally into center of cutlet registers 165°F.

2 Meanwhile, with knife, cut peel and white pith from orange; discard. Cut on either side of membrane to remove each segment from orange; place half of segments in 2-quart saucepan; set remaining segments aside. Squeeze juice from membranes into saucepan.

3 To same saucepan, add celery, green onions, vinegar, and remaining ¼ teaspoon ginger and ⅛ teaspoon salt. Heat to boiling over high heat. Reduce heat to simmer; cook 7 minutes or until celery is crisp-tender, stirring occasionally. Remove from heat; stir in cilantro and reserved orange segments.

4 Cook couscous as label directs. Serve chicken with relish and couscous.

320 CALORIES
PER SERVING. 30G PROTEIN | 45G CARBOHYDRATE | 3G TOTAL FAT (1G SATURATED) 8G FIBER | 63MG CHOLESTEROL | 245MG SODIUM ♥ 🌾

MAKE IT A MEAL: For a crunchy starter, nibble on a celery stalk stuffed with 1 tablespoon herbed goat cheese or one-half a small red pepper, sliced and dipped in 1½ tablespoons hummus. Each is just 50 calories, so you could even enjoy both—total calories for the meal would be 420.

ALMOND-CRUSTED CHICKEN

These quick-cooking chicken cutlets get their oven-crisped coating from chopped almonds, which are chock-full of healthy fats.

ACTIVE TIME: 20 MINUTES · **TOTAL TIME:** 30 MINUTES
MAKES: 4 MAIN-DISH SERVINGS

2 ORANGES	½ TEASPOON GROUND BLACK PEPPER
4 CUPS THINLY SLICED RED CABBAGE (12 OUNCES)	1 TABLESPOON ALL-PURPOSE FLOUR
2 LARGE CARROTS, PEELED AND CUT INTO THIN MATCHSTICKS	½ CUP ALMONDS, VERY FINELY CHOPPED
1 LARGE YELLOW PEPPER, VERY THINLY SLICED	1 LARGE EGG WHITE
2 TABLESPOONS SNIPPED CHIVES	¼ TEASPOON GROUND CUMIN
3 TABLESPOONS WHITE WINE VINEGAR	¼ TEASPOON NO-SALT-ADDED CHILI POWDER
4 TEASPOONS CANOLA OIL	4 CHICKEN BREAST CUTLETS (4 OUNCES EACH)
½ TEASPOON SALT	

1 Arrange one oven rack in lowest position; place 15" by 10" jelly-roll pan on rack. Preheat oven to 450°F with pan inside.

2 Cut peel and white pith from oranges; discard. Cut oranges into segments, slicing on either side of membranes, and drop segments into large bowl; squeeze juices from membranes into bowl. Add cabbage, carrots, yellow pepper, chives, vinegar, 1 teaspoon oil, and ¼ teaspoon each salt and pepper. Toss well; let slaw stand.

3 Spread flour on medium plate; spread almonds on second plate. In pie plate, beat egg white until foamy. Sprinkle cumin, chili, and remaining ¼ teaspoon each salt and pepper over chicken. Press one side of each cutlet in flour; shake off excess. Dip same side in egg white; press into nuts.

4 Remove hot pan from oven; brush with remaining oil. Add cutlets, nut side down; roast 10 to 12 minutes, until instant-read thermometer inserted horizontally into cutlet registers 165°F. Serve with slaw.

 350 CALORIES **PER SERVING.** 30G PROTEIN | 28G CARBOHYDRATE | 15G TOTAL FAT (2G SATURATED) 7G FIBER | 63MG CHOLESTEROL | 425MG SODIUM

MAKE IT A MEAL: If you want to add on, pair with a wedge of our Roasted Acorn Squash (150 calories; page 410) for a 500-calorie dinner. Bake the squash above the chicken, on the top oven rack.

325 CALORIES

Mango Chicken Lettuce Wraps (page 391)

SALADS, WRAPS & SANDWICHES

Chicken salads and sandwiches make energizing lunches and light but satisfying dinners. Try our creative twists on traditional chicken salad, including our pretty Chicken and Raspberry Salad; Buffalo Chicken Salad, made with cayenne pepper-coated chicken tenders and blue cheese dressing; and Mango Chicken Lettuce Wraps that you can eat out of hand. For sandwiches, our offerings include Chicken Quesadillas with an avocado-tomato salsa for dipping and chicken Caesar salad stuffed in a pita. Or sink your teeth into our Chicken Apple Burgers; shredded apple lends moisture and flavor to the chicken patties without adding fat.

KEY TO ICONS

🔵 30 minutes or less   ❤️ Heart healthy   🌾 High fiber   🟩 Make ahead   🍲 Slow cooker

CHICKEN AND RASPBERRY SALAD

This satisfying, healthful salad features grilled avocado to provide a buttery counterpart to fresh berries and grilled chicken.

TOTAL TIME: 35 MINUTES
MAKES: 4 SERVINGS

2 TABLESPOONS FRESH LEMON JUICE	1 POUND SKINLESS, BONELESS CHICKEN BREAST HALVES
2 TABLESPOONS REDUCED-FAT SOUR CREAM	1½ TEASPOONS OLIVE OIL
1 TABLESPOON HONEY	1 AVOCADO, CUT IN HALF, PITTED BUT NOT PEELED
1 TEASPOON DIJON MUSTARD	1 PINT RASPBERRIES (3 CUPS)
⅜ TEASPOON SALT	6 OUNCES MIXED GREENS
⅜ TEASPOON GROUND BLACK PEPPER	¼ CUP SLICED TOASTED ALMONDS
1 TEASPOON POPPY SEEDS	

1 Prepare outdoor grill for direct grilling over medium heat.

2 In bowl, whisk lemon juice, sour cream, honey, Dijon, and ⅛ teaspoon each salt and pepper. Stir in poppy seeds. Cover dressing; refrigerate up to 1 day.

3 With meat mallet, pound chicken to even ½-inch thickness. Rub 1 teaspoon oil over chicken; sprinkle with remaining ¼ teaspoon each salt and pepper. Rub cut sides of avocado with remaining ½ teaspoon oil. Place chicken and avocado on grill. Grill avocado 3 to 5 minutes or until grill marks appear, turning over once. Cook chicken 8 to 10 minutes, until instant-read thermometer inserted horizontally into thickest part of breast registers 165°F. Let chicken and avocado rest 5 minutes. Discard avocado peel; slice. Slice chicken.

4 In bowl, toss raspberries with 1 tablespoon dressing. In large bowl, toss greens with remaining dressing; divide among plates. Top with raspberries, chicken, avocado, and almonds.

300 CALORIES

PER SERVING. 27G PROTEIN | 19G CARBOHYDRATE | 14G TOTAL FAT (3G SATURATED) 8G FIBER | 67MG CHOLESTEROL | 320MG SODIUM 🌾 ❤️

MAKE IT A MEAL: For a 400-calorie lunch with added fiber, serve with a whole-grain roll (100 calories). Try some of the grilled avocado spread on the roll.

CURRIED CHICKEN SALAD

Fragrantly spiced, studded with sweet red grapes and crunchy celery slices, and served on a bed of romaine, this chicken salad is sure to dazzle guests.

ACTIVE TIME: 15 MINUTES · **TOTAL TIME:** 35 MINUTES
MAKES: 4 MAIN-DISH SERVINGS

4   SKINLESS, BONELESS CHICKEN BREAST HALVES (1½ POUNDS)

1   ONION, CUT INTO QUARTERS

½   TEASPOON SALT

¼   CUP PLAIN NONFAT YOGURT

¼   CUP LIGHT MAYONNAISE

1   TABLESPOON FRESH LIME JUICE

1½ TEASPOONS CURRY POWDER

1   TEASPOON GRATED, PEELED FRESH GINGER

1¼ CUPS SEEDLESS RED GRAPES, EACH CUT IN HALF

2   STALKS CELERY, THINLY SLICED

1   BAG (10 OUNCES) CUT-UP HEARTS OF ROMAINE

1 Place chicken breasts in deep 12-inch skillet. Add onion quarters, ¼ teaspoon salt, and enough *water* to cover chicken; heat to boiling over high heat. Remove skillet from heat; cover and let chicken sit in poaching liquid 20 minutes or until chicken loses pink color throughout. Instant-read thermometer inserted horizontally into thickest part of breast should register 165°F. Transfer chicken to cutting board; cool until easy to handle.

2 Meanwhile, in large bowl, whisk yogurt, mayonnaise, lime juice, curry powder, ginger, and remaining ¼ teaspoon salt until blended. Stir in grapes and celery.

3 Cut chicken into ½-inch chunks and add to mixture in bowl; toss to coat. Serve salad right away, or cover and refrigerate to serve chilled. Spoon chicken salad onto romaine to serve.

315 CALORIES **PER SERVING.** 42G PROTEIN | 18G CARBOHYDRATE | 8G TOTAL FAT (2G SATURATED) 3G FIBER | 104MG CHOLESTEROL | 455MG SODIUM ❤️ 🥗

MAKE IT A MEAL: For added flavor and a wholesome crunch, toss in 1 tablespoon toasted walnuts, chopped, per serving (45 calories). You can enjoy this delicious lunch for just 360 calories.

BUFFALO CHICKEN SALAD

This quick main-dish salad is ready in just 30 minutes. Full of lean protein and bursting with flavor from the cayenne-coated chicken, it's a fun and filling lunch.

TOTAL TIME: 30 MINUTES
MAKES: 4 MAIN-DISH SERVINGS

1¼ POUNDS CHICKEN BREAST TENDERS, EACH CUT CROSSWISE IN HALF, THEN LENGTHWISE IN HALF

¼ TEASPOON CAYENNE (GROUND RED) PEPPER

¼ TEASPOON SALT

3 TABLESPOONS CAYENNE PEPPER SAUCE

1 TABLESPOON BUTTER

1 TABLESPOON WATER

1 LARGE HEAD BOSTON LETTUCE, TORN INTO BITE-SIZE PIECES

1 CUP SHREDDED CARROTS

2 STALKS CELERY, THINLY SLICED

½ CUP BOTTLED BLUE CHEESE DRESSING

1 Preheat oven to 450°F. Spray 15½" by 10½" jelly-roll pan with nonstick cooking spray. Toss chicken with cayenne and salt. Place on prepared pan and bake 10 minutes.

2 Meanwhile, in microwave-safe small bowl, heat pepper sauce, butter, and water on High for 30 seconds or until butter is melted. Add sauce to chicken in pan; stir to coat. Bake 2 to 3 minutes longer, or until instant-read thermometer inserted into thickest part of chicken registers 165°F.

3 To serve, arrange lettuce on dinner plates; top with chicken. Sprinkle with carrots and celery and drizzle with dressing.

360 CALORIES **PER SERVING.** 35G PROTEIN | 7G CARBOHYDRATE | 21G TOTAL FAT (5G SATURATED) 2G FIBER | 96MG CHOLESTEROL | 1,085MG SODIUM

MAKE IT A MEAL: For a 405-calorie lunch, add 1 cup cubed watermelon (45 calories) for dessert. It's a perfect lunch for lazy summer days.

WARM CHICKEN SALAD WITH BACON

This filling, flavorful combo of poultry and bacon tossed with arugula and frisée will win you over to the salad-as-stand-alone-meal idea.

ACTIVE TIME: 25 MINUTES · **TOTAL TIME:** 30 MINUTES
MAKES: 4 MAIN-DISH SERVINGS

4   SLICES BACON (3 OUNCES), CUT INTO ½-INCH PIECES

OLIVE OIL, IF NEEDED

1½   POUNDS SKINLESS, BONELESS CHICKEN BREAST HALVES, CUT INTO ½-INCH-WIDE STRIPS

¼   TEASPOON SALT

1   MEDIUM SHALLOT (2 OUNCES), FINELY CHOPPED

1   POUND CREMINI MUSHROOMS, SLICED

1   CUP CANNED REDUCED-SODIUM CHICKEN BROTH OR HOMEMADE BROTH (PAGE 330)

2   TABLESPOONS BALSAMIC VINEGAR

1   BAG (5 TO 6 OUNCES) BABY ARUGULA

1   SMALL HEAD FRISÉE (3 OUNCES), STEM ENDS TRIMMED AND DISCARDED

1 In 12-inch skillet, cook bacon over medium heat 5 to 6 minutes or until browned, stirring occasionally. With slotted spoon, transfer bacon to paper towels to drain; remove fat from skillet and reserve 4 teaspoons. (If necessary, add enough olive oil to bacon fat to equal 4 teaspoons.)

2 To skillet, return 2 teaspoons reserved fat and heat over medium heat. Add chicken and salt; cook 7 to 8 minutes or until chicken is browned outside and no longer pink inside, stirring occasionally. Transfer to bowl.

3 Add remaining 2 teaspoons fat and shallot to skillet; cook 1 minute, stirring. Add mushrooms; cover and cook 5 minutes. Uncover, raise heat to medium-high, and cook, stirring frequently, 4 to 5 minutes longer or until mushrooms are browned and tender and most liquid has evaporated. Add broth and vinegar; heat to boiling. Remove skillet from heat.

4 In large bowl, combine arugula and frisée; add chicken and mushroom mixture and toss until well combined. Serve topped with reserved bacon.

330 CALORIES

PER SERVING. 48G PROTEIN | 9G CARBOHYDRATE | 10G TOTAL FAT (3G SATURATED) 4G FIBER | 108MG CHOLESTEROL | 535MG SODIUM

MAKE IT A MEAL: This hearty salad needs no embellishment. For a sweet and icy finale, add 14 frozen grapes (50 calories) to make a 380-calorie lunch.

ASIAN CHICKEN SALAD

This fast, easy chicken salad recipe is full of Asian-inspired flavors.

TOTAL TIME: 30 MINUTES

MAKES: 6 MAIN-DISH SERVINGS

3	LIMES
4	SKINLESS, BONELESS CHICKEN BREAST HALVES (1½ POUNDS)
1	BAG (10 TO 12 OUNCES) FROZEN SHELLED EDAMAME (SOYBEANS)
⅓	CUP REDUCED-SODIUM SOY SAUCE
¼	CUP LOOSELY PACKED CILANTRO LEAVES, CHOPPED

1	TABLESPOON GRATED, PEELED FRESH GINGER
2	TEASPOONS ASIAN SESAME OIL
1	POUND (½ SMALL HEAD) NAPA CABBAGE (CHINESE CABBAGE), SLICED
1	BUNCH RADISHES, TRIMMED AND THINLY SLICED

1 Cut 2 limes into thin slices. From remaining lime, squeeze 2 tablespoons juice; set aside.

2 In covered 12-inch skillet, heat half of lime slices and 1 *inch water* to boiling over high heat. Add chicken; cover, reduce heat to medium-low and cook 13 to 14 minutes or until chicken loses pink color throughout and instant-read thermometer registers 165°F when inserted into thickest part of breast. With slotted spoon or tongs, remove chicken from skillet and place in large bowl of *ice water;* chill 5 minutes. Discard poaching liquid. Drain chicken well; with hands, shred into bite-size pieces.

3 Meanwhile, cook edamame as label directs; drain. Rinse with cold running water to stop cooking and drain again. In large bowl, whisk together soy sauce, cilantro, ginger, sesame oil, and reserved lime juice. Add cabbage, edamame, radishes, and shredded chicken to bowl; toss to combine.

4 To serve, transfer to deep bowls and garnish with remaining lime slices.

285 CALORIES

PER SERVING. 39G PROTEIN | 14G CARBOHYDRATE | 8G TOTAL FAT (1G SATURATED) 6G FIBER | 66MG CHOLESTEROL | 560MG SODIUM

MAKE IT A MEAL: Our Summer Fruit in Spiced Syrup (125 calories; page 435) is a bright and colorful finish to this chicken salad—and makes for a refreshing 410-calorie lunch.

MANGO CHICKEN LETTUCE WRAPS

Mango, mint, and jicama add Latin American zing to these speedy, no-cook chicken wraps. For photo, see page 382.

TOTAL TIME: 20 MINUTES
MAKES: 4 MAIN-DISH SERVINGS

1 LARGE RIPE MANGO, PEELED, SEEDED, AND CHOPPED	½ TEASPOON ASIAN CHILI SAUCE (SRIRACHA), PLUS MORE TO TASTE
1 CUP FINELY CHOPPED JICAMA	¼ TEASPOON SALT
½ CUP PACKED FRESH MINT LEAVES, FINELY CHOPPED	3 CUPS COARSELY SHREDDED CHICKEN MEAT (FROM ½ ROTISSERIE CHICKEN)
¼ CUP FRESH LIME JUICE	12 BOSTON LETTUCE LEAVES
2 TABLESPOONS EXTRA-VIRGIN OLIVE OIL	

1 In large bowl, combine mango, jicama, mint, lime juice, oil, chili sauce, and salt. Toss well. If making ahead, cover bowl and refrigerate mixture up to overnight.

2 To serve, add chicken to mango mixture; toss to combine. Place 3 lettuce leaves on each serving plate; divide chicken mixture equally among lettuce leaves.

325 CALORIES **PER SERVING.** 32G PROTEIN | 17G CARBOHYDRATE | 15G TOTAL FAT (3G SATURATED) 4G FIBER | 94MG CHOLESTEROL | 400MG SODIUM

MAKE IT A MEAL: For a quick, low-cal dessert, add on our Chocolate-Dipped Dried Fruit (55 calories; page 431); you can make them ahead and store them in an airtight container, so they'll be ready when you need a sweet bite. Total calories for this lunch: just 380!

CHICKEN CAESAR PITAS

Chicken Caesar salad served in whole-wheat pitas makes for a terrific sandwich. Healthy and easy, this recipe takes only twenty minutes!

ACTIVE TIME: 10 MINUTES · **TOTAL TIME:** 20 MINUTES
MAKES: 4 PITA SANDWICHES

3	TABLESPOONS OLIVE OIL, PLUS ADDITIONAL FOR GREASING PAN	1	GARLIC CLOVE, CUT IN HALF
¾	POUND CHICKEN BREAST TENDERS	4	WHOLE-WHEAT PITAS, EACH CUT IN HALF
¼	TEASPOON SALT	1	HEART OF ROMAINE LETTUCE, CHOPPED
¼	TEASPOON GROUND BLACK PEPPER	¼	CUP FRESH BASIL LEAVES, SLICED
2	TABLESPOONS FRESH LEMON JUICE	¼	CUP FRESHLY GRATED PARMESAN CHEESE
1	TABLESPOON RED WINE VINEGAR	1	CUP GRAPE TOMATOES, EACH CUT IN HALF
1	TEASPOON DIJON MUSTARD		
1	TEASPOON ANCHOVY PASTE		

1 Heat ridged grill pan over medium-high heat until hot. Lightly brush with olive oil. Sprinkle chicken tenders with ⅛ teaspoon each salt and pepper. Cook 6 to 7 minutes, or until chicken is browned and instant-read thermometer inserted into thickest part registers 165°F, turning over once.
2 Transfer chicken to cutting board and let cool completely. While chicken cools, in large bowl, with wire whisk, stir lemon juice, vinegar, mustard, remaining ⅛ teaspoon each salt and pepper, and anchovy paste, if using, until well mixed. Continuing to whisk, add oil in slow, steady stream until incorporated.
3 Rub cut sides of garlic all over insides of pitas; discard garlic. Microwave pitas on High for 15 seconds to soften.
4 Cut chicken into 1-inch pieces. In bowl with dressing, combine lettuce, basil, Parmesan, tomatoes, and chicken, tossing to coat. Divide mixture among pitas.

340 CALORIES

PER SANDWICH. 25G PROTEIN | 29G CARBOHYDRATE | 15G TOTAL FAT (3G SATU-RATED) | 4G FIBER | 52MG CHOLESTEROL | 540MG SODIUM

MAKE IT A MEAL: Serve with a cup of strawberries for a 390-calorie portable lunch. Or pair with our Warm Dijon Potato Salad (150 calories; page 418) for a relaxed 490-calorie dinner.

CHICKEN APPLE BURGERS

Shredded apple keeps these chicken patties moist and flavorful without adding any extra fat. Serve with potato salad or coleslaw dressed with a mustard vinaigrette.

ACTIVE TIME: 15 MINUTES · **TOTAL TIME:** 25 MINUTES
MAKES: 4 BURGERS

2 GRANNY SMITH APPLES, CORED
½ TEASPOON POULTRY SEASONING
½ TEASPOON SALT
¼ TEASPOON GROUND BLACK PEPPER

1 POUND GROUND CHICKEN
¼ CUP FINELY CHOPPED CELERY (ABOUT ½ STALK)
4 HAMBURGER BUNS
½ CUP WHOLE-BERRY CRANBERRY SAUCE

1 From each apple, cut 6 thin slices crosswise from center (for a total of 12 apple rings). From remainder, coarsely shred ¾ cup apples. Spray ridged grill pan with nonstick cooking spray; heat pan over medium-high heat until hot.
2 In medium bowl, stir shredded apple with poultry seasoning, salt, and pepper until blended. Mix in chicken and celery just until combined, but do not overmix. Shape into four ½-inch-thick burgers, handling mixture as little as possible.
3 Place burgers in grill pan; cook 10 to 12 minutes or just until chicken loses pink color throughout, turning over once. Instant-read thermometer inserted horizontally into thickest part of patty should register 165°F. Serve burgers on buns with apple rings and cranberry sauce.

385 CALORIES

PER BURGER. 24G PROTEIN | 47G CARBOHYDRATE | 12G TOTAL FAT (1G SATURATED) 4G FIBER | 0MG CHOLESTEROL | 610MG SODIUM

MAKE IT A MEAL: You're already shredding apples for these burgers, so why not shred some cabbage, carrots, and yellow peppers too to create our Tricolor Slaw (40 calories; page 402)? Or, if you prefer, match with our Light and Lemony Slaw (80 calories; page 405). Either one adds crunch to a tasty meal that's well under 500 calories.

GREEK CHICKEN DIPPERS

Fast and fresh, this Greek-style combination of chicken, vegetables, and pita doesn't skimp on flavor, thanks to a lemony herbed yogurt topping.

TOTAL TIME: 25 MINUTES
MAKES: 4 MAIN-DISH SERVINGS

1 CUP PLAIN FAT-FREE GREEK YOGURT	2 TABLESPOONS FRESH LEMON JUICE
2 TABLESPOONS PACKED FRESH MINT LEAVES	4 TEASPOONS EXTRA-VIRGIN OLIVE OIL
	¼ TEASPOON DRIED OREGANO
2 TABLESPOONS DILL LEAVES, CHOPPED, PLUS MORE FOR GARNISH	1 POUND CHICKEN BREAST TENDERS
	½ ENGLISH (SEEDLESS) CUCUMBER
¾ TEASPOON GROUND CUMIN	1 LARGE RIPE TOMATO
1 GARLIC CLOVE, CRUSHED WITH PRESS	4 WHOLE-WHEAT PITAS, CUT IN HALF
⅝ TEASPOON SALT	

1 In small bowl, combine yogurt, mint, dill, ¼ teaspoon cumin, one-third of garlic, and ¼ teaspoon salt. Let stand.

2 In pie plate, combine 1 tablespoon lemon juice, 1 tablespoon oil, oregano, ¼ teaspoon salt, remaining ½ teaspoon cumin, and half of remaining garlic. Add chicken, turning to coat. Let stand. Meanwhile, prepare outdoor grill for direct grilling (or preheat grill pan) over medium-high heat.

3 Grill chicken 10 to 12 minutes or until no longer pink in center, turning over once.

4 Meanwhile, cut cucumber and tomato into chunks; toss, in large bowl, with remaining ⅛ teaspoon salt and remaining 1 tablespoon lemon juice, 1 teaspoon oil, and garlic.

5 Transfer chicken to serving plates. Grill pitas until toasted, turning once. Serve alongside chicken, yogurt sauce, and cucumber mixture; garnish with dill.

330 CALORIES **PER SERVING.** 33G PROTEIN | 31G CARBOHYDRATE | 9G TOTAL FAT (2G SATURATED) 5G FIBER | 63MG CHOLESTEROL | 685MG SODIUM

MAKE IT A MEAL: Enjoy this Greek salad plate on its own for lunch. Or add our Tabbouleh salad (185 calories; page 425) for a 515-calorie dinner.

CHICKEN QUESADILLAS

This tasty Tex-Mex uses reduced-fat tortillas and cheese. The splurge: an avocado-tomato salsa. Though avocado is high in fat, it's mostly the heart-healthy kind; plus, avocados contain a natural cholesterol reducer.

ACTIVE TIME: 10 MINUTES · **TOTAL TIME:** 35 MINUTES
MAKES: 4 MAIN-DISH SERVINGS

2 TEASPOONS CANOLA OIL	1 CUP REDUCED-FAT SHREDDED MEXICAN CHEESE BLEND
1 GREEN ONION, THINLY SLICED	
1 LIME	4 BURRITO-SIZE LOW-FAT FLOUR TORTILLAS
1 POUND SKINLESS, BONELESS THIN-SLICED CHICKEN BREASTS, CUT INTO 1-INCH STRIPS	½ AVOCADO, PEELED, SEEDED, AND CUT INTO ½-INCH PIECES
¼ TEASPOON SALT	¾ CUP PREPARED SALSA
⅛ TEASPOON GROUND BLACK PEPPER	

1 In nonstick 12-inch skillet, heat oil over medium heat 1 minute. Add green onion and cook, stirring occasionally, until tender, about 6 minutes.

2 Meanwhile, from lime, grate 1 teaspoon peel and squeeze 2 tablespoons juice. Season chicken strips on both sides with lime peel, salt, and pepper.

3 Add chicken to green onion in skillet; cook 10 minutes or until chicken is no longer pink inside. Transfer chicken and green onion to bowl; stir in lime juice.

4 Evenly divide chicken mixture and cheese among tortillas, placing filling on one half of each; fold over to make 4 quesadillas.

5 In same skillet, cook quesadillas over medium heat, in two batches, 7 to 8 minutes per batch or until browned on both sides and heated through. Cut each quesadilla into thirds. Stir avocado into salsa; serve with quesadillas.

400 CALORIES

PER SERVING. 38G PROTEIN | 31G CARBOHYDRATE | 14G TOTAL FAT (5G SATURATED) 8G FIBER | 86MG CHOLESTEROL | 970MG SODIUM ✿

MAKE IT A MEAL: The quesadilla with avocado salsa makes a great lunch on its own. For a 505-calorie dinner, add on our summery salad of Watercress and Peaches (105 calories; page 407).

FAVORITE ADD-ONS

To make your meal-planning a breeze, we've organized the add-on recipes in the following chapters by calorie count—from lowest to highest. Choose your main dish from the preceding chapters, then select one or more of these tempting add-ons. So if you're preparing our Finger Food Feast, a yummy 335-calorie main dish of panko-crusted drumsticks and fresh veggies with a yogurt dipping sauce, you could add our Confetti Rice Pilaf (165 calories) to create a 500-calorie dinner. Or you could enjoy two lower-calorie add-ons instead: Warm Dijon Potato Salad (150 calories) plus three Lemon Meringue Cookies (5 calories each)—and your meal still adds up to 500 calories total!

205
CALORIES

Grilled Vegetables with
Thai Pesto
(page 413)

VEGGIES & SIDE SALADS

Once you've selected a succulent chicken main, you'll want to pair it with an equally delicious vegetable side. We provide a colorful, vitamin-packed assortment, from Carrots and Parsnip Coins and Oven-Roasted Brussels Sprouts to fresh green beans, two ways. Our Roasted Acorn Squash is a natural match for roasted or baked chicken. Looking for a side salad? Our Watercress and Peaches is a sophisticated option, while our Garden Macaroni Salad is just the thing for a backyard barbecue. If you're grilling chicken, add on our Corn on the Cob with Molasses Butter or Grilled Vegetables with Thai Pesto.

KEY TO ICONS

🕐 30 minutes or less   ❤️ Heart healthy   🌾 High fiber   🟩 Make ahead   🍲 Slow cooker

TRICOLOR SLAW

Toss red cabbage, carrots, and yellow pepper with an apple cider vinaigrette to make a colorful, crunchy coleslaw.

TOTAL TIME: 20 MINUTES
MAKES: 4 CUPS OR 6 SIDE-DISH SERVINGS

In serving bowl, stir **1 small garlic clove,** crushed with press; **3 tablespoons cider vinegar; 1 tablespoon vegetable oil; ¾ teaspoon sugar; ¼ teaspoon celery seeds;** and **½ teaspoon salt** until mixed. Cut **¼ small cabbage** (8 ounces) in half; thinly slice using slicing blade on box grater or sharp chef's knife, discarding tough ribs. Add cabbage; **1 carrot,** peeled and shredded; and **½ small yellow pepper,** thinly sliced, to dressing in bowl and toss until evenly mixed. If not serving right away, cover and refrigerate up to 1 day.

 40 CALORIES **PER SERVING.** 1G PROTEIN | 5G CARBOHYDRATE | 2G TOTAL FAT (0G SATURATED) 1G FIBER | 0MG CHOLESTEROL | 200MG SODIUM

CANTALOUPE AND CUCUMBER SALAD

Juicy, ripe cantaloupes and crunchy English cucumbers make a tempting pair in this fresh summer salad.

TOTAL TIME: 20 MINUTES
MAKES: 4½ CUPS OR 5 SIDE-DISH SERVINGS

In large bowl, whisk **2 tablespoons lime juice, ⅛ teaspoon salt,** and **pinch ground black pepper** until blended. Add **½ large English (seedless) cucumber,** peeled in alternating strips and coarsely chopped; **1 ripe cantaloupe,** coarsely chopped; **2 green onions,** thinly sliced; and **¼ cup loosely packed fresh cilantro,** chopped. Toss to coat.

 45 CALORIES **PER SERVING.** 6G PROTEIN | 25G CARBOHYDRATE | 5G TOTAL FAT (1G SATURATED) 5G FIBER | 0MG CHOLESTEROL | 160MG SODIUM

BLOODY MARY TOMATO SALAD

This fresh salad combines lemon juice, hot pepper sauce, and Worcestershire sauce with tomatoes and celery for delicious results. Be sure to leave enough time to chill the salad before serving.

TOTAL TIME: 15 MINUTES PLUS CHILLING
MAKES: 3½ CUPS OR 4 SIDE-DISH SERVINGS

1 TABLESPOON PREPARED HORSERADISH

1 TABLESPOON OLIVE OIL

1 TABLESPOON VODKA (OPTIONAL)

2 TEASPOONS FRESH LEMON JUICE

¾ TEASPOON HOT PEPPER SAUCE

½ TEASPOON WORCESTERSHIRE SAUCE

¼ TEASPOON SALT

¼ TEASPOON GROUND BLACK PEPPER

1½ PINTS GRAPE OR CHERRY TOMATOES, CUT IN HALF

2 STALKS CELERY, CUT INTO ¼-INCH-THICK DIAGONAL SLICES, LEAVES RESERVED FOR GARNISH

In large bowl, whisk together horseradish, oil, vodka (if using), lemon juice, pepper sauce, Worcestershire, salt, and pepper until blended. Add tomatoes and celery; toss to combine. Cover and refrigerate 2 hours. To serve, toss again to coat with dressing and garnish with celery leaves.

65 CALORIES

PER SERVING. 1G PROTEIN | 7G CARBOHYDRATE | 4G TOTAL FAT (1G SATURATED) 2G FIBER | 0MG CHOLESTEROL | 190MG SODIUM ♥

SKINNY DRESSINGS FOR VEGGIES

Boost the flavor—without loading on the fat—with these simple alternatives to classic butter, cheese, and cream sauces.

FOR GREEN BEANS OR BROCCOLI

- Blend prepared horseradish, Dijon mustard, and light mayonnaise; drizzle over steamed green beans.
- Whisk together seasoned rice vinegar, soy sauce, and grated, peeled fresh ginger to taste. Use as a dipping sauce for tender-crisp broccoli.

FOR YELLOW SQUASH OR ZUCCHINI

- Toast bread crumbs with chopped garlic in 1 teaspoon olive oil. Sprinkle the crumbs over steamed yellow squash or zucchini along with some chopped parsley.

FOR DARK, LEAFY GREENS (SPINACH, SWISS CHARD, COLLARDS)

- Sauté minced garlic and a pinch of red pepper flakes in 1 teaspoon olive oil until fragrant. Add fresh spinach or Swiss chard to the pan and cook until it wilts.
- Add a handful of yellow raisins to steamed bitter greens such as collards.

FOR ASPARAGUS OR CAULIFLOWER

- Prepare a mock hollandaise by mixing light mayonnaise with Dijon mustard, fresh lemon juice, and a pinch of ground black pepper. Drizzle the cool sauce over steamed cauliflower, broccoli, or—the classic hollandaise partner—asparagus spears.
- Chop some mango chutney (available in the international section of most supermarkets) and toss it with steamed cauliflower.

FOR EGGPLANT

- Heat chopped fresh tomato with crushed fennel seeds in a skillet until hot. Spoon over baked or broiled eggplant slices.

FOR NEW POTATOES

- Toss chopped mixed fresh herbs (such as basil, mint, rosemary, or oregano) and grated lemon zest with boiled new potato halves.

ROASTED CAULIFLOWER

Roasting brings out the natural sweetness of cauliflower and contributes a delectable brown crust.

ACTIVE TIME: 10 MINUTES · **TOTAL TIME:** 45 MINUTES
MAKES: 4 SIDE-DISH SERVINGS

Preheat oven to 450°F. Trim **1 head cauliflower** and separate into 1-inch flowerets. In large bowl, toss cauliflower, **1 coarsely chopped onion, 2 tablespoons reduced-sodium soy sauce, 1 tablespoon olive oil,** and **1 garlic clove,** crushed with press, until evenly mixed. Spread mixture in 15½" by 10½" jelly-roll pan and roast, stirring occasionally, about 35 minutes or until cauliflower is tender and browned. Spoon cauliflower into serving bowl; garnish with **fresh chives.**

70 CALORIES

PER ¾-CUP SERVING. 3G PROTEIN | 7G CARBOHYDRATE | 4G TOTAL FAT (1G SATURATED) | 3G FIBER | 0MG CHOLESTEROL | 300MG SODIUM ♥

LIGHT AND LEMONY SLAW

Lower in fat than the typical deli slaw, the subtle sweetness of this slaw is a nice change of pace.

TOTAL TIME: 25 MINUTES
MAKES: 6 SIDE-DISH SERVINGS

In large bowl, with wire whisk, mix **1 teaspoon lemon peel** and **2 tablespoons lemon juice** (from 1 lemon), **¼ cup light mayonnaise, 2 tablespoons reduced-fat sour cream, ½ tablespoon sugar, ½ teaspoon salt, ¼ teaspoon coarsely ground black pepper,** and **⅛ teaspoon celery seeds,** crushed. Add **1 small head cabbage** (1½ pounds), quartered, cored, and thinly sliced, and **2 carrots,** peeled and shredded, to dressing in bowl; toss to coat. Serve at room temperature, or cover and refrigerate up to 4 hours.

80 CALORIES

PER SERVING. 2G PROTEIN | 10G CARBOHYDRATE | 4G TOTAL FAT (1G SATURATED) 2G FIBER | 5MG CHOLESTEROL | 298MG SODIUM ● ♥

GREEN BEANS WITH SHALLOTS

Enjoy this simple, low-cal recipe or the (even lower calorie) variation.

ACTIVE TIME: 30 MINUTES · **TOTAL TIME:** 45 MINUTES

MAKES: 5 SIDE-DISH SERVINGS

3	QUARTS WATER	½	POUND SHALLOTS, THINLY SLICED (1¼ CUPS)
¾	TEASPOON SALT	¼	TEASPOON GROUND BLACK PEPPER
1½	POUNDS GREEN BEANS, TRIMMED	1½	TABLESPOONS DIJON MUSTARD WITH SEEDS
1	TABLESPOON BUTTER OR MARGARINE		

1 In covered 4- to 5-quart saucepot, heat water and ½ teaspoon salt to boiling over high heat. Add green beans and cook, uncovered, 5 to 7 minutes or until tender-crisp. Drain. Plunge beans into large bowl filled with ice water to chill quickly. Drain well. If you like, you can place well-drained beans in plastic storage bags and refrigerate until ready to use.

2 In same saucepot, melt butter over medium-low heat. Add shallots; cook 12 to 15 minutes or until tender and golden, stirring occasionally.

3 To mixture in saucepot, add green beans, pepper, and remaining ¼ teaspoon salt; increase heat to medium-high, and cook about 5 minutes longer or until beans are heated through, tossing occasionally with tongs. Stir in mustard.

90 CALORIES

PER SERVING. 4G PROTEIN | 16G CARBOHYDRATE | 3G TOTAL FAT (1G SATURATED) 4G FIBER | 0MG CHOLESTEROL | 185MG SODIUM ♥ 🛍

GREEN BEANS WITH GARLIC

Prepare green beans as above in step 1. In step 2, omit shallots, and in place of butter, heat **1 tablespoon olive oil** over high heat. Complete recipe as in step 3, adding **2 garlic cloves,** finely chopped, after beans are heated through; omit mustard. Cook 1 minute longer or until garlic is fragrant, tossing.

50 CALORIES

PER SERVING. 2G PROTEIN | 9G CARBOHYDRATE | 2G TOTAL FAT (0G SATURATED) 4G FIBER | 0MG CHOLESTEROL | 125MG SODIUM ♥ 🛍

OVEN-ROASTED BRUSSELS SPROUTS

Perfect for a busy weeknight, these tender roasted Brussels sprouts are low-cal and take just minutes to prepare.

ACTIVE TIME: 5 MINUTES · **TOTAL TIME:** 25 MINUTES
MAKES: 4 SIDE-DISH SERVINGS

Preheat oven to 450°F. Trim and halve **1¼ pounds Brussels sprouts;** toss in jelly-roll pan with **1 to 2 tablespoons olive oil.** Roast 20 to 25 minutes or until tender and browned, stirring once or twice. Toss with **2 tablespoons rice vinegar;** add **ground black pepper to taste.**

95 CALORIES

PER SERVING. 4G PROTEIN | 14G CARBOHYDRATE | 4G TOTAL FAT (0G SATURATED) 5G FIBER | 0MG CHOLESTEROL | 295MG SODIUM

WATERCRESS AND PEACHES

Peppery watercress complements sweet juicy summer peaches in this quick side salad, ready in 10 minutes.

TOTAL TIME: 10 MINUTES
MAKES: 4 SIDE-DISH SERVINGS

In large bowl, combine **6 to 7 ounces watercress, 2 pitted and chopped peaches, 2 tablespoons fresh lemon juice,** and **⅛ teaspoon each salt and ground black pepper.** Toss gently until coated. Drizzle with **1 tablespoon extra-virgin olive oil**; gently toss again. Top with **¼ cup shelled roasted salted pistachios.**

105 CALORIES

PER SERVING. 3G PROTEIN | 9G CARBOHYDRATE | 8G TOTAL FAT (1G SATURATED) 2G FIBER | 0MG CHOLESTEROL | 155MG SODIUM

105 CALORIES

Corn on the Cob with Molasses Butter (opposite)

CORN ON THE COB WITH MOLASSES BUTTER

Cayenne pepper and coriander add kick to the molasses-sweetened butter. For photo, see opposite.

ACTIVE TIME: 10 MINUTES · TOTAL TIME: 20 MINUTES
MAKES: 4 SIDE-DISH SERVINGS

Prepare outdoor grill for direct grilling over medium-high heat. In small bowl, with fork, stir **1 tablespoon softened butter or margarine, 1½ teaspoons light (mild) molasses, ¼ teaspoon coriander, ¼ teaspoon salt,** and **pinch of cayenne (ground red) pepper** until well combined. Place **4 ears corn,** husks and silk removed, on hot grill rack. Cover grill and cook, turning frequently, until corn is brown in spots, 10 to 15 minutes. Transfer to platter; serve with molasses butter.

105 CALORIES

PER SERVING. 3G PROTEIN | 18G CARBOHYDRATE | 4G TOTAL FAT (2G SATURATED) 2G FIBER | 8MG CHOLESTEROL | 186MG SODIUM 💙 ❤️

CARROT AND PARSNIP COINS

This cheerful, orange-scented side dish combines the sweetness of carrots with the mellow sharpness of parsnips.

ACTIVE TIME: 15 MINUTES · TOTAL TIME: 25 MINUTES
MAKES: 4 SIDE-DISH SERVINGS

From **1 navel orange,** grate ½ teaspoon peel and squeeze ¼ cup juice. In 12-inch skillet, combine **1 tablespoon butter or margarine, ¾ cup water, 1 pound peeled and thinly sliced carrots, 8 ounces peeled and thinly sliced parsnips, ¼ teaspoon ground nutmeg,** and **½ teaspoon salt.** Cover and heat to boiling over medium-high heat. Reduce heat to medium and cook, covered, 3 minutes. Stir in orange juice and cook, uncovered, 6 to 8 minutes longer or until vegetables are tender-crisp and most liquid has evaporated. Stir in orange peel.

115 CALORIES

PER SERVING. 2G PROTEIN | 21G CARBOHYDRATE | 3G TOTAL FAT (1G SATURATED) 6G FIBER | 0MG CHOLESTEROL | 370MG SODIUM 💙

ROASTED ACORN SQUASH

A traditional accompaniment to roasted chicken, this squash side dish is as colorful as it is tasty. If you'd like to adjust the flavor profile to match your main dish, try one of these variations on the melted butter mixture: For a sweet and spicy twist, stir ⅛ teaspoon cayenne (ground red) pepper into the melted butter. For an herb-scented acorn squash, omit the brown sugar and stir in 1 teaspoon chopped fresh rosemary or oregano. For garlicky squash, omit the brown sugar and stir in one large clove chopped garlic.

ACTIVE TIME: 10 MINUTES · **TOTAL TIME:** 40 MINUTES
MAKES: 4 SIDE-DISH SERVINGS

Preheat oven to 450°F. Spray 15½" by 10½" jelly-roll pan with nonstick cooking spray. Cut **2 small acorn squashes (1 pound each)** lengthwise in half; scoop out seeds and discard. Cut each half into 2 wedges. Place squashes in pan. In cup, stir together **2 tablespoons melted butter or margarine, 2 tablespoons packed brown sugar, ½ teaspoon salt,** and **⅛ teaspoon coarsely ground black pepper.** Brush cut sides of squash halves with butter mixture and bake 30 minutes or until lightly browned and fork-tender.

TIP To ensure that the squash wedges sit flat, trim about ¼ inch off the bottom of each wedge.

150 CALORIES **PER SERVING.** 2G PROTEIN | 26G CARBOHYDRATE | 6G TOTAL FAT (1G SATURATED) 3G FIBER | 26MG CHOLESTEROL | 375MG SODIUM

GARDEN MACARONI SALAD

This summery salad is sprouting with a rainbow of veggies.

ACTIVE TIME: 25 MINUTES · **TOTAL TIME:** 40 MINUTES
MAKES: 8 CUPS OR 10 SIDE-DISH SERVINGS

8	OUNCES CORKSCREW (ROTINI) PASTA	5	RADISHES, CUT INTO ½-INCH CHUNKS
1	LARGE LEMON	1	SMALL ZUCCHINI (6 OUNCES), CUT INTO ½-INCH CHUNKS
⅔	CUP LIGHT MAYONNAISE	1	CARROT, PEELED AND SHREDDED
⅓	CUP MILK	½	YELLOW PEPPER, CUT INTO ½-INCH PIECES
½	TEASPOON SALT		
½	TEASPOON GROUND BLACK PEPPER	¼	CUP CHOPPED FRESH CHIVES
1	CUP FROZEN PEAS, THAWED		

1 Cook pasta as label directs.

2 Meanwhile, from lemon, grate 1 teaspoon peel and squeeze 3 tablespoons juice. Transfer peel and juice to serving bowl; add mayonnaise, milk, salt, and black pepper. With whisk, stir mixture until smooth.

3 Drain pasta. Rinse with cold running water; drain again.

4 Add pasta, peas, radishes, zucchini, carrot, yellow pepper, and chives to mayonnaise mixture in bowl; toss until evenly mixed. If not serving right away, cover and refrigerate up to 1 day.

160 CALORIES

PER SERVING. 5G PROTEIN | 23G CARBOHYDRATE | 6G TOTAL FAT (1G SATURATED) 2G FIBER | 6MG CHOLESTEROL | 295 MG SODIUM ❤️ 🟩

GRILLED VEGETABLES WITH THAI PESTO

Pesto takes a Thai-inspired twist when we add fresh lime and sweet chili sauce to the mix. For photo, see page 400.

ACTIVE TIME: 25 MINUTES · **TOTAL TIME:** 35 MINUTES
MAKES: 4 SIDE-DISH SERVINGS

THAI PESTO

1   LARGE LIME

½   CUP WALNUTS

1   CUP PACKED FRESH BASIL LEAVES

1   TABLESPOON THAI SWEET CHILI SAUCE

3   TABLESPOONS WATER

¼   TEASPOON SALT

GRILLED VEGETABLES

4   PLUM TOMATOES, EACH CUT LENGTHWISE IN HALF

2   YELLOW PEPPERS, EACH CUT INTO QUARTERS, SEEDED, AND STEMMED

½   MEDIUM EGGPLANT, CUT CROSSWISE INTO ¾-INCH-THICK SLICES

1   LARGE ZUCCHINI, CUT DIAGONALLY INTO ½-INCH-THICK SLICES

½   LARGE SWEET ONION, CUT THROUGH ROOT END INTO 6 WEDGES

OLIVE OIL NONSTICK COOKING SPRAY

¼   TEASPOON SALT

1 Prepare pesto: From lime, grate ½ teaspoon peel and squeeze 2 tablespoons juice. In skillet, toast walnuts over medium heat 5 minutes, stirring, until fragrant. Set aside.

2 In food processor with knife blade attached, blend nuts, basil, chili sauce, water, lime peel and juice, and salt. Store covered in refrigerator up to 2 days. Makes about ⅔ cup.

3 Prepare vegetables: Prepare outdoor grill for direct grilling over medium heat, or heat large ridged grill pan over medium heat until hot. Lightly spray tomatoes, peppers, eggplant, and onion with cooking spray. Place all vegetables on hot grill grate, cover, and cook until tender, turning each vegetable over once during cooking time. Cook tomatoes and zucchini 6 to 8 minutes, peppers and onion 8 to 10 minutes, and eggplant 10 to 12 minutes. As vegetables finish cooking, transfer to serving plate. Sprinkle with salt and serve with pesto.

205 CALORIES

PER SERVING. 6G PROTEIN | 28G CARBOHYDRATE | 11G TOTAL FAT (1G SATURATED) 7G FIBER | 0MG CHOLESTEROL | 365MG SODIUM

125 CALORIES
*Herbed Roasted Potatoes
(page 416)*

POTATOES, BEANS & GRAINS

What could be more comforting than chicken paired with potatoes, stuffing, or rice? With our lighter takes on classic sides, you can enjoy a full meal minus the high calories and fat. Savory Pear Stuffing, Herbed Roasted Potatoes, or Confetti Rice Pilaf are scrumptious with any of our oven-baked or roasted chicken mains. Or, if you're making one of our grilled chicken dishes, add on Warm Dijon Potato Salad or Three-Bean and Corn Salad. Fiber-filled whole grains are a must for any healthy diet, too, so be sure to try our Tabbouleh and Red Quinoa Pilaf.

KEY TO ICONS

🔵 30 minutes or less   ❤️ Heart healthy   🌾 High fiber   🟩 Make ahead   🍲 Slow cooker

SAVORY PEAR STUFFING

Spruce up packaged cornbread stuffing mix with Bartlett pears, green onions, and fresh parsley.

ACTIVE TIME: 10 MINUTES · **TOTAL TIME:** 40 MINUTES
MAKES: 8 SIDE-DISH SERVINGS

Preheat oven to 425°F. In 4-quart saucepan, heat **1 tablespoon olive oil** over medium-high heat until hot. Add **2 chopped stalks celery** and cook 5 minutes, stirring occasionally. Meanwhile, cut **2 large ripe Bartlett pears** into ½-inch chunks, slice **4 green onions,** and chop **¼ cup packed fresh parsley leaves.** Add **3 cups water** to saucepan; cover and heat to boiling. Remove from heat; stir in **1 package (12 ounces) corn bread stuffing mix,** pears, green onions, and parsley. Spoon stuffing into shallow 3½-quart casserole; cover with foil. Bake 20 minutes; uncover and bake 10 minutes longer.

110 CALORIES — **PER SERVING.** 3G PROTEIN | 19G CARBOHYDRATE | 3G TOTAL FAT (0G SATURATED) 2G FIBER | 0MG CHOLESTEROL | 385MG SODIUM

HERBED ROASTED POTATOES

Potato chunks tossed with parsley and butter cook into tender morsels when foil-wrapped. For photo, see page 414.

ACTIVE TIME: 15 MINUTES · **TOTAL TIME:** 45 MINUTES
MAKES: 6 SIDE-DISH SERVINGS

Preheat oven to 450°F. In 3-quart saucepan, melt **2 tablespoons butter or margarine** over medium-low heat with **1 tablespoon chopped fresh parsley, ½ teaspoon freshly grated lemon peel, ½ teaspoon salt,** and **⅛ teaspoon coarsely ground black pepper.** Remove saucepan from heat; add **1½ pounds halved small red potatoes** and toss well to coat. Place mixture in center of 24" by 18" sheet of heavy-duty foil. Fold edges over and pinch to seal tightly. Place packet in jelly-roll pan and bake until potatoes are tender when pierced (through foil) with knife, about 30 minutes.

125 CALORIES — **PER SERVING.** | 2G PROTEIN | 20G CARBOHYDRATE | 4G TOTAL FAT (2G SATURATED) 2G FIBER | 10MG CHOLESTEROL | 241MG SODIUM ❤

LIGHT MASHED POTATOES

Fat-free half-and-half gives these potatoes the same silky texture you'd get with heavy cream but without the fat and cholesterol.

ACTIVE TIME: 15 MINUTES · **TOTAL TIME:** 30 MINUTES
MAKES: 4½ CUPS OR 6 SIDE-DISH SERVINGS

In 4-quart saucepan, combine **2 pounds Yukon Gold potatoes,** peeled and cut into 1-inch pieces, with water to cover; heat to boiling over high heat. Reduce heat to low; cover and simmer 8 to 10 minutes or until potatoes are fork-tender. Reserve **¼ cup cooking water.** Drain potatoes and return to saucepan. Mash with **1 tablespoon butter or margarine** and **¾ teaspoon salt.** Gradually add **½ cup warm fat-free half-and-half,** continuing to mash until mixture is smooth and well blended; add some of reserved cooking water if necessary.

145 CALORIES

PER SERVING. 3G PROTEIN | 29G CARBOHYDRATE | 2G TOTAL FAT (0G SATURATED) 2G FIBER | 0MG CHOLESTEROL | 345MG SODIUM

WARM DIJON POTATO SALAD

We season this warm potato salad with plenty of zesty red onion, Dijon mustard, and slightly sweet cider vinegar—a winning combination.

ACTIVE TIME: 15 MINUTES · **TOTAL TIME:** 25 MINUTES
MAKES: 6½ CUPS OR 6 SIDE-DISH SERVINGS

2 POUNDS SMALL RED POTATOES, EACH CUT INTO QUARTERS

1½ TEASPOONS SALT

2 STALKS CELERY, THINLY SLICED

½ CUP THINLY SLICED RED ONION

¼ CUP CIDER VINEGAR

¼ CUP DIJON MUSTARD

¼ TEASPOON COARSELY GROUND BLACK PEPPER

¼ CUP LOOSELY PACKED FRESH PARSLEY LEAVES, COARSELY CHOPPED

1 In 4-quart saucepan, place potatoes, enough *water* to cover, and 1 teaspoon salt; heat to boiling over high. Reduce heat to medium-low; cover saucepan and simmer potatoes about 8 minutes or until just fork-tender.
2 Meanwhile, in large bowl, stir together celery, red onion, cider vinegar, Dijon, remaining ½ teaspoon salt, and pepper.
3 Drain potatoes well, then add hot potatoes to bowl with celery mixture. With rubber spatula, gently toss to coat thoroughly.
4 Spoon potato salad into serving bowl; sprinkle the top with parsley and serve warm.

150 CALORIES

PER SERVING. 4G PROTEIN | 33G CARBOHYDRATE | 1G TOTAL FAT (0G SATURATED) 3G FIBER | 0MG CHOLESTEROL | 370MG SODIUM

POLENTA AND SPINACH GRATIN

A creamy spinach topping layered over slices of ready-made polenta is a satisfying side dish (or serve a double portion as a main-dish!). You can assemble this casserole up to one day ahead, then cover and refrigerate it before baking it. When you're ready to serve it, heat it in a 425°F oven for about 40 minutes, until it's hot and bubbly.

ACTIVE TIME: 20 MINUTES · **TOTAL TIME:** 55 MINUTES
MAKES: 8 SIDE-DISH SERVINGS

1 LOG (24 OUNCES) PRECOOKED PLAIN POLENTA	1¾ CUPS WHOLE MILK
1 TABLESPOON OLIVE OIL	1 TABLESPOON CORNSTARCH
1 MEDIUM ONION, CHOPPED	½ TEASPOON SALT
1 GARLIC CLOVE, MINCED	½ CUP FRESHLY GRATED PARMESAN CHEESE
⅛ TEASPOON CRUSHED RED PEPPER	
2 PACKAGES (10 OUNCES EACH) FROZEN CHOPPED SPINACH, THAWED AND SQUEEZED DRY	

1 Preheat oven to 425°F. Cut polenta log crosswise in half, then cut each half lengthwise into 6 slices. In 8" by 8" ceramic or glass baking dish, place half of polenta slices, overlapping slightly.

2 In 4-quart saucepan, heat oil over medium heat until hot. Add onion and cook until tender and golden, 10 to 12 minutes, stirring occasionally. Add garlic and crushed red pepper and cook 1 minute, stirring. Add spinach and cook 3 minutes to heat through, stirring frequently.

3 In medium bowl, with wire whisk, mix milk and cornstarch. Stir in salt and all but 2 tablespoons Parmesan. Add milk mixture to spinach mixture in saucepan; heat to boiling over medium-high heat. Reduce heat to low; cook 2 minutes, stirring occasionally.

4 Spoon half of spinach mixture over polenta slices in baking dish. Repeat layering with remaining polenta slices and spinach mixture. Sprinkle with reserved Parmesan. Bake until hot and bubbly, about 20 minutes.

155 CALORIES **PER SERVING.** 8G PROTEIN | 19G CARBOHYDRATE | 5G TOTAL FAT (3G SATURATED) 2G FIBER | 12MG CHOLESTEROL | 625MG SODIUM

CORN AND BARLEY SALAD

In the height of summer, corn is so fresh and sweet that you can eat it raw, which is how we use it in this salad.

ACTIVE TIME: 20 MINUTES · **TOTAL TIME:** 40 MINUTES PLUS CHILLING
MAKES: 4 CUPS OR 6 SIDE-DISH SERVINGS

1 CUP WATER	¼ TEASPOON GROUND BLACK PEPPER
½ CUP PEARL BARLEY	¾ CUPS FROZEN SHELLED EDAMAME (SOYBEANS), THAWED
¼ TEASPOON SALT	
3 EARS CORN, HUSKS AND SILKS REMOVED	¼ CUP PACKED FRESH MINT LEAVES, CHOPPED, PLUS ADDITIONAL SPRIGS FOR GARNISH
¼ CUP RICE VINEGAR	
1 TABLESPOON OLIVE OIL	

1 In covered 2-quart saucepan, heat water to boiling over high heat. Stir in barley and salt; heat to boiling. Reduce heat to low; cover and simmer 30 to 35 minutes or until barley is tender and liquid is absorbed.

2 Meanwhile, with sharp knife, carefully cut corn kernels from cobs (see Tip); discard cobs. In large bowl, with wire whisk or fork, whisk vinegar, oil, and pepper until blended; stir in warm barley, corn kernels, edamame, and mint. Cover salad and refrigerate at least 1 hour or up to 8 hours. To serve, garnish salad with mint sprigs.

TIP To remove kernels from corn cob, trim tip of cob to create a smooth surface. Stand the ear on trimmed end, then slice down to cut off the corn kernels, cutting close to the cob. Rotate the ear and cut off additional rows of kernels until all of the corn has been removed from the cob.

155 CALORIES

PER SERVING. 6G PROTEIN | 25G CARBOHYDRATE | 5G TOTAL FAT (1G SATURATED) 5G FIBER | 0MG CHOLESTEROL | 160MG SODIUM 🌱 ❤️ 🥗

THREE-BEAN AND CORN SALAD

This classic salad is always a hit at a picnic or potluck.

ACTIVE TIME: 25 MINUTES · **TOTAL TIME:** 35 MINUTES PLUS CHILLING
MAKES: 7 CUPS OR 12 SIDE-DISH SERVINGS

1¾ TEASPOONS SALT

12 OUNCES GREEN AND/OR WAX BEANS, TRIMMED AND CUT INTO 1-INCH PIECES

1 SMALL SHALLOT, FINELY CHOPPED

¼ CUP OLIVE OIL

3 TABLESPOONS FRESH LIME JUICE

2 TABLESPOONS WHITE WINE VINEGAR

2 TABLESPOONS HONEY

1 TABLESPOON CHOPPED FRESH TARRAGON LEAVES

1 TABLESPOON DIJON MUSTARD

¼ TEASPOON GROUND BLACK PEPPER

4 EARS CORN, HUSKS AND SILKS REMOVED

1 CAN (15 TO 19 OUNCES) RED KIDNEY BEANS, RINSED AND DRAINED

1 CAN (15 TO 19 OUNCES) WHITE KIDNEY BEANS (CANNELLINI), RINSED AND DRAINED

1 RED PEPPER, CUT INTO ½-INCH PIECES

1 In 2-quart saucepan, heat *1 inch water* with 1 teaspoon salt to boiling over high heat. Add green beans; heat to boiling. Reduce heat to medium-high; simmer 5 minutes or until beans are tender-crisp.

2 Meanwhile, prepare dressing: In small bowl, with whisk, mix shallot, oil, lime juice, vinegar, honey, tarragon, Dijon, pepper, and remaining ¾ teaspoon salt until blended.

3 Drain green beans. Rinse with cold running water to stop cooking; drain again. Transfer beans to large serving bowl. With sharp knife, carefully cut corn kernels from cobs; discard cobs and add kernels to bowl. Add both canned beans and red pepper to bowl.

4 Pour dressing over bean mixture; toss until evenly coated. Cover and refrigerate to blend flavors, at least 1 hour or up to 8 hours.

160 CALORIES

PER SERVING. 5G PROTEIN | 24G CARBOHYDRATE | 5G TOTAL FAT (1G SATURATED) 6G FIBER | 0MG CHOLESTEROL | 375 MG SODIUM

CONFETTI RICE PILAF

Tender rice is cooked with a festive mix of peas, carrots, and green onions.

ACTIVE TIME: 10 MINUTES · **TOTAL TIME:** 30 MINUTES
MAKES: 6 SIDE-DISH SERVINGS

---

1 TABLESPOON BUTTER OR MARGARINE

1 CARROT, PEELED AND DICED

1 CUP REGULAR LONG-GRAIN WHITE RICE

1 CUP CANNED OR HOMEMADE CHICKEN BROTH (PAGE 40)

1 SMALL BAY LEAF

¼ TEASPOON SALT

⅛ TEASPOON COARSELY GROUND BLACK PEPPER

1 CUP WATER

1¼ CUPS FROZEN PEAS

1 GREEN ONION, SLICED

1 In 3-quart saucepan, melt butter over medium heat. Add carrots and cook 2 to 3 minutes, until slightly softened, stirring occasionally. Add rice and cook 1 minute, stirring, until grains are coated. Stir in chicken broth, bay leaf, salt, pepper, and water; heat to boiling over high heat. Reduce heat to low; cover and simmer 15 to 20 minutes, until all liquid is absorbed and rice is tender.

2 Discard bay leaf. Stir in peas and green onions; heat through.

---

165 CALORIES

PER SERVING. 4G PROTEIN | 29G CARBOHYDRATE | 3G TOTAL FAT (0G SATURATED) 0G FIBER | 0MG CHOLESTEROL | 260MG SODIUM ♥

SWEET-POTATO CORN STICKS

Your family is going to love these. Sweet potatoes are rich in beta-carotene and vitamin C, and vitamin B$_6$ too.

ACTIVE TIME: 20 MINUTES · **TOTAL TIME:** 45 MINUTES
MAKES: 14 CORN STICKS

2   MEDIUM SWEET POTATOES (¾ POUND EACH), EACH PEELED AND CUT INTO QUARTERS

1¼ CUPS ALL-PURPOSE FLOUR

1   CUP YELLOW CORNMEAL

2½ TEASPOONS BAKING POWDER

1   TEASPOON SALT

¼   CUP BUTTER-FLAVOR SHORTENING

1¼ CUPS MILK

⅓   CUP PACKED BROWN SUGAR

1   LARGE EGG

1   In 3-quart saucepan, heat sweet potatoes and enough *water* to cover to boiling over high heat. Reduce heat to low; cover and simmer until sweet potatoes are fork-tender, 15 to 20 minutes; drain.

2   Meanwhile, preheat oven to 400°F. Thoroughly grease 14 corn-stick molds (2 pans, 7 molds each).

3   In large bowl, combine flour, cornmeal, baking powder, and salt. With pastry blender or two knives used scissor-fashion, cut in shortening until mixture resembles coarse crumbs.

4   In small bowl, with potato masher, mash sweet potatoes with milk, brown sugar, and egg until smooth. Stir into dry ingredients until batter is just blended. Spoon batter into prepared molds.

5   Bake until toothpick inserted in center comes out clean, 10 to 15 minutes. Cool corn sticks in molds on wire rack 5 minutes. Remove from molds; cool completely on wire rack. (Freeze in zip-tight plastic bags up to 3 months, if you like.) Just before serving, reheat, if desired.

170 CALORIES   **PER PIECE.** 4G PROTEIN | 29G CARBOHYDRATE | 5G TOTAL FAT (3G SATURATED) 2G FIBER | 20MG CHOLESTEROL | 316MG SODIUM

TABBOULEH

Cracked wheat, herbs, and plum tomatoes make tabbouleh wholesome and delicious.

ACTIVE TIME: 20 MINUTES PLUS SOAKING
MAKES: 6 SIDE-DISH SERVINGS

---

1   CUP BULGUR

2   PLUM TOMATOES, COARSELY CHOPPED

2   GREEN ONIONS, THINLY SLICED

2   CUPS LOOSELY PACKED FRESH
    PARSLEY LEAVES, CHOPPED

1   CUP LOOSELY PACKED FRESH MINT
    LEAVES, CHOPPED

⅓   CUP FRESH LEMON JUICE

¼   CUP EXTRA-VIRGIN OLIVE OIL

¾   TEASPOON SALT

1 In medium bowl, place bulgur and enough *water* to cover by 2 inches; soak at room temperature 1 hour. Drain bulgur in sieve, then rinse under cold running water. Drain well and return to bowl.

2 Stir tomatoes, green onions, parsley, mint, lemon juice, oil, and salt into bulgur until evenly mixed. If not serving right away, cover and refrigerate up to 1 day.

---

 185 CALORIES **PER SERVING.** 4G PROTEIN | 23G CARBOHYDRATE | 10G TOTAL FAT (1G SATURATED) 7G FIBER | 0MG CHOLESTEROL | 315MG SODIUM

GREAT GRAINS TO TRY

These days, side dishes aren't just about rice or potatoes—try these healthier options.

Bulgur: Steam, dry, and then crack wheat berries and you've got bulgur. This quick-cooking grain is high in fiber and has a light, nutty taste that's great in soups, salads, pilafs, or even stuffing. Or try it in our Tabbouleh (page 425).

Barley: Whole-grain barley is as nutritious as whole-grain wheat. With 8 essential amino acids, it's a hearty add-in to soups. Or try it in our Corn and Barley Salad (page 421).

Quinoa: Gluten-free quinoa is the new star of the whole-grain world, even even though—technically—it's a seed, not a grain. Packed with amino acids, quinoa is considered a super-food. Enjoy it in our Red Quinoa Pilaf (opposite).

RED QUINOA PILAF

We tossed red quinoa with green onions, cashews, and yellow raisins to create a colorful pilaf. Substitute white or black quinoa if you prefer.

ACTIVE TIME: 5 MINUTES · **TOTAL TIME:** 20 MINUTES
MAKES: 4 SIDE-DISH SERVINGS

Toast **1 cup red quinoa** in 2-quart saucepan over medium-high heat 3 minutes, or until fragrant and popping, stirring. Stir in **1½ cups water.** Heat to boiling, cover, and simmer over low heat 15 minutes or until water is absorbed. Transfer to large bowl and toss with **2 thinly sliced green onions** and **¼ teaspoon each salt and ground black pepper.** Let cool slightly. Chop **¼ cup roasted salted cashews** and add to bowl along with **¼ cup golden raisins** and **1 teaspoon extra-virgin olive oil.** Toss well.

250 CALORIES

PER SERVING. 7G PROTEIN | 40G CARBOHYDRATE | 7G TOTAL FAT (1G SATURATED) 3G FIBER | 0MG CHOLESTEROL | 255MG SODIUM ♥♥💚

5
CALORIES
Lemon Meringue Drops
(page 430)

SWEET BITES

It's easier to stick to a low-calorie diet if you indulge in the occasional treat. Here, we provide recipes for irresistible desserts that will satisfy your sweet tooth without sacrificing your waistline. Fruit is a natural choice when it comes to skinny desserts, so we've included recipes for Chocolate-Dipped Dried Fruit and Summer Fruit in Spiced Syrup, plus baked goods like Apricot Oatmeal Cookies and Jam Crumble Bars that incorporate both fruit and whole grains. Looking for a completely guilt-free sweet treat? Nibble on a couple Lemon Meringue Drops—they're just five calories apiece!

KEY TO ICONS

🔵 30 minutes or less   ❤️ Heart healthy   🌾 High fiber   🟩 Make ahead   🍲 Slow cooker

LEMON MERINGUE DROPS

These melt-in-your-mouth meringues are both crunchy and cloud-light—and require only five ingredients. For photo, see page 428.

ACTIVE TIME: 45 MINUTES · **BAKE TIME:** 1 HOUR 30 MINUTES PLUS 1 HOUR STANDING
MAKES: 60 COOKIES

---

3 LARGE EGG WHITES	½ CUP SUGAR
¼ TEASPOON CREAM OF TARTAR	2 TEASPOONS FRESHLY GRATED LEMON PEEL
⅛ TEASPOON SALT	

1   Preheat oven to 200°F. Line two large cookie sheets with parchment.

2   In medium bowl, with mixer on high speed, beat egg whites, cream of tartar, and salt until soft peaks form. With mixer running, sprinkle in sugar, 2 tablespoons at a time, beating until sugar dissolves and meringue stands in stiff, glossy peaks when beaters are lifted. Gently fold in lemon peel.

3   Spoon meringue into decorating bag fitted with ½-inch star tip. Pipe meringue into 1½-inch stars, about 1 inch apart, on prepared cookie sheets.

4   Bake meringues until crisp but not brown, 1 hour 30 minutes, rotating cookie sheets between upper and lower racks halfway through. Turn oven off; leave meringues in oven until dry, 1 hour.

5   Remove meringues from oven and cool completely. Remove from parchment with wide metal spatula. Store in an airtight container up to 1 month.

5 CALORIES

PER COOKIE. 0G PROTEIN | 2G CARBOHYDRATE | 0G TOTAL FAT (0G SATURATED) 0G FIBER | 0MG CHOLESTEROL | 10MG SODIUM ❤ 🍱

CHOCOLATE-DIPPED DRIED FRUIT

These sweet nibbles make a satisfying treat and cost you only 55 calories and 1 gram of fat. Dip the larger pieces of fruit first, then use the smaller pieces to scrape up the melted chocolate remaining in the pan. Store them in an airtight container for up to 1 week.

ACTIVE TIME: 10 MINUTES · **TOTAL TIME:** 15 MINUTES PLUS COOLING
MAKES: 32 PIECES DIPPED FRUIT

---

4   SQUARES (4 OUNCES) SEMISWEET CHOCOLATE, CHOPPED

1   TEASPOON VEGETABLE SHORTENING

1   POUND MIXED DRIED FRUIT, SUCH AS APRICOTS, APPLES, PEARS, PINEAPPLE, AND MANGO

3   OUNCES CRYSTALLIZED GINGER (OPTIONAL)

1 Place sheet of waxed paper under large wire rack. In top of double boiler or in small metal bowl set over 2-quart saucepan (but not touching simmering water), melt chocolate and shortening, stirring often, until smooth.
2 Dip one piece of fruit at a time halfway into chocolate. Shake off excess chocolate or gently scrape fruit across rim of double boiler, being careful not to remove too much chocolate. Placed dipped fruit on wire rack; allow chocolate to set for at least 1 hour.
3 Layer fruit between sheets of waxed paper in airtight container. Store at room temperature up to 1 week.

55
CALORIES

PER SERVING. 1G PROTEIN | 12G CARBOHYDRATE | 1G TOTAL FAT (1G SATURATED)
1G FIBER | 0MG CHOLESTEROL | 2MG SODIUM

HEALTHY MAKEOVER BROWNIES

The rich texture and chocolaty goodness of these brownies speak of decadence—but compare each square's 95 calories, 3 grams of fat, and complete lack of cholesterol to a regular brownie's doubly high calories, nearly quadrupled fat, and 60 milligrams of cholesterol, and you'll feel virtuous (and satisfied). Our cheats? Swapping nonfat cocoa for chocolate and cholesterol-free spread for not-so-heart-healthy butter.

ACTIVE TIME: 15 MINUTES · **BAKE TIME:** 22 MINUTES PLUS COOLING
MAKES: 16 BROWNIES

1 TEASPOON INSTANT COFFEE POWDER OR GRANULES	1½ TEASPOONS SALT
2 TEASPOONS VANILLA EXTRACT	1 CUP SUGAR
½ CUP ALL-PURPOSE FLOUR	4 TABLESPOONS TRANS-FAT-FREE VEGETABLE-OIL SPREAD (60 TO 70% OIL)
½ CUP UNSWEETENED COCOA	3 LARGE EGG WHITES
¼ TEASPOON BAKING POWDER	

1 Preheat oven to 350°F. Line 8-inch square metal baking pan with foil; grease foil. In cup, dissolve coffee powder in vanilla extract.

2 On waxed paper, combine flour, cocoa, baking powder, and salt.

3 In medium bowl, whisk sugar, vegetable-oil spread, egg whites, and coffee mixture until well mixed, then blend in flour mixture. Spread in prepared pan.

4 Bake 22 to 24 minutes or until toothpick inserted 2 inches from edge comes out almost clean. Cool brownies completely in pan on wire rack, about 2 hours.

5 Lift foil, with cooled brownie, out of pan; peel away from sides. Cut brownies into 4 strips, then cut each strip crosswise into 4 squares (see Tip). These freeze well: Pack in zip-tight plastic bag and freeze up to 3 months.

TIP If brownies are difficult to cut, dip knife in hot water; wipe dry, then cut. Repeat dipping and drying as necessary.

95 CALORIES

PER BROWNIE. 2G PROTEIN | 17G CARBOHYDRATE | 3G TOTAL FAT (1G SATURATED) 1G FIBER | 0MG CHOLESTEROL | 75MG SODIUM

FROZEN FRUIT YOGURT

Make yummy low-cal frozen yogurt in just ten minutes!

TOTAL TIME: 10 MINUTES

MAKES: 2½ CUPS OR 4 SERVINGS

12 OUNCES FROZEN STRAWBERRIES, CHERRIES, OR PEACHES (2¾ CUPS)

1 CONTAINER PLAIN LOW-FAT YOGURT (8 OUNCES)

6 TABLESPOONS GRANULATED SUGAR

1 TABLESPOON FRESH LEMON JUICE

⅛ TEASPOON ALMOND EXTRACT

1 In food processor, with knife blade attached, blend frozen fruit until fruit resembles finely shaved ice, stopping processor occasionally to scrape down sides. If fruit is not finely shaved, dessert will not be smooth.
2 Add yogurt, sugar, lemon juice, and almond extract and process just until mixture is smooth and creamy, scraping down sides occasionally. Serve immediately.

100 CALORIES

PER SERVING. 3G PROTEIN | 17G CARBOHYDRATE | 1G TOTAL FAT (1G SATURATED) 1G FIBER | 3MG CHOLESTEROL | 35MG SODIUM ❤ 🍱

CREAMY BANANA SORBET

This all-natural frozen treat contains a touch of maple syrup.

TOTAL TIME: 20 MINUTES PLUS FREEZING

MAKES: 3 CUPS OR 6 SERVINGS

4 MEDIUM VERY RIPE BANANAS

⅓ CUP MAPLE SYRUP

1 TEASPOON VANILLA EXTRACT

1 PINCH SALT

1 Peel bananas and place in large self-sealing plastic bag; freeze overnight or until very firm.
2 Slice frozen bananas. In food processor with knife blade attached, blend bananas with maple syrup, vanilla, and salt until creamy but still frozen, about 2 minutes. Serve immediately.

115 CALORIES

PER SERVING. 1G PROTEIN | 29G CARBOHYDRATE | 1G TOTAL FAT | 1G FIBER 0MG CHOLESTEROL | 25MG SODIUM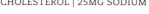

SUMMER FRUIT IN SPICED SYRUP

This is the perfect sweet ending to a brunch or backyard barbecue.

ACTIVE TIME: 15 MINUTES · **TOTAL TIME:** 25 MINUTES PLUS CHILLING
MAKES: 6 CUPS OR 4 SERVINGS

¾ CUP WATER

½ CUP SUGAR

3 WHOLE CLOVES

1 CINNAMON STICK (3 INCHES)

1 STAR ANISE

1 STRIP LEMON PEEL (3" BY ¾")

2 TABLESPOONS FRESH LEMON JUICE

6 CUPS FRESH FRUIT, SUCH AS SLICED NECTARINES, PLUMS, STRAWBERRIES, BLUEBERRIES, AND/OR RASPBERRIES

1 In 1-quart saucepan, combine water, sugar, spices, and lemon peel; heat to boiling over medium-high heat, stirring frequently. Reduce heat to medium-low; simmer 5 minutes.

2 Remove saucepan from heat and stir in lemon juice. Cool syrup to room temperature.

3 In large bowl, combine fruits and spiced syrup. Cover and refrigerate 2 hours, stirring occasionally.

125 CALORIES

PER SERVING. 1G PROTEIN | 32G CARBOHYDRATE | 1G TOTAL FAT (0G SATURATED) 4G FIBER | 0MG CHOLESTEROL | 2MG SODIUM ❤ 🧺

APRICOT OATMEAL COOKIES

These cookies are chock-full of sweet, tart, chewy, crunchy ingredients!

ACTIVE TIME: 40 MINUTES · **BAKE TIME:** 14 MINUTES PER BATCH
MAKES: 54 COOKIES

---

1 CUP (2 STICKS) BUTTER OR MARGARINE, SOFTENED

1 CUP PACKED LIGHT BROWN SUGAR

½ CUP GRANULATED SUGAR

2 LARGE EGGS

1½ CUPS ALL-PURPOSE FLOUR

1 TEASPOON BAKING SODA

1 TEASPOON GROUND CINNAMON

1 TEASPOON ALMOND EXTRACT

½ TEASPOON SALT

3 CUPS OLD-FASHIONED OR QUICK-COOKING OATS, UNCOOKED

1 CUP CHOPPED DRIED APRICOTS

¾ CUP DRIED CRANBERRIES

¾ CUP SWEETENED FLAKED COCONUT

¾ CUP SLIVERED ALMONDS, TOASTED

1 Preheat oven to 350°F; arrange two racks in upper and lower thirds of oven.

2 In large bowl, with mixer on medium speed, beat butter and both sugars until creamy, 2 minutes, occasionally scraping bowl with rubber spatula. On low speed, beat in eggs, flour, baking soda, cinnamon, almond extract, and salt just until blended. Stir in oats, all dried fruits, coconut, and almonds.

3 Drop dough by rounded measuring tablespoons, 2 inches apart, onto two ungreased large cookie sheets. Bake until tops are golden, 14 to 15 minutes, rotating pans between upper and lower oven racks halfway through. Using wide metal spatula, transfer cookies to wire racks to cool. Repeat with remaining dough if necessary.

4 Store cookies in cookie jar up to 1 week, or pack in zip-tight plastic bags and freeze up to 3 months.

130 CALORIES

PER COOKIE. 3G PROTEIN | 18G CARBOHYDRATE | 6G TOTAL FAT (3G SATURATED) 2G FIBER | 18MG CHOLESTEROL | 85MG SODIUM ♥ 🛒

JAM CRUMBLE BARS

A food processor makes quick work of these delicious bars. For variety, spread alternating stripes of different-colored jams over the crust or drop spoonfuls of contrasting jams and swirl them together for a marbled effect.

ACTIVE TIME: 15 MINUTES · **BAKE TIME:** 40 MINUTES PLUS COOLING
MAKES: 16 BARS

1¼ CUPS ALL-PURPOSE FLOUR

½ CUP PACKED LIGHT BROWN SUGAR

¼ TEASPOON BAKING SODA

¼ TEASPOON GROUND CINNAMON

½ CUP (1 STICK) COLD BUTTER OR MARGARINE, CUT INTO PIECES

¼ CUP PECANS, CHOPPED

½ CUP JAM (SUCH AS RASPBERRY OR BLACKBERRY)

1 Preheat oven to 350°F. Line 9-inch square baking pan with foil. In food processor with knife blade attached, process flour, sugar, baking soda, and cinnamon until mixed. Add butter and process until mixture resembles coarse crumbs and, when pressed, holds together. Transfer ½ cup crumb mixture to small bowl; stir in pecans and reserve for topping. Press remaining mixture firmly onto bottom of prepared pan.

2 With small metal spatula, spread jam evenly over dough, leaving ½-inch border all around. With fingers, crumble reserved topping over jam.

3 Bake until top and edges are browned, 40 to 45 minutes. Cool completely in pan on wire rack.

4 When cool, lift foil, with pastry, out of pan; peel foil away from sides. Cut pastry into 4 strips, then cut each strip crosswise into 4 pieces. (These freeze well: Pack in zip-tight plastic bag and freeze up to 3 months.)

150 CALORIES

PER BAR. 1G PROTEIN | 21G CARBOHYDRATE | 7G TOTAL FAT (4G SATURATED) 0G FIBER | 16MG CHOLESTEROL | 85MG SODIUM ❤ 🍱

GRILLED ANGEL FOOD CAKE WITH STRAWBERRIES

Store-bought angel food cake goes gourmet when it's grilled and topped with sweetened balsamic-soaked strawberries.

ACTIVE TIME: 10 MINUTES · **TOTAL TIME:** 15 MINUTES PLUS STANDING
MAKES: 6 SERVINGS

1½ POUNDS STRAWBERRIES, HULLED AND EACH CUT IN HALF, OR INTO QUARTERS IF LARGE

2 TABLESPOONS BALSAMIC VINEGAR

1 TABLESPOON SUGAR

1 (9 OUNCE) STORE-BOUGHT ANGEL FOOD CAKE

WHIPPED CREAM (OPTIONAL)

1 In medium bowl, toss strawberries with balsamic vinegar and sugar. Let stand at room temperature until sugar dissolves, at least 30 minutes, stirring occasionally.

2 Meanwhile, prepare outdoor grill for direct grilling over medium heat. Cut angel food cake into 6 wedges.

3 Place cake on hot grill rack and cook 3 to 4 minutes or until lightly toasted on both sides, turning over once. Spoon strawberries with their juice onto 6 dessert plates. Place grilled cake on plates with strawberries; serve with whipped cream, if you like.

PER SERVING. 3G PROTEIN | 35G CARBOHYDRATE | 1G TOTAL FAT | 3G FIBER
0MG CHOLESTEROL | 320MG SODIUM ❤

GENERAL INDEX

V

INDEX OF RECIPES BY ICON

This index makes it easy to search recipes by category, including 30 minutes or less, heart-healthy, high-fiber, make-ahead, and slow-cooker dishes.

● 30 MINUTES OR LESS

These easy weekday meals and treats are perfect for busy home cooks. Each require 30 minutes or less to prepare—from kitchen to table!

♥ HEART HEALTHY

If you're looking for heart-healthy options, look no further. Each main dish contains 5 grams or less saturated fat, 150 milligrams or less cholesterol, and 480 milligrams or less sodium. Each appetizer or side dish contains 2 grams or less saturated fat, 50 milligrams or less cholesterol, and 360 milligrams or less sodium.

✹ HIGH FIBER

Want to get more fill-you-up fiber into your diet? Incorporate the following high fiber dishes into your regular repertoire. Each of these recipes contains 5 grams or more fiber per serving.

▇ MAKE AHEAD

For convenience, you can make all (or a portion) of these recipes ahead of time. The individual recipes indicate which steps you can do-ahead or how long you can refrigerate or freeze the completed dish.

🍲 SLOW COOKER

These slow-cooked dishes make it easy to get dinner on the table. Just put all the ingredients in the bowl of your slow cooker in the a.m., and you'll have a delicious, ready-to-serve main dish in the p.m.

ⓥ VEGAN

Following a diet that's free of animal products like dairy and eggs? These recipes are 100-percent vegan—and sure to satisfy.

PHOTOGRAPHY CREDITS

Antonis Achilleos: 20, 217, 243, 252, 301, 346

James Baigrie: 36, 42, 102, 105, 117, 124, 129, 144, 188, 198, 203, 226, 235, 247, 254, 276, 328, 340, 396, 411

Monica Buck: 11, 39, 140, 191, 225

Tara Donne: 288

Getty Images: Annabelle Breakey, 408; Dennis Gottlieb, 142; Alexandra Grablewski, 417; Tom Grill, 304; Image Source, 46 (top); Richard Jung, 137; Brian Leatart, 305; Michael Rosenfeld, 157; Yuenkel Studios, 24

Brian Hagiwara: 74, 290, 302, 435

Lisa Hubbard: 32

iStockPhoto: Alea Image, 158; Andyd, 229; Mariya Bibikova, 14; Kevin Dyer, 367; Eric Hood, 303; Uyen Le, 439; Luigidi Maggio, 17; James McQuillan, 285, 423; Judd Pilosoff, 428; Tarek El Sombati, 304 (bottom); Laura Stanley, 117; Alasdair Thompson, 431

Frances Janisch: 123, 419, 425, 438

John Kernick: 262

Yunhee Kim: 248

Rita Maas: 68, 112, 114, 201 (right), 122, 212, 436

Kate Mathis: 16, 23, 47, 49, 53, 65, 77, 201 (left), 126, 135, 138, 177, 180, 193, 204, 214, 232, 264, 270, 282, 294, 308, 363, 381, 385, 393, 400, 433

Ellie Miller: 196

Ted Morrison: 265

Con Poulos: 80, 155, 209, 293, 311, 364, 368

David Prince: 85, 286, 317, 325, 332

Alan Richardson: 13, 220, 349

Charles Schiller: 376

Kate Sears: 29, 57, 60, 88, 93, 99, 108, 130, 151, 164, 169, 172, 258, 261, 299, 315, 320, 337, 353, 357, 358, 373, 388, 403

Shutterstock: Teresa Azevedo, 132; 171

Ann Stratton: 185

Studio D: Philip Friedman, 9, 46 (bottom), 153, 207; J Muckle 426

Anna Williams: 54, 73, 94, 231, 238, 268, 345, 427

METRIC EQUIVALENTS

The recipes that appear in this cookbook use the standard United States method for measuring liquid and dry or solid ingredients (teaspoons, tablespoons, and cups). The information on this chart is provided to help cooks outside the U.S. successfully use these recipes. All equivalents are approximate.

METRIC EQUIVALENTS FOR DIFFERENT TYPES OF INGREDIENTS
A standard cup measure of a dry or solid ingredient will vary in weight depending on the type of ingredient. A standard cup of liquid is the same volume for any type of liquid. Use the following chart when converting standard cup measures to grams (weight) or milliliters (volume).

Standard Cup	Fine Powder (e.g. flour)	Grain (e.g. rice)	Granular (e.g. sugar)	Liquid Solids (e.g. butter)	Liquid (e.g. milk)
1	140 g	150 g	190 g	200 g	240 ml
¾	105 g	113 g	143 g	150 g	180 ml
⅔	93 g	100 g	125 g	133 g	160 ml
½	70 g	75 g	95 g	100 g	120 ml
⅓	47 g	50 g	63 g	67 g	80 ml
¼	35 g	38 g	48 g	50 g	60 ml
⅛	18 g	19 g	24 g	25 g	30 ml

USEFUL EQUIVALENTS FOR LIQUID INGREDIENTS BY VOLUME

¼ tsp	=					1 ml
½ tsp	=					2 ml
1 tsp	=					5 ml
3 tsp	=	1 tbls	=		½ fl oz	=	15 ml
		2 tbls	=	⅛ cup	=	1 fl oz	=	30 ml
		4 tbls	=	¼ cup	=	2 fl oz	=	60 ml
		5⅓ tbls	=	⅓ cup	=	3 fl oz	=	80 ml
		8 tbls	=	½ cup	=	4 fl oz	=	120 ml
		10⅔ tbls	=	⅔ cup	=	5 fl oz	=	160 ml
		12 tbls	=	¾ cup	=	6 fl oz	=	180 ml
		16 tbls	=	1 cup	=	8 fl oz	=	240 ml
		1 pt	=	2 cups	=	16 fl oz	=	480 ml
		1 qt	=	4 cups	=	32 fl oz	=	960 ml
						33 fl oz	= 1000 ml	= 1 L

USEFUL EQUIVALENTS FOR DRY INGREDIENTS BY WEIGHT
(To convert ounces to grams, multiply the number of ounces by 30.)

1 oz	=	¹⁄₁₆ lb	=	30 g
2 oz	=	¼ lb	=	60 g
4 oz	=	½ lb	=	120 g
8 oz	=	¾ lb	=	240 g
16 oz	=	1 lb	=	480 g

USEFUL EQUIVALENTS LENGTH
(To convert inches to centimeters, multiply the number of inches by 2.5.)

1 in	=		2.5 cm	
6 in	= ½ ft	=	15 cm	
12 in	= 1 ft	=	30 cm	
36 in	= 3 ft	= 1 yd	= 90 cm	
40 in	=		100 cm	= 1 m

USEFUL EQUIVALENTS FOR COOKING/OVEN TEMPERATURES

	Fahrenheit	Celsius	Gas Mark
Freeze Water	32° F	0° C	
Room Temperature	68° F	20° C	
Boil Water	212° F	100° C	
Bake	325° F	160° C	3
	350° F	180° C	4
	375° F	190° C	5
	400° F	200° C	6
	425° F	220° C	7
	450° F	230° C	8
Broil			Grill

THE GOOD HOUSEKEEPING TRIPLE-TEST PROMISE

At *Good Housekeeping*, we want to make sure that every recipe we print works in any oven, with any brand of ingredient, no matter what. That's why, in our test kitchens at the **Good Housekeeping Research Institute,** we go all out: We test each recipe at least three times—and, often, several more times after that.

When a recipe is first developed, one member of our team prepares the dish and we judge it on these criteria: It must be **delicious, family-friendly, healthy,** and **easy to make**.

1 The recipe is then tested several more times to fine-tune the flavor and ease of preparation, always by the same team member, using the same equipment.

2 Next, another team member follows the recipe as written, **varying the brands of ingredients** and **kinds of equipment.** Even the types of stoves we use are changed.

3 A third team member repeats the whole process **using yet another set of equipment** and **alternative ingredients.** By the time the recipes appear in our books, they are guaranteed to work in any kitchen, including yours. **We promise.**